Healthy Markets?

Healthy Markets?

The New Competition in Medical Care

Edited by Mark A. Peterson

DUKE UNIVERSITY PRESS   Durham / London, 1998

© 1998 Duke University Press
All rights reserved
Printed in the United States of America on acid-free paper ∞
Typeset in Berkeley by Keystone Typesetting, Inc.
Library of Congress Cataloging-in-Publication Data appear
on the last printed page of this book.

To my daughter Sophie Ainur,
whose future knows no bounds

Contents

Introduction: Health Care into the Next Century

Mark A. Peterson

A t the dawn of the twentieth century's final decade, the United States was poised for yet another intense political debate about whether or not to join other advanced industrial democracies in guaranteeing health care insurance coverage as a signature feature of citizenship while simultaneously using the power of the public sector to bring fiscal discipline to medical care expenditures. A few years into the decade, Democrat Bill Clinton was elected president with a campaign promise of sweeping health care reform. He explicitly linked the reputation of his administration to the successful enactment of a Health Security Act that would maintain Medicare for the elderly and ensure that the rest of the nation would enjoy the protections of standardized comprehensive benefits furnished through competing private insurance plans operating within the confines of both market pressures and potential premium caps. The political failure of this complex and controversial initiative was not, in itself, surprising. No previous president had been able to enact health care reform, although many had tried. No other nation had implemented a system of universal coverage in the context of a technologically developed medical industry consuming one-seventh of the economy (Jacobs 1995). For many reform advocates in the 1990s, hope may have triumphed over experience, but few could honestly be shocked that the bold gambit of comprehensive reform had once again succumbed to the power of antagonistic stakeholders, a public paralyzed by the fears of disrupting what it already had, and the challenge of coalition building engendered by the highly decentralized character of American government. Status quo ante continued to be the lament of all twentieth-century health reformers.

As we view the health care system at the century's end, however, the status quo is anything but static. The next century in health care at the outset will be decidedly different from the one present as the 1990s began and the reform debate ensued, despite the formal public policy stalemate. Only in retrospect is this dynamic readily apparent. We now know that the health care system stood at a crucial fork in the road. Down one lane was the passage of federal legislation that would at least set the trajectory for achieving a universal health care system under the guidance of the public sector and with cost control a government responsibility. Down the other was not more of the same, it turns out, but rather an unleashing of private-sector initiative that literally transformed the status of patients, the physician-patient relationship, interactions among different types of providers, the meaning and role of insurance, the very structure of health delivery and financing institutions, and, at least perceptually, the course of medical inflation. These changes are probably every bit as profound as any that would have been prompted by public statute. Indeed, the title of a forum organized at Carnegie Mellon University in spring 1996 raised a question few would even have considered just a short while before: "Healthcare: Does the Government Matter Any More?" As Yogi Berra once said, "When you see a fork in the road, take it." We did. Having done so, we need to ask how the particular path of our future was taken and with what implications for the health care system and the American public.

The advance of both public policy and private decision making are historically and institutionally bounded. The choices of one period are intimately linked to the choices grasped or missed in a previous era. In the argot of social science, the sequence of events that shape any sector are path dependent, or, for the econometrically inclined, autoregressive (North 1990; for a health care application, see Wilsford 1995). At any given moment, more than one path is possible, but the range of plausible paths and the decisions affecting them are heavily influenced by what has come before, often long before—what policy approaches have worked or failed, what options have proven politically attractive or anathema, what institutions and administrative capacities have been generated or denied, what interests have been nurtured or thwarted, and what participants have been acclaimed or vilified (see Putnam 1993; Skocpol 1992). At the same time, there can be building pressures—the modeler's "exogenous shocks" (although in social systems they are rarely truly exogenous), the econometrician's "disturbances"—that shift the center of gravity of policy deliberation and private action, perhaps in ways not easily anticipated. Health care in the United States in the 1990s illustrates precisely both of these tendencies.

The reform debate that came to a head in 1994 had obvious ties to the past. The rhetoric was often the same, with each side harkening to claims long associated with distinct dimensions of American public philosophy: "universal coverage," a "right" to health care, the "moral" imperative of granting everyone real access to medical care as part of a commitment to equal opportunity versus "socialized medicine," and a "government takeover" that would, by definition, destroy the world's best health care system and even rob us of our individual liberty. Institutional dynamics over time had transformed the policy positions and political places of numerous organized interests, but, as before, various interests had either existing fundamental stakes in the system to defend (providers) or proposed future burdens to prevent (small business), and each had access to veto points within a decentralized governing system (Peterson 1994a, 1994b, 1995; Steinmo and Watts 1995). The proposals themselves sometimes represented new conceptual amalgamations, such as the president's "liberal synthesis" of managed competition under a budget (Hacker 1997; Starr 1994). The essential elements, however, whether involving incentives and competition, or mandates and budgets, had enjoyed some status in health care debates long ago. And the outcome, with the inability of a pro-reform coalition to attain enough stature even to secure a formal vote on either floor of Congress, was an exact repeat of the past.

What is distinctly different, however—the "disturbance"—is how, and to what effect, private actors responded in the wake of government indecision. From the early 1970s well into the 1990s, there had been a general clarion call about an intensifying health care cost crisis in the United States. Those employers who provided their employees with health insurance benefits and financed most of the premium costs were, after households themselves, a major category of payers of health care services and supplies. In 1989, business picked up 30 percent of the bill, compared with 37 percent for households, and 16 percent and 14 percent, respectively, for the federal government and state governments (Levit and Cowan 1990: 131). From 1970 to 1989, employers witnessed a dramatic rise in the costs of providing health benefits, an increase so substantial that it probably could not be countered by freezing or lowering cash compensation. During this period, employer spending on health benefits went up, in constant dollars, 163 percent. Wages and salaries were held to a 1 percent real increase (Morrison, Morrison, and Edwards 1991: 104).[1] These cost pressures brought many large employers to the health care reform table—in the states and at the national level, more than once—and some even advocated a shift to public financing of health services (Bergthold 1990, 1994; Martin 1994, 1995).

When the federal government failed to act, however, for the third time since the pronounced cost escalations began (the legislative paralysis on the comprehensive initiatives of the Nixon, Carter, and Clinton administrations), employers who granted health coverage to their workers concentrated harder than ever on actions that they could take independently to stem the tide, as described by Cathie Jo Martin in her chapter in part 2 of this book. One strategy was to reduce their costs by limiting benefits: dropping eligibility for dependents, eliminating coverage for some employees, and elevating direct employee contributions to the cost of their care through higher premium shares and greater out-of-pocket payments (Pear 1996d). The other strategy was to move their covered employees even more rapidly into managed care plans. Using gatekeeping by primary care providers to control access to specialists and high-tech services, selective contracting with providers and altered payment mechanisms to ensure adherence to plan procedures and attention to cost efficiency, and practice guidelines with utilization review to promote cost-effective treatments, these plans offered the promise of less intense utilization of services at lower payment rates per service. State Medicaid programs, which had experienced rapid increases in expenditures, followed suit. Using waivers from the Health Care Financing Administration, more and more states transferred—by incentive or by mandate—their Medicaid beneficiaries from fee-for-service medicine to managed care organizations. The Medicare program experimented with managed care, too. Many private insurers and providers joined this game to demonstrate their capacity to hold down costs without being compelled by the unwanted force of law.

Managed care was not a new technology that suddenly appeared from nowhere. Prepaid group practice—the term for health maintenance organizations before policy entrepreneur Paul Ellwood came along—had a long history. Employers had attempted to exploit the potential benefits of managed care for decades. Managed care had also long ago been promoted by federal legislation, such as the Health Maintenance Organization Act of 1973 (Brown 1983). Despite these precedents, it had never taken off. The stated goals of the HMO Act—establishing 1,700 federally qualified HMOs by the end of the 1970s—had been missed by more than a country mile. It was not until the 1990s reform debate and its aftermath that the private transformation of the health care system shifted into overdrive. The conceptual framing of Clinton's Health Security Act around the idea of stimulating "managed" competition among private, primarily managed care plans no doubt facilitated the changing configuration of the health care system. Many insurers—especially the "Big

Five"—and providers sought to reconstitute themselves in ways that would be advantageous in the health care world that the president envisioned. But despite the resistance of many other insurers, providers, other interests, and politicians to this managed care orientation, once the president's plan had no legs, managed care went into full sprint. And with it has come an emergent vision of health care—for those with employer-based insurance, as well as for the beneficiaries of Medicaid and Medicare—that incorporates the notion of private health plans in some kind of regulated competition with one another (Schlesinger 1997; Etheredge 1998). The potential paths that lie before us now are the product of the institutional, political, and social dynamics that shaped the health care reform debate and the new set of imperatives generated by market change and the so-called managed care revolution. What choices people make in the years ahead—employers, insurers, providers, policy makers, and consumers/patients/voters—cannot escape the intersection of these historical roots and contemporary shocks. The latter have altered alignments of resources, prompted a redistribution of power, and opened the door to new participants. They have reconfigured avenues of "exit" for disaffected individuals, changed the mechanisms for using "voice" to challenge institutional policy, and imposed new standards of "loyalty" for those who retain their previous relationships with existing plans and institutions (Hirschman 1970; Emanuel and Emanuel 1997).

The recasting of the U.S. health care system as we cross into the next century is thus a subject with potentially profound implications. It merits close review from a number of perspectives. It has rightly been the subject of innumerable conferences, forums, and seminars over the past few years. Most of these have accepted the private-sector transformations as given, settled, and accepted, with only a passing glance at both remaining government responsibilities and many of the issues, such as the uninsured and underinsured, that were frequent subjects of discussion during the reform debates of our era and of those past. Some assessments of the changes in the health care system have been explicitly celebratory, with some cause. The cost-escalation bugaboo of the late twentieth century seems, for now, to have been tamed, even more so than would have been projected under health care reform plans. By almost every measure—percentage of gross domestic project, changes in the real per capita expenditures, the rate of medical inflation, and nominal percentage changes in business health insurance costs—health care spending is well under control.[2] The fears that some analysts expressed just a few years ago—that health care would consume as much as a fifth of our national income by the year 2000—now seem quaint. To be sure, there is reason to question whether this is a permanent shift—an almost completely parallel change occurred in 1978 and 1979 when health care reform was last debated and created pressure on private-sector actors, and in 1997 premiums began to rise again at more than the general rate of inflation—but at least the current evidence suggests that one of the major motivations for pursuing reform through the public sector has abated (Levit, Lazenby, and Sivarajan 1996: 133–134; Health Care 1997). Indeed, a recent projection for health care expenditures in the year 2000 is well under what would have been anticipated with the adoption of the Clinton Health Security Act (Pearlstein 1996).

Whether or not the disciplining of health care spending is a short-term or long-term phenomena, the structural changes in the health care system itself are likely to endure in one form or another. Certainly for a period of indeterminate length, they have set the context in which all decision makers—public and private; at the national, state, and community levels—will have to act and help to define what are acceptable as policy options. Because of its significance, however, the transformation of the health care system demands more than quiet acceptance or uncritical celebration. We need to know much more about how the system has changed and to what effect, with what consequences, and for whom. We make little headway settling on essentially teleological views that the health care system has reached a kind of homeostasis, adapting in a logical and functionalist way to the need for cost control, rationalization, and quality improvement—the public-relations message of managed care plans and other "market romantics" who exhort the virtues of the new environment (see Morone and Goggin 1995b: 558).

These fundamental changes in medical care financing and delivery have roots in political, social, and historical dynamics, as well as economic. They also harbor political, social, and economic ramifications beyond (or perhaps more important than) some uncritical notion of unyielding progress toward greater efficiency, expressed as delivering higher quality care at lower cost. There are questions about the very meaning of efficiency and quality in the health care setting. There are implications for how relationships change as patients become consumers and physicians transmogrify into business representatives. There are distributive consequences, matters of who gains and who loses, and why. There are concerns about how federal and state policy makers, who presumably, by virtue of their election, represent to some degree public concerns and preferences, can continue to advance public needs and values in both existing programs and new ones. There are challenges like determining the role and contours of the individual and the community in this new regime. These are the kinds of questions that prompted the

Journal of Health Politics, Policy and Law, in its twentieth year, to sponsor the May 1996 conference on "Health Care into the Next Century: Markets, States, and Communities" that produced the work that first appeared in various issues of the journal and that we are now publishing here—significantly reorganized, revised, and updated.

The Health Care System at Century's End

Just what is this new health care system I have alluded to, so rapidly transforming at the century's end? That will become more apparent in the chapters that follow this introduction. But it is worth previewing descriptively various indicators of the rapid changes, motivated by the health care market, that have been taking place since the late 1980s and early 1990s, and sometimes in the space of just the last few years. The most obvious and frequently discussed shift is the one from indemnity insurance in a fee-for-service medical delivery system to one dominated by managed care. When health care reform became an issue in the 1992 presidential race, just over 40 million Americans were enrolled in HMOs, and 50 million were in more loosely organized preferred provider organizations (PPOs). In the late 1980s, nearly six in ten physicians still did not have any managed care patients, and their incomes continued to climb. Just a few years later, during 1995, HMOs covered nearly 70 million individuals and PPOs upward of 90 million. More than 80 percent of physicians worked with at least one managed care contract, and their incomes dropped for the first time. Over roughly the same period, managed care enrollment in Blue Cross/Blue Shield plans went from around 10 percent to nearly half of plan memberships. Medicaid beneficiaries in managed care grew from three in a hundred to four in ten, and the numbers were rising rapidly as almost all states used waivers from the Health Care Financing Administration to design and implement managed care programs. Medicare was trailing, but major change was also under way in that program. A total of 78 percent of managed care organizations reported that by the end of 1996 they planned to have Medicare risk contracts, and 14 percent of beneficiaries had enrolled by August 1997. Market penetration of health maintenance organizations was climbing throughout the nation, averaging more than a quarter of covered lives in metropolitan areas of a million or more people. Minnesota hit 45 percent in 1995. For those with employer-provided coverage about three-quarters were subscribers to some kind of managed care plan. The U.S. health care system in the early twenty-first century will be a system of managed care, in all of its permutations.[3]

It will also be a system rapidly reconfigured through vertical and horizontal consolidation. New York City, previously the home of dozens of independent hospitals, is heading toward a half dozen competing networks. Other cities are following similar patterns. Major hospital systems are also being built nationally. Columbia HCA, for example, before becoming the target of federal auditors, purchased or became affiliated with forty-one hospitals in 1995 alone. Nationally, only a fifth or fewer hospitals expect to be freestanding institutions by the end of the decade, neither bought nor part of an alliance or network. Physicians increasingly came together, too. By 1995, a third were in group practice. By the summer of 1996, there were 4,000 independent practice associations (IPAs)—involving an average of 300 physicians per IPA—up from 1,500 in 1990. Physicians, hospitals, and clinics also started banding together in their own provider-managed networks, in some cases contracting directly with employers and supplanting managed care plans. Minnesota, once foremost in the development of managed care, is leading experimentation with such networking. Insurers themselves got together or were taken over by others. The 120 independent Blue Cross/Blue Shield plans that existed in 1975 were down to 63 by the middle of 1996. Even the big insurance carriers were buying up one another, such as the $8.9 billion acquisition of U.S. Healthcare by Aetna Life and Casualty. The pharmaceutical industry, medical equipment manufacturers, and other kinds of providers were also part of the hyperkinetic restructuring of the health care industry. Taken together, just in 1995 there were 623 mergers and acquisitions in the health care sector.[4] These activities obviously raise antitrust concerns and are certain to receive considerable attention from the U.S. Department of Justice and the Federal Trade Commission, as well as from analysts interested in their microlevel impacts on efficiency, prices, and quality. They also raise larger issues of political economy in health care. They create new and different kinds of political as well as institutional players, redistributing resources in ways that have implications for both political and economic power.

The rise of managed care and the consolidation of health care institutions has brought with it corporatization and a move away from traditional not-for-profit institutions. By 1994, for-profit health maintenance organizations had more enrollees than their not-for-profit counterparts, which had previously dominated the scene (by mid-1996, almost three-quarters of HMOs were for-profits, accounting for 61 percent of HMO enrollments). Formerly nonprofit Blue Cross/Blue Shield plans were either formally becoming profit-making entities or joining corporate networks. A decentralized system with myriad local- or state-based carriers and providers is being supplanted by giant regional and national enterprises in search of a profit. All of this was being accomplished with little prodding from federal or state policy makers, and with little reaction from them. Only recently have both the federal government and the states begun in earnest to consider and enact legislation that seeks to promote consumer interests that can, at least on occasion, be overwhelmed by the imperatives of the corporate bottom line. Even so, at the contemporary table of health care decision makers, capitalists—investors, shareholders, and the managers of capital markets—demand greater recognition, and by the nature of their activities, wield increased control over both public and private policy agendas. The results may often be socially beneficial. Private-sector entrepreneurs and managers operating in this environment may be able to squeeze out truly excess capacity and inefficiencies that eat up social resources and distort health care delivery, setting needed priorities and appropriately imposing losses that elected officials are decidedly not wont to do. It is also questionable whether many formally nonprofit health care institutions, including various hospitals and Blue Cross/Blue Shield plans, always earned the benefits of their nonprofit status by making significant contributions to the community (see Schlesinger, Gray, and Bradley 1996). But, again, there are social and political as well as economic questions to raise about this transformation. The corporatization of the health care system leads to the commodification of medical services, with the conversion of patients into consumers and healers into entrepreneurs. It diverts attention from the uninsured, the underinsured, and distributive equity to a concentrated focus on efficiency as defined by market forces and desired by shareholders. Borrowing from Arthur Okun's (1975) characterization of the "big trade-off" in democratic market-based systems, efficiency prevails over equality.[5]

Assessing the New Health Care System

Understanding, explaining, and analytically coming to terms with what all of these changes mean for the health care system in the next century is no small task. In many respects, as Theodore Marmor notes in the closing essay, the transformation has been so swift and dramatic that the individual changes have been unpredictable, at least in their range and intensity. The metamorphosis is also not over. Evaluating the context and impact of such a profound shift in the health care sector as it is in progress presents a significant challenge even to the best social scientists and health policy specialists. Our ambitions here are thus decidedly tempered, but nonetheless important. The first is to fill some of the lacunae in the issues covered and the perspectives brought to bear on the study of health system change. Many forums have provided rich detail about very specific aspects of restructuring the health care sector, such as the impact of managed care on mental health services. Some have furnished various participants in the health care sector—physicians, hospital administrators, employer benefit managers, managed care executives, investors, and even consumers—with the guidance they need to maneuver successfully in this new environment from the vantage point of their own interests. Others have offered broad economic assessments of the health market in transition or commended the successes of reform instigated by the private sector. We need not pass over that same territory. Instead, our objective is to give some moment to specific economic, social, political, and organizational issues frequently overlooked or given scant attention in previous reviews of contemporary health system change. We also seek to bring a synthesis to many of the issues associated with the transformation of American health care by tracing the impact of health system change through a number of intersecting perspectives and venues. The objective of this volume is to grapple with central questions about the character of the contemporary American health care system as we pause at the historical antechamber of the next century.

The Meaning of "Market" in U.S. Health Care

Before launching into an analysis of the market transformation of health care in the United States, however, it is imperative to recognize the slippery character of the term *market*. What do we mean when we speak of markets in the health care setting? One might have in mind a general consonance with the conventional wisdom about core American preferences—among elites and the public—for private markets as opposed to government intervention. Taken to the extreme, however, relatively few people, beyond selected libertarian and right-wing politicians, believe that all matters pertaining to the delivery of medical care services should be left to the marketplace, however conceived. Some individuals may believe that health care is no different from toothpaste (see Herzlinger 1997), but that is a view shared by few analysts and citizens. Most market advocates, such as health economists Alain Enthoven and Mark Pauly, support major interventions by the government to subsidize coverage for those who remain uninsured and to promote new rules of the game to mitigate the well-recognized inefficiencies of the market (see, for example, Enthoven 1993 and Pauly et al. 1991). Analysts across the spectrum of opinion reject the simplistic dichotomies of government versus the market, or regulation versus competition (Health Care Study Group 1994). More pertinent are questions about where, when, in what form, and under what conditions both market mechanisms and government policies have a role.

In the health care setting, the market rubric is typically a reference to a diverse set of marketlike instruments or arrangements. These include privately owned or managed institutions, which can range from stockholder-owned insurance companies to nonprofit sickness funds in the German tradition. They often refer to the use of incentives embedded within institutions of whatever sort (private or public) that are designed to encourage more efficient individual-level behavior. Fully capitated payments to physicians by corporate HMOs, which shift risk to the doctor and reward the utilization of fewer services, would certainly be encompassed by the market orientation. But one would also have to consider the hospital payment methodology of diagnosis-related groupings (DRGs) used by a public program like Medicare. The market frequently is taken to refer to a process of decision making; for example, using competition among substitutable entities to identify and select the best choice according to some measure of utility. That competition, however, can be among private firms, nonprofit institutions, or even public agencies or employees. It can occur within an unregulated marketplace or within the bowels of the public sector. The same can be said of another marketlike arrangement: contractual agreements between relevant parties.

Even agreement on the meanings of these marketlike instruments and arrangements in the abstract does not necessarily yield a consistent understanding of their meaning or impact in practice. How they are used and to what effect is highly contingent. Because various health care systems around the world have experimented with or implemented design features that look similar to some of these instruments or mechanisms, it is all too easy to accept the claim that market forces, and the "American model" that embodies them, are diffusing around the world. To do so, however, ignores the differing effects that are generated when similar looking instruments—for example, contracts, competition among providers for patients, and capitated payments—are introduced in quite different historical, institutional, and cultural settings (Morone and Goggin 1995a; Jost et al. 1995; Jacobs 1998).

For our purposes, the market concept has developed a fairly distinct if imprecise set of features specific to the contemporary American scene (they need not go together as a matter of underlying principle nor in other settings). First, although payers may be either private or public, private institutions typically regulate the flow of funds between payers and providers of care. Second, those private institutions are moving toward payment mechanisms that use incentives to promote cost-effectiveness. Those payment mechanisms generally fall under the rubric of managed care, itself a slippery and highly inclusive term for everything from staff-model HMOs with salaried physicians and their own hospitals, to capitated payments to panels of physicians and other providers, to discounted fee-for-service payments and bonuses paid to otherwise independent providers. Saying that everyone is in managed care is somewhat akin to suggesting that everyone has a mode of transportation: some fly in airplanes, some drive cars, some use public buses, some ride bicycles, and some walk, with obviously variegated implications for speed, costs, and the quality of the experience. It is easier to identify what is not included in managed care than what is, but that nonetheless remains a meaningful distinction, because all forms of managed care, no matter how weak, create behavioral incentives for providers and patients opposite those promoted by open-ended fee-for-service arrangements. Third, contracting is a dominant mode of establishing formal relationships between purchasers of coverage and insurers, between insurers and providers, among providers, and sometimes directly between purchasers and providers. Fourth, although private institutions, whether insurers or providers, need not be profit-seeking entities in order to perform in the market, commercial firms are acceptable, perhaps even idealized, participants. Fifth, although the federal and state governments have enacted a number of policies that affect individual and institutional behavior in the market—such as financing Medicare and Medicaid, shielding employee health benefits from taxation, imposing some regulation of insurance practices, and isolating from state regulation self-insured companies with the federal Employee Retirement Income Security Act (ERISA)— decisions about insurance products and the delivery of medical care services are primarily made by private actors.

The Market Model

In part 1 of this volume, various perspectives on the market as a model for medical care organization and financing are presented. The essays and the associated commentaries and responses explore the overall market model or aspects of it seriously, critically (in the constructive sense), and sometimes very contentiously. As these essays will reveal, even within the discipline of economics there are deep-seated differences about how to view markets in the health care context, both in terms of what markets can do (compared to government) and what analytical advantages for policy making are to be gained from the core assumptions and tools of economic analysis.

Given the fact that market change has taken off outside the confines of government-defined rules of the game and largely at the behest of private actors, for noneconomists it is worth returning to general market theory and assessing its applicability to the health care sector. As I noted earlier, almost every analyst and serious economist is aware of the deficiencies of the health care market as it exists in practice. Even prominent "market romantics" wish to exploit the positive power of government to introduce market corrections. Mark Pauly rightly concludes in his accompanying commentary that our discussions always have to be about imperfect markets and imperfect governments as we actually experience and can realistically recraft each of them in their respective settings.

But as the market is glorified in the rhetoric of many politicians, as the apparent fiscal discipline and product innovation of the current health care market are celebrated, as private actors launch major restructuring of health care institutions and relationships thus far largely lacking the presence of a guiding regime constructed by public policy, we all need to be reminded about where unfettered market forces are likely to take us in the financing and delivery of health care services. That is the task that Thomas Rice assumes in his essay, "Can Markets Give Us the Health System We Want?" The answer to that question, readers will discover, depends a great deal on what is included in the words *we* and *want,* but Rice highlights where the health care market, left to its own devices, can go wrong even within its own terms. Robert Evans goes a step further. He explores the political economy of the health care market, identifying how the social and financial interests of many proponents of market-driven organization are advantaged by private rather than public approaches to health care reform. As Gary Belkin later suggests, the market is often characterized as an objective set of instruments that can be neutrally applied to various health care problems. The concern for Evans is that market arrangements, due to their inherent distributive impact on different categories of individuals, inevitably produce their own winners and losers. The apparent neutrality (and virtues) of the market can be exploited as a cover protecting a particular political agenda. Some individuals may well view the distribution of resources and the resulting winners and losers as either an optimal outcome or at least not a priori inferior to any other. Rooted in the Canadian experience, Evans takes a different view. Although theirs are not the individual material stakes so fervently nurtured by market imperatives, economists and other health care specialists who highlight the virtues of market arrangements, Evans argues, lend credence to the rhetoric of politically influential market advocates.

The Rice and Evans essays are the focus of two commentaries, one by Mark Pauly and another by Martin Gaynor and William Vogt. These authors offer a fundamentally different assessment of health economics, the role of the market, and associated political-economic issues. They suggest that the critical insights of Rice and Evans range from being obvious to simply being wrong, mischaracterizing the meaning and overstating the vulnerability to real-world applicability of principle components of economic analysis. They further contend that Rice and Evans fail to shine the same critical light upon government in practice as they do on markets in practice.

A reader being introduced to these disputes for the first time will understandably come away from this debate confused about what to make of the market and what specialists in the field have to say about it. In some senses that confusion is healthy, because it reflects the lack of analytical consensus that is too often hidden by the simplified arguments made by politicians and nonscholar advocates in the public arena. But there are also appropriate ways to put these strongly stated disagreements in context. When forging into these particular chapters and commentaries, I recommend that readers keep the following issues in mind: First, despite their differences, all of these health economists agree that the medical care market, as we currently experience it, is a far cry from the pure competitive model of microeconomic theory. In addition, I believe that they all would agree with Victor Fuch's comment that "the most important contribution we make is the economic point of view." Economic thinking forces a recognition that "resources are inherently scarce," that populations of individuals embody a "heterogeneity of preferences," and that choices involve making decisions at the margin among substitutable goods (Fuchs 1996: 3–4). These are all factors that have to be considered in any health care system no matter how it is organized.

Second, the sources of the disagreements among these authors can be identified and evaluated by readers in their own terms. To be sure, some of the contention has to do with the core values that any analyst brings to the table, either explicitly or implicitly, including what kinds of institutions one trusts more intuitively and what meaning one brings to such things as the scientific enterprise. More specifically, however, these authors are engaged in substantive dissension about what assumptions are appropriate to make when evaluating individual and institutional behavior. Some health economists, such as the commentators in this volume, are more comfortable treating individual preferences or tastes as the product of processes beyond the domain of economics (they are matters about which economists have little, if anything, to contribute). The values encompassing those preferences and the utility functions according to which individuals make decisions at the margin are taken to be essentially stable. Preferences are thus exogenous factors, accepted as given, from which analysis can begin.

Others, such as Rice and Evans, share the perspective expressed by Henry Aaron that values cannot be treated as axiomatically stable and that behavior, which both affects and is affected by the larger community and community norms, can influence preferences (Aaron 1994: 6–7). Starting the analysis with preferences as given, without incorporating the process by which preferences are formed, will, from this perspective, lead to erroneous conclusions. Additionally, analysts differ over how to view the highly skewed distribution of resources among individuals that establishes the budget constraints within which choices at the margin over substitutable goods have to be made. One can assume, as some market enthusiasts often do, that the original distribution of resources was judged fair by society, and thus subsequent distributions generated by the market can be accepted as given without making any value determinations (see Nozick 1974), or that this issue, too, is beyond the domain of economic analysis and rests with political and value decisions that the society has to make with respect to fairness. Market skeptics counter that neither view is appropriate for analysis. Material resources afford individuals political power—and thus influence over what issues are on the agenda and how they should be addressed—and influence preferences. Both effects, according to this view, subvert the neutrality or objectivity of analyses predicated on treating the distribution of resources as external to economic analysis.

Yet another area of potential conflict has to do with assumptions about efficiency and equity taken together. Many economists consider efficiency—making optimal choices given resource constraints—as one of the prime benefits of market arrangements. From this perspective, society must make value judgments about what it wants to accomplish, including whether or not to redistribute resources to achieve greater equality, but once that value judgment is cast, and it can only be a decision based on values, economic principles can be used to achieve that objective in the most efficient manner. Fuchs and others remind us, however, that it may be inappropriate to assume that "efficiency is society's only goal" or perhaps that it is even a primary goal (Fuchs 1996: 4). The emphasis on efficiency in itself may be a value judgment that cannot be offered as a first principle. To the extent that efficiency and equality represent a "big trade-off," in Arthur Okun's words, *neither* can be a starting assumption for objective analysis.

The market model applied to health care also raises issues not traditionally associated with economic analysis. A few are considered in the two essays that conclude part 1. Gary Belkin explores present claims about objectivity and the value of applying aggregate clinical outcomes to guide individual treatment decisions—hallmarks of managed care in the market environment—by exploring what he terms the "technocratic wish." Proponents of change often seek to trump political divisions and contests among competing claims of legitimacy by tying their favored approaches to the long-term logic of scientific and technocratic progress. These emergent practices in the American medical marketplace are not the result of battles over competing values, they are the rational result of the march of objective science. The history of science, however, reveals that this appeal to the technical fix is an oft-repeated pattern and that the claimed linkages to scientific advancement are at least partially socially constructed. Alternative and quite different formulations could compete for legitimacy in the same terms. Such is the case with managed care in the contemporary health care market.

The essay by Deborah Stone, "The Doctor as Businessman: The Changing Politics of a Cultural Icon," pursues another aspect of social construction affected by the market and managed care, the cultural perceptions of the physician. Physicians, the major point of contact for patients seeking medical care, are at the core of any health care system. Previous cultural norms in the United States promoted the perceptual convention—or pleasant fiction—that physicians performed their services free of financial considerations. They did what was best for their patients, regardless of the cost (albeit, often to their own significant financial benefit). Managed care arrangements grounded in the market model, especially those that spread financial risk to physicians, explicitly promote the opposite norm, making economic issues an essential feature of treatment decisions. That shift in cultural norms alters physician-patient relationships in ways that favor insurance interests and discourage treatment of individuals lacking insurance or those representing higher risks of utilization even if they are nominally covered by insurance.

The Market in Practice

Having assessed and critiqued the market model, as well as contentious claims about it, in part 2 of this book we turn to an evaluation of how market forces affect aspects of the current U.S. health care system. This subject has been and will keep health policy analysts busy for some time to come. Here we can only focus on a select number of issues. We begin by providing an overview of what is happening to the health care system across the board in the 1990s, the myriad activities by numerous participants in the process that are prompting the major shifts in institutional arrangements and norms. Paul Ginsburg, from his vantage point as president of the Center for Studying Health System Change, describes these organizational trends in "The Dynamics of Market-Level Change." He presents an initial broad survey of the factors that have spurred changes in the health care market, the strategies advanced by market competitors to succeed in this environment, and the implications for various kinds of participants—private and public purchasers of care, health plans, hospitals, physicians, safety-net providers, and consumers.

Next we want to know what effect these changes have had on the substance of health care in the nation. The widespread concerns about "care, cost, and coverage" that brought health care reform back to the agenda in the late 1980s and early 1990s did not disappear with the demise of reform legislation and an altered political environment. They have been affected in major ways by the rise of private-sector change and the spread of managed care, which Kenneth Thorpe examines in detail. Although the overall health care cost explosion has been mitigated, albeit with mixed results for different kinds of payers and with an uncertain future, the emergent competitive forces in the health care system are imposing new pressures on providers, especially hospitals, that historically used cross-subsidies to provide "uncompensated" care to the uninsured. Market restructuring in the health care sector has, at best, not diminished the ranks of the uninsured, but competitive contracting with hospitals is shrinking the resource base for treating them. Will the uninsured continue to have access to care? As Thorpe notes, with providers expected to be squeezed even further in the future by managed care organizations and public programs, the circumstances of the uninsured are likely to deteriorate, especially if federal and state policy makers are unable to enact programs to expand coverage.

Given these concerns about the health care market and managed care, what has brought about the rapid ascent of market approaches in the wake of health care reform's defeat? Business interests, Cathie Jo Martin reports, seemingly natural allies of marketlike approaches, understandably took the lead in promoting managed care. As the purchasers of most private insurance coverage, worried about unabated health care costs and seeing that government would not institute an effective system of fiscal discipline, employers and their benefit managers took the initiative to promote private solutions more than ever before. However, once the Republican majorities in the 104th Congress—the nominal political allies of business—sought to extend these market-oriented changes from private insurance to existing public programs like Medicare, the benefits for business interests were not so clear, and major divisions emerged between large and small employers.

Like publicly funded or directed health insurance programs throughout the world, Medicare and Medicaid reflect concrete cultural acceptance of the provision of medical care as a social good that should not be distributed substantially on the basis of ability to pay, at least for arguably "deserving" individuals. Both programs, although in different ways, socialize the financing of medical benefits made universally available to each of the defined populations of eligible individuals. These social attributes of the two programs are quite different from those that motivate overall market-oriented organization of health care. That makes it particularly important to evaluate the effects and implications of using an expanded range of market instruments, such as managed care and private plans, in these publicly financed programs.

Jonathan Oberlander's essay evaluates the specific initiative to expand the use of managed care in the Medicare program. Risk contracts under Medicare were already on the rise by the mid-1990s, but Medicare managed care—and with it the emergence of beneficiaries as consumers choosing among competing private health plans—is certain to accelerate rapidly as a result of the 1997 balanced budget agreement enacted by Congress and signed by President Clinton, which introduced the largest substantive changes in the program since its inception in 1965. Although the coordinating functions of managed care can be beneficial for a population that makes extensive use of myriad medical services and many specialties, often simultaneously, Oberlander flags concerns about an approach to delivering medical care that has strong economic incentives to shun the kinds of people for whom Medicare is most important: the old and the sick. Medicare and managed care need not be mutually exclusive, but they are not an easy fit.

The Medicaid program offers a potentially different story. States are rapidly moving to replace their publicly administered fee-for-service programs with systems built on public contracts with competing private managed care organizations. Managed care for the acute-care portion of Medicaid, serving primarily poor women and children, can actually expand the range of providers available to the poor and provide easier (and maybe first-time) access to primary caregivers. But it can wreak havoc on a vulnerable, politically weak population with special needs. As Marsha Gold shows in her comparison of the implementation of Medicaid managed care in Oregon and Tennessee, the success of using this particular market-oriented instrument in a publicly funded health care program mixing state and federal administration is highly contingent on a number of factors, such as a state's previous experience with managed care in the private sector, the manner in which the new program is formulated, and the expectations that are imposed upon it. Gold concludes that managed care is neither a "poison pill" nor a "silver bullet" for Medicaid.

Reflections on the Road Ahead

Policy issues are never finally settled. The tremendous changes taking place in the U.S. health care market have all the hallmarks of a revolution, but revolutions are as much beginnings as they are endings. Private actors and public officials will continue to react to change, promote new avenues of policy, and project alternative interpretations of the existing reality at any given moment. After having remained relatively mute, standing as quiet spectators on the sidelines of private-sector change, elected officials at both the state and federal level are again considering formal public policy responses to the exigencies of the health care market. The partisanly polarized 104th Congress and President Clinton came to agreement on modest insurance market reforms with the Health Insurance Portability and Accountability Act, providing some additional security primarily to those who already have private insurance as a benefit of employment. With growing public concerns about some of the ways managed care is practiced, Congress enacted legislation, with the President's support, that requires insurers to pay for forty-eight hour maternity hospital stays and mandates a version of parity in lifetime limits for coverage of mental health and physical illness (Clinton 1996b; Pear 1996c). More proposed legislation is in the hopper. In 1996, Clinton also announced that he would establish an Advisory Commission on Consumer Protection and Quality in the Health Care Industry to "recommend ways of protecting consumers against changes in the health care industry that threaten the quality of care" (Executive Order 1996; Pear 1996b). The commission quietly took up its mandate during the president's second term, recommending its own version of a consumer's "bill of rights," but without specifying how it should be implemented (Pear 1997). Responding to the same pressures, state legislators introduced hundreds of bills to regulate the managed care industry in ways small and large, from requiring insurance coverage for in-patient mastectomies to instituting comprehensive consumer protection acts. Most states have enacted at least some of these provisions (Families USA 1996). In addition, Congress and the president began down the road of Medicare reform. Long-term changes to meet the challenges of the baby-boom generation's retirement remain in the hands of a commission and future legislative action, but in the meantime the reforms enacted in 1997 ensure that Medicare will effectively be merging with the private market of competing managed care plans. Within both the employer-based and Medicare domains, too, we now have experiments going on in the promotion of medical savings accounts (MSAs).

Will policy makers in the future pursue and implement approaches to policy that incorporate appropriate lessons from the assessments of market approaches presented in this book and in other forums? As I argue in the opening essay of part 3, that depends on the character of the social learning process, the means by which policy makers learn about both the substantive effectiveness and political viability of different policy options. There are compelling reasons to be skeptical of how well our state and federal officials will respond to the transformation of the medical marketplace. When the issues are highly salient to more than the career bureaucrats in the implementing agencies, the analytical dimension of policy learning tends to be overwhelmed by political considerations. That is especially true when powerful interests have significant stakes to protect and the expert community is divided within itself. Lawrence Brown's essay, "Exceptionalism as the Rule? U.S. Health Policy Innovation and Cross-National Learning," notes that policy learning about health care markets is not restricted to U.S. officials. Policy makers in Europe and elsewhere are looking to both our own market experience and the expertise generated by American health services research to develop marketlike methods to enhance fiscal discipline and efficiency within their own systems. Brown emphasizes that they "adapt" rather than "adopt" elements of the American model, and in the process of employing them in the very different context of established social solidarity on health care coverage may once again be the source of important lessons for future policy making in the United States.

In the final chapter of the book, Theodore Marmor asks whether we can derive reasonable predictions about the future direction of the U.S. health care system carefully conditioned on plausible alternative political and economic scenarios. Revisiting predictions along these lines that he and Paul Starr presented in the early 1980s, Marmor demonstrates the relative utility of such an approach. The dramatic speed and broad scope of the market changes we have witnessed over the past couple of years, however, challenge the efficacy of making any predictions at all, even contingent ones based on different combinations of political and economic conditions.

One will not finish reading this book, therefore, confident about what the U.S. health care system will look like in 2010. We do know, however, that it will be different from the system that would have been produced had federal and state health care reform initiatives not failed and the health care market not transformed itself so thoroughly. Our best hope is that private actors and government officials will make decisions individually and collectively that produce arrangements for health care financing and delivery that grant all Americans full access to affordable, high quality health care at the lowest possible social and individual cost. This book does not provide the answer for how to achieve the normative objectives of equity *and* efficiency, but it is intended to yield analytical guidance for making reasoned judgments about the transition that is underway from the twentieth-century health care system to that of the twenty-first century.

Acknowledgments

Major conferences and the publications that follow do not happen without the support of myriad institutions and individuals. This particular undertaking was made possible in the most literal sense of the word by a generous grant from the Robert Wood Johnson Foundation. As usual, RWJF vice presidents Robert Hughes and James Knickman not only endorsed the project but were actively involved in the program. The Robert Wood Johnson Foundation contributed indirectly as well to the enterprise through two of its recent initiatives invigorating the social sciences in the study of health care policy. One author in this volume (Jon Oberlander) was a participant in the Scholars in Health Policy Research Program. Two others (Mark Schlesinger and I) have benefited from the Investigator Awards in Health Policy Research Program.

Additional support for the conference was provided by the Center for Health Policy Research and Education. I am grateful to Frank Sloan, the center's director, for his gracious assistance and participation. Duke University Press, the publisher of the *Journal of Health Politics, Policy and Law* throughout its history, did a superb job of coordinating conference activities. We are indebted to Stephen Cohn and Rachel Toor for their hard labors and dedication to the project. The journal production staff at

Duke University Press, especially Angela Williams, Mike Brondoli, and Rob Dilworth, had their lives disrupted by the "elephant in the python" that the conference issues proved to be. I appreciate their patience and unstinting dedication to the journal. Creating this book from the foundation of this previous work depended on the enthusiasm, encouragement, and solid advice provided by Valerie Millholland. As usual, Paula Dragosh and other members of the Duke University Press staff provided superb assistance. I would also like to thank a set of individuals whose words do not appear in these pages, but whose facility as panel moderators at the conference helped to make the project gel intellectually: Rashi Fein, Harvard University; Beth Fuchs, Congressional Research Service; Robert Hughes, Robert Wood Johnson Foundation; Carol Rissman, Families USA; Karen Schimke, New York Department of Health; Carolyn Tuohy, University of Toronto; and Debbie Ward, Group Health Cooperative of Puget Sound.

Three individuals in the journal's editorial office bore the burden of organizing the conference and managing the paper flow associated with moving the conference papers first to journal publication, and then, revised, to inclusion in this book. Jacquelyn Stephanou, the journal's former managing editor, led the initial effort, aided by Ranjan Chaudhuri, the journal's editorial assistant. Their long hours, hard work, attention to detail, and diplomacy in maneuvering through the university bureaucracy are deeply appreciated by everyone involved in the project. Hope Kurtz became the journal's managing editor just as the mass of papers from the conference hit the journal's production stream, made all the more complicated by the new bimonthly publication schedule. She has now also overseen the assemblage of this book. It was a baptism by fire. Her perseverance in the face of multiple and conflicting deadlines literally made this project possible.

Two other individuals contributed significantly to this project in ways that cannot, thankfully, be measured by even the best analyst. In the course of late nights at the office, travel, and the burdens of competing projects, Jane Margolis and Sophie Margolis-Peterson afforded me patience beyond the call, unconditional support, and the best of all possible rewards, the essential joys of life.

Notes

1   Neoclassical economists typically argue that, generally speaking, employers should not be particularly concerned about the costs of providing health care insurance coverage to their employees. All employers care about, with regard to labor, are the

total costs of compensation. Increases in one area of compensation, such as health insurance benefits, can be countered by reductions in other forms of compensation, including wages and salaries. Indeed, employees pay the total costs of their health care coverage by accepting lower wages equivalent to the cost of benefits. As long as that trade-off is a practical possibility, business does not have a specific interest in health care costs, and any perceptions to the contrary are misplaced. However, if the direct employer share of health care costs rises faster than can be neutralized by changes in wages or reductions in other nonwage forms of compensation, perhaps due to collective bargaining agreements and other sources of "stickiness" in wages, then the health care cost spiral merits more attention. The 1970s and 1980s arguably generated such real pressures on employers.

2   See Levit, Lazenby, and Sivarajan 1996, A Look at Employers' Costs of Providing Health Benefits, and Clinton 1996a.

3   Information in this paragraph comes from HMO Industry Report 1996, 1995 AAHP HMO and PPO Trends Report 1996, HMO-PPO Digest 1997, Blues Growth Tied to Managed Care 1996, Managed Care in Medicare and Medicaid 1997, The *Competitive Edge* Regional Market Analysis 1996, Popularity of HMOs Grows 1996, Rosenthal 1996, Berger 1996, Simon and Born 1996, and Jensen et al. 1997.

4   Information for this paragraph comes from Haas-Wilson and Gaynor 1996, U.S. Hospitals 1996, 1995 National Hospital Merger and Acquisition Survey 1996, and Olmos 1996.

5   Information for this paragraph comes from Mega Managed Care Deal 1996, HMO-PPO Digest 1996, *Competitive Edge* HMO Industry Report 7.1 1997, and Levinson 1996.

Part 1 *The Market Model*

Can Markets Give Us the Health System We Want?

Thomas Rice

n recent years there has been a surge of interest in reforming health care systems by replacing government regulation with a reliance on market forces. Although much of the impetus has come from the United States, the phenomenon is worldwide. Spurred by ever-increasing health care costs, many analysts and policy makers have embraced the competitive market as the method of choice for reforming health care. This belief stems from economic theory, which purports to show the superiority of markets over government regulation.

This has led advocates to champion a number of policies, including:

- providing low-income people with subsidies to allow them to purchase health insurance, rather than paying directly for the services they use;
- having people pay more money out-of-pocket in order to receive health care services, especially for services whose demand is most responsive to price;
- also requiring that they pay more in premiums to obtain more extensive health insurance coverage;
- letting the market determine the number and distribution of hospitals and what services they provide, as well as the total number of physicians and their distribution among specialties;
- removing regulations that control the development and diffusion of medical technologies;
- eschewing government involvement in determining how much a country spends on health care services.

This essay attempts to show that economic theory does not support the specific belief that such policies will enhance economic efficiency, or the more general one that they will increase social welfare.[1] This is because the theory is based on a large set of assumptions that are not and cannot be met in the health care sector. Although it is well known among economists and noneconomists alike that some set of assumptions needs to be met to ensure that market forces will result in socially desirable outcomes, what is less understood are the specific assumptions that comprise the list.[2] This essay reviews a number of assumptions that are particularly relevant to health care competition and the theory of demand for care.[3] The above list comprises only a fraction of the total number of assumptions upon which conclusions about the superiority of market forces are based.[4]

This essay is aimed at both health economists and noneconomist health policy researchers. It is an attempt to remind economists that it is inappropriate for them to bring into their work any preconceptions that relying on market forces in health care provides the preferred set of social policies. The arguments are also intended to cast doubt on the validity of various tools that health economists often use to analyze the health care sector.

For noneconomists, this essay should help clarify what economic theory can and cannot conclude about the desirability of market-based health care reforms. Because economics uses a language of its own, it is often difficult for the other professions to comprehend fully the methods used, and evaluate the conclusions reached, by health economists. (In this regard, Joan Robinson stated, "Study economics to avoid being deceived by economists," quoted in Kuttner 1984: 1.) It is hoped that this essay can be used by noneconomists to level the playing field when competing with economists for the ear of policy makers.

The essay is divided into two main sections: The first focuses on the economic theory of market competition, and the second on the theory of demand. The competition section discusses three assumptions that affect economic analyses of markets in general, although the applications provided all pertain to health. The section on demand focuses more specifically on applying the assumptions of demand analysis to health care. Each section is divided into three parts: a short review of the relevant economic theory (which can be skipped by those who are familiar with microeconomics), a discussion of problems with the theory, and implications for health policy.

Market Competition

Review of economic theory
The field of microeconomics is devoted to the study of competition— mainly its virtues, but also some of its pitfalls. Although many of the

techniques used by economists are fairly new, the emphasis on competition is not, dating back to the writings of Adam Smith over two hundred years ago. Smith believed that people, driven by their own economic interest in the marketplace, are guided by an "invisible hand" to act in a manner that ultimately is most beneficial to society at large.

The notion of competition is intuitively appealing. In a competitive market, people are allowed—but not compelled—to trade their stock of wealth, including their labor, to purchase goods and services. Firms are compelled to produce only those things that people will be willing to purchase, and to do so in the least costly manner. Once everyone stops trading because they see no more advantage, the market is in *equilibrium*. Such an outcome is desirable for several reasons: (a) people are making their own choices; (b) the only goods and services produced are those that people demand, and they are produced without wasting economic resources; and (c) by not engaging in any more trades, people *reveal themselves*[5] to be as satisfied with their economic lot as possible, given the resources with which they began.

There are two facets to competitive theory: consumption and production. In consumer theory, people seek to maximize their *utility*, which is determined by the bundle of goods and services that they possess. To do so, they purchase their ideal bundle based on their desire or *taste* for alternative goods, and based on the prices of these alternatives (subject, of course, to how much income they have available to spend). In production theory, firms seek to maximize profits. To do so, they purchase inputs and transform them into outputs through the application of some sort of technology. How many inputs of each type are purchased depends on how each affects output, as well as their prices.

When both the consumption and production markets are in equilibrium, and when some other conditions are met,[6] the economy will be in a position called *Pareto optimality* (named after Italian economist Vilfredo Pareto). If the economy is in a Pareto optimal state, it is impossible to make someone better off (i.e., increase their welfare) without making someone else worse off. In such a situation, the economy has reached a state of *allocative efficiency*, although as we shall see next, this rests on a number of assumptions.

How does an economy reach Pareto optimality? Economists have shown that if certain conditions are met, a free or competitive market operating on its own will reach such a Pareto optimal state. As a result, allowing competition to occur will result in a situation where it is impossible to make someone better off without making someone else worse off. Taxes and subsidies can then be used to redistribute income so that society's overall welfare can be maximized.

This last point—the need to redistribute income once competition brings about Pareto optimality—is extremely important. A competitive equilibrium can occur when one person has nearly all of the output, and another has almost none. In fact, this can easily occur if the former person begins with the vast majority of initial wealth. This point was made graphically by Amartya Sen (1970: 22), who wrote:

> An economy can be [Pareto] optimal . . . even when some people are rolling in luxury and others are near starvation as long as the starvers cannot be made better off without cutting into the pleasures of the rich. If preventing the burning of Rome would have made Emperor Nero feel worse off, then letting him burn Rome would have been Pareto-optimal. In short, a society or an economy can be Pareto-optimal and still be perfectly disgusting.

Although it might seem desirable to transfer wealth from the rich person to the poor person, this cannot be viewed as improving the economy from a Paretian viewpoint because it will involve making the rich person worse off. If society cares about both efficiency and equity, then it will have to redistribute income—a process that obviously involves value judgments—for it to reach its highest level of welfare.

Problems with the economic theory

It would appear that the traditional economic model of competition has a strong grip on health economists. This is supported by a 1989 survey of health economists in the United States and Canada (Feldman and Morrisey 1990). One of the questions asked was whether the competitive model cannot apply to the health care system. Respondents were evenly divided on this question; half thought the model could apply, and half did not. More noteworthy, perhaps, were some of the response patterns to the question. Two-thirds of respondents who received their doctorates from top economics departments thought that the competitive model could apply, versus 53 percent with degrees from other economics departments. Few of those who received their training in noneconomics departments believed that the competitive model could apply to the health care system. Similarly, in his recent survey of health economists, Victor Fuchs (1996) found a great deal of agreement on so-called positive issues, but very little on normative ones, which would presumably include whether health economists believe that the competitive model should be applied to the health care market.

There is thus evidence that many, if not most, health economists believe that the competitive model is an appropriate means for studying (and perhaps reforming) health care systems. The remainder of this section examines three reasons why such a belief is not warranted; each of these reasons is tied to one of the assumptions around which the purported superiority of the market-based model is based. The following section then applies this to health care.

The Pareto Principle. As noted here, if certain assumptions are met, then allowing competition to occur will result in a state of the world called Pareto optimality, where it is impossible to increase one person's welfare without lowering that of another. Rarely do economists step back and consider whether Pareto optimality is indeed a desirable state of the world. But if the Pareto principle is thought to be problematic, then market competition—which leads to Pareto optimality—would not necessarily be the best way to bring about socially desirable outcomes. Rather, other policies, involving perhaps the regulation of certain industries and even restrictions on what consumers can purchase, could be superior.

It is not hard to see the appeal of the Pareto principle. Why not let people engage in trade until they are satisfied with their lot and no longer wish to engage in further trades? Similarly, why not enact policies that convey benefits to some people and no cost to others? Wouldn't encouraging such trade and enacting such policies be in everyone's best interest?

The answer to this last question is, perhaps surprisingly, "not necessarily." As noted before, under the standard economic theory, consumers derive utility from the quantity of each of the alternative goods that they possess. It is important to think about what is *not* part of this conception of utility. There is no consideration given to how one's bundle of goods and services compares to, and affects or is affected by, those possessed by other people. Stated simply, only one's absolute amount of wealth matters; one's relative standing is irrelevant.

We therefore need to ask, Which conception of utility best represents people's actual behavior—one in which only absolute wealth matters, or one where relative standing is important as well? Intuition would tell us that the Pareto conception, in which only one's own possessions matter, is implausible if not downright wrong. It implies that people are indifferent to their rank or status in society. Rather, all that they care about is what they themselves have, irrespective of whether this is more or less, better or worse, than others with whom they have contact. Suppose that this is not the case, and that people do care about these issues. Then the fact that one person has increased his or her utility by obtaining more goods could in fact lower the utility of another person who does not obtain more goods.

In this regard, A. C. Pigou (1932: 90), one of the founders of modern economics, quoted and affirmed John Stuart Mill's statement, "Men do not desire to be *rich,* but to be richer than other men." In a lighter vein, Robert Frank (1985: 5) noted that "H. L. Mencken once defined wealth as any income that is at least one hundred dollars more a year than the income of one's wife's sister's husband." Lester Thurow (1980: 18) has stated that once incomes exceed the subsistence level, "individual perceptions of the adequacy of their economic performance depend almost solely on relative as opposed to absolute position."

Is there any evidence to support the belief that people care about their relative standing in addition to their absolute level of wealth? Richard Easterlin's (1974) study of human happiness in fourteen countries is particularly relevant here. He found that in a given country at a particular time, wealthier people tend to be happier than poorer people. Within a given country over time, however, happiness levels are surprisingly constant, even in the wake of rising real incomes. Furthermore, average levels of happiness are fairly constant across countries; people in poor countries and wealthy countries claim to be about equally happy. The only way such findings can be reconciled is if both relative wealth and absolute wealth matter.[7] Easterlin's findings contradict the notion that people care only about their own level of wealth.

Suppose that one accepts the notion that people are concerned with how they compare with others. It could still be argued that, even so, it is an irrational and/or flawed character trait that should not be respected by the analyst or policy maker. But this argument doesn't hold up for two reasons. First, the traditional economic theory does not evaluate where preferences come from or whether they are good or bad. Instead, it views them as what has to be satisfied in order for an individual, and ultimately, a society to be in a best-off position. Second, concern about one's status, rather than being irrational or even undesirable, is an essential element of human nature allowing not only individuals, but also a society, to prosper. In this regard, Tibor Scitovsky (1976: 115) has written: "The desire to 'live up to the Joneses' is often criticized and its rationality called into question. This is absurd and unfortunate. Status seeking, the wish to belong, the asserting and cementing of one's membership in the group is a deep-seated and very natural drive whose origin and universality go beyond man and are explained by that most basic of drives, the desire to survive." What others have can also be viewed as necessary information for a person in formulating his or her individual desires: It shows what can be had, what is reasonable to expect.

Why is the Pareto principle so important to the belief that markets are superior? It is because markets are able to satisfy individuals only if people care about their absolute bundle of possessions rather than how they stand relative to others. Although health applications will be provided later, an example may help illustrate this. Suppose that an extremely expensive therapy is developed that can substantially reduce the chance of contracting a fatal disease, but only a few people can afford it. Under a market model, this therapy will be available only to those few. This will obviously increase their utility, but it would likely reduce the utility of a far greater group who would know that a life-saving technology was available—but not to them. Relying on markets would therefore tend to reduce overall social welfare. To improve society's overall lot, it might be better if government intervened either to ensure equal access to the technology, or perhaps even to thwart its availability.

Externalities of Consumption. Another assumption necessary for showing the superiority of market competition is that there are no externalities of consumption, or alternatively, that any such externalities are explicitly dealt with through public policy. A consumption externality exists when one person's consumption of a good or service has an effect on the utility of another person. There are positive and negative externalities of consumption. With a positive externality, one person's consumption of a good raises the utility of another person. With a negative externality, it lowers another person's utility.

The existence of important externalities like these means that the operation of a competitive market, by itself, will not result in a socially optimal outcome. One possible way to improve matters is through government intervention. In the case of a positive externality, like immunizations, government can subsidize their provision, even providing them free of charge. By funding such a program through taxes, most taxpayers would help contribute, which would seem desirable because so many people are benefiting. Dealing with a negative consumption externality, like smoking, is somewhat more problematic. Although it is easy to tax smokers by enacting special taxes on the production or consumption of cigarettes, it is much harder to ensure that this revenue is dispersed to those who are most affected by smoking. As a result, governmental bodies in the United States have taken an additional step of prohibiting smoking in many public places.

In this section we will deal with a different type of consumption externality, which has received far less consideration from economists: *concern about the well-being of others.* If we care about other people's needs as well as our own—be they specific ones like food or medical care, or somewhat more vague concerns about how happy they view themselves—then there is a positive externality of consumption.[8] As just mentioned, a competitive market, by itself, will not provide the desirable amount of goods and services for which there is a positive externality. Note that this does not contradict the previous discussion about people feeling envy or having concern about status. It is not unreasonable to believe that people would envy those who have more than they do, and have benevolence toward those who have less.

It is important to understand that this issue is not just about equity: It concerns efficiency as well. Suppose for a moment that I care about poor people and want them to have more food and medical care. In order to increase my own utility, I would want to give some of my resources to the poor.

Why doesn't everyone just donate their optimal amount to charity, which in turn should maximize their personal utility? The problem is that many, if not most, people will attempt to become "free riders," recognizing that the poor will do about as well if everyone except themselves provides donations. This, in turn, will result in less redistribution than is economically efficient; people would feel better if there were a way to redistribute the optimal amount of resources rather than the lesser amount that occurs through the free market.

There is a standard "answer" to this problem in traditional economics. That is to rely on markets to allocate resources efficiently, and then to employ just the right amount of a special kind of tax and subsidy to redistribute income. These are called *lump-sum* taxes and subsidies. It is important to understand the nature of these lump-sum transfers. The idea is to come up with a way to tax, say, the wealthy, to subsidize, perhaps, the poor, without changing in any important way the efficiency-enhancing incentives of a competitive market.

The problem with this lump-sum solution is the virtual impossibility of establishing true lump-sum taxes and subsidies;[9] no such taxes exist that would also be politically acceptable.[10] But if no such methods are feasible, then use of market competition becomes problematic when there are consumption externalities. If we do not redistribute income, the market is inefficient because people want the poor to be better off than they are. But if we do redistribute income—say, by the traditional method, the income tax—we damage the efficiency that the marketplace is designed to create.

Thus, in making policy, it is impossible to separate issues of resource allocation from issues of resource distribution. Rather, they both must be dealt with simultaneously. But this is not in keeping with the traditional method often preached by economists, in which markets are allowed to operate in an unfettered fashion and redistribution is only done afterward, usually through cash transfers rather than through the direct provision of goods and services.

This anomaly—the impossibility of separating allocative and distributional activities of the economy—has been raised, in a variety of contexts, by several economists, but has received little attention from the profession at large.[11] The primary implication for policy makers is a crucially important one: Allocative and distributive decisions by a society should be made in conjunction with each other, not separately.

This concern would be eased if income were redistributed to the degree desired by members of society. But if it is not, then other strategies are necessary to deal with both the inefficiencies and inequities that arise when there are positive externalities of consumption. One of the best ways is to enact policies to ensure that those in need obtain goods and services even if they do not have the economic resources to purchase them in the marketplace. Programs like Medicare and Medicaid, which are not in keeping with some economists' recommendations to rely on competition and then redistribute resources through cash subsidies, offer good examples of how society grapples with problems like these.

Consumer Tastes Are Predetermined. Of all of the assumptions in the traditional economic model, perhaps the one that is most often forgotten is that consumers' tastes are already established when they enter the marketplace. This turns out to be very important; this section will attempt to show that this assumption is not realistic, and that when it is dropped, the competitive model loses many of its advantages.

Economics is almost universally viewed as a social science. The common element among all social sciences is that they seek to understand how individuals and/or groups of people behave, and each has its own way of viewing human behavior. Sociology, for example, focuses on how behavior is affected by society's organization, social stratification, group dynamics, and the like (Mechanic 1979). Political science examines how individuals and groups attempt to obtain what they want through such means as "conflict, influence, and authoritative collective decision making in both public and private settings" (Marmor and Dunham 1983: 3). Social psychology attempts to understand "the influences that people have upon the beliefs or behavior of others" (Aronson 1972: 6).

One facet of these other social sciences is that, in general, they seek to determine how people and groups *actually* behave, not how they *ought to* be behaving. In economics, on the other hand, one commonly sees the word *ought* (e.g., people *ought* to maximize their utility, or otherwise they are being "irrational"; to maximize social welfare, a society *ought* to depend on a competitive marketplace).

In economic theory, individual tastes and preferences "simply exist— fully developed and immutable—" (Thurow 1983: 219). This is what Kenneth Boulding (1969: 1) has referred to as the "Immaculate Conception of the Indifference Curve," because "tastes are simply given, and . . . we cannot inquire into the process by which they are formed." Milton Friedman (1962b: 13) provided one explanation for this: "Economic theory proceeds largely to take wants as fixed . . . primarily [as] a case of division of labor. The economist has little to say about the formation of wants; this is the province of the psychologist. The economist's task is to trace the consequences of any given set of wants."

Henry Aaron (1994: 7) recently pointed out one of the problems with this viewpoint, when individuals' behavior influences the community and is influenced by it. He noted: "It is then essential to recognize how changes in individual beliefs and values alter the environment in which individual actions occur. The environment is important both because people's preferences are shaped by pressure from peers and neighbors and because community attitudes shape the actual payoffs to various kinds of individual behavior."

The unrealistic nature of the assumption of predetermined tastes is easy to see. Consider the case of advertising. The reader, who is likely well versed in the tactics of the media, probably will admit that most advertising is not aimed at providing objective information so that consumers can obtain the best value. Rather, it is designed to (a) *minimize* the consumer search process, and more generally, (b) change consumer tastes, in part by exerting social pressure. It is hard to claim that the tastes people come to have, as the result of exposure to this sort of advertising, are sacrosanct. In fact, people often make "bad" or nonmaximizing decisions by acting on the message: the hallmark of a successful advertising campaign!

Why, then, does economics consider tastes predetermined rather than subject to the forces of change? Readers who are most familiar with economic theory will understand one possible reason. The primary tenet of modern economics is the sanctity of consumer choice. Most economists believe that the consumer is the best judge of what will maximize his or her utility. Consequently, to maximize overall social welfare, we should set up an economic system that is best at allowing consumer choices to be satisfied. Where these choices come from, as Friedman said, is beside the point.[12]

In contrast, it might be true that your current tastes are determined not on the basis of preferences that are endemic to you, so much as on what you consumed in the past. This implies a strong advantage for whatever is the status quo; familiarity breeds preference (as opposed to contempt), so what exists now will be demanded in the future. But if that is the case, it could be argued that in demanding goods and services in the marketplace, you are *wanting what you got* rather than getting what you want (Pollak 1978).

If what you want depends on what you had in the past, or on the influence of advertisers, then it is not clear that a competitive marketplace is the best way to make people better-off. In the following paragraphs, three examples are provided in which people's market behaviors are not predetermined, but rather are a result of their past or present environments. In each case, it is not clear that fulfillment of their personal choices would make them best-off.

The first example, and perhaps the least important of the three given, concerns addiction. Suppose that, while growing up, you are in a peer group that smokes cigarettes, and you become addicted. Once you leave that peer group, you will still have a "taste" for cigarettes and are more likely to demand them than someone who is not addicted. Can we really say, in such an instance, that satisfying this taste through the marketplace is efficient from a societal standpoint—in the same way as satisfying the demand for bread or literature? Might not you be better off if cigarettes are taxed so prohibitively (or even banned) by the government as to make you stop smoking?[13]

A second and much more general application is habit formed by past consumption patterns.[14] Suppose you live in a community that has not discovered the joys of music. A resident of such a place will, therefore, not have developed a taste for music. But, as Alfred Marshall (1920: 94), one of the founders of modern economics, once noted, "The more good music a man hears, the stronger is his taste for it likely to become." The aforementioned resident might likely be better off with music than without, but he or she has not been sufficiently "educated" to know this. Government intervention, in the form, perhaps, of funding for the arts, could make people better off than pure reliance on the marketplace.

The third example concerns occupational choices. In the traditional economic model, it is assumed that people make occupational choices by weighing all alternatives; factors considered would include how much satisfaction they obtain from the work and the wages that it offers. Whatever choice is made in a competitive labor market is assumed to be utility maximizing. But this might not be the case if tastes are a product of one's environment. Suppose, for example, that a person grows up in a factory town and later decides to work in the factory. This might not necessarily be utility maximizing; it is possibly a poor choice for such a person, which was made because of his or her limited opportunities. As another example, imagine that one person works to perform house-cleaning services for another. This may not reflect the personal preferences as much as lack of good alternatives (Buchanan 1977). In this regard, John Roemer (1994: 120) stated that "people learn to live with what they are accustomed to or what is available to them. . . . Thus the slave may have adapted to like slavery; welfare judgments based on individual preferences are clearly impugned in such situations." Again, we see that the status quo would be favored by competitive markets, even though people might be better off if society, in some way, intervened in these choices. A public job-training program would be an example of the type of intervention that could be beneficial to society.

If this is true and people's tastes are indeed the product of their environment, why is this an indictment of market forces? It is because people's demand for goods and services might not reflect the things that would make them best-off.[15] In health care, for example, people may not demand certain preventive services that would make them better-off, in part because they grew up in an environment in which more high-tech medical interventions were stressed. In such an instance, having the government provide or subsidize such services would then be superior to relying on the market, where they are not purchased in sufficient quantity. But if consumer tastes are viewed as predetermined, as they are in the market model, people become "stuck" with whatever they demand, because they are assumed to always know best.

Implications for health policy

The previous discussion attempted to show that, despite popular belief to the contrary, economic theory does not provide a strong justification for the superiority of market competition in the health care area because the competitive model is based on certain assumptions that do not appear to be met. This section provides some implications of these conclusions for health care policy.

Equalizing Access to Health Care Services. The Pareto principle states that if society can make someone better off without making someone else worse off, it should do so. At first glance, it might appear that most developed countries do believe in the Pareto principle when it comes to health policy. After all, almost all countries, even those with comprehensive universal health insurance programs, allow their citizens to spend their own money on additional health care services if they wish to go outside the government-sanctioned program.

But upon closer examination, it can be demonstrated that health care policy has been (and continues to be) conducted on principles quite contrary to the Pareto principle. This is even true in the United States, where, it will be argued, society has not tended to tolerate large differences in access to care.

Evidence supporting this belief dates back many years. Beginning with the post–World War II period, public funding for building and expanding hospitals under the Hill-Burton Act directly reflected a belief that poorer, rural areas of the United States should not be disadvantaged relative to wealthier, urban areas of the country. By defining the need for hospitals based on the per capita availability of beds, the philosophy behind Hill-Burton was that no areas of the country should be given greater access than others to hospital care.

Further evidence can be seen by examining the political fallout that arose from the Oregon proposal for Medicaid reform, which was dubbed as requiring "rationing" of services. Early versions of the proposal engendered a great deal of opposition, mainly because program beneficiaries would not be able to receive coverage for the same services as the rest of the insured population. Rather, what services would be paid for would depend on how much money was available. Less cost-effective services would not be covered if program money was exhausted after paying for more cost-effective services. This prompted Bruce Vladeck (1990: 3), who later became director of the federal government's Health Care Financing Administration, to write: "This will be the first system in memory to explicitly plan that poor people with treatable illnesses will die if Medicaid runs out of money or does not budget correctly, and providers will be excused from liability for failing to treat them. The Oregonians argue that it is healthier for society to make such choices explicitly, but it is hardly healthy to establish rules of the game that require such choices." In fact, the proposal was cleared by federal officials only after the methodology was revised to ensure that disabled individuals would not face discrimination in coverage (Fox and Leichter 1993), and after the state made it clear that all essential services would be provided.

A final, and probably the most compelling, example of how health policy operates in conflict with the Pareto principle concerns coverage for new health care technologies. Traditionally, when new and potentially effective technologies become available, they are viewed as experimental until their safety and efficacy are established. But once they are established, insurers almost always cover them; failure to do so first results in strong pressure from policyholders, and eventually lawsuits that the insurer is withholding necessary medical care. Having these technologies covered by public and private insurance ensures their access to the large majority of the population who possess health insurance. In this regard, Uwe Reinhardt (1992: 311) wrote:

> Suppose [that a] new, high-tech medical intervention [is available] and that more of it could be produced without causing reductions in the output of any other commodity. Suppose next, however, that the associated rearrangement of the economy has been such that only well-to-do patients will have access to the new medical procedure. On these assumptions, can we be sure that [this] would enhance overall *social welfare?* Would we not have to assume the absence of *social envy* among the poor and of guilt among the well-to-do? Are these reasonable assumptions? Or should civilized policy analysts refuse to pay heed to base human motives such as envy, prevalent though it may be in any normal society?

If public policy were based on the Pareto principle, then we would see a market-driven gap between the services that are available to the wealthy and those available to the rest of the population. This would likely result in reduced social welfare, as noted by Reinhardt. But we do not see such a gap; once a procedure is found to be safe and effective, everyone with private health insurance is potentially eligible to receive it. And, if insurers are not sufficiently quick to adopt new procedures, states can and do mandate their provision.[16]

What Comes First: Allocation or Distribution? In the traditional economic paradigm, a competitive market ensures that resources are allocated efficiently. But if there are positive externalities of consumption, for example, if society wants poorer people to have more resources, then the free-rider effect will prevent a competitive economy from achieving allocative efficiency. The traditional economic solution to this problem is to institute lump-sum taxes and subsidies because they do not distort incentives and reduce efficiency, but in practice, no such mechanisms are available.

Rather than relying on this economic paradigm, what all developed countries do, instead, is confront allocative and distributive issues concurrently. In the United States, public programs like Medicare and Medicaid were established outside the competitive marketplace in order to ensure that their priority—access to medical care services for the elderly and the poor—was met. There is now much discussion about introducing more competition into both programs, and perhaps that will occur.

Nevertheless, such proposals have engendered a tremendous amount of opposition because it is contended that the introduction of more competition will jeopardize the principles that formed the basis of these programs in the first place.

The belief that we should start with principles of fairness, and then proceed to considerations of efficiency, is also the foundation upon which most other health care systems have been built. In their comprehensive study of health care financing and equity in nine European countries and the United States, Adam Wagstaff and Eddy van Doorslaer (1992: 363) found that:

> There appears to be broad agreement . . . among policy-makers in at least eight of the nine European countries . . . that payments towards health care should be related to ability to pay rather than to use of medical facilities. Policy makers in all nine European countries also appear to be committed to the notion that all citizens should have access to health care. In many countries this is taken further, it being made clear that access to and receipt of health care should depend on need, rather than on ability to pay.

No countries have adopted the economic approach of starting with a market system and then engaging in redistribution policies so that the poor can afford to purchase privately provided care. There are many good reasons for this. The key one, however, is that it would provide no assurance that people who find themselves without insurance would purchase it. This, in turn, would lower the welfare of a society where people feel better in knowing that the poor can receive health care services.

Competition and Prevention. Another manifestation of the problems associated with the free-rider effect concerns prevention. Traditionally, HMOs have encouraged preventive services both through low service copayments, and by covering services not traditionally included in many fee-for-service health plans, such as annual preventive examinations and diagnostic tests. One of the reasons HMOs have given for providing these services to members is that they will reduce future health care costs. This will not be the case, however, if plan members regularly switch between competing (and often nearly identical) health care plans. In this regard, Donald Light (1995: 151) writes,

> Prevention by any given [health] plan only makes economic sense within a contract year, or else one's competitors may benefit from one's efforts when subscribers switch plans in the next contract

year. . . . Why should a given plan, for example, make efforts to reduce drug abuse or smoking at the schools of a given town when only some of the children are their customers, and their parents may move or switch plans next year?

Recent data show that individuals are willing to switch their health plans in the wake of very small premium differences—particularly when there are few discernible differences between these alternatives (Buchmueller and Feldstein, 1996; Christianson et al., 1995).

It is too early to know whether, in fact, the provision of preventive services is indeed declining as a result of this free-rider effect. Documentation of such an effect would provide further reason to consider limiting the number of health plan choices available to consumers, or to move toward a more publicly funded system.

Should Cost Control Be a Public Policy? A larger issue that arises if consumer tastes are pliable concerns cost control. Health economists often point out that we cannot say that a country spends too much of its national income on health care. Who is to say that 14 percent or even 25 percent is "too much"? It is contended that there is nothing necessarily wrong if a society wants to spend more of its money on, say, expensive technologies. But this viewpoint is harder to justify if one views consumer tastes, not as predetermined, but rather as the product of previous experiences.

Take the example of medical technology. People are likely to demand the fruits of new technologies in part because they come to expect them. Dale Rublee (1994) has provided data on the relative availability of six selected medical technologies in Canada, Germany, and the United States. For all six technologies studied, the number of units per million persons is far higher in the United States than in Canada and Germany. With regard to open heart surgery, the figures are almost three times as high in the United States as in Canada, and nearly five times as great as in Germany. For magnetic resonance imaging, availability in the United States is ten times as great as in Canada and three times as great as in Germany.

Because of this, the U.S. public—and perhaps more importantly, their physicians—are likely to have developed greater expectations of such technologies. Some analysts argue that it is the growth of these technologies, or, as Joseph Newhouse (1993: 162) termed it, "the enhanced capabilities of medicine," that is primarily responsible for rising health care costs in the United States.

The point—that perhaps people would be equally well-off without so many expensive (not to say duplicative) life-saving interventions—is made only tentatively. One would not want to claim that people want to live longer because they are inculcated into believing that is desirable. Clearly, though, quality-of-life issues become relevant to such a discussion, as does the fact that the United States ranks near the top of the world in only one major vital-statistic category: life expectancy after reaching age eighty.[17] One must take pause when considering Easterlin's (1974) results presented earlier—that people in poor countries seem to be equally as happy as those in wealthier ones—or perhaps more relevant to health care, the fact that citizens of other countries, which spend far less money on medical care, tend to be much happier with their health care systems. This latter point is supported by Robert Blendon et al.'s (1990) research on the satisfaction that citizens in ten developed countries have in their health care systems. Only Italians show as low satisfaction levels as do Americans. Ten percent of Americans thought that only minor changes were needed in their health care system, compared to 56 percent of Canadians, 41 percent of Germans, 32 percent of Swedes, and 27 percent of British. Thus, more spending on technologies, in and of itself, does not seem to be increasing utility levels very much.

As was argued previously, if tastes are based on past consumption, then perhaps in demanding things like more medical technology, patients and their physicians are, in part, wanting what they *got* rather than getting what they *want*. It follows that greater medical spending to support more of these technologies might not enhance social welfare so much as it represents the fulfillment of expectations that were built on the availability of such technologies in the past. Having said this, one must be very careful, because in the case of health care, people's utility would appear to depend a great deal on absolutes rather than relatives. (If you feel pain, it is little consolation if your neighbor does too.) Nevertheless, the belief that more and more spending on technologies may not increase utility levels very much—because it raises people's expectations to unrealistic levels—is consistent with a rather sober quotation from E. J. Mishan (1969b: 81):

> As I see it, the main task today of the economist at all concerned with the course of human welfare is that of weaning the public from its post-war fixation on economic growth; of inculcating an awareness of the errors and misconceptions that abound in popular appraisals of the benefits of industrial development; and also, perhaps of voicing an occasional doubt whether the persistent pursuit of material ends, borne onwards today by a tidal wave of unrealisable

expectations, can do more eventually than to agitate the current restlessness, and to add to the frustrations and disillusion of ordinary mortals.

Demand

Review of economic theory

Just as market competition represents the core concept in microeconomics, demand theory is the key to understanding market competition. Demand, which economists often define as how many goods and services would be purchased at alternative prices, is the mechanism that drives a competitive economy. Under demand theory, how much of a commodity is produced and consumed is determined by people's demand for it. If people's tastes change for some reason, and they want more of one good and less of another, prices will change, prompting firms to adjust their production. Unless there is some sort of constraint on obtaining the necessary inputs for production, in the long run, supply adjusts to satisfy demand.

But demand theory implies more than just this. It also forms the basis by which economic theory evaluates social welfare. If people demand a certain bundle of goods and services, it means that they prefer it to all other ways in which they could spend their money. And if everyone acts in such a way as to maximize their utilities, given their available income, society will also be at a welfare maximum.[18]

How, then, can we ascertain people's demand? One way is to ask them which alternative bundle of goods they would prefer. There are two problems with this technique, however. First, it is difficult to imagine administering such a population survey, given the nearly countless possible bundles of goods from which people can choose. Second, it is entirely possible that people would not tell the truth, or even if they did, that they would not know how they would actually behave when faced with such market choices.

The concept of *revealed preference* is designed to eliminate these problems. Under this theory, pioneered by Paul Samuelson (1938, [1947] 1976), people are simply assumed to prefer whatever bundle of goods they choose to consume. If they purchase one bundle, but could afford another one, we can say that they have revealed themselves to prefer the former. One significant aspect of this theory is that it does not rely on understanding the psyche of the individual. Rather, as Robert Sugden (1993: 1949) noted: "The most significant property of the revealed preference approach . . . is that we do not need to enquire into the reasons why one thing is chosen rather than another. We do not look into the factors that go into the deliberation which leads to a choice; we look only at the results of that process." The derivation of demand through revealed preference leads to an important implication: The goods and services that people demand are the ones that make them best-off. That is to say, the act of demanding one set of goods implies that a person is better-off than with any other bundle of goods that he or she can afford. And if this is the case, it is a fairly small leap to say then, that an economic system that allows people to choose their bundles is best for society.

Thus, when a person demands a good, revealed preference theory implies that he or she prefers it to all alternatives. One of these alternatives is, of course, not spending the money in the first place. Consequently, the utility obtained from purchasing a good or service must be at least as great as the price paid—or it would not have been purchased in the first place. What a demand curve therefore shows is the *marginal utility* of a particular purchase. If a person buys six apples when they are priced at fifty cents each but buys seven when they are priced at forty cents, then the marginal or additional utility derived from the purchase of the seventh apple is at least forty cents. We would expect rational consumers, therefore, to demand a seventh apple only if the price is less than or equal to forty cents.

Problems with the economic theory

In *Candide,* the philosopher Dr. Pangloss attempts to prove that the obviously flawed state of nature and society is, nevertheless, the best of all possible worlds. Voltaire ([1759] 1981: 18) quoted his character as stating:

> It is demonstrated that things cannot be otherwise: for, since everything was made for a purpose, everything is necessarily for the best purpose. Note that noses were made to wear spectacles; we therefore have spectacles. Legs were clearly devised to wear breeches, and we have breeches. . . . And since pigs were made to be eaten, we have pork all year round. Therefore, those who have maintained that all is well have been talking nonsense: they should have maintained that all is for the best.

Although perhaps not recognized by most economists, the theory of revealed preference in particular, and consumer theory in general, bears a striking resemblance to Pangloss's philosophy. By choosing a particular bundle of goods, people demonstrate that they prefer it to all others; consequently, it is best for them. And, if all people are in their best position, then society, which is simply the aggregation of all people, is also in its best position. Therefore, allowing people to choose in the marketplace results in the best of all possible economic worlds.

This section questions this line of reasoning because it is based on assumptions that are difficult to support, particularly in the health area. In doing so, it questions the conventional meaning of the demand curve—that it represents the marginal utility obtained by consumers through the purchase of alternative quantities of a good. If one accepts the arguments presented here, there are profound implications concerning the wisdom of relying on competitive markets in health care financing and delivery.

Recall that an economic system that allows for consumer choice will, subject to some caveats, result in Pareto optimality.[19] Then, if society can reach some agreement on the distribution of wealth, social welfare can be maximized. Here, we will make the assumption that an acceptable redistribution does indeed take place. By doing so, we can focus on the resulting implication about competitive markets under economic theory—that reaching Pareto optimality through market competition will ultimately lead to the maximization of social welfare. With this assumption about redistribution in hand, we can form the following syllogism:

> *If* (A) Social welfare is maximized when individual utilities are maximized,
> *And* (B) Individual utilities are maximized when people are allowed to choose,
> *Then* (C) Social welfare is maximized when people are allowed to choose.

This is obviously a strong conclusion because it implies that the type of consumer choice brought about by market competition will result, as Dr. Pangloss would say, in the best of all possible worlds. In the health care field, it would provide strong ammunition for the superiority of competitive approaches. But if either Proposition A or B does not hold, then such a conclusion about the superiority of competition is not warranted. The following two sections will attempt to cast doubt first on Proposition B, and then on Proposition A.

Are Individual Utilities Maximized When People Are Allowed to Choose?
One of the basic tenets of market competition is that people can achieve the highest level of utility when they are allowed to make their own choices. If, instead, some entity such as government makes the choices for them, it would be extremely unlikely that consumers would fare as

well; each person is different, and it would seem to be impossible for an outsider to appreciate an individual's exact desires. Although this is a persuasive argument, this section will attempt to demonstrate that, at least in the health care field, allowing people to make their own choices does not necessarily make them best-off.

The belief that consumers will find themselves in a best-off position when they have sovereignty over their market choices is based on several assumptions in the competitive economic model:

- People know what's best for themselves.
- People have the ability to make choices that are in their best interest: There is sufficient information available, and they have the internal wherewithal to do so.
- The resulting choices indeed reveal their preferences.

Each of these will be considered in turn.

Do People Know What's Best for Themselves? The first question that needs to be addressed when considering if sovereignty is best for consumers is whether they know what is best for themselves. In many instances they unquestionably do, but they may not in all areas. If, in some instances, consumers are not the best judge of what is in their interest, then such choices might be better handled through public intervention.

There is no way to test the proposition directly. Thus, we consider how society goes about making allocation decisions about particular goods and services. In many instances, societies set rules that are explicitly designed to thwart the sanctity of individual choice.

Some of the activities that a libertarian, that is, a person who believes in the sanctity of individual sovereignty, would likely believe should be left up to the individual rather than be proscribed by society include personal use of narcotic drugs, gambling, prostitution, riding a motorcycle without a helmet, selling one's own organs, and suicide. This list was chosen specifically because these are all decisions that mainly affect the individual in question rather than others.

Why would society act in a way to abridge individual choice when consumer theory indicates that people can and do make welfare maximizing choices themselves? Robert Frank (1985) suggested an interesting possibility: People are overly concerned with their status and will make the wrong economic, social, and/or moral decisions in order to enhance this status. But this does not seem to account fully for such laws. There is nothing status-raising about going to Mexico to purchase a supposed cure for cancer. Thus, another reason for paternalistic laws that limit individual choice is that some types of spending decisions are simply a waste of money or an unnecessary danger; society is protecting people from their own foolishness. A final reason, and the one that is usually raised in this regard, is that in health care there are often "experts" who know much more than individual consumers. This would also help account for the laws against the sales of remedies that have not been approved by governmental authorities.

Do People Have the Ability to Make Choices That Are in Their Best Interest? Even if people know what is in their best interest, they may not have the ability to make choices that are in their best interest. There are both external and internal reasons for this. On the external side, they may not have sufficient information or might be unable to process adequately the information that is available. With respect to their internal resources, they may not behave in a rational manner. Each will be considered in turn.

Beginning with the information issue, the first question is whether people have enough information available to make the health care choices that are best for them. This obviously depends on the type of health service being considered, and unfortunately, there is very little research available upon which to rely.

Some empirical research has been conducted on how consumers go about trying to collect information on the alternatives they face in the health care market. A number of fairly old studies have found relatively little evidence of "consumerism" in health care, with one physician observer sardonically noting that consumers "devote more effort selecting their Halloween pumpkin than they do choosing their physician."[20] A more recent study, by Thomas Hoerger and Leslie Howard (1995), examined how pregnant women search for a prenatal care provider. The sample included women from Florida who gave birth in 1987. Women who believed that they had a choice of prenatal providers were asked: "Before you selected your actual prenatal care provider, did you seriously consider using another prenatal care provider?" If they answered that in the affirmative, they were further queried: "Did you actually speak with or have an appointment with another prenatal care provider?" Curiously, only 24 percent of respondents seriously considered using another provider, and only 14 percent actually had contact with another provider. Hoerger and Howard (1995: 341) concluded: "This amount of search is surprisingly low, given the importance of childbirth, the ample opportunity for choice, and the relative surplus of information about prenatal care providers compared to providers of other physician services. Recall that we expected the choice of prenatal care providers to establish a benchmark or *upper bound* on the extent of search for other physician services" (italics added).[21]

A related issue is whether consumers are able to use information successfully that is made available to them. Judith Hibbard and Edward Weeks (1989a, 1989b) conducted studies of how being given information about physician fees affects consumer knowledge levels and their use of services. They found little if any resulting change in behavior, as measured by asking about the costs of visits, procedures, tests, or medications, or changing physicians or insurance plans. They also found that receipt of the information had no effect on costs per physician visit, on the number of visits, or on annual health care expenditures.

A final informational concern is whether consumers can predict the results of their choices. If they cannot, then another entity might be better able to make some choices for them. This issue is best understood by considering something known as the "counterfactual." Counterfactual questions are those that are hypothetical in a special way: They concern what would have happened if history had been different. Questions such as these obviously can never be answered with certainty.

Health care poses many counterfactual questions. Suppose a person seeks health care from a primary care physician and tries to determine what was learned from the experience. It turns out to be very difficult for the person to conclude whether or not he or she made the right decision in seeking care from that provider, because to do so would involve answers to several counterfactual questions, for example: Would the problem have gone away if I had left it untreated? What would have happened if I had sought the care of a specialist instead of a primary care physician? Would the result have been different if I had seen a different primary care physician than the one I sought? In this regard, Burton Weisbrod (1978: 52) wrote:

> For ordinary goods, the buyer has little difficulty in evaluating the counterfactual—that is, what the situation will be if the good is not obtained. Not so for the bulk of health care. . . . Because the human physiological system is itself an adaptive system, it is likely to correct itself and deal effectively with an ailment, even without any medical care services. Thus, a consumer of such services who gets better after the purchase does not know whether the improvement was because of, or even in spite of, the "care" that was received. Or if no health care services are purchased and the individual's problem becomes worse, he is generally not in a strong position to determine whether the results would have been different, and better, if he had purchased certain health care. And the consumer, not being a medical expert, may learn little from experience or from friends' experience . . . because of the difficulty of determining whether the coun-

terfactual to a particular type of health care today is the same as it was the previous time the consumer, or a friend, had "similar" symptoms. The noteworthy point is not simply that it is difficult for the consumer to judge quality before the purchase . . . but that it is difficult even after the purchase.

Moving on to internal or cognitive reasons that individuals may be unable to make choices in their best interest, we consider the issue of consumer rationality. Here, we define rationality as indicating *reasonable* behavior.[22] For example, if an adult in the United States smokes cigarettes, we would not necessarily regard this as irrational. This is because there are several potentially reasonable bases for some people to smoke: pleasure, vanity, or addiction. Thus, smoking can be a reasonable decision if these benefits outweigh the various costs. Now suppose that such a person also claims that smoking does nothing to harm health. If the person is even minimally educated, that sort of behavior should be viewed as irrational because it is not based on reason. To deny that cigarette smoking can harm one's health simply does not make sense.

Economists, in contrast to social scientists in other disciplines, sometimes suppose that consumers must be rational and must therefore act to maximize their utility. But that supposition would seem to be false. In this regard, Harvey Leibenstein (1976: 8) has noted that "the idea of utility maximization must contain the possibility of choice under which utility is not maximized." Similarly, Lester Thurow (1983: 217) wrote that "revealed preferences . . . is just a fancy way of saying that individuals do whatever individuals do, and whatever they do, economists will call it 'utility maximization.'"

Obviously, the topic of whether consumers are rational or not is a broad one. To confine the issue a bit, only one such issue will be discussed here, because it has been well researched in the field of social psychology, but only touched upon by economists: cognitive dissonance. The theory of cognitive dissonance concerns a central aspect of human behavior: self-justification or rationalization. As explained by Elliot Aronson (1972: 92–93), "Basically, cognitive dissonance is a state of tension that occurs when an individual simultaneously holds two cognitions (ideas, attitudes, beliefs, opinions) that are psychologically inconsistent. . . . Because [its] occurrence . . . is unpleasant, people are motivated to reduce it."

Whether people act in a way that we might define as rational or irrational depends on how difficult it is to change the behavior in question versus the cognition. Smoking offers one of the best examples.

Suppose that a person smokes but knows that it is very dangerous to health. This causes cognitive dissonance; how can you continue to do something that is so self-destructive? If the person is not addicted or has a particularly strong will, he or she may quit. But an addict or weaker person will typically find it easier to change the cognition than the behavior, by either attributing more pleasure to smoking than is truly obtained, or by denying that it is dangerous (Aronson 1972). Although this latter type of behavior has been repeatedly confirmed and is certainly understandable, it would seem to be a violation of the English language to deem it rational.

Economists George Akerlof and William Dickens (1992) have used cognitive dissonance to explain various economic behaviors. Examples include explaining the choice of risky jobs, technological development, advertising, social insurance, and crime. Regarding social insurance, they wrote:

> If there are some persons who would simply prefer not to contemplate a time when their earning power is diminished, and if the very fact of saving for old age forces persons into such contemplations, there is an argument for compulsory old age insurance. . . . [They] may find it uncomfortable to contemplate their old age. For that reason they may make the wrong tradeoff, *given their own preferences,* between current consumption and savings for retirement. (317; italics added)

Note that saving is what would make the person best-off in his or her own eyes, but the person fails to do it anyway. Hence, society makes the decision to override individual choice by establishing social insurance programs, like Social Security and Medicare. In summary, when cognitive dissonance is important, there is little reason to suppose that people will act in a rational manner, that is, make decisions that maximize their utility.

Do Individuals Reveal Their Preferences through Their Actions? The final aspect of whether market choices are best left to the individual concerns a perhaps more abstract issue: whether people's actions really reflect their preferences. Demand theory assumes that what people choose to buy or do reflects their preferences. This might not be the case.

Amartya Sen (1982, 1987, 1992) has written several persuasive essays and books on this issue. The basic problem concerns an issue addressed earlier: interdependencies in people's utility functions. If people make their choices based not only on their own preferences but on those of others as well, then these choices will not necessarily reflect their own preferences. This becomes important because it casts doubt on the conventional meaning of demand curves, which purport to show the marginal utility that people obtain from additional units of consumption.

One argument that Sen makes is that much human behavior flies in the face of the notion that your actions indicate your personal preferences. He does this by distinguishing two concepts: sympathy and commitment. A person who acts on feelings of sympathy is indeed showing his personal preferences through his actions; you feel better if you help. Commitment, however, is different; you would rather do something else, but you don't because you are committed to a particular cause. Sen used recycling as an example. He argued that people don't recycle because they enjoy it or because they think that their own actions will convince anyone else to do it. In spite of that, they do it anyway because of their commitment to a cleaner environment. Sen (1982) summarized this point: "One way of defining commitment is in terms of a person choosing an act that he believes will yield a lower level of personal welfare to him than an alternative that is also available to him" (92), and that this concept "drives a wedge between personal choice and personal welfare, and much of traditional economic theory relies on the identity of the two" (94).

People's actions therefore seem to be motivated by things other than selfishness, and thus, the choices one observes do not necessarily indicate the level of welfare derived by the individual or by society. (In this regard, Sen [1982: 99] wrote, "The *purely* economic man is indeed close to being a social moron.") But the results of this behavior can go in either direction: either choosing something that enhances social but not personal welfare (e.g., commitment), or choosing not to help others when it would be personally beneficial to do so. S. K. Nath (1969) provided a useful example of the latter behavior.

Suppose we observe a person *not* giving to a charity aimed at improving the health of the poor. Using revealed preference, one would conclude that the person would rather have something else—the good or service purchased with the money that could have been given to the charity. This might not be the case, however. It may be that the person would benefit from providing such a donation because his utility function contains an element encompassing the health of the poor. But he may believe that his contribution will not be of much help because others are not compelled to follow suit. Thus, the person would like the poor to have better access to health care, but this is not evident by examining his or her market behavior. Nath (1969: 141) stated that there is a "fallacy in the assumption that an individual's welfare function coincides with his utility function as revealed by his market choices. This is a very common fallacy in economic writings."

In summary, what I have tried to show is that Proposition B in the syllogism presented earlier—that individual utilities are maximized when people are allowed to choose—very well may not be met in the health care area. The next section examines the validity of the other proposition that must be met in order for consumer choice necessarily to result in what is best for society.

Is Social Welfare Maximized When Individual Utilities Are Maximized? This section examines Proposition A of the syllogism presented earlier, that social welfare is maximized when individuals maximize their own utility.[23] Although the proposition that social welfare is based solely on individuals' welfare is a philosophical issue and cannot be proven true or false, there are two reasons to question its validity. The first of these arguments is also from Sen (1982, 1987, 1992), who disputed this notion that individual welfare is the only legitimate component of social welfare. He called such a philosophy "welfarism," which "is the view that the only things of intrinsic value for ethical calculation and evaluation of states of affairs are individual utilities" (1987: 40). His arguments, which span several books, are too lengthy to be summarized properly here. One reason that Sen rejected the welfarist approach is that it does not allow us to distinguish between different *qualities* of utility. An example he gave is that if you get pleasure from my unhappiness, that counts as much under the welfarist approach as anything else. Alternatively, one might believe that a society should devote its resources to meeting somewhat more lofty desires. Another reason is that the concept of individual welfare does not seem to be well captured simply by the goods one has; other aspects of life, such as freedom, would also seem to be important. In this regard, Robin Hahnel and Michael Albert (1990) pointed out that conventional theory would make you equally well-off if you were *assigned* a bundle of goods, versus a situation in which you *choose* the bundle. It does not take much introspection to realize that the latter may indeed result in higher utility.

A second and more fundamental reason to doubt that social welfare is not the sum of individual welfare was brought up by Robert Frank (1985), who noted that much of what individuals seek out is status or rank. But these are relative things; if my status goes up, yours goes down by definition. This leads to a situation where people engage in consumption that does not add to the social welfare. For example, if I buy a fancy car, I get utility both from the various characteristics of the car, as well as from the fact that I have distinguished myself from you. Once you (and others like you) buy the car, the latter part of my utility is canceled out. Total utility (or social welfare) is thus lower than the sum of individual utilities.

Implications for health policy

The previous section has attempted to show that there are various problems with inferring that the goods and services people demand in a competitive marketplace will necessarily make them best-off. This section provides a number of implications concerning the tools used, and the issues studied, by health economists.

Is Comprehensive National Health Insurance Necessarily Inefficient?[24] Health economists have long contended that people in the United States and other developed countries are "overinsured." That is, they have more insurance than is optimal for them or for society at large. To the non-economist, this might seem like an odd belief given the great concern about the number of uninsured people in the United States. In fact, nearly all economists would agree that a risk-averse person would do better by purchasing fairly priced health insurance.[25] Nevertheless, many contend that people with health insurance have too much coverage, that is, they do not have to pay enough of the costs of care out-of-pocket.

To understand this argument better, it is necessary to review a concept in insurance called *moral hazard*. Moral hazard exists when the possession of an insurance policy increases the likelihood of incurring a covered loss, and/or the size of a covered loss. In health care, moral hazard implies that people use more services when they are insured, or more fully insured. But as Mark Pauly (1968: 535) pointed out, "The response of seeking more medical care with insurance than in its absence is a result not of moral perfidy, but of rational economic behavior." For a fully insured person, the cost of using an additional service will be shared by everyone who pays premiums. Thus, the person is likely to use more services than if he or she paid the full cost of the additional service.

Despite the fact that moral hazard in health care is an example of rational economic behavior, many economists are nevertheless troubled by its existence. This is because when people are fully insured, they may demand services that only provide a small amount of benefit. But these services are likely to cost just as much as any other service. Thus, the benefits people derive from the purchase of these "marginal" services might be swamped by their cost.

The existence of moral hazard that results from the possession of health insurance has made many economists conclude that there is a societal "welfare loss" associated with the ownership of too much health insurance: One recent set of estimates puts this loss somewhere between $33 and $109 billion (in 1984 dollars), representing between 9 and 28 percent of U.S. health care spending (Feldman and Dowd 1991). The implication of these welfare loss estimates is that society would be better-off if its members did not have complete health insurance coverage. In this regard, a 1989 survey of U.S. and Canadian health economists found that 63 percent strongly or mildly agreed with the statement that health insurance causes societal welfare loss (Feldman and Morrisey 1990).

The argument supporting the notion of welfare loss from full health insurance, and estimates of its magnitude, are based on the assumption that the demand curve shows the marginal utility a person derives from an additional service. Consumers determine exactly how much an additional service is worth to them, and then compare this to its price to determine if it is worthwhile to purchase the service. (In the previous section I questioned whether consumers can and do behave in such a manner.)

There is a method of testing whether in fact consumers do exhibit such behavior. It will be recalled that welfare loss occurs because consumers with health insurance have an incentive to purchase additional services that provide little benefit to them. We can therefore examine whether this occurs by observing the kinds of services that consumers forgo when they are provided with less comprehensive insurance coverage. The results from the RAND Health Insurance Study and other research show that utilization will go down in the presence of coinsurance (Newhouse and the Insurance Experiment Group 1993; Feldstein 1988a; Phelps 1992). Welfare loss theory tells us the types of services that ought to be forgone: those that provide relatively little utility.

The nature of this test is clarified in Figure 1, which is taken from an earlier work of mine (Rice 1992). The horizontal line indicates the marginal cost of producing a service, which can be viewed as the cost to society, that is, the resources that must be expended to provide a service. The curved line, which is a demand curve, shows the marginal utility of each additional service. At a zero price, that is, with comprehensive insurance, the consumer will demand Q_0 services; the last such service provides very little utility.

Now suppose that there are two types of services: those that are highly effective (HE) and those that are less effective (LE). Further suppose that the person no longer has health insurance, and his or her demand for care declines from Q_0 to Q_1. It is clear from Figure 1 that the person would be expected to forgo the low-effectiveness service, LE, because its benefits are now outweighed by its costs. But service HE would still be

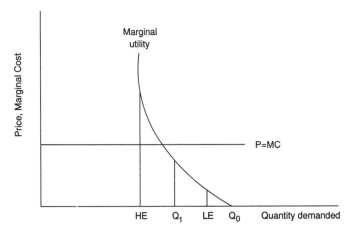

Figure 1. Change in demand for services of differing effectiveness.

purchased because its benefits exceed costs, even in the absence of insurance coverage. If people actually behave as predicted, then we would have some confidence that the demand curve for medical care really shows the marginal utility consumers obtain from additional services. This, in turn, would provide support for the welfare loss estimates discussed previously.

The problem with operationalizing this test is finding a way to determine the marginal utility consumers receive from a service. The proxy used here is a measure of the medical effectiveness of a service—as judged by medical experts. Although consumers and experts may differ in what they think is important, it seems logical that consumers would prefer those services that are thought to be the most effective.

As part of the RAND study, Kathleen Lohr et al. (1986) grouped services into several categories based on their expected medical effectiveness and found that "cost sharing was generally just as likely to lower use when care is thought to be highly effective as when it is thought to be only rarely effective" (S32), and that it "did not seem to have a selective effect in prompting people to forego care only or mainly in circumstances when such care probably would be of relatively little value" (S36).[26]

What does all this mean for the theory of welfare loss from excess health insurance? It is that consumers do not seem to be able to evaluate the usefulness of medical services and to make the type of decisions that economic theory calls for them to make. This view—that patient-demand curves show how much consumers buy at different prices, but not necessarily the utility they derive from such services—runs very much against the grain of conventional economic theory. It is not, however, unique among economists. One noteworthy example is from an article by Randall Ellis and Thomas McGuire (1993: 142), who wrote: "We are skeptical that the observed demand can be interpreted as reflecting 'socially efficient' consumption, [so] we interpret the demand curve in a more limited way, as an empirical relationship between the degree of cost sharing and quantity of use demanded by the patient."

If one is skeptical that there is such a large welfare loss from excess health insurance, a related issue naturally arises: Are there other substantial sources of waste in the provision of medical care services? Over the years, health services researchers have shown strong agreement that many of the services provided are not medically necessary: Estimates go as high as 30 percent (Leape 1989). Indeed, probably the major research effort being conducted by the health services research community today is determining what services are and are not medically effective.

Under the traditional theory, the source of the waste is clear: Patients demand too many services when they have complete or nearly complete insurance coverage. The alternative being presented here is that most of the waste is in the provision of services that do little or no good to improve patients' health.[27] The policy implications of the two approaches are very different. If one believes the conventional theory, policies should be enacted that make the users of services more sensitive to price. In contrast, if the problem is provision of services that are not useful, one should target the *provider* of services.

Many analysts—economists as well as practitioners of other disciplines—believe that managed care strategies that are based on capitating health plans offer the best hope for improving efficiency and controlling U.S. health care costs. In doing so, they are (perhaps unbeknownst to themselves) eschewing their own belief in the traditional economic model of competition! Managed care strategies are aimed almost entirely at changing what services are provided by providers, rather than changing the demand by consumers. In fact, what is perhaps most noteworthy about the HMO approach to cost containment is that copayments are *lower* than in fee-for-service medicine. If these strategies are designed to reduce waste, it would seem clear that the waste is thought to be generated through the provision of unnecessary services, far more so than through excess demand by patients.

Indeed, most policies aimed at controlling health care costs not only in the United States, but in the rest of the developed world, are aimed at the supply-side rather than demand-side. By focusing on the supply-side, other countries find themselves able to provide the population with comprehensive national health insurance. This can improve equity, and, if supply-side measures are more effective than demand-side ones in bringing about other policy goals, can enhance the efficiency of their health care systems as well.

Should Patient Cost Sharing Be Encouraged, or Should We Use Other Policies? As indicated before, the thrust of the welfare loss literature is that more patient cost sharing will be beneficial to society. There is a danger in this sort of analysis, which was noted by Robert Evans (1984: 49): "The welfare burden is minimized when there is no insurance at all." If one takes this reasoning very far, it becomes apparent that the conventional analysis will always find that the country with higher patient cost-sharing requirements will have the more efficient health care system (Reinhardt 1992). Thus, the U.S. system would be deemed the most efficient in the world, not because of a comparison of outcomes to costs, but rather simply from the fact that the United States imposes patient copayments, which in turn reduce utilization.

Non-U.S. health economists have been more amenable to the idea that a fee-for-service system could be efficient in the absence of patient cost sharing. Evans, Barer, and Stoddart (1993: 26) argued that the case for patient cost sharing is difficult to make if four questions can be answered in the affirmative: (1) Is the service really health care? (2) Does the service work? (3) Is the service medically necessary? and (4) Is there no better alternative? If a service passes all of these tests, "the standard argument against user charges, that they tax the sick, seems wholly justified."

Currently there is a great deal of policy interest in the United States in medical savings accounts (MSAs), which rely heavily on patient cost sharing. Under most MSA proposals, people (usually employees) would be able to choose a health plan with a very large annual deductible (often several thousand dollars), but that covers medical expenses above that amount in full. The savings in premiums could be used to make payments toward the deductible, or alternatively, could be spent (or saved) on anything that the consumer desires.

Here I will focus on three criticisms of MSAs that derive from the preceding discussion. First, it is not clear that MSAs will indeed quell the demand for services. Although it is likely that those with MSAs will forgo some minor services, the vast majority of health care spending goes toward "big ticket items." Two percent of the U.S. population in a particular year, for example, are responsible for over 40 percent of expenditures (Berk and Monheit 1992). Because any hospitalization or procedure is likely to meet the annual deductible, patients will not have much of a financial incentive to curb medical spending. For that reason, there is also little reason to expect that MSAs would result in depressed demand for expensive medical technologies.

Second, the idea behind MSAs is that individuals can make informed choices about whether treatment should be sought for a particular illness. It was shown earlier, however, that there is evidence that makes one doubt consumers' ability to perform this task very well. Findings from the RAND Health Insurance Study indicate that patients are as likely to forgo effective medical services in the presence of cost sharing as they are to forgo less effective care (Lohr et al. 1986; Siu et al. 1986).

Third, selection bias could cause various problems for a country embarking on MSAs. One would expect that those who are less likely to need medical care will be the most likely to purchase the accounts. This would cause two problems. First, patients who are sicker—and who therefore might need more incentive to consider costs when making medical care decisions—would not tend to enroll in MSAs, and therefore would not be subject to any efficiency-enhancing incentives that derive from cost sharing. Second, it would mean that the health care market would be segmented, with healthier people in the less expensive plans and sicker people pooled together in non-MSA plans, making the latter even more expensive.

Returning to the issue of patient cost sharing, there are two broad arguments that can be made against employing this cost control technique. First, of course, is the issue of equity. It is frequently argued that cost sharing is more burdensome on people with lower incomes, as it comprises a larger proportion of their disposable income (and even more, when one considers that they tend to have lower health status). As a result, its imposition leads to decreased service utilization, which in turn can impair health status. In this regard, one of the key findings of the RAND Health Insurance Experiment was that the sick and the poor had the most adverse health consequences as a result of cost sharing (Newhouse and the Insurance Experiment Group 1993).[28]

The other issue concerns efficiency: Specifically, are there alternative ways of encouraging efficiency and containing health care costs besides cost sharing? Various supply-side policies were mentioned earlier. Here, a *demand-side* lever is noted that is not concerned with price: influencing behavior. Although estimates about the cost of so-called bad behaviors— smoking, alcohol consumption, drug abuse—abound, economists rarely consider these to be social welfare losses in the sense that too much health insurance is considered to be a loss. This is particularly curious given the estimated sizes of these losses: in the United States alone, an estimated $67 billion annually for drug abuse, $99 billion for alcohol abuse, and $91 billion for smoking (Robert Wood Johnson Foundation 1994). These figures far exceed all estimates of the welfare losses from health insurance.

Sociologists and psychologists have been concerned about the factors that influence behavior, and ways in which it can be altered. (In contrast, economic theory views behavior as either immutable or something that should *not* be altered because it reflects individual choices.) The field of health education focuses, to a large degree, on how behaviors can be changed. David Mechanic (1979: 11) stated:

> Reducing needs involves the prevention of illness or diminishing patients' psychological dependence on the medical encounter for social support or other secondary advantages. Reducing desire for services requires changing people's views of the value of different types of medical care, making them more aware of the real costs of service in relation to the benefits received, and legitimizing alternatives for dealing with many problems.

The task of changing behavior is not easy, however. In this regard, Mechanic (1979: 12) wrote: "It is prudent to recognize the difficulty of the task, the forces working against change, and the depths of ignorance concerning the origins of these behaviors and the ways in which they can best be modified." The point is not that health economists need to be conducting this research. Rather, it is that policy levers like these need to be recognized by policy makers even if these levers are not derived from traditional economic analyses.

Should People Pay More for Price-Elastic Services? Another common economic conclusion is that the magnitude of patient coinsurance rates should be directly related to the price elasticity of demand.[29] More specifically, services for which consumers show a high demand elasticity should have higher cost-sharing requirements than services for which consumers are less price sensitive (Ellis and McGuire 1993).

The intuition behind this result is straightforward. If the possession of insurance leads to a large increase in utilization, then welfare loss will be larger because more services will be purchased where the marginal costs exceed marginal benefits. Thus, one would improve social welfare by assessing higher patient coinsurance rates for such services, thereby reducing usage. In contrast, if utilization rates are not very sensitive to the possession of insurance, then there is little welfare loss and less need to charge high coinsurance rates.

Table 1. Arc Price Elasticities of Medical Spending in the
RAND Health Insurance Experiment

Range	Acute	Chronic	Well	Total out-patient	Hospital	Total medical	Dental
0–25	−0.16	−0.20	−0.14	−0.17	−0.17	−0.17	−0.12
25–95	−0.32	−0.23	−0.43	−0.31	−0.14	−0.22	−0.39

What services are the most price-elastic and therefore should, according to theory, have the highest patient cost-sharing requirements? The major source of data to answer this question is the RAND Health Insurance Experiment (Newhouse and the Insurance Experiment Group 1993). Its results in this regard are somewhat ambiguous, because the calculated elasticities vary depending on the level of coinsurance.[30]

These elasticities, shown in Table 1, do not vary a great deal by type of service. One noteworthy exception is that so-called well-care services, although showing a comparable elasticity to other outpatient services (acute and chronic) in the 0–25 percent range, had a much larger elasticity in the 25–95 percent range. Dental services also showed a relatively high elasticity in the 25–95 percent range. The well-care services considered in the study would include not only preventive care, but other services as well. This, unfortunately, is most of what is currently known about the elasticity of demand for preventive services.

The implications of the standard economic model are nevertheless clear: If preventive services are the most price responsive, they should have the highest patient coinsurance rates, which in turn will discourage their usage. This would be true even if it were shown that some of these services were particularly effective in improving health and/or well-being.

There are, of course, alternative criteria that one could use in determining patient copayment levels that are in the best interest of society. One model, popular in a number of recent proposals for U.S. health reform, would have made preventive services free of any copayments: the *opposite* of what the economic model would recommend.

There are several possible justifications for basing copayment rates on factors other than price elasticities, all of which have been discussed in other contexts here. First is the issue of whether consumers have sufficient information. If they do not, then they may underestimate the value of investing in preventive services. Second, even if the appropriate information is available, people may not use it correctly. As noted, it is difficult for people to make counterfactual choices. Furthermore, because of people's tendency toward cognitive dissonance, they may avoid seeking some types of services that are of value to them. Third, medical experts may be better aware of the benefits of certain services than are individuals, and they routinely recommend more preventive services than people obtain. Fourth, people might be shortsighted in their views, particularly when they are young. Finally, there is a public-good aspect of preventive care: If it makes you healthy, I want you to have it, but the free-rider effect will prevent me from subsidizing you; subsidized, low copayments for preventive care, therefore, could improve social welfare.

Can People Choose the Right Health Plan? A successful competitive market depends on information: the availability of good information about alternative choices, as well as consumers' ability to use this information properly. The success of most market-based approaches to health care reform relies on people choosing the right health plan: one that delivers high-quality services in a cost-effective manner. To accomplish this, people need to have and use information about alternative plan choices.

Researchers, however, know very little about how well consumers can discern plan quality from the written materials that would be distributed through so-called health care report cards. Even if the information were collected by an independent organization—something that is *not* the case currently—consumers have never shown themselves to be able to use such information effectively. It is far from clear, for example, that consumers would know the best choice when presented with plan-by-plan comparisons of age- and sex-adjusted utilization rates for mammograms, cholesterol screening, low-birthweight infants, hospital-acquired infections, and the like. The extent of this problem would be heightened by our current inability to risk-adjust these figures accurately. Although plan satisfaction figures would be easier to interpret, there is little evidence that higher satisfaction levels are highly correlated with clinical measures of health care quality.

Relevant here is a study on the type of information consumers look for on report cards, which was conducted by Judith Hibbard and Jacqueline Jewett (1996). They found that most consumers indicate that the key type of information for them in choosing a health plan are so-called desirable events, such as utilization rates for mammograms, cholesterol screening, and pediatric immunizations. Less important to them were "undesirable events," such as hospital death rates from heart attacks, rates of low birthweights, and hospital-acquired infections. Curiously, then, when given report cards on two alternative health plans—one with a better record on desirable events and the other with a better record on undesirable events—consumers overwhelmingly chose the latter. Although far more research is needed in this area, this sort of inconsistent behavior casts doubt on how well consumers can use report card information to make the best choices for themselves. The mere existence and dissemination of information, even if objective and complete, does not guarantee that it will be used properly by an individual.

Finally, under competitive-based reform proposals, there is an intense pressure on the part of health plans to attract enrollees by keeping premiums at a competitive level. One way to do this is by enacting true efficiencies, but another is to try to obtain a *favorable selection* of patients. It is in plans' interest to avoid groups whose costs are likely to be high, and individuals with chronic conditions (Light 1995). In addition, because enrolling in better health plans is likely to be more expensive, it is possible that the lowest-cost plans in an area will be the least desirable ones, for example, having a limited provider network, providing little choice, only paying for the most basic services, making it difficult to obtain referrals, and so on (Rice, Brown, and Wyn 1993). Indeed, to the extent that putting providers at considerable financial risk is effective in controlling costs, one would expect less expensive plans to have more severe physician incentives to conserve resources.

Conclusion

This is a long piece; no effort will be made to summarize it. Although the content may be viewed as somewhat downbeat, I will end it on a positive note.

If one accepts the viewpoint that economic theory does not demonstrate the superiority of market forces in health, the obvious corollary is that all important questions must be answered empirically. And, to a large extent, that is exactly what most health economists and health services researchers are trying to do. I have few reservations about the kinds of research studies being conducted; they address many key issues. I am, however, very concerned that the work will suffer if researchers come in with preconceived notions of what the results *ought* to be.

In spite of the fact that most questions in health policy can be answered only through empirical research, getting the theory right is nevertheless extraordinarily important to the enactment of sound health care policies. If analysts misinterpret economic theory as applied to health—by assuming that market forces are necessarily superior to alternative policies, and that other tools of the trade neatly translate to health care—then they will blind themselves to policy options that might actually be best at enhancing social welfare, many of which simply do not fall out of the conventional, demand-driven competitive model. Market forces may indeed have a prominent place in health care organization and delivery, but, as I have tried to show, economic theory does not show them to be necessarily a superior approach to health care policy.

Notes

1 Economic efficiency can be thought of as occurring when the fewest economic resources are used to satisfy consumer demand for alternative goods and services. Social welfare is maximized when the distribution of these goods and services is concordant with society's desires.

2 In this regard, Lester Thurow (1983: 22) has written, "Every economist knows the dozens of restrictive assumptions . . . that are necessary to 'prove' that a free market is the best possible economic game, but they tend to be forgotten in the play of events."

3 A book that evaluates assumptions in the other two areas—the theories of supply and redistribution—will be published in 1998 (Rice 1998).

4 The assumptions analyzed in the paper come from several sources: Graaff 1971, Henderson and Quandt 1980, Mishan 1969a, 1969b, Nath 1969, Ng 1979, and Rowley and Peacock 1975.

5 The section on demand for care will focus on the concept of *revealed preference*.

6 The main one is that consumers' relative desire between different pairs of goods are equal to the economy's ability to transform one good into the other.

7 The idea that relative wealth drives people's behavior was pioneered by James Duesenberry (1952).

8 In this regard, Henry Aaron (1994: 15–16) suggests that people simultaneously possess multiple utility functions: "In one or more of these sub-functions the arguments, as in the standard theory, are particular goods and services. In others the arguments are intangible objectives such as adherence to duty, altruism, or spite."

9 For further discussion on problems in enacting such taxes and subsidies, see Graaff 1971: 77–82; and Samuelson 1947: 247–249.

10 There is, in theory, one sort of tax and subsidy that might work, but it has no practicality. This is a *poll tax*—a tax that is levied on everyone irrespective of income.

11 Some examples of economists who have raised this issue include Arrow 1963; Mishan 1969a, 1969b; Thurow 1983; and Blackorby and Donaldson 1990.

12 For a discussion of alternative models of preference formation, see March 1978.

13 Note that this argument for government intervention does not rely at all on any externalities associated with cigarette smoking.

14 For a good discussion of these issues, see Hahnel and Albert 1990.

15 This line of reasoning is pursued in the second part of the essay, which concerns demand for health care.

16 States cannot currently mandate provision of services under employer-sponsored health plans that fall under the jurisdiction of the Employee Retirement Income and Security Act (ERISA). Although this has effectively reduced the strength of state mandates, there is little doubt that such mandates would still exist if ERISA were repealed.

17 Data from twenty-four developed countries show that female life expectancy in the United States at age eighty is rivaled only by Canada, and male life expectancy at that age, only by Canada and Iceland. In contrast, fifteen countries exceed the United States in female life expectancy at birth, and seventeen in male life expectancy. See Schieber, Poullier, and Greenwald, 1992.

18 This assumes that society is satisfied with the distribution of income, an issue discussed elsewhere in this paper.

19 The primary caveat is that externalities are unimportant. That is why economists often say that the presence of important yet uncorrected externalities results in "market failure."

20 This quote, from Dr. Harvey Mandell, is from Hoerger and Howard 1995, which contains a good review of the literature on consumer search for physicians.

21 Interestingly, experience from previous births did not explain the results. For most women the birth examined was the first child, and furthermore, women with previous births were more likely to search for a provider than those who were having their first child.

22 Economists often use a more technical definition, in which choices are consistent and transitive (see Mishan 1982).

23 Recall that we are making the assumption that society can and does redistribute income so that any Pareto optimum that is reached through a competitive marketplace will result in maximum social welfare. This allows us to explicitly examine the advantages of allowing for consumer choice in the health care market without worrying about issues of equity.

24 For a more detailed discussion of this issue, see Rice 1992.

25 A risk-averse person can be thought of as someone who prefers "a bird in the hand to two in the bush." The specific definition is that a person is risk-averse if the marginal utility of additional income declines. In other words, if you make $30,000 a year, the last $1,000 you make brings about more utility than an additional $1,000 (that would make your income $31,000). It can be shown that such a person would generally want to buy insurance if the administrative or "loading" charges are small. For derivations of this, see Feldstein 1988a and Phelps 1992.

26 Another component of the RAND study (Siu et al. 1986) reached a similar conclusion regarding the impact of coinsurance on appropriate versus inappropriate hospitalization.

27 Other writers have also advocated calculating welfare losses based on the provision of unnecessary services. See Phelps and Parente 1990; Phelps and Mooney 1992; Dranove 1995; and Phelps 1995.

28 For a summary of literature on the impact of cost sharing, see Rice and Morrison 1994.

29 This is defined as the percentage change in the quantity of a good demanded divided by the percentage change in its price.

30 In the study, patients were assessed 0 percent or 25 percent or 95 percent of the total charge. Some patients were charged 50 percent coinsurance rates, but they were not used in the demand elasticities presented by authors of the study.

Going for the Gold: The Redistributive Agenda

behind Market-Based Health Care Reform

Robert G. Evans

Summary Propositions

Fundamental economic principles . . . put efficient, competitive health care markets in the same class as powdered unicorn horn.
"Health Care without Perverse Incentives," *Scientific American,* July 1993

1 There is in health care no "private, competitive market" of the form described in the economics textbooks, anywhere in the world. There never has been, and inherent characteristics of health and health care make it impossible that there ever could be. Public and private action have always been interwoven.

2 The persistent interest in an imaginary private competitive market is sustained by distributional objectives. These define three axes of conflict.

a The progressivity or regressivity of the health care funding system: Who has to pay, and how much?

b The relative incomes of providers: Who gets paid, and how much?

c The terms of access to care: Can those with greater resources buy "better" services?

3 The real policy choices fall into two categories.

a The extent of use of marketlike mechanisms within publicly funded health care systems.

b The extent to which certain services may be funded outside the public sector, through quasi markets, and under a mix of public and private regulation.

4 Proposals to shift toward more use of quasi markets, through the extension of private funding mechanisms, are distributionally driven. They reflect the fact that, compared with public funding systems, privately regulated quasi markets have to date been:

a less successful in controlling prices and limiting the supply of services (more jobs and higher incomes for suppliers);

b supported through more regressive funding sources (the healthy and wealthy pay less, whereas the ill and wealthy get preferential access);

c off-budget for governments (cost shifting in the economy looks like cost saving in the public sector).

5 Marketlike mechanisms within publicly funded health care systems constitute a particular set of management tools that might be used along with other more established mechanisms to promote the following generally accepted social objectives:

a effective health care, efficiently provided and equitably distributed across the population according to need;

b fair but not excessive reimbursement of providers; and

c equitable distribution of the burden of contributions according to ability to pay; within

d an overall expenditure envelope that is consistent with the carrying capacity of the general economy, or rather of its members' collective willingness to pay.

6 These general objectives seem to be widely shared internationally. Their specific content is of course much more controversial—they are fundamentally political statements—and, as usual, God and the devil are in the details. But the key point is that these social objectives have their origins prior to, and at a higher level than, the choice of any particular set of mechanisms for trying to attain them. They are *ends;* the mix and blend of public and private actions are *means* to those ends. (Markets were made for and by men, not vice versa.)

7 Marketlike mechanisms, as a class, have no inherent or a priori claim to superiority as mechanisms for achieving these public objectives. Nor is there, to date, any overwhelming empirical support for their widespread use. There are a number of interesting examples, in different countries, of the use of economic incentives to motivate desired changes, and these bear close watching. But this is still very much an experimental technology for system management. Moreover, there are grounds for serious concern about negative side effects from transforming the structure of motivations and rewards in health care.

8 The central role of governments remains that of exercising, directly or more traditionally by delegation, general oversight of and political responsibility for each country's health care system. Governments are increasingly acting as a sort of "consumers' cooperative" or prudent purchaser on behalf of their populations. They should choose what-

ever managerial tools seem to work best for this purpose, subject to the political constraints created by the fundamental conflicts of distributional interests detailed previously. In particular, they may delegate some parts of this role, but should not be permitted to divest themselves of it. In the one country where a coalition of private interests has prevented government from taking up this responsibility, the results have been spectacularly unsatisfactory.

The proper role of governments in health systems is an ancient debate. Its longevity reflects the permanence of certain fundamental conflicts of economic interest among the different groups involved in the organization and financing of health services. The form and extent of government involvement, and its relation to the activities of nongovernmental agents, significantly affect the balance of advantage in these conflicts.

The current worldwide resurgence of interest in the topic is driven by a number of different motives, covert as well as overt. There is, however, an unfortunate tendency to frame the issue as "government *versus* the market," or "regulation *versus* independent action," as if these were alternative, mutually exclusive frameworks for economic organization. Such juxtapositions grossly misrepresent the relationships among the various institutions and actors composing modern health care systems.

State and private institutions have always interpenetrated each other, to the extent that in most national systems it is often difficult, and inherently arbitrary, to classify a particular institution as "public" or "private." In reality, there is a continuum along the line from civil service at one end, to the privately owned, strictly for-profit corporation at the other. Most health care, in most countries, is provided by people and organizations that fall into neither category. The public regulatory framework (set by government) typically gives them much more autonomy than civil servants, while conferring both privileges and responsibilities that distinguish them in essential ways from participants in "normal" markets. The most obvious example of such interpenetration, so obvious that it long ago disappeared from the consciousness of most of those who approach health care systems from a market perspective, is professional self-regulation. Provider associations exercise the coercive authority of the state, the police power, to regulate and sometimes to suppress competitive behavior among their members. Even more important, they are vigilant in preventing intrusions into their fields of practice by unlicensed persons. This process goes on, one way or another, in all systems, and has very deep historical roots.

The presumption, widely if not universally shared, is that professional self-regulation promotes more general social interests. There is room for considerable disagreement over the balance of public and private interests actually served, in general or in particular circumstances. But in any case, the thing *happens*. Public regulatory authority and (collective) private interest are woven together in a complex way.[1] Where markets for health care exist, they are always managed markets. There may be, at different times and places, bitter political struggles over *who* should manage the market, but no one seriously questions the need for management.[2]

Another example: The state confers monopoly rights, in the form of patents, on the developers of new drugs and devices. This blatant government interference with the free market is traditionally justified as encouraging further innovation: short-run costs for long-run gains. But the traditional story highlights the role of government in responding to "failure" in private markets and regulating in the public interest. Patent-holding firms thus prefer to speak of "intellectual property," implying that there is some sort of "natural right" to exercise monopoly power (and to call upon the state to enforce it) that is prior to, and more fundamental than, whatever interpretation might be given to the public interest by the government of the day. This is legal nonsense, but can be very effective politics.

So are patents regulatory interference with free markets, or simply recognition and protection of private property rights? Certainly, when a government tries to modify patent rights within its own jurisdiction, for example, by introducing compulsory licensure as Canada did during the 1970s, patent holders worldwide react to this as public intrusion into private markets. They may then be supported by their home governments, essentially claiming a modern form of "extraterritoriality," backed up by a modern form of gunboat diplomacy.[3] Self-governing professional associations react with equivalent outrage when governments try to modify the (public) legislation from which they derive their power. In general, those who exercise and benefit from delegated public authority come to regard that authority as private property, and try to convince their fellow citizens to share this view. Whether they succeed or fail, the process makes clear the foundation of private property in political consensus. How could it be otherwise?

The long and complex relationship between the state and providers of health care thus goes far beyond the role of public agencies as payers for care. Economic analysts, in particular, tend to focus on the latter as if it were the only point of contact. This restricted view can lead to the representation of the supply-side of health care systems in terms of the traditional categories of the microeconomic theory textbooks. Such an imaginary system may then be hypothesized to be actually or potentially "competitive," in the full textbook sense, with all that that implies for the potential role of private markets. These representations are both analytically convenient and intellectually familiar (to economists)— advantages that seem to compensate for their gross inadequacies as descriptions of actual institutions or behavior.

But the convenience is not only for the analyst. The pretense that the provision of health services either is, or ever was, or ever could be, organized along the lines of markets for shoes or ships or sealing wax serves to draw a veil over the activities of those who *do* in fact exercise power, and to screen them from public accountability for its use: "Nobody here but us competitors, all obeying the laws of the market." Attempts to modify the institutional rules in order to align private activity more closely with public interests or objectives can then be portrayed, by those with private interests to defend or advance, as simply wrongheaded political meddling in an otherwise smoothly functioning private marketplace.

The primary concern of this essay is to identify the economic interests defended or advanced by the extension of private market mechanisms in health care. The companion essay by Thomas Rice (1997) in this volume provides a comprehensive survey of an extensive literature demonstrating that the simple-minded application to health care of economic theories about competitive markets is both descriptively invalid and theoretically unsound. Here we consider *why* advocates of the private marketplace might continue to rely on just such analyses.

Standard economic analyses of the market suppress its inevitable distributional implications. If market advocates do, in fact, have a distributional agenda, but one that is not widely shared, then they have an obvious interest in promoting the use of an intellectual framework that makes distributional questions difficult or impossible to ask. If that framework also yields a conclusion (valid or erroneous) that private markets are socially "optimal" in some technical sense (bearing no relation to the common use of the word), so much the better.

Distributional questions may be suppressed in economic analysis, but they remain at the forefront of public policy debates. Private markets have been reduced to a subsidiary role in all developed countries other than the United States, largely on the basis of distributional concerns. This may explain why advocates of private markets tend to make their arguments as if the last forty years had never occurred. The issues that were contentious in the 1950s and 1960s are being dragged out again, with all sorts of old a priori arguments being dusted off, repainted, and presented as new thinking about the role of the private sector.

But we *have* now had several decades of international experience with different mixes of public and private funding systems, and the broad lessons are pretty clear. In the developed world, a general consensus has evolved that White (1995) labeled "the international standard" for health care systems. Behind wide variations in detail, there is a broad similarity of system characteristics (White 1995: 271):

- universal coverage of the population, through compulsory participation
- comprehensiveness of principal benefits
- contributions based on income, rather than individual insurance purchases
- cost control through administrative mechanisms, including binding fee schedules, global budgets, and limitations on system capacity

Although the processes may vary, there seems to have been a progressive convergence in both the mechanisms used for administrative management of system costs, and the understanding of system dynamics on which these are based. Cost control is always incomplete; in all countries there are powerful interest groups arrayed on the other side trying to promote continuous system expansion. But in all developed countries, Wildavsky's (1977: 109) law of medical money ("costs will increase to the level of available funds . . . that level must be limited to keep costs down") has been understood and acted upon through the development of countervailing public authority (Abel-Smith 1992; Abel-Smith and Mossialos 1994).

The turning point seems to have come, for most countries, at some time during the 1970s. Figure 1 displays the share of GDP spent on health care, averaged (unweighted) across all the countries of the Organization for Economic Cooperation and Development (OECD) for which data are continuously available from 1960 to 1996 (OECD/CREDES 1997). This average is bracketed by the experience of the United States and of the United Kingdom, as representing high and low-cost countries. For the first half of the period the aggregate international cost experience paralleled that of the United States, with the United Kingdom becoming more and more of an outlier on the low side. But since the mid-1970s the average experience is of substantially slower growth in health expenditures relative to GDP—roughly paralleling the U.K. trend—with the United States progressively diverging.[4] From 1960 to 1976, the OECD average share of health spending in GDP rose 75.4 percent, or an average rate of 3.57 percent per year. But over the last twenty years it has risen only 22.4 percent, or 1.02 percent per year. Since 1993 it has actually fallen slightly and is now just below its 1991 level.

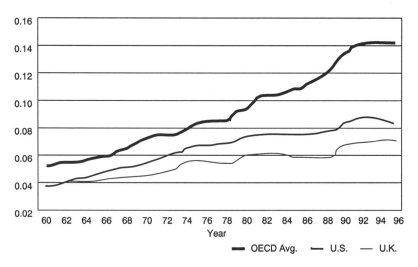

Figure 1. Health expenditures as a share of GDP: OECD Average, U.S. and U.K. *Source.* OECD/CREDES 1997.

The United States is of course the exception to White's (1995) generalization, departing in a major way from his "international standard" in both structure and performance. The same point was made ten years earlier by Abel-Smith (1985), observing that the United States was the "odd man out" among modern health care systems. As such, it provides an enormously valuable point of comparison for the rest of us. What happens if a country does *not* move toward a central role for government in the financing of health care? The decade between Abel-Smith's observation and White's review has reinforced the earlier conclusion. The United States has a health care system that is, by most measures, not only unique in the developed world but also uniquely unsatisfactory. Within the United States it may be daring (Blendon et al. 1995) or heretical (Lamm 1994) to question (publicly) the axiom that "America is number 1," but most external observers (and some internal ones) would put its health care system closer to the *bottom* of the league tables.

This is not to say that the health *care* provided in the United States is of poor quality. Some is, but much is excellent; some is the best in the world. And American patients typically express a high degree of satisfaction with their own care, as do patients in Canada, or the United Kingdom, or most other countries. But as a *system* for organizing, delivering, and particularly for financing health care, the American approach is, by international standards, grossly inefficient, heartbreakingly unfair, monumentally top-heavy with bureaucracy, and off the charts in both the level and the rate of escalation of costs.[5] And for all that, Americans are not particularly healthy, relative to the rest of the developed world.

Yet, even though the United States maintains the institutional forms and the rhetoric of a private system, it has, over time, shifted more than half its health care funding to the public sector. By 1996, 47.0 percent of total health expenditure were reported as coming from some level of government (OECD/CREDES 1997). But the tax expenditure subsidy for private health insurance, the failure to tax employer-paid premiums as income in the hands of the employee, represents an additional public contribution of nearly 10 percent in the form of foregone tax revenue.

This American reality, in the face of the most powerful expressions of antigovernment ideology, suggests that it may simply be impossible to support a modern health care system predominantly from private funds. One can, however, have public funding without comprehensive public oversight and control, at least as long as one is willing to put up with pretty dismal results.

These observations are not always put so bluntly, but their substance is not in dispute. No serious student of health care systems, inside or outside the United States, tries to defend the American status quo. Indeed, American citizens have also figured this out, and give their system very low marks. Figure 2 combines responses by citizens of different countries to a standard set of questions constructed by the Harris polling organization (Blendon et al. 1990) with expenditure data from the OECD Health Datafile (OECD/CREDES 1996).[6]

What is most striking is not simply that Americans expressed a relatively low level of satisfaction with their health care system (*not* with their own personal health care), but that they depart so markedly from the pattern found across all other countries surveyed. There is a surprisingly close linear relationship, among the countries that have evolved an institutional framework conforming to White's (1995) international standard, between per capita spending on health care and the average level of public satisfaction with the health care system. More spending leads to more satisfaction.[7] The United States is different, and Americans are not happy about it.[8]

But for them, the international standard appears to be politically inaccessible. Managed care and competition have thus emerged as a sort of lateral move in response to failure and frustration, marketed as an opportunity for the United States to innovate and leap over the experience of other countries to a position of leadership: "If we cannot do what everyone else does, well then we'll do something else. And it will be

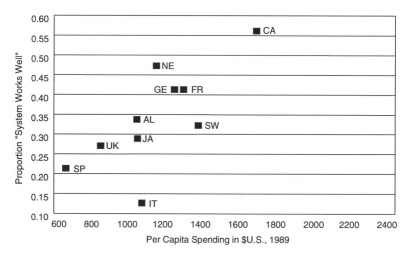

Figure 2. Satisfaction with health care: selected OECD countries. *Source.* Blendon et al. 1990.

much better!" Desperation may explain the high level of enthusiasm, despite the lack of any record of success. The triumphs of managed care are still, as they always have been, in the future.

But is the future finally here? American advocates of "the market" may well see vindication at last in the less rapid growth of health expenditures since 1992. The OECD (using a slightly more restrictive definition of GDP than the U.S. Department of Commerce) reports that from 1992 to 1996, the American ratio of health spending to GDP has fluctuated in a narrow band just above 14 percent (OECD, 1997). Such sustained control is unique in the record of the last fifty years; previous periods of stability have lasted only a couple of years before ending in rapid escalation. There seems no doubt that, whatever else may be going on, there has been a fundamental change in the dynamics of cost expansion in the United States.[9] Hair-raising scenarios in which health absorbs nearly twenty percent of the American GDP by the year 2000 now look decidedly out of date, the products of another era.

But before accepting the post-1992 experience as proof that "the market," in its current American form, finally offers a superior alternative for organizing health care systems, those of us in other countries would be wise to consider some additional observations.

First, "cost control" in the United States is at a level of expenditure nearly 50 percent higher, as a share of GDP, than that in the next most expensive countries. (In per capita terms it is twice as high.) And the spread between the Americans and the rest of us is still widening, although much more slowly now, because the average for OECD countries has begun to fall. On the very narrow criterion of cost control, the American performance has improved from "much worse than average" to "at or slightly below average"—hardly a ringing endorsement for the market!

Second, this control is associated with growing restrictions on patient choice and on the clinical freedom of physicians, as well as an increasingly inequitable financing system. More people are uninsured, while more of those who are insured find that their insurance plan dictates which physicians they may see, and what forms of care those physicians may offer. Those with sufficient personal resources can, of course, buy their way around such restrictions; the distributional consequences are discussed in more detail below.

Third, while the cost control after 1992 has been sustained longer than ever before, there is still room for considerable doubt as to whether it represents a new equilibrium. It has been accompanied by increasing public and provider unhappiness, reflected in a wave of legislation to regulate the various techniques that competitive health plans have used to limit their own outlays. This public dissatisfaction is likely to increase markedly when the elderly population, until 1997 largely insulated from such restrictions by the national Medicare program for those over 65, discover that they, too, are now being forced into the world of competing, for-profit health plans. Many of them will have to give up long-standing relationships with providers or pay out of pocket.

At the same time, providers who have lost both autonomy and income since 1992 are organizing to strike back. Moreover, a significant expansion in numbers of physicians is already underway, and pharmaceutical manufacturers have a large number of potent but expensive new drugs "in the pipeline" soon coming to market. The former will want to be paid for their services, and the latter for their products. If these can ally with an angry public, the peculiar combination of circumstances that has supported effective cost control—through whatever set of institutions—may dissolve as rapidly as it emerged. After all, competitive "managed care" of one form or another has been around for years in the United States without yielding cost control, and most other countries have achieved cost control without such "managed care." There may be an element of post hoc fallacy in the presumption that the one has been the sole cause of the other. At the very least, the question is still open.

Thus, when managed care is offered in other countries as a compromise between public regulation and private action, it looks rather more like a compromise between success and failure. Nobody pretends that other countries do not have substantial problems with their health care systems. But they are typically problems that most Americans would be very relieved to have to face.[10]

So there is a puzzle. The record of the last forty years seems to show that the United States took the wrong road in trying to rely on private action to organize and finance health care. The rest of us groped our way to what now seems to be a reasonably satisfactory road, albeit one needing a good deal of further work. Why, then, would anyone want to rerun the ancient state-versus-market debates of the 1950s? And why, in particular, would other countries be thinking of expanding the role of the private market, and importing American ideas?[11] Have we gotten the military maxim backward: "Expedite failure, and abandon success?"

A good part of the answer, I think, lies in the loose use of *we*. It implies a commonality of interest, suppressing the rather obvious fact that choices with respect to health care finance, as with any other aspect of public policy, have significant distributional consequences. Some gain, and some lose, and the gains and losses can be very large.

The persistence of the same old arguments over health care finance, the resilience of ancient policy proposals in the face of contrary experience, is rooted in the fact that the broad pattern of gainers and losers resulting from particular policy choices in health care has changed little, if at all, over the decades (Barer et al. 1994). The relative size of the particular interest groups is now very different, in different countries, and the stakes are much larger. But the interests are the same.

Figure 3 and Equation 1 provide an accounting framework—a stripped-down sectoral version of the national income accounts—within which to represent the different interests involved. Abstracting from both international trade and changes in asset stocks, there is a fundamental identity linking total *expenditures* on health goods and services, total *revenues* raised to pay for those services, and total *incomes* earned from the provision of services:

$$T + C + R \equiv P \times Q \equiv W \times Z. \tag{1}$$

The definition of what does or does not constitute a health service, the basket of commodities included in this sector, is in principle arbitrary, although in practice there is good agreement on the broad categories of medically necessary hospital, medical, and pharmaceutical services. The gray areas are many, but quantitatively pretty small (with the exception of institutional care of the frail elderly or otherwise disabled).

Revenues may be raised through three main channels: taxation (*T*),

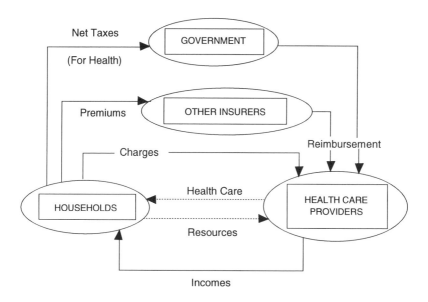

Figure 3. Alternative ways of paying for health care.

direct charges (C), and private insurance premiums (R).[12] Total expenditure can be factored into the unit prices of the various health care commodities, and the quantities of each. P and Q are thus vectors whose elements refer to all the different types of commodities provided in the system. These, in turn, are produced by combining various inputs or resources Z that are paid at a rate per unit W. An element of the vector W might be a wage rate, for example, corresponding to a type of labor input measured in hours and making up an element of Z.

Health care goods and services are provided by various kinds of firms: professional practices, hospitals, government agencies, private corporations. A real exchange takes place between these firms and households, as the latter both receive and consume the products of the former, and supply the resource inputs that firms combine (i.e., "transform") into commodities. The revenues received by firms for their products then all flow back to households as incomes, in payment for the resources provided.[13]

Reference to "provider incomes" is a convenient shorthand, but introduces a source of semantic confusion that has become much more important as a result of the major changes that have taken place in the American health care system. Providers are usually professional persons or institutions who actually give care: doctors and nurses, or hospitals and nursing homes. But the W and Z in Equation 1 refer to all the resources that are reimbursed from health care expenditures. Total incomes earned from the provision of health care are not restricted to the incomes of providers.[14]

They include, for example, the fees of the lawyer reimbursed by the insurer to whom the physician pays premiums for malpractice insurance. They also include the dividends (and retained earnings) of shareholders in the for-profit managed care firm that contracts with physicians and collects premiums from patients. To the extent that the managed care revolution results in lower fees, salaries, or workloads for particular caregivers, it lowers the incomes of providers as commonly defined. But if total costs continue upward, then the flow of funds through the health care system will have been redirected to benefit a different group of households: suppliers of managerial services and investment capital, marketers, accountants, and the whole administrative overhead of business enterprise. The components of W and Z will be rearranged—less for some, more for others—but taken in total, incomes earned from the provision of health care continue to increase.

The fundamental point, however, is that the relationship depicted in Figure 3 and written out in Equation 1 is an *identity*, and must hold, as a matter of logic and mathematical consistency. Any change to one component must be either offset or balanced by corresponding changes elsewhere in the equation. To this identity, we can annex various side equations, or additional relationships that are postulated to involve components of the basic identity. At a minimum these would include:

1 A health production function that links the outputs of health services Q to the health status of the members of the population. This relationship is both complex and controversial, but the very definition of health services implies that they bear a special relationship to health. Absent that relationship, and most of us would much prefer to forego the services themselves: Consuming health care is not in itself a source of satisfaction.

2 A health care production function that links the outputs of services Q to the levels of inputs Z. Dollars do not produce services; but people, know-how, capital, and raw materials do. One cannot make bricks (at least not very good ones) without straw.

3 A demand relationship linking the level of direct charges paid by

users, C, to the level of utilization, Q. The typical assumption from the economics textbooks is that as C goes up, Q goes down, and indeed ceteris paribus that appears to be true. But the ceteris are rarely, if ever, paribus, which is why this relationship must be considered in the context of the overall identity.

4 A capacity relation linking levels of service provided Q to some maximum available stock of inputs. The inputs, Z, used at any point in time do not necessarily represent the full capacity of the health care system; we might think of that capacity being determined (in the short run) by some maximum level, $Z,*$ of total resources that could be made available. $Z^* \geq Z$; actual resource use must be less than or equal to this maximum. The capacity relation by which Q depends upon Z^* expresses the observation that there is a strong tendency for patterns of health care use to adapt to the capacity available (Roemer's Law) (see, e.g., Wennberg et al. 1988, esp. chs. 3 and 6). Supply creates its own demand.

The production functions need not hold as equalities; they are boundary conditions that place limits on the possible. But providers of care routinely assert, and often sincerely believe, that both of these boundaries have been reached, and also that there would be a high payoff in improved health from further increasing (the right form of) health care. The system is underfunded! Needs are not being met! Send more resources, and especially more money!

Such claims are part of the political theater in which struggles over income shares are played out. Occasionally they may be supported with actual examples of unmet needs; rarely are the boundary assumptions made explicit, let alone supported. But whatever its relation to "unmet needs," more expenditure always yields an increase in incomes. ($W \times Z$ goes up, although the split between W and Z will depend on other factors.) This is the driving force behind Wildavsky's law (1977).[15]

There is, likewise, a great deal more assertion about the strength—and normative significance—of the demand relationship than ever appears in actual system experience. On the contrary, providers in publicly funded systems commonly advocate the expansion of direct charges as a way of *increasing* the total flow of funds into health care, implying that if there is any net negative effect on Q, it will be offset by corresponding increases in P. At the system-wide level, the evidence seems to be consistent with this view.[16] In practice, increases in user charges serve to *shift* costs from one payer to another, while increasing, not decreasing, the total. Providers, and especially their representatives, are not economically naive.

On the other hand, the direct impact of capacity on use is one of the most solidly grounded empirical relationships in health economics. It has been observed for hospital beds, physicians, and new drug products or types of technical equipment. But it is conditional on the availability of payment. Roemer's law, that a built bed is a filled bed, abruptly ceased to hold in the United States when Medicare shifted to case-based reimbursement. And fund-holding general practitioners in the United Kingdom, who have to bear the resulting costs, seem much less willing than previously to hospitalize their patients.

The side equations however remind us that we are dealing with individual people (or households) as well as with commodities and units of currency. Money is fungible, but people are not. If we simply rewrite Equation 1 in notation that provides labels for each of the persons, commodities, and inputs involved, it becomes obvious that the identity holds in aggregate, but not for any one individual. Thus,

$$\Sigma_i\{tY_i + \Sigma_j(C_j \times q_{ij}) + R_i\} \equiv \Sigma_{ij}(P_j \times q_{ij}) \equiv \Sigma_{ik}(W_k \times z_{ik}) \qquad \text{(1a)}$$

Here persons are indexed by i, health care services by j, and factor inputs by k. In addition, the taxes paid by any individual that are directed toward health care are assumed to be a constant proportion t of that person's income. The user charges paid by an individual are the product of that person's use of a particular commodity, q_{ij}, multiplied by the level of charge, C_j, applicable to that service, and summed over all services. The user charge will typically lie between zero and the actual price/cost P_j of the service, although there is no logical reason why it could not be outside that range.

Stripped of the summations across individuals, the relationships in Equation 1a divide the population into two groups according to whether $W \times Z$ for a particular individual exceeds or falls short of both $T + C + R$ and $P \times Q$. The group for whom $W \times Z$ is higher are (net) recipients of health spending; they receive more in income from health care than they contribute to its financing or receive in services. The remainder, with low $W \times Z$, are (net) users of/payers for care: the rest of us.

A change in the funding arrangements for health care that increases expenditure (relative to what it would otherwise have been) will typically be advantageous for the first group, and costly for the second.[17] Most obviously, an increase in expenditure that takes the form of rising P and W, however it is financed, unambiguously transfers income from payers/users to providers—no surprises there.

But the user/payer group is not homogeneous; it can, in turn, be subdivided according to whether $T + C + R$ exceeds or falls short of $P \times Q$. The former can be labeled as the healthy and/or wealthy, contributing

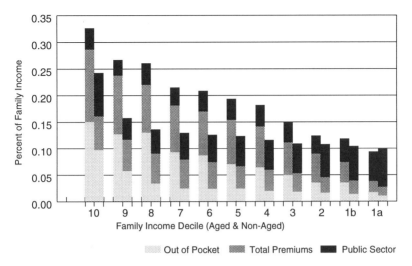

Figure 4. Family expenditures for health care by income decile and age of head. *Source.* Rasell, Bernstein, and Tang 1993.

more to the financing of the system than the value of the services they receive from it. Conversely, those for whom $P \times Q$ exceeds $T + C + R$ are net beneficiaries, at least financially.[18] Again, any change in the sources of funding for a health care system will transfer income between the members of these two groups.

Thus one finds, for example, that people with higher incomes are more likely to favor greater reliance on user charges as a source of system finance, and less use of general public revenues. A priori it should be pretty obvious that, whereas tax liabilities tend to be more or less proportionate to income, illness is not. For any given level of total national expenditure on health, more will come out of the pockets of wealthier individuals if the system is tax-financed, and less if it is user-paid. Private insurance premiums, being based on expected use of care, not on income level, also take a bigger share of the incomes of people at lower incomes.[19]

Empirical confirmation comes from studies in both the United States and the European Community. Rasell, Bernstein, and Tang (1993) and Rasell and Tang (1994) have shown that in the United States the share of health spending that comes through public budgets is progressively distributed, taking a larger share of the incomes of people at higher income levels. But both user fees and private insurance are strikingly regressive, taking a much larger share of the incomes of lower-income people (Figure 4).[20]

Moreover this pattern is particularly apparent among those over sixty-five, who are virtually all enrolled in the national Medicare program for the elderly. The various deductibles, coinsurance rates, and exclusions in that program, and the corresponding private "Medigap" insurance market, produce a highly regressive financing structure even for this universal public program.

Similar findings emerge from the large-scale ECuity project directed by van Doorslaer, Wagstaff, and Rutten (1993), a detailed empirical study of the pattern of distribution of health, health care, and financing burdens across income classes in the countries of the European Community, as well as the United States. They conclude:

> The two countries with predominantly private financing systems—Switzerland and the US—have the most regressive structures overall. This is scarcely surprising in view of just how regressive private insurance and out-of-pocket payments are when used to finance such a large proportion of health care expenditures for such a large proportion of the population. The group of countries with the next most regressive systems are the countries operating the so-called social insurance model, . . . countries which . . . rely mainly on tax-finance . . . have the least regressive financing systems. (ibid.: 44)

But while "out-of-pocket payments tend to be a highly regressive means of financing health care" (ibid.: 42), the impact of private insurance is more nuanced. Private insurance that is purchased as supplementary cover in a more or less universal public system appears to be a "luxury" that is more commonly bought by people with higher incomes; such payments are thus progressively distributed. But if, as in the United States, private insurance is purchased by a large proportion of the population because public coverage is restricted or nonexistent, the distribution of its costs is highly regressive. Private coverage for deductibles or copayments in the public system tends to be progressive or regressive depending upon the scale of such charges. In general, the larger the user charges and the more people who must pay them, the more regressive are the costs of private insurance to cover them.

These observations form the empirical context for proposals for "reform" of financing systems; the identity provides the underlying algebra. In Equation 1a, if one holds total expenditure constant and makes offsetting changes in t and C, those whose share of total income exceeds their share of total health expenditures (either because their incomes are large or because their expenditures are small) will gain more from tax reductions than they lose from increased user charges (Evans, Barer, and

Stoddart 1994).[21] And these are the people who then advocate, on various grounds and through a multitude of channels, increased reliance on "private" funding (Barer et al. 1994).

Several attempts have been made over the years to confuse this essentially straightforward distributional issue. Proposals for integration of user charges with the income tax, or the creation of medical savings accounts, are financing gimmicks that obscure or appear to change the direction of the income transfer. But when one works through the details, at their core is health insurance with greatly increased deductibles and rates of coinsurance: more user pay and less tax finance. So long as tax liability is related to income, and service use is not, any such changes must transfer income from the less to the more healthy and wealthy.[22] Thus, debates over public or private financing, whatever other issues they may draw in, are always and inevitably about who pays what share of the bill.

The standard claim by market advocates has always been that placing more of the cost burden on individual users will lead to lower utilization and more careful purchasing by consumers/patients, more competitive behavior by providers, and thus to a less costly, more responsive, and more efficient health care system. If this does not occur, it must be because the user charges are not high enough.

As observed previously, the international comparative experience of the last forty years is flatly in contradiction with this claim. But the point emphasized here is that, whether or not the claim is true, it must be the case, from the basic accounting, that shifting the cost burden from taxpayers to users will, on average, redistribute wealth from lower- to higher-income individuals. When people persistently advocate a particular policy by making a claim A, which (I believe) the evidence rejects, while consistently avoiding discussion of effect B, which the policy *must* bring about, one should at least consider that B may be the real objective.

Interestingly, Hsiao (1995) provides a recent evaluation of Singapore's experience with medical savings accounts, as part of a more general reform based on precisely the claims of the market advocates. He concludes that, contrary to those claims, increasing the role of private financing has led to more rapid cost escalation, an overcapitalized system of duplicated and underutilized facilities, and rapid increases in physician incomes. Even when patients are paying prices in nominally "free" markets, hospitals do not compete on price, but on technology, in order to attract the physicians who will bring in the paying patients. Nor can this be blamed on mismanagement; Hsiao describes the Singapore funding system as carefully planned and well executed. It was the fundamental theory that was in error.

In 1993, the Singaporean authorities concluded that "the health care system is an example of market failure. The government has to intervene directly to structure and regulate the health system" (quoted in Hsiao 1995: 263). Their observation is a bit late to be original; indeed, one does wonder, given the accumulation of international experience, how they could ever have imagined otherwise. But it is significant because it follows a decade-long effort, under the most favorable circumstances, to make the market work.[23]

Contributors at different income levels are not, however, the only participants in the conversation over the state versus the market. The split between those who pay and those who are paid has had an even more powerful and long-term impact on the evolution of health care policy. It has always fueled the conflicting perceptions of system under-funding versus excessive costs that seem to emerge in all systems, whatever the evidentiary base.

The comparative success of governments in developing mechanisms for cost control—although not always in deploying them—has led to increasing efforts by providers to enhance their incomes by drawing in more private funds. These efforts underlie the peculiar "conversation of the deaf" between those who are trying to limit public responsibility for payment by defining "core services," and turning the rest over to the private market, however defined, and those who are trying to improve system management by eliminating ineffective services. The root of the problem is that people get paid for doing things, whether or not these are effective.[24] If the movement for evidence-based health care leads to a slimmed-down health care system, with fewer ineffective services and lower costs, then, as the identity makes obvious, there will be fewer and/or lower income streams generated. Population health status may be maintained, or may even increase, but Q, Z, and T, C, and/or R all fall.

On the other hand, the core-services approach finesses the question: Does the service do any good? Health drops out of consideration. Q is split into two components: *core* paid for from the public budget, and *noncore* paid for through direct charges or private insurance. The original bundle of services, or rather types of services, now draws in more money in total. Private funding (C and/or R) increases; unless there are equal or greater reductions in public funding, the health care system as a whole expands: Prices, incomes, and perhaps jobs are up.

Are the noncore services effective in improving health? Well, once they are out in the private market, who cares? Containing the exuberance of private medicine (or drugs, or dentistry, etc.) is technically difficult and politically expensive, unless there is some egregious public scandal (e.g., thalidomide). Governments—or employers—will only take on the task if they must bear the financial consequences of not doing so. And even then, success is not guaranteed. But if someone else is paying, the prudent response is to hide behind the rhetoric of the "sovereign consumer" (who is after all "freely choosing" to spend his or her own money), and perhaps to try to promote a voluntary code of ethical conduct by providers.

The key distinction is that the evidence-based approach to classifying services identifies activities that do no good, and thus should not be provided *by anybody, in any setting*. In aiming to reduce total system costs while maintaining or improving population health status, it threatens provider incomes. The core-services approach is instead a program for tapping more private funds to supplement those provided by increasingly tough-minded governments—cost shifting rather than cost control. In this way, advocates hope to expand total system costs while limiting or reducing public outlays. Different objectives, different constraints, but again, the debate about private funding turns out to be about incomes.

Not all providers, however, believe that they can successfully draw in private funds. Those who offer well-defined and easily marketable procedures to anxious middle-aged businessmen may do very well, but those whose clienteles have complex problems and few resources would gain little from an opportunity to market their services privately. From them, one hears support for the evidence-based approach, but with the proviso that any savings should be put back into other forms of care to meet other needs. Resources (and incomes) would then be redirected within the health care sector, while blunting the threat to total expenditures/incomes. Unlike the core services approach, however, this does not offer governments a way to limit *their* outlays.

Proposals to expand the role of private insurance link the interests of both providers and upper-income contributors. Governments have proven to be quite tough as budgetary negotiators, and are imposing increasingly stringent controls on health care expenditures as their own fiscal positions weaken. Private insurers, on the other hand, have no particular incentive to limit cost escalation—if anything, the contrary—and in any case have not done so. From the point of view of providers, the optimal situation, at least in economic terms, is to have complete freedom to set prices and choose treatment patterns, but to have a high level of insurance coverage in the population so that the resulting bills will be paid.

American experience indicates that a high level of coverage requires very large public subsidies, both directly for the elderly and poor, and through tax expenditures for those with private coverage. But the tax expenditure subsidies for private insurance can be, and in the United States are, structured to yield the greatest benefits for people in higher income brackets. At the same time, the tax-supported public program for the elderly has extensive user charges—deductibles and coinsurance—built into it in the name of cost control. These charges are in turn covered, in whole or in part, by private medigap insurance policies or through extensions of employer coverage as a retirement benefit. Such private coverage is highly correlated with income.[25]

Thus, increases in Medicare user charges serve primarily to shift costs from a funding source that is related to income (taxes) to one that is not (private insurance premiums). Their deterrent effect, which as noted above has no effect on aggregate system cost anyway, is faced only by those whose employers did not provide (or can no longer sustain) postretirement coverage, or who cannot afford private medigap coverage (or were sold a bad policy), or who are not poor enough for (or do not know about) Medicaid coverage.

Viewed in aggregate, the combination of Medicare user charges to control costs, plus private insurance to cover those charges, plus tax expenditure subsidies for private insurance, all overlaid with the capricious effects of highly imperfect markets, makes no sense at all. Indeed, it borders on lunacy. But, if one looks at the combination instead as a (nontransparent) way of keeping health care expenditures and incomes *up* by fragmenting funding sources while shifting the burden of contributions down the income scale, with a cover story that holds the ill accountable for their "choices" to "consume" health care, then it begins to make sense. The whole system produces much higher costs, and a much more regressive contribution structure, than would be politically acceptable in any single-payer public system funded from general revenue.[26]

But all this administrative apparatus does not come cheap. This point emerged very clearly from an analysis of OECD data by Gerdtham and Jönsson (1991), in which they identified the effects of differences in the relative prices of health care services, from one country to another, on international comparisons of health care costs. They found, as displayed in Figure 5, that a large proportion of the difference in per capita expenditures between the United States and all other countries of the OECD was a result of higher relative prices of health care in the United States.[27]

Americans receive, on average, no more care than Canadians, very little more than Japanese, and much less than Swedes. But they pay much more, relatively, for what they get. In terms of the preceding identity, P (price) is higher in the United States than anywhere else.[28]

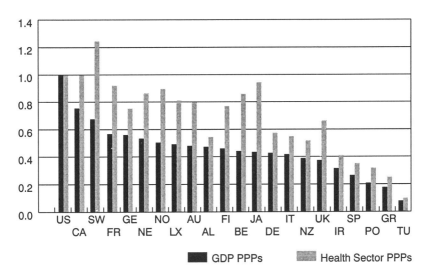

Figure 5. Health care spending per capita, 1985, as percent of U.S. purchasing power parities. *Source.* Gerdtham and Jönsson 1991.

Defenders of the American health care system may claim, and even believe, that this price differential corresponds to some unmeasured difference in quality, but the discussion rapidly becomes circular. It is, in fact, a natural extension of the American exceptionalism claim (see note 8): "American health care costs more because Americans face greater threats to their health, and need more care." "But they do not *get* much more care, they just pay much more for it." "Well, then the care they get must be of higher quality." In effect, expenditure is *defined* as quality. The only way out of this (il)logical trap is to place the burden of proof on the apologist. Let him find some evidence of benefit—not just for the wealthy but population-wide, not just inferred from some theory but actually documented—to correspond to the extra cost of the system as a whole.

The extreme case frames the general issue. The expansion of private insurance, within a public system of health care finance, offers benefits to both providers (higher prices) and upper-income payers (a more regressive financing structure). It thus supports a potent political alliance. If, in addition, providers are able (selectively) to recruit people into the private insurance system by offering them the reality, or even just the perception, of superior services, this reinforces the financial advantages.

But the complex administrative mechanisms for achieving these redistributional objectives are themselves costly. They result not only in higher incomes for (some) providers, but also in an increasing flow of real resources into the overhead costs of managing the health care system. And this is inevitable. The inherent instability of private health care financing—Wildavsky's law (1977) again—leads to uncontrolled cost escalation. This in turn generates an administrative arms race as each payer struggles to shift the ever-increasing costs onto others. Such efforts are highly rational, indeed necessary for survival, at the level of the individual institution. From the perspective of the society as a whole, they generate an ever-increasing level of pure waste motion.[29]

The dynamics of the relationship between public and private insurance depend upon a number of institutional characteristics that are quite system-specific. God and the devil are again both in the details. The point emphasized here is the more general one, that distributional conflicts are central to all arguments for and against private insurance—the relative balance of state and private action. Depending upon how it is structured, expanding private insurance offers opportunities for transfer of incomes both from payers to providers, and from the less to the more healthy and wealthy payers. Conversely, the historic shift to public coverage moved incomes the other way, although the amounts were not so large in earlier decades. Associated with these inherently political choices over distribution, however, are significant differences in the real resource costs of system administration, and corresponding differences in income opportunities for the financial services industry.

If governments, and behind them electorates, can be induced to focus their attention on public budgets alone, rather than the balance of costs and benefits from the health care system as a whole, then the stage is set for an unholy alliance in which all three parties can gain by (a) lowering public expenditures, but (b) increasing overall expenditures, and (c) shifting a larger share of costs onto the relatively less healthy and wealthy. A perfectly reasonable public objective of reconstructing a highly dysfunctional health care sector can then be deflected and perverted into a program for regressive income redistribution and protection of health sector revenues, all under the ideological cover of shrinking big government.

All of which is rather banal and obvious (Political Economy 101), and one might reasonably ask whether the whole excursion was necessary. The justification, I think, is that so much of the debate over health care policy, particularly among economists, and particularly over the relative roles of the state and the market, continues to be carried on as if it *were* possible to abstract from distributional issues, when out in the real world, the conflicts are in fact about very little else.

The tone of economic discourse was set about twenty-five years ago, and Arrow (1976) sounded a warning at the time that was generally ignored. In an analysis of the welfare effects of coinsurance rates, originally written in 1973, he declared at the outset that "I ignore distributional considerations and assume a single person in the economy" (4). On the next page, however, he stated: "To avoid distributional considerations I assume that all individuals have identical endowments and identical utility functions. I further assume a very large population" (5).

The confusion is understandable. In a single-person economy, who buys insurance, and from whom? But in an economy of *differentiated* individuals, it is impossible to derive general a priori conclusions about aggregate welfare. Arrow (1976) therefore assumed that the economy consists of many identical individuals. They vary in their actual health experience (or why buy insurance?) but they are identical in their *expectation* of illness, so they have equal access to insurance coverage as well as equal incomes. Moreover, they all work for the same proportion of their time in the "medical" industry. Thus, there is no distinction between providers and users: Everyone is both, and to an equivalent degree. Under Arrow's assumptions, Equation 1a *does* hold for each of the individuals i, not just for the aggregate. One need only substitute an expected value for the actual quantities of services used by each person.

As an approximation to the real world, Arrow's (1976) assumptions were ridiculous—as he very well knew. What he was showing is that *without* such assumptions, one cannot, at the theoretical level, ignore "distributional considerations" and generate any conclusions at all about the desirability or otherwise of any particular policy.[30]

Of course, one can do so if one is prepared to make interpersonal comparisons of well-being, balancing one person's loss against another's gain, and this happens every day in the real world of public policy. But as a number of leading theorists, Arrow included, have pointed out, one cannot do so on the basis of "value-neutral" economic theory. Theory by itself does not, and logically cannot, provide a normative basis for policy prescriptions. Rice's (1997) essay in this book provides a more detailed discussion; see also Culyer 1989, Reinhardt 1992, and Culyer and Evans 1996. Normative judgments, in or out of economics, cannot be derived from positive propositions alone, or in Archibald's paraphrase of Hume: "No ethics in, no ethics out."

Yet respected economic analysts do so routinely, making firm declarations as to the efficiency or optimality of particular arrangements, or their welfare costs or benefits. In doing so they are making value judgments about the relative deservingness of different individuals, and approving or disapproving the transfer of substantial funds from one set of people to another. But these judgments are implicit, unaccountable, and typically unconfessed—sometimes even denied. There is also some reason to believe that the values implicit in proposals for more reliance on private markets in health care are quite unrepresentative of the views of the populations who use and support health care systems. Yet, they are confidently offered as guides for public policy. So, what is going on?[31]

Well, the suppression of distributional considerations through the (implicit) assumption of identical individuals *can* provide an analytic cloak for what would otherwise be a naked redistributional agenda. Deliberately redistributive policies can be promoted as optimal on a priori grounds, allegedly on the basis of value-free economic theory. The essential feature of all such policies is a shift in funding sources in order to link individual contributions more closely to either care use or risk status, while weakening the link to ability to pay. Often they will also give providers greater discretion in price setting, which may include offering patients various forms of preferential treatment in return for additional private payments.[32] ·

One need not, however, assume that the provision of an analytic cloak for redistributional objectives is the deliberate intent of analysts in the tradition of neoclassical economic theory, even if their work may be useful for this purpose. There is an important distinction to be drawn between two quite different groups of participants in the debate over the role of the state in health services, whom we may label fundamentalists and instrumentalists. The latter advocate particular structures or policies because they expect certain consequences to result; but the former are "advocates without predicates," holding particular forms of economic organization to be good per se. In an earlier day, socialists regarded state control of the means of production, or at least of the "commanding heights" of the economy, as good per se, on a priori grounds. At present, advocates of the market on theoretical grounds enjoy the same absolute conviction.

Debates with fundamentalists about the proper scope of public and private action are ultimately futile. Initial impressions to the contrary, they do not, in fact, base their case for the market on (testable) claims that their preferred institutions or policies will lead to lower costs, or healthier people, or better performance on any other externally defined criterion (Frankford 1992). When pressed, fundamentalists explicitly reject such external standards (e.g., Pauly 1994a, 1994b). Their position is rather that *whatever* results—prices, quantities, distribution of services, health outcomes—emerge from market processes, such results are optimal *because* they have been generated by those processes. The private marketplace is the source of ultimate objectives rather than merely a means to their achievement. Individual willingness to pay for the products of private, competitive firms is not the best criterion for efficient resource allocation: It is the only criterion.

The fundamentalist argument for private action in health care, although clothed in economic rhetoric, is in fact a form of religion. It converts Side Equation 3, linking the level of use of health care services to the direct charges that users must pay, from a *positive* statement about an (in principle) observable relationship between two variables, into a *normative* statement about how the level, mix, and distribution of health care services, the q_{ij}, *ought* to be determined. But normative statements are the province of priests. (And also of politicians, but those suffer the inconvenience of having to secure public support.) The normative views of economists, qua economists, have no more (or less) significance than those of T. C. Pits.[33]

But these theoretical arguments, mostly in the economic literature, are primarily icing on the cake. Very few people (if any) share the underlying value system on which they are based. When we come to the point, most of us do *not* agree that it is a misallocation of resources when people receive lifesaving care that they cannot themselves afford, and that our societies would be in some sense more efficient (better) if this did not occur. We do not want to live in that kind of society, we do not have to, and we will not.

Accordingly, most of those on the political stage who consistently advocate (or oppose) a larger role for private markets in health care do so because they anticipate particular consequences, rather than from religious conviction. These instrumentalists, however, may have very different objectives. Roughly, we may draw a distinction between those whose aims are primarily distributional, and those who are genuinely concerned with system performance.

All, of course, use the rhetoric of system improvement, and of public interest more generally—even the fundamentalists can sometimes be found in this camouflage. And it is a gross oversimplification to suggest that a population can be thus neatly partitioned into two distinct groups. People's motives are usually mixed, and are often far from clear even to themselves. Nevertheless, it is important to recognize explicitly that debates over health policy, and particularly over the role of the state, are motivated by these two quite different classes of objectives.

The mixture of motives is well illustrated in the major changes to the American Medicare system that were introduced in the summer of 1997.

For a number of years, that program had been developing mechanisms similar to those in the universal systems of other countries, to contain overall payments to providers on behalf of its insured population. But the political will to apply these in full force was often lacking—as it has been in other countries. During the post-1992 period costs have escalated more rapidly in Medicare than in the private sector. An obvious inference was that public budgetary controls did not work and that competitive private-market pressures did. The new approach will thus move beneficiaries from their present coverage to enrollment in private, competitive health plans. The expectation is that this will lead to further savings.

The federal government would pay a fixed sum per beneficiary to each such plan, limiting the liability of the Medicare program itself. It thus accepts the traditional provider argument—limit public expenditures, not total payments to providers—and is in effect a voucher system. The catch from providers' point of view is that, if the post-1992 patterns persist, the result will be a shift of revenue from providers of clinical services to providers of managerial and financial services.

But that will not be the only form of financial redistribution. The amount of public payment to a private plan on behalf of each individual beneficiary will never match that beneficiary's risk status. (The matching formula is the Holy Grail that a subindustry of economists has failed to find.) The incentive for plans to select the most profitable (i.e., usually, the healthiest) enrollees is obvious and powerful. To the extent that they can do so, a multitiered system of plans is likely to emerge as the healthy and/or wealthy are welcomed into more attractive plans and the unhealthy or unwealthy take what they can get.

For the prospective patient with means, however, the point-of-service plan offers another option. Enroll in a low-cost plan, then if something serious goes wrong, pay out-of-pocket to get the provider and the care you (believe you) need. Alternatively, purchase supplementary insurance to cover such eventualities. Recalling that the Medicare system (both Part A and the voluntary Part B) is largely tax-supported, the containment of Medicare costs and the expansion of private outlays is a profitable exchange—if one is sufficiently healthy and/or wealthy.

The net effect of a huge and complex "reform" to privatize the Medicare payment system will thus be to shift costs from taxes to private sources, i.e., from the healthy and wealthy to the unhealthy and unwealthy, while ensuring preferred access for the wealthy and unhealthy. Other objectives—efficiency, effectiveness, sustained cost control, deficit reduction—may or may not be advanced. But the redistribution of costs is pretty well guaranteed.

But is anyone surprised? The interest groups that for decades have re-iterated the same arguments for private markets, regardless of the evidence accumulated against them, see their own interests clearly enough. Their members hope to earn more (providers), or to contribute less and have preferred access to services (healthy and/or wealthy users).

To the extent that they are right, there is, as with the fundamentalists, little to debate. The analyst's role is only to make the proposed redistributional agenda as explicit as possible. Its advocates can then compete directly for broader public support without drawing upon misinterpretations of economic theory or other claims of general public benefit. Because, in practice, people as citizens do not appear to be motivated solely by perceptions of their own economic interests, greater transparency of policy effects may well lead to different, and more satisfactory, collective choices. (If it were not so, interest groups would not be so careful to disguise the full impact of their proposals.)

Moreover, redistributional processes turn out to be more complex than they look, and alternative choices *do* have consequences for the overall functioning of a health care system. Quite clearly, private funding mechanisms can be used to generate a more regressive distribution of contributions, if that is what one wants. But international experience indicates that the overall system will be more expensive because providers' prices will be higher, because inappropriate use will be harder to control, and especially because the complex mix of public and private financing and management mechanisms will add substantially to the administrative overhead costs of providing care.

The past explosion of costs in the United States, for example, did not, as noted above, all go into the pockets of providers as traditionally defined. An increasing proportion has been appropriated by members of the managerial and financial services industries, who now appear to be cutting into, and pushing down, the incomes of caregivers. The management thus financed has, to date, involved a good deal of extra trouble and work for both caregivers and patients, not all of which is included in statistics on health care costs. But if the most recent data do in fact herald a new world of stable or even declining American health care expenditures, the struggle between providers of care and providers of managerial overhead is likely to become increasingly bitter.

In any case, although upper-income Americans may pay a smaller *share* of the costs of their health care system than they would if it conformed to White's (1995) international standard, many of them actually pay more in total because their system is so much more expensive. Public sector spending on health care in the United States, at $1,742 per capita in 1996, was among the highest in the OECD, up with Luxembourg, Switzerland, and Germany, even without including the American tax expenditure subsidy. Canada, for example, with universal public first-dollar coverage for hospital and medical care, spent about U.S. $300 less in public funds; most European countries spent substantially less (OECD/CREDES 1997). Americans thus pay more *in taxes* for health care, in addition to (or despite) their massive contributions through the private sector.

The more interesting instrumentalist debates arise, however, after it is accepted that the public purpose of health care systems is indeed what most people in every society say it is: the maintenance and improvement of health, and the humane treatment of the ill (Labelle, Stoddart, and Rice 1994). Indeed, as van Doorslaer, Wagstaff, and Rutten (1993: 11) reported, and as public surveys confirm, most people seem to have a rather Marxist view of health care systems: "From each according to his ability, to each according to his needs." Side Equation 3 then moves from the center of the stage and we focus instead on Side Equations 1 and 2. Are our health care systems efficient producers of effective services? Do they respond to patients' needs in a humane and timely fashion? How can their performance be improved while maintaining fiscal constraints?

If a health care system *were,* in fact, on the frontier of both the health care and the health production functions, then there would be a direct link between resource inputs and (someone's) health status. In such circumstances, cutbacks do cost lives—or at least put health at risk—as care is long delayed, or denied altogether. And overstrained providers may be brusque, perfunctory, uncommunicative, and inconvenient to access. Faced with such prospects, a majority of our populations might well support more resources for health care, particularly if they perceive themselves personally to be at risk. Nurturing that belief is the cornerstone of the public relations strategy of provider representatives in all countries.

If, on the other hand (as is widely, if not universally, believed by students of health care systems), there is a great deal of inappropriate, unnecessary, and sometimes downright harmful care being paid for in all modern health care systems, and if the process of production is none too efficient either, then the key question becomes one of moving closer to both production frontiers.

The instrumentalist case for systemic reform through private market mechanisms is simply that these could be structured either to embody incentives for greater efficiency in production than is possible in governmentally administered systems, or (which is not at all the same thing) to encourage a more appropriate mix—perhaps less in total—of services, more responsively provided. In the process, of course, these mechanisms must not result in an unacceptable (to whom?) redistribution of incomes, or a re-ignition of cost escalation.

At a very basic level, this proposition does not seem particularly contentious. Opening hospital laundry or dietary services to competitive bids from private firms may raise issues in labor relations, but not for health policy.[34] Implicitly, it is assumed that the quality control problems are similar regardless of the choice of supplier.

Matters become more interesting, however, when the incomes of those making clinical or managerial decisions are linked to the choices they make. Empirically, it is now well established that the therapeutic decisions of providers *are* sensitive to how they are paid, although the terrain is far from fully mapped. When the American Medicare program introduced prospective payment in 1983, for example, and began paying hospitals a predetermined price per inpatient case, treatment patterns promptly changed and inpatient bed use fell. Even more dramatic reductions have since taken place in response to pressures from private payers. In Germany, claims for public reimbursement of prescription drugs fell by 20 percent in the first six months of 1993, following the government's declaration that drug billings that exceeded a preset target would be paid from the fund for physician reimbursement (Henke, Murray, and Ade 1994). When physicians are financially at risk for increased drug bills, they change their prescribing habits.

In general, it seems quite clear that (some) service patterns can be powerfully influenced by linking them directly to provider incomes—making W depend on Q. Aneurin Bevan's comment in 1948 that if you want to send a message to doctors, you should write it on a check, has been confirmed. Furthermore, if you want to make changes in the mix and volume of health care, you *have* to send a message to doctors.

But there are a number of ways of doing this, involving different mixes of economic, regulatory, and educational messages. In the German case, for example, the economic message was combined with closer scrutiny, by professional colleagues, of the prescribing practices of individual physicians (Henke, Murray, and Ade 1994). Which intervention was critical? Rates of performance of certain surgical procedures—extracranial/intracranial bypass grafting, carotid endarterectomy, mammary artery ligation—have been powerfully affected by the results of effectiveness trials. But others, tonsillectomy, for example, or diagnostic procedures such as PSA testing or routine EFM in childbirth, have been remarkably resistant to contrary evidence. In Canada, the transition from inpatient to same-day surgery proceeded at a slow and stately pace over nearly twenty years after the supporting evidence first became available. The process sped up remarkably in the 1990s, when tighter hospital global budgets forced bed closures.

Economic incentives of various forms, particularly directed at providers of care, are thus only one potentially useful class of tools in the overall mix of mechanisms for health care system management. There is as yet no evidence at the systemwide level to justify a wholesale shift to decentralized decision making based on market-type signals. Moreover, all interventions have side effects. One should never underestimate the power of economic incentives, but neither should one overestimate the ability of economists (or anyone else) to predict how people will respond.[35]

The British experience with general practitioner (GP) fund-holding and hospital trusts is of particular interest in this regard; so far, no close observers of that system seem willing to commit themselves as to whether or not it is working. The introduction of the total package of reforms seems to have been associated with a significant *increase* in system costs, particularly in managerial overhead. There are very clear warnings from the United States that more management may simply mean more money for more managers. Reported declines in waiting lists in the United Kingdom may merely show that with more money, one can buy more services.

The test will be whether the new, more marketlike system can deliver better performance, for the same or less money, on meaningful outcome measures. The downside risk, apart from the extra costs of a managerial bureaucracy that fails to pay for its keep, is that it may simply open up new opportunities for income redistribution to providers, and among payers. GP fund holders may find—as American managed care systems have found before them—that selecting and enrolling relatively healthy patients yields a much higher return than more carefully analyzing the care they give and recommend. (The Blair government's shift from fund-holding to "commissioning" appears to reflect similar concerns.)

More generally, if subjected to stronger economic incentives, providers will respond. But their responses will probably go beyond what is contemplated or desired by governments, and may be difficult or impossible to control through contracts. As Ham (1994) pointed out, the market will always have to be managed. But the management task may be a good deal more difficult if providers think of themselves less as professionals with public responsibilities, and more as private businessmen beating the system any way they can. In the United States, that horse has already left the barn, but not elsewhere, and cooperative relationships, however grudging, should not be lightly put at risk.

In any case, the notion that some sort of automatic, self-regulating market-like structure can be established that will *substitute* for public management and yet achieve public objectives is a fantasy: powdered unicorn horn. In particular, it seems very clear that no incentives at the individual or institutional level, economic or otherwise, will set an upper limit on overall system expenditures. Ultimately, governments have to set these limits and maintain them with whatever mechanisms will do the job.

The use of competition among providers, and market mechanisms generally, as simply one set of tools among others for the pursuit of public objectives seems quite well understood and accepted by many of those responsible for managing the health care systems of western Europe. Morone and Goggin (1995: 568) referred to "guarded optimism about the proposed marriage of medical markets and social welfare universalism. Competition . . . may add efficiency and consumer control without subverting traditional collective visions."

It may be that the confusion between market as means and market as end, and the use of currently fashionable private sector rhetoric as a cover for distributional objectives, are more characteristic of North America, at least at the moment. But these ideas *are* being energetically exported, and will find receptive audiences among the same set of potential gainers, in all countries.

The short message of this essay is:

There are powerful redistributional motives behind parts of the health care reform agenda, in all countries.

Much analysis, particularly by economists, misdirects attention by assuming these issues away.

Competition, and market mechanisms generally, are particularly suited to both facilitating and concealing the process of redistribution.

Accordingly, to come back to Morone and Goggin (1995: 568), "The great question for the future turns on whether that optimism is justified." Keep your eyes open, and watch your back.

Notes

This essay is a somewhat revised version of a paper first presented at the International Conference on Governments and Health Systems: Implications of Differing Involvements, Jerusalem, Israel, 17–22 December 1995 and is published as chapter 1.1 of D. Chinitz and J. Cohen, eds., *Governments and Health Systems: Implications of Differing Involvements* (Chichester: John Wiley, 1998), pp. 7–34. It is reprinted with permission.

1 One of the best treatments of this relationship is Trebilcock, Tuohy, and Wolfson 1979: chaps. 2–3.

2   *Managed markets* is Ham's (1994) term for the interaction between purchasers and providers of health care in the post-reform British National Health Service; in this case "management" is very clearly by the central government, in pursuit of public objectives as interpreted by that government. Kessel (1958) is the classic source in the economic literature for a historical analysis of various forms of collusion and market management among American physicians; there is a large international institutional literature on this subject.

3   The rights of the stronger *do* seem more natural, at least to the stronger.

4   It is interesting to note that cost escalation in the United Kingdom seems to have accelerated, relative to the OECD average, in the early 1990s, subsequent to the "internal market" reforms.

5   Although the specific numbers may be controversial, the broad empirical facts do not appear to be in dispute. And these are so glaring as to render the details essentially unimportant.

      No one denies, for example, that the uniquely American form of health insurance generates very large administrative costs, much higher than in any other national system. Woolhandler and Himmelstein (1991) have done the most to focus attention on these excess costs; their estimates relative to, say, the costs of administering a Canadian-style universal system, would now be well over $100 billion per year. Others have generated lower estimates, but the point is that whether unnecessary paper-pushing costs Americans $80 billion or $120 billion, the amount is *large*.

      Similarly, one can debate whether the number of Americans without health insurance at any point in time is closer to 35 or to 40 million, or whether one should count only those uninsured for a full year, or only citizens—and how much care do the uninsured really get anyway? Again, the point is that the number is very large, both in total and as a share of the population, and would not be tolerated in any other developed country.

      And while international comparisons of health care (or any other) expenditures are subject to a number of sources of bias and distortion, as well as periodic revision, no amount of statistical adjustment is likely to narrow the gap between the United States, now spending roughly 14 percent of its national income on health care, and the next most costly countries at about 10 percent.

6   The Clinton health reform plan was defeated, not because the populace suddenly discovered a new affection for the existing system, but because highly sophisticated and very well-financed disinformation campaigns by those whose incomes would be threatened by reform—$1 trillion fills a lot of large war chests—were successful in generating myths, confusion, and considerable fear of the unknown. These undermined support for any specific change, paralyzing the broad consensus that some change was essential (Barer, Marmor, and Morrison 1995).

7   These observations are not good news for the cost cutters of the 1990s. Moreover, they have the curious feature that reported satisfaction is related to total *spending*. As the relative price of health care varies considerably across countries (see the following), this figure would look quite different if per capita spending were adjusted to reflect the varying per capita quantities of services available in each country. The linear relationship would tend to break down. This implies that Figure 2 does *not* simply reflect the crude economic assumption that people are happier when they use more services. What then is the connection between spending and satisfaction?

8   The regularity of the international relationship, and the remarkable deviation of the

United States, form a context for a claim sometimes made to explain the American experience, that the threats to health are simply greater in the United States, so the health care system has to work harder and needs more resources. This is the international version of "costs are higher in this hospital because our patients are sicker" (alternatively, Americans' expectations are higher). Figure 2, however, indicates that this American exceptionalism argument requires them to be "very different," not just from some other country, but from the general pattern shown by all developed countries surveyed.

A priori, one might have expected that the differences among "the rest" would have been greater than the differences between the United States and, say, Canada. The only obvious factor differentiating the United States from *all* these other countries is, as Abel-Smith (1985) and White (1995) have pointed out, its health care system.

9   "Whatever else may be going on" covers a vast field, from improved effectiveness, efficiency, and responsiveness to patients at one end, to deliberate underservicing and exploitation of patient vulnerability at the other. A broader discussion is far beyond the scope of this essay. A recent and very extensive review by *Consumer Reports*, including a survey of over 30,000 of its members, concluded: "The new age of managed care . . . [is] an appealing picture—but today, it's a mirage" (How Good Is Your Health Plan 1996: 41). Likewise, Zwanziger and Melnick (1996: 190): "The transformation is not yet over. In fact, we are far from the finish, and the process is so complex that we cannot easily predict the outcome."

10 Most, but not all. Those who work in the private insurance industry, or the rapidly growing managed care industry, know that in any other country their incomes—and the costs they represent—would not exist.

11 Enthoven, one of the most prominent advocates of competitive managed care, declared flatly in 1989 that "it would be, quite frankly, ridiculous . . . to suggest that we in the United States have achieved a satisfactory system that our European friends would be wise to emulate" (49). Whatever the changes that have since taken place in the American health care system, the fundamental problems of cost and coverage, efficiency and equity, which motivated his comment, have only become worse.

12 For some purposes, one might wish to subdivide taxes into social insurance premiums and general taxation; alternatively, one can treat that distinction under the general head of the progressivity or regressivity of the overall tax system.

13 Any revenues remaining "in the firm" are attributed back as income to the firm's owners, who are also members of households in this (by assumption, closed) economy. To suppress a swarm of arrows, Figure 3 implicitly assumes that no real resources are used up by governments, and no incomes generated therein. One could insert a resource-using process for each financing channel, but the result would be total loss of transparency.

14 Strictly speaking, provider incomes are also not restricted to incomes from health care. They may include earnings on capital investments (outside the health care sector), and other sources of nonprofessional income.

15 Providers, naturally enough, prefer to talk about the "infinite demand" of "consumers." Patient demands may, in fact, escalate pretty rapidly in response to *perceived* threats to life and limb, or health and function. But this demand is endogenous: It depends upon the behavior of providers themselves.

The cholesterol industry in the United States, for example, has done a remarkable job of creating demand for testing of blood lipids, in complete defiance of the experimental evidence. Those who undergo the tests believe that their life expectancy will be increased by detection and treatment of elevated blood lipids. Understandably enough, they demand the test. Unfortunately, for most of them (the asymptomatic ones), the experimental evidence does not support this belief: ditto mammography in the under-fifty population, ditto PSA testing, ditto routine ultrasound in normal pregnancy, ditto bone density measurement. . . . But there is too much money to be made, not only from testing, but from all the associated services of interpretation, monitoring, and therapy (especially sales of pharmaceuticals) to let lack of evidence impede medical progress.

16 Emphasis here is on "system." A number of studies have found that the utilization of health care by individuals does seem to respond in the conventional direction when user charges are imposed. But it is a logical error, the fallacy of composition, to infer from this observation that the *overall* costs of a health care system will be lower if patients are required to pay more out-of-pocket. Cross-system observation suggests the reverse, and supports the position taken by providers and their representatives. User charges provide a means of evading the more effective price and quantity controls in public payment systems, and thus of raising overall system costs—and provider incomes.

17 Strictly speaking, this statement depends upon an assumption that the rates of payment for factor inputs in health care exceed their opportunity costs. Because rents and quasi rents are so pervasive in health care earnings, the assumption is easy to defend. Translated from "economese," the basic idea is that, for a variety of good and less good reasons, people and firms supplying health care tend to be paid prices for their products that are greater, often much greater, than their current costs of production (marginal cost, variable cost), where the latter includes the value of the provider's own time and skills. They are thus made better off by increases in expenditures that support increases in output at constant prices, as well as by those that simply increase prices.

18 Use of words like "benefits," however, can obscure the obvious fact that, on the whole, one would prefer not to be among the heavy users of health care! Try it, you won't like it.

19 There are, however, two aspects to the regressivity of private insurance financing, as compared with tax financing. Because private insurance premiums are independent of income, lower-income people will have to pay a larger share of their incomes for the same coverage. This will be true even of a community-rated private plan, or a plan covering a large employee group, in which the covered pool is large enough that an individual's premium does not depend upon his or her own illness experience. Tax-financed coverage charges people in some proportion to their incomes.

In small employee groups, however, experience rating by the insurer implies that the amount of the premium will also be sensitive to extreme individual experiences. Insofar as today's insured outlays are recouped by the insurer in the form of higher premiums tomorrow, insurance becomes, in part, a delayed user charge. This will increase the *variance* of health care costs as a share of income; to the extent that illness is correlated with low income, it will also increase the regressivity of the financing system. And if and as the labor market evolves away from large employee groups toward smaller firms and individual contractors, this aspect of regressivity will become more pronounced.

20 Both the accounting and the observations are point-in-time snapshots of people

moving through a life cycle. Wealth and health change over time; being healthy or wealthy today provides no absolute guarantee for tomorrow. In theory, then, one could imagine that point-in-time status differences might be evened out over the life cycle. But in reality they are not; these states are highly autocorrelated. If you are healthy (or wealthy) today, your chances of being in that state tomorrow are a good deal higher than if you are unhealthy (or unwealthy) today. And the strength of the autocorrelation increases with age. Illnesses become chronic, and wealth becomes predominantly financial assets. Moreover, the two states are cross-correlated. The wealthier (healthier) you are today, the more likely you are to be healthy (wealthy) tomorrow, and this correlation appears to reflect causality in *both* directions. Life does not even out over time.

21 The assumption that taxes are proportionate to income simplifies the algebra without doing much violence to reality. A sufficiently regressive tax structure would of course reverse this conclusion, but that is all hypothetical. Payroll or other social insurance taxes are less progressive than general income taxes, and revenues from these may be earmarked for health care. But this is simply a labeling exercise if, *at the margin,* public payments for health care come from general revenue sources. In that case, it is the progressivity or regressivity of the tax system as a whole that is relevant, not that of a particular revenue component, whatever its label.

22 There is a qualification here. Health status is negatively correlated with income, but service use may not be if there are sufficiently large income-related barriers to access. So long as any (positive) correlation between income and use is weaker than that between income and tax liability, however, the transfer is as described.

23 Massaro and Wong (1995) offer a much less critical commentary on the Singaporean experience, though drawing upon many of the same observations as Hsiao (1995). Where Hsiao pointed to health care costs outrunning a national income that was itself growing rapidly, they state that nations "rationally invest" (269) a larger share of their income in health care as they become wealthier, leaving it unclear whether they consider cost control a proper objective in the first place. On the other hand, they suggest that because costs did not rise as rapidly as they have in some other fast-growing economies, medical savings accounts may have tended to control costs. In any case, "hospitals are profitable and physicians are well paid" (ibid.), and high-technology services are readily available. But that is exactly Hsiao's point: The system is overcapitalized, and (some) providers have made out like bandits.

Massaro and Wong share Hsiao's view that Singapore provided the most favorable environment for competitive markets in health care, and they emphasize the necessary interplay between market mechanisms and detailed public regulation. But they seem to miss the point that the increasing regulation of physician supply, hospital budgets, and prices/fees in both the public and the private sectors is (according to Hsiao) an explicit response by Singaporean authorities to what they regard as failure of the private market system to control costs and promote efficiency. Consequently, they have now adopted the cost control measures that are common in public insurance systems all over the developed world.

As for medical savings accounts, a country with a very small proportion of elderly people, a low birthrate, and a recent very rapid rise in life expectancy would be wise to accumulate savings any way it can. If fear of illness makes people willing to accept a compulsory savings program, then so be it.

24 This generalization is not restricted to fee-for-service payment. Hospital employees

may be salaried, and the institution may receive a global budget. But if workloads fall, sooner or later people will be laid off. And eventually, although the adjustment may take some years or even decades, institutions will close.

25   The very poorest are eligible through the Qualified Medicare Beneficiary program for reimbursement of their user charges by Medicaid, if they know about and qualify for the program.

26   Interestingly, France also combines user charges in the public system, the *ticket moderateur*, with private insurance coverage against these charges. The cover story is the same: User charges are needed to hold down costs, but private insurance is needed to ensure access. French health care costs have steadily increased until, by 1995, they were the second highest (relative to GDP) in the OECD. As Marmor says, "Nothing that is regular, is stupid."

27   Gerdtham and Jönsson (1991) began with the usual calculation, converting health care expenditures per capita in each of the OECD countries into U.S. dollars using purchasing power parities (PPPs). When PPPs are based on comparisons of the relative prices of all the commodities in the GDP, one finds very large differences between per capita spending in the United States and in all other countries.

But when other countries' currencies were converted into U.S. dollars using PPPs specific to the health care sector, much of this differential disappeared. In this alternative comparison, every country in the OECD moves up relative to the United States, some by a small amount and others by a great deal.

The point is not that prices for health care goods and services are higher in the United States than elsewhere. They are, but what Figure 5 shows in that the *ratio* of health care prices to the general price level is higher in the United States than in other countries.

28   Other studies support this finding. Schieber, Poullier, and Greenwald (1994) showed significantly higher rates of relative inflation of health sector prices in the United States than in other OECD countries. Several comparisons of the Canadian and American health care systems have shown rates of service use that are on average very similar, with Canadians receiving more of some forms of care, and less of others (Fuchs and Hahn 1990; Nair, Karim, and Nyers 1992; Redelmeier and Fuchs 1993). Higher prices in the United States account for the cost differences.

29   Some have challenged the identification of excessive administrative costs with waste (e.g., Thorpe 1992). They point to the extraordinarily sophisticated management techniques in the United States, the extent and detail of data generated, and the leading-edge research in health services. In these, the United States clearly does lead the world.

Such responses, however, miss the point. Managerial (and even research) activities are not ends in themselves. They are only valuable insofar as they contribute to the ultimate ends of a more efficient and effective health care system, and a healthier and more satisfied population. As the United States achieves much worse results than systems that spend much less, the extra administrative expenditure is wasted, regardless of how much sophisticated management it may buy. It appears to support a vast negative-sum game of interinstitutional competition over cost transfer and benefit appropriation.

30   Strictly speaking, Arrow (1976) did not ignore distributional considerations. Rather, he imposed very specific distributional assumptions, without which his conclusions have no significance. Nor are there any grounds for arguing that Arrow's results

approximate what might emerge from a more realistic analysis. They are simply irrelevant to a world of differentiated individuals.

31 Economists who serve as market advocates will sometimes reply that they are simply taking as given whatever distributional outcomes have been generated by the wider society/economy, and are implicit in current arrangements. This argument slides over the fact that changes in health care organization and finance will *change* the pattern of burdens and benefits that the analyst claims to take as given. Preserving the status quo would require offsetting policy changes that are not identified, let alone advocated. In fact, however, their work typically shows little interest in redistributional effects, and even less in the social and political processes that determine underlying patterns.

32 Policies of this form may be described as making more use of the market and of competitive forces to determine the allocation of resources to and within the health care sector. In practice, however, they are always embedded within pseudomarkets, hedged about with extensive regulation and formal or informal collaboration by providers. Much of the regulation may be privately administered, but nowhere outside theoretical analyses does one find anything approximating the free competitive markets of the economics textbooks.

33 The Celebrated Man in the Street, updated.

34 Squeezing down costs does not necessarily represent improved efficiency. If private managers achieve their savings by cutting W rather than Z, then there has been no saving in resource inputs, but only a transfer of incomes from workers in this sector out to whoever enjoyed a decrease in contributions. It is far from clear, at least to me, to what extent contracting out is driven by true efficiency gains as opposed to opportunities to negotiate more favorable input prices. But does it matter: Should we be concerned by the latter?

35 Law 4: "Beware of Incentives. Economists and other rationalists restlessly tinker with people's incentives. This is a dangerous game. Although incentives are important for understanding problems and fashioning solutions, they are also tricky devils, always veering off in unanticipated ways. . . . People are complicated, social systems almost infinitely so. A great many uninvited incentives lurk in each policy change" (Morone 1986: 818).

Commentary

Who Was That Straw Man Anyway?

A Comment on Evans and Rice

Mark V. Pauly

I have been asked to comment on the essays by Evans and Rice (this volume) from the perspective of someone who looks with favor on the use of markets to organize and finance the provision of medical services. These two essays do not deal with what actually happens in medical markets, or even with the actual politics of health reform. Instead, they reflect an argument economists have with each other about what advice we do and should give to policy makers.

While what economists think is surely not the most important or influential thing in the world, the views of economists do matter to some extent, because financing necessarily reflects economic issues. I fear that readers of these two essays will get an incorrect impression of many aspects of the work of the set of economists who have done so much to explore how markets might solve resource allocation problems in medical care. It is obviously both presumptuous and unnecessary for me personally to defend these scholars from the Evans-Rice critique—for many reasons, they need no defense and are perfectly capable of defending themselves. Nevertheless, there are some claims in these essays that are so mistaken that there needs to be some defense. This is especially the case for the Evans article, which actually says relatively little about the substance of ideas of market-oriented health economists, but offers a great deal of ad hominem speculation about their hidden motives. Here again, I cannot presume access to insights about what motivates people, and any defense against a charge of selfishness or self-interest always leaves the defendant protesting too much. I can say a little about my own motives, and what I gather to be those of others, but my primary argument here will be about the distributional consequences of what these economists have actually proposed, compared to the status quo in the United States, arrangements in other countries, or other proposed arrangements.

The certain conclusion one can draw from Evans's essay is that he does not like the current U.S. health care system. Neither do I, and neither do the other analysts who have written about market-based health reform. As far as I can determine, there are no "fundamentalist" analysts who defend the current U.S. system as ideal or near ideal. They all propose something different from the current system. This is, as Evans notes, rather slippery behavior for his opponents, because it would be much easier to nail them if they were defenders of what is, rather than advocates of what might be. It does mean that Evans's vigorous attacks on the defects of the current U.S. system are entirely beside the (intellectual) point. The real issue does not concern the merits of current markets in the United States. Rather, it is a debate about whether the best way to reform is to build on the market system or to dismantle it.

Is what these "fundamentalists" propose part of a hidden distributional agenda? This seems to be Evans's major claim. My reading of this literature is that virtually without exception, proposals for reform involve a redistribution of both medical services and the burden of financing them that would be substantially more progressive than at present. Specific proposals differ, and when made by economists, they are usually qualified with the comment that the precise nature and extent of redistribution cannot be determined by economic analysis but is ultimately a political judgment. Speaking specifically of my own "Responsible National Health Insurance" proposal, we envisioned a set of progressive refundable tax credits—equal to the premium for a generous policy for the poor, and then declining in value as incomes rose—to be financed in large part by abolition of the current super-regressive tax exclusion of employer premium payments.[1] The net impact of this scheme would be a substantial redistribution away from higher-income people like me and toward those at the bottom end of the income distribution. So far one of our big disappointments is finding so little support among political decision makers for this proposal for self-harmful redistribution by academics and lawyers. In any case, the redistribution embodied in all market-oriented proposals is away from the upper-middle-income class which (U.S.) academics inhabit and specifically and especially toward those at or near the poverty line.

Are market-based approaches instead a secret plot to make sure that people who work in health care earn higher incomes than they should? It is true that the period of high growth in medical spending in the United States was accompanied by substantial growth in real income for nurses, technicians, and even unskilled health care workers—and that these people are paid better in the United States than they are in other countries (Pauly 1993). Physicians also gained, of course. However, my reading of the fundamentalist market reform creed is that it is very hostile to physicians and their income. When Alain Enthoven thunders against the old "guild free choice" system that is to be replaced by managed cared, he means the physician-dominated system. It is probably correct to say that advocates of market reform, as true economists, saw the best form of cost containment as one which primarily reduced resource use in the medical services sector, rather than one which reduced incomes of people who work there, and that envy of the incomes earned by physicians or by people who own drug company stock was not as great a motivating factor for them as it has been for some who are more ideologically committed to fully public systems. However, in many public systems, the doctors and the drug companies have historically done quite well in any case; it is usually the less influential, less skilled workers who earn less than they would in a market-based system.

It is also true that market-based approaches have been unwilling to endorse the view held in Canada (but not in western Europe) that people whom society allows to have more income should not be allowed to spend freely some of that income on more, better, or more convenient medical care for themselves and their families. (Of course, there is considerable research to indicate that their greater financial "access" largely wastes the resources of the well-to-do on unnecessary care; allowing the rich to throw their money away is a potential method for improving the overall equity of final consumption patterns.)

Not that the Canadian view has been ruled out—you can find discussions of taxing excess consumption of medical services—but it has not been elevated to the level of unequivocally acceptable social policy. The main reason for taking a more open-minded view, I believe, is that, at least in the United States, "society" has not expressed itself of one mind on this question. From the Capron Commission's endorsement of "appropriate medical care" as a flow below which no one should sink, rather than a ceiling above which no one may rise, to the success of the Harry and Louise commercials that raised apprehension about government limiting citizens' choices of what they buy, there is evidence that perfect equality in the use of medical services is neither desired nor expected by citizens. Economics is capable of handling a desire for "health-care-specific" equity; it just doesn't assume it as a given.

Advocates of the use of markets always envisioned a sizable role for government, one greater than its current role in the United States for the nonelderly—in specifying minimum coverage, in subsidizing people so they can afford that level or even better coverage, and in making sure that information is available to help people make informed choices.

Once those prerequisites are in place, these advocates then thought that markets might be a good (though not necessarily the only good) way for citizens to choose what medical services they would get. Of course, a government staffed by angels could undoubtedly do a better job than markets run by humans. But in the real governments versus real markets contest, the plea was not to rule markets out on a priori grounds. There may yet be some hidden evil in this, or hidden greed, but I do not think Evans has identified the culprit.

Rice's essay is much more serious and much less polemical; paradoxically, this means I will have less to say about it. I do think that the extended and laborious proof that medical markets as a whole fall short of the textbook competitive model is unnecessary, since I certainly know no one who maintains that current medical markets fit that case. Moreover, even those who "embrace the competitive model as the method of choice for reforming health care" do not base this belief on the economic theory which shows the market as superior to government regulation. The reason they do not do so is that there is no such economic theory. If I understand welfare economics correctly, it says that a competitive market can in theory achieve an optimal outcome. It does not say that government cannot also do so, and indeed, the welfare economists' ideal welfare-maximizing government, without more, by definition *will* do so. That is, theory tells us that, at best, the ideal market can tie an ideal government, not that it can do better.

There are other positive theories of government behavior, some based on elegant public choice or impossibility theorem analyses, which show that one should not generally expect actual governments to behave in this ideal fashion. This analysis is entirely ignored by Rice, but it leads to the right (if really difficult) second-best question raised above: imperfect markets versus imperfect government. In my view, this is what we should be talking about, not bashing old textbooks with other old textbooks.

I believe that most analysts already know this. The question in the Morrisey-Feldman survey asked economists whether there was any *conceivable* applicability of the model of perfect competition to medical care, not whether medical markets now were perfectly competitive. When I filled it out, I answered that, yes, I could conceive of some medical markets being reasonably competitive; I was thinking of things like routine pediatric care and the purchase of drugs for chronic illness, and I interpreted *applicable* to mean whether positive theory—like supply and demand and the tendency of profits to fall in the long run—might help explain how these markets work. From what I have already said above, and regrettably, the elegant normative economics that enshrines the perfectly competitive equilibrium as first-best optimal will not fit much of the rest of medical care; we must choose between imperfect governments and imperfect markets.

What about economists' use of welfare economics, the Pareto principle, and all that? I think that we use them not because we believe them to be perfect, but because we do not know of a better normative criterion. Despite Rice's attack on the Pareto principle, I submit that his argument falls prey to the same failing of not specifying any better alternative. As a case in point, consider his discussion of envy as affecting the evaluation of a costly new therapy that only the wealthy choose to buy. If we postulate envy as motivation on the part of the nonrich, it is true that this technology will make them worse-off; still, it is preposterous to propose forbidding technologies that make one envious person just a tiny bit more jealous. Rice concludes with the economically correct answer: "To improve society's overall lot, it might be better if government intervened either to ensure equal access to the technology, or perhaps even to thwart its availability" (p. 33). But how could one tell whether, say, forbidding the technology would "improve society's overall lot"? To answer this question, one needs a definition of "society's overall lot," which Rice has not furnished. There is one definition—measure how much worse-off envious people feel by how much you would have to pay them to get them to allow the rich to use the new technology. If that amount is greater than the net value of the new technology to the rich, forbid it; if it is less, permit the technology to be used, but tax the rich to compensate the envious. But what is the form of this analysis? It is Paretian welfare economics, with negative consumption externalities—something neither novel nor efficiently handled by markets, even in the view of economic fundamentalists. What seems to be a fatal flaw only turns out to be a familiar wrinkle.

Likewise, the old saws about positive consumption externalities, the effect of advertising, and free riding by the uninsured are familiar fare to economists, who know that they have already been discussed a lot and that such theoretical discussion has been, is now, and probably always will be inconclusive. As someone who has advocated mandatory subsidized universal insurance coverage and public provision of information as important correctives to the market, I surely would not disagree that their absence is a problem. But I do not believe that such discussion about theoretical possibilities, backed up by citations to speculative thinking of the greats, helps us much.

And perhaps such humility is best spread around. Rice appears to be arguing against "those" (whoever they are) who assert that "economic theory demonstrates the superiority of market forces in health." I would assert that this is an empty set. What is true is that there are "those" (myself included) who would assert that no one, not even Evans in full cry, can demonstrate the theoretical *inferiority* of market forces in health either. What one ought to do, in my view, is outline the best model of the use of market forces (something I have tried to do), outline the best model of government management of health care (something few have tried to do), and then invite people of good will to compare the two, both in theory and (insofar as we can divine from fragmentary evidence) in terms of how they might work in practice. This is trial-and-error work, not rocket science, but it is all we know how to do.

Does what is currently happening in the U.S. market change the terms of the debate? Current success—for at least three years in a row—in "containing costs" for the privately insured has shown that high growth rates are not inevitable. Since I do not accept the current system as ideal, I would not claim that one could prove that these low rates are necessarily good, any more than I thought that one could prove that the former high rates were necessarily bad. But they certainly are low, and their presence has certainly taken out whatever steam was left in arguments for government price or spending control. The downside of what is happening now is a continued increase in the numbers of uninsured and probably a reduction in access to uncompensated care. No fundamentalist would ever have claimed that competitive markets redistribute, so these developments come as no surprise (Pauly 1996a). Eventually, perhaps, they will stimulate citizens to correct the government failure that is the source of most problems in the health care sector.

I optimistically believe that there is more commonality of views among the authors of these two essays and those they criticize than is ordinarily believed. It is the mule-headed reluctance of the U.S. political process to listen to any of us, especially when it comes to universal coverage, that leads us to fight among ourselves.

Notes

1 By *super-regressive,* I mean a taxation policy that redistributes from the poor to the rich, as the tax exclusion does.

Commentary

What Does Economics Have to Say about Health Policy

Anyway? A Comment and Correction on Evans and Rice

Martin Gaynor and William B. Vogt

We have been asked to write a commentary on the essays on market reform appearing in this volume. Since we are economists, we concentrate on the essays by Evans and Rice, which directly address the application of economics to health policy. The Evans essay attacks market-oriented reforms of health care systems. There are four elements to his argument: (1) A redistributive "rent-seeking" agenda lies behind support for market-oriented policies; (2) markets are not optimal for the production and distribution of health care; (3) government is; and (4) economic analysis is not applicable to health care, hence it is not useful and is actually harmful. Rice's essay contains two intertwined but distinct themes. The first of these is an attack upon the application of a textbook model of perfect competition to the health care sector. The second is an attack upon several of the tools used by economists to study markets in general and health care markets in particular.

The essays by Evans and Rice, while different in many ways, do share some important factors. The main themes in both essays are that market-oriented health systems do not work well, that government-run health systems are superior to market systems, and thus economic analysis is not applicable to health care and thus its application can be misleading or harmful. In what follows we comment on the arguments presented in support of these claims.

The logical and factual flaws in the articles are too many to enumerate individually here. Instead, we concentrate on what we view as the major problems in the essays: a misunderstanding or mischaracterization of the nature and implications of modern economics, in particular welfare economics and political economy; and flaws in the logical arguments, in particular logical inconsistencies and the use of ad hominem arguments, unsupported allegations, and innuendo. Additionally, both essays confuse ideology with analysis. The Evans essay is particularly egregious in this regard. If analysis of health policy is to have any claim to objective scholarship, it is absolutely essential to make a serious, honest effort to separate the two. While some important issues have been raised in these articles, it remains for serious scholarship to grapple with them.

Our commentary is divided into three sections. Section 1 addresses the applicability of economics to health policy. While this theme is present in both essays, it is most extensively developed in the essay by Rice, hence most of our comments in section 1 are directed toward the arguments in this essay. We address political economy in health care in section 2. Since this issue is only raised by Evans, the comments in section 2 are directed toward his essay. Section 3 contains a summary and conclusions.

Economics and Health Policy

Both the Rice and Evans essays contain arguments seeking to show that the textbook model of perfect competition does not apply to the health care sector. This argument is clearly a straw man. The fact that health care markets are not textbook competitive markets is not news to economists. If Evans or Rice were to read almost any major economics textbook, they would find manifold descriptions of markets in which the assumptions of perfect competition fail, and analyses of policy options in the presence of market failure. Indeed, the vast bulk of work in health economics has been concerned with understanding the nature of markets for health care. The classic paper by Nobel laureate Kenneth Arrow (1963) describes differences between markets for health care and textbook competitive markets, and goes on to analyze the implications for the workings of health care markets. The literature in health economics spawned by Arrow's paper has been concerned to a great extent with analyses of the types of market failure likely to occur in health care markets, and with potential policy options in the face of such failure.[1] Surely Rice and Evans cannot have failed to notice this.

It is worth mentioning, however, that there are results in economic theory which provide a set of *sufficient* (as distinct from *necessary*) conditions under which markets must be superior (in the sense of *Pareto optimality* described below) to any other institution for organizing economic affairs.[2] What this means is that if the assumptions of the textbook competitive model are truly satisfied, then it follows that markets are the optimal form of organizing economic activity. However, if a market is not textbook competitive, there is *no implication about what the optimal organization of exchange might be.* It might be pure government activity, it might be pure market activity, or it might be a mixture of the two.

In beating the perfect competition straw man, Rice also claims to be "cast[ing] doubt on the validity of various tools that health economists often use," and it is toward the validity of these tools that we direct our comments. In particular, Rice attacks the relevance of the Pareto criterion for evaluating alternative economic arrangements, and impugns economists' methods for assessing the preferences of consumers.

In performing evaluations, economists typically evaluate alternative means for organizing economic activity in terms of the Pareto principle. The Pareto principle says, in essence, that if every member of a society prefers one alternative, say A, to another alternative, say B, then A is better than B. To say that Sally prefers A to B is to say she would choose A over B were she to be faced with such a choice. So, the Pareto principle says that society prefers A to B if every member of society would choose A over B were each of them to be in a position to make the choice. A choice is said to be *Pareto optimal* if there is no other choice which would be preferred to it under the Pareto principle.

There are several important things to recognize about the Pareto principle. First, it will not always distinguish between two alternatives. For example, if Sally prefers A to B, but Bob prefers B to A, then the Pareto principle is silent on the question of which is best. The canonical example of an alternative on which the Pareto principle is silent is wealth distribution. If either Sally or Bob can own a piece of property, and Sally prefers that Sally own the property, and Bob prefers that Bob own the property, the Pareto criterion is silent on who should own it. Second (and relatedly), there are typically very many Pareto optimal choices, each with a different distribution of wealth. Third, the Pareto principle only tells us which of A and B is better from the point of view of the members of a society. If consuming music or Snickers bars is beneficial to society in the view of a social planner, but members of that society unanimously agree that they prefer not to consume the music or the Snickers bars, the Pareto principle will call for a lower consumption of music or Snickers bars than would the social planner. Fourth, the notion of preference as defined above depends only on how people would behave, rather than on some external measure of what is good for them.[3] Neither economists nor moral philosophers can claim consensus on what the "right" standard is for judging the social good, and progress in this area would obviously be welcome. It is worth pointing out that, contrary to Rice's innuendo, it is not only market advocates who use the Pareto criterion; supportive studies of socialism (Lange 1938; Lerner 1946) also use Pareto optimality in their evaluations.

Rice mounts a number of criticisms of the use of the Pareto principle in economics for evaluation purposes. First, he observes that economics, unlike other disciplines, is normative (i.e., it evaluates). It is not clear to us in what way an economist saying "trade barriers make everyone worse-off than" is any more or less normative than an engineer saying "bridges made out of cardboard will fall down more frequently than." Each is a technical statement and can be evaluated as such on its merits. A social planner may *choose* to build bridges of cardboard or erect trade barriers if those policies are preferred on nontechnical grounds.

A second criticism by Rice is that the Pareto criterion cannot take proper account of people's preferences over their relative rankings (status) in society. This is false, and his discussion on this point is confused. He asserts that "summing" over utilities in these models is inappropriate since status is a relative thing. In arguing for this point, however, he does what can only be interpreted as summing over utilities. When each person's utility is not influenced by any other person's consumption, the change in total utility from Rice buying a car is just the same as the change in Rice's utility. However, when status is important, the change in total utility when Rice buys a car includes both the gain to Rice's utility from the purchase, and the loss to someone else's utility generated by that person's envy. Thus, when status is important, the change to total utility from one consumer's action can only be calculated by summing over the effects of this consumer's action on everyone else's utilities. This appears to be nearly the opposite of what Rice argues. In fact there are economic models (e.g., Frank 1985; Akerlof 1995; Bernheim 1994; Varian 1974) in which relative rankings matter (this implies that distribution matters) and in which Pareto optima may be calculated. Indeed, Pareto optimum is the welfare criterion used in evaluating outcomes in these models.

Another criticism is that Pareto optima are not relevant when people have "sticky" preferences, and that perfect competition does not lead to good outcomes in such circumstances. By "sticky" preferences, we mean preferences which have the property that past consumption affects the relative desirability of current consumption, as Rice says: "wanting what you got." These sorts of dynamic effects in preferences are consistent with the standard textbook models of economic behavior, so that Pareto optima are well defined and have their usual interpretation. It is worth noting that the textbook competitive model deals with such preferences in both finite and infinite horizon models, and welfare economics' claims vis-à-vis the desirability of markets are unaffected by such concerns (Stokey and Lucas 1989: sections 5.11–5.13, 16.7, and references therein; Debreu 1979).

Although the Pareto criterion remains applicable in the case of "sticky" preferences, Rice does raise a second issue here. Consider the case of a woman who, because she consumed cigarettes previously, is now addicted to them, and continues to consume them, say in order to stave off the symptoms of withdrawal. In the economist's usual conception of the Pareto criterion, these preferences "count" just as much as do any other preferences. Rice does not approve of the economist's decision on this count, and claims that the addict might be "better-off" if she is forced to stop smoking. No support is provided for this judgment, and it is far from obvious to us that the addict's pain of withdrawal is somehow less valid than any other motive for preference formation. It is possible to rigorously analyze issues of addiction and welfare (e.g., Pollak 1970, 1976; Winston 1980; Schelling 1984; Becker and Murphy 1988), but Rice has not done so.

A final theoretical criticism of Pareto optima from Rice is that the social planner may care about things in addition to or instead of Pareto optima. Rice says that a social planner may care about the quality of utilities, about wealth distribution, or about freedom, all in addition to or instead of Pareto rankings. Rice notes that what a social planner should care about is a philosophical issue, and goes on to point out other things which might motivate her. In moral philosophy, there appears not to be a consensus on what the appropriate objects are for the benevolent social planner to consider, and the "welfare" position does have its defenders (e.g., Arneson 1990).

Rice does not make a case, however, for the irrelevance of Pareto rankings in social decision making. In fact, even a perfectly venal and totally self-interested social planner is compelled to consider the Pareto rankings of her subjects in pursuing her goals (McGuire and Olson 1996).[4] If the point is merely that Pareto rankings are not the sole criterion for social choice, then it is hard to see with whom Rice argues, as this is something on which essentially all economists agree. If his point is that Pareto rankings are irrelevant, this simply does not follow from the arguments presented, and, indeed, other critics of the Pareto criterion have been careful to avoid the claim that preferences (and thus the Pareto criterion) are irrelevant to social choice (e.g., Sen 1982: 363–364).

Rice also makes an empirical criticism of the Pareto criterion. He claims that governments do not appear to follow the Pareto criterion in making health policy. Suppose one accepts the assertion. It is unclear how this bears on the validity of Pareto rankings. Observing that political choices do not appear to follow the Pareto criterion does not tell us that it is useless, but simply that there are other factors affecting political decisions. This is hardly surprising.

There is also a confusion here, and in the Evans essay, between *is* and *ought*. There is no obvious reason to believe that observing what a particular government does with regard to health policy reveals what is socially optimal. Evans claims that the forms of health systems adopted by western European countries and Canada are optimal (or superior) (e.g., the "general consensus" on the "international standard" for health care systems, p. 71). This may or may not be true, but taking observations on what "is" as evidence of what "ought" only makes sense if it is known that the political process in those countries leads to the adoption of socially optimal health policies. Evans's trenchant criticism of the susceptibility of policy making to rent seeking by special interests is in direct contradiction to this view. Further, it is difficult to see how anyone possessed of a nodding familiarity with modern political economy or even with the history of the twentieth century would accept such an assumption. We elaborate on issues of political economy in the next section.

Pareto optimality may not be the exclusive criterion one might use in assessing forms of economic organization, but it is likely to be a relevant criterion both to a hypothetical benevolent social planner and to any real social planner. This is the case for both philosophical and practical reasons. Making everyone better off by their own lights may not be the exclusive criterion for good social policy, but exclusivity is not what is required. A benevolent social planner need only be partially concerned with making her citizens better off by their own lights in order for her to want to use Pareto rankings as part of her decision making.

For practical purposes, calculation of Pareto rankings is also useful. First of all, for whatever goal the social planner is pursuing, knowledge of the structure of Pareto rankings is likely to be of great use, since policies leading to Pareto improvements are likely to lead to a larger amount of resources from which to finance whatever goal the planner pursues (McGuire and Olson 1996). Second, a social policy which is not Pareto optimal leaves gains from trade unrealized, or "left on the table." Private mechanisms frequently arise to realize these gains. To use a standard example, the food stamp program forces some recipients to consume more food than they would prefer to consume were they just given cash. This means that the policy is not Pareto optimal, for we could make everyone better-off, by their own lights, were we to give the recipients cash (or to permit them to trade their food stamps for cash). But the possibility of this gain from exchange is realized in the real world, as there is an active black market for food stamps. So, policy which ignores Pareto rankings and which thereby leaves gains from trade "on the table" may bring about private actions directed toward realizing these gains and which work at cross-purposes to the policy.

Although it is not made explicit, Rice does provide some hint as to what his vision of social choice might entail. As Rice points out, the Pareto criterion typically would not endorse in-kind transfers to the poor. An in-kind transfer means providing a person with goods, like food (or food stamps), or housing, or health insurance, rather than providing him with the cash equivalent and letting him choose whether or not to purchase the good.

In arguing for providing the poor with free health care rather than with an equivalent amount of money with which they could choose to purchase health care or to purchase something else, Rice says, "[cash payments] would lower the welfare of a society where people feel better knowing that the poor *can* receive health care services" (our emphasis). Before commenting on this proposal, we undo the rhetorical sleight of hand embodied in the word *can*. The poor *can* buy health services (or health insurance) under either the cash transfer or the in-kind transfer policies. The difference between the two is that under the in-kind transfer the poor *must* either consume the health services or nothing. Society, in Rice's example, does not care about either the preferences of the poor or about whether the poor *can* purchase health care, for both of these goals are served as well or better by the cash transfer. Rather, society cares about the amount of health services consumed by the poor, regardless of their preferences.[5]

Let's consider an example to illustrate the costs of such a policy choice. Coronary artery bypass graft (CABG) is a frequently performed and expensive surgical procedure. It costs (roughly) $25,000, and in some subpopulations, many CABGs are performed in cases where the primary or only benefit is the relief of the pain of angina (it does not prolong life in some groups) (see Leape et al. 1991). Obviously, no one disputes that the relief of pain is a worthy goal, to be pursued for rich and poor alike. But consider a poor person covered by Rice's compulsory medical insurance scheme. To most Americans $25,000 is a great deal of money (the *median* family income in the United States in 1994 was $32,264), and it is easy to imagine that some people with income substantially below this figure would wish to have the money to pursue some personal goal, rather than to receive the reduced pain.[6] The Pareto criterion calls for the poor person to be paid the money, which she can either use to buy the surgery or for some other purpose. Rice's plan calls for her to receive the surgery. The in-kind transfer makes this person worse-off (according to her own assessment) than does the cash transfer. It is not our purpose to argue that the Pareto criterion makes the right choice here, but to point out that deviations from Pareto optimality always entail frustrating someone's preferences, someone whose preferences we could satisfy at no cost to anyone else. In many practical applications, such as this one, it is the poor who bear the brunt of this inefficiency, since they are more often the target and are less often in a position to escape government policy. Now, under some scheme of social choice, it may in fact be better to deny this hypothetical consumer her preferred outcome. But to make an argument for this scheme, it is surely incumbent upon the proponent to face the problem squarely, and not to hide *musts* behind *cans*.

To calculate Pareto rankings, it is necessary to measure consumer preferences. The method favored by most economists is to infer what people prefer from what they actually choose. In the simplest case, where a consumer buys an apple at a price of $1, we infer that the apple is worth at least $1 to the consumer. If the consumer does buy the apple at a price of $1, but refrains at a price of $1.01, we infer that the apple is worth exactly $1 to the consumer.

One might imagine estimating preferences in other ways. To find the value of an apple to a consumer, we might simply ask him what he would be willing to pay for an apple. Alternatively, we could try to measure happiness directly and then try to correlate happiness with apple consumption to infer how much happiness an apple generates. Both Evans and Rice evidently are of the opinion that such methods are desirable, as both use them to bolster various arguments; however, Rice is of divided sentiment on the point, accepting relatively uncritically the international comparisons of happiness presented in Easterlin 1974, but regarding with skepticism the value of satisfaction surveys in comparing different health plans.

Most economists are skeptical of measuring preferences in either of these ways. The first approach is sometimes used (as in contingent valuation in environmental economics), but is regarded with considerable caution for several reasons. First, people responding to surveys typically have very poor incentives to tell the truth or to think carefully about the questions. There may even be systematic biases toward deception (see Kuran 1995; Bjornstad and Kahn 1996; Hausman 1993). An amusing example can be found in the responses of Americans to surveys about whether or not they vote. About 50 percent of eligible Americans turn out to vote in presidential elections, but if we believed what Americans tell people conducting surveys, we would conclude that turnout must be 15 percent to 20 percent greater than this. About 15 percent to 20 percent more people say they vote than actually do (Seppa 1996)! Second, survey questions necessarily leave out details which would affect actual choices ("How much would you be willing to pay for a pound of steak?" leaves out the type, quality, age, fat content, etc.).

The second approach, directly measuring happiness or satisfaction, suffers from all the defects of the first, but also suffers from problems of comparability among individuals. What *happy* means is likely to vary from person to person, from culture to culture, and from time to time, and has no obvious physical referent. The responses are contextual, and made relative to an often unsolicited reference point for the individual. One example of this difficulty is presented in Freeman and Medoff 1984. When workers are asked about job satisfaction, union members indicate significantly greater dissatisfaction with their jobs, relative to similar nonunion employees. Nonetheless, it is also true that union members would require significantly more pay to accept nonunion jobs. These two findings are inconsistent, casting doubt on any straightforward interpretation of the measures of satisfaction. It is hard to know what, if anything at all, can be learned from comparing measures of happiness across people, let alone countries.

As Rice notes, the usual economic approach to assessing preferences also has potential problems. His primary point, raised repeatedly in various guises, is that a consumer operating under imperfect information about the product he is considering may make choices which are not easily interpreted in terms of his fully informed preferences. The world is not always so simple as our example of the apple above. Perhaps not all apples are the same; perhaps there are good apples worth $1.50 and bad apples worth $0.50 to the fully informed consumer, but perhaps the consumer cannot tell the difference before buying them. If (say) the consumer assesses a 50 percent chance that the apple is a good one and a 50 percent chance that it is a bad one, he may be willing to pay $1 for the apple. In this case, the consumer's choice does not tell us about his fully informed preferences for apples, but it tells us about a mixture between his true preferences and his assessment of the likely quality of apples. Notice, though, that his choice does tell us something. It tells us that he expects to get at least $1 worth of satisfaction from his apple purchase. It is also not clear that there is any social welfare problem here. People make decisions under uncertainty all the time, and by necessity some will turn out badly ex post. That does not imply, however, that the individual could have, or should have, done anything differently ex ante. Unless information can be improved ex ante, bad outcomes ex post do not render observed ex ante decisions bad decisions.[7]

Another potential problem Rice raises is the possibility of some indirect effect. If, for example, our hypothetical consumer's parents are apple growers, he may consume apples not out of some preference for apples per se, but because he believes his parents will regard him more poorly if he does not. Rice also raises the problem of externalities in consumption, which can lead to incorrect assessments of Pareto rankings if they are not recognized. Although these are clearly important limitations of standard demand theory, they are also widely recognized by economists. Furthermore, they do not justify blanket condemnation of demand theory. Detecting circumstances in which these problems arise and inferring "primitives" (like preferences for consumers, and costs for firms) from observed market behavior in conditions such as these are areas of active research and progress in economics. As a single example, great progress has been made over the last twenty years in drawing inferences concerning the structure of costs, demand, and the nature of competition only from market data on prices and quantities (Bresnahan 1989; see also Reiss 1996). Keeler (1995) and McClellan (1995) provide analyses of the effects and implications of imperfect information for demand and welfare analysis in the health care sector.

Rice also presents an empirical analysis which he believes poses a significant challenge to the usual interpretation and use of demand analysis. It does not. This particular example has been published before (Rice 1992) as a part of an extended exchange regarding the meaning of demand curves for health services (Feldman and Dowd 1991; Rice 1992; Feldman and Dowd 1993; Rice 1993a; Peele 1993; Rice 1993b; Keeler 1995; McClellan 1995). Although Rice's position has been adequately refuted in that exchange, we repeat and augment the criticisms. Rice analyzes data from the RAND Health Insurance Experiment (HIE) reported in Lohr et al. 1986. The HIE was a social experiment in which consumers were assigned randomly to health insurance plans with different deductibles and coinsurance rates. Rice's reasoning is as follows: When price rises, demand theory asserts that consumers will reduce their consumption, beginning with the units of a commodity yielding the least marginal (additional) utility. In Lohr and colleagues' study, when faced with an increased rate of coinsurance, consumers reduced their consumption, but reduced their consumption of "highly effective" services by the same amount that they reduced their consumption of "less effective" services. Thus, Rice contends, demand theory is falsified.

This reasoning is wrong for several reasons. First, demand theory claims that units yielding the least *marginal* utility will be foregone when price rises. To the extent that the highly effective and least effective categories have any economic interpretation at all, they are about the *average* utility of the services consumed within each category of procedures.[8] Even if one grants the identity of marginal and average utility[9] of services, it is far from clear that standard demand theory predicts what Rice claims. The experiment considered is not a price change but a change in coinsurance. When the coinsurance rate rises, it is not the units with the smallest marginal utility which are foregone first, but the units with the smallest marginal utility net of price. That is, a high-marginal utility, high-price item may be forgone in favor of a low-marginal utility, low-price item. Consequently, the observations on the ways in which consumers reduce their consumption of medical care in the HIE (at least as presented) do not support Rice's assertion.

The test Rice constructs is not objectionable on theoretical grounds alone, however. Demand theory predicts the behavior of *individual* patients vis-à-vis what they consume, and it is questionable whether the procedure used to categorize services as highly effective and least effective reveals anything about the marginal utility of various services to individual patients. The categorizations of "highly effective" and "less effective" care were made after the fact by physicians who did not examine the relevant patients and who did not know the history of the relevant patients. Furthermore, there was not agreement among the physicians categorizing the services as to the categories to which they belong (Lohr et al. 1986; Newhouse 1993: chap. 5). While Rice may find it "logical that consumers would prefer those services that are thought to be the most effective," others may find it logical that consumers disregard the after-the-fact, non-unanimous opinions of people who do not know them or their history, who have never examined them, and who have no strong incentives to think carefully about which treatment is best for them.

Unsurprisingly, Lohr and colleagues interpret their results with more caution than does Rice. They note the great breadth of their service definitions, and point out that their methodology may falsely lead to a finding of no differential response if there are errors in classification of services to categories, if there is substantial heterogeneity in patients' valuations of health status, or if there is substantial heterogeneity in patients' valuations of health status, or if there is substantial heterogeneity in the effectiveness of medical treatment among patients. Obviously, these are empirical issues, but Rice's position depends upon these heterogeneities not being important. This does not exhaust the list of problems with Rice's interpretation of the results, however. The measure, as constructed by Lohr and colleagues, counts only *whether* a consumer sought care. Seeking care one time, two times, or one hundred times are each counted the same. Also, the amount of care sought in each visit is not considered. If the differential demand effect operated along either of these dimensions, the cited study would not be able to detect it.

In another HIE study, O'Grady et al. (1985) found that the effect of higher copayments on emergency room use was to reduce use of the emergency room for "less urgent" diagnoses more than it did for "more urgent" diagnoses. Obviously, for all the reasons we discuss above, this study is no more evidence for demand theory than Lohr and colleagues' findings are a refutation of it; it serves only to show that the result Rice relies upon is not robust, since the results of this study go in the direction which Rice would presumably interpret as validating the standard theory.

Although Rice's evidence is weak indeed for the falsification of standard demand theory, there is evidence from the health insurance experiment bearing on the subject. What other evidence from the HIE is there? Adopting an argument from Feldman and Dowd (1993), if consumers do reduce their consumption of effective care, we should expect to see some deterioration in their health status, relative to consumers who do not. What evidence is there for this in the health insurance experiment? When people's coinsurance rates were increased, they reduced their consumption of health services significantly, but their health outcomes were not changed (Newhouse 1993: chaps. 3, 4, 6).[10] This is not conclusive evidence in favor of consumer rationality, but it is consistent with the theory and inconsistent with Rice's hypothesis.[11]

In defending the use of Pareto optimality and of demand analysis in health economics, we do not claim that these tools are perfect, free of error, and incapable of improvement. However, demand analysis represents the best tool currently available for assessing people's preferences over economic alternatives, and if we wait to use it until the tool is perfect, we will surely wait forever. Neither is the Pareto criterion the only basis for social choice. No economist we are aware of claims that Pareto optimality is a fit candidate for the sole criterion of social choice, and an examination of any introductory microeconomics textbook should dispel any misapprehension on this score.[12] The Pareto criterion is useful in decision making for any hypothetical social planner who has any regard for satisfying the preferences of her charges, and for any actual policy maker whose activities are goal oriented.

Political Economy

An important aspect of the Evans essay is the emphasis on the political economy of health policy. Self-interested attempts to affect government policy are certainly present in health, as they are with respect to other policies. This sort of analysis is present in health economics, but more is certainly called for.[13] While Evans is to be commended for drawing attention to these issues, the presentation in the article is strangely unbalanced and is therefore unconvincing.

In summarizing his essay, Evans states that the short message of the piece is that there are powerful redistributional motives behind part of the health care reform agenda; that much analysis, particularly by economists, misdirects attention by assuming these issues away; and that competition and market mechanisms generally are particularly suited to facilitating and concealing the process of redistribution.

There are four major flaws with the arguments presented in the article. First, as indicated previously, the analysis is incomplete. Evans only considers the political economy of rent seeking by private beneficiaries of market-oriented policies (he uses the term *redistributional motives*).[14] He ignores, however, the political economy of public system-oriented policies. Further, he only analyzes rent seeking, when there are many other potential sources for government failure. Second, he misrepresents modern economic analysis and the uses to which it can be put. Third, he employs conspiracy theories and ad hominem arguments in attempting to make his case. Fourth, he employs unsupported assertions to back his argument. In what follows we review these flaws in turn.

The study of political economy in economics derives from a long tradition of trying to understand the role and limitations of government in the economy (see Schumpeter 1954 for an intellectual history). This analysis arises from two fundamental observations. First, there is an essential interdependence between the economy and the polity of a country. Neither economic activity nor politics occurs independently of one another. Second, this interdependence will lead individuals to try to influence policy to their own benefit. Private interest groups will try to influence policy to increase their economic gains (these are referred to by economists as *economic rents,* hence the term *rent seeking*). In the public sector, politicians and bureaucrats will try to influence the economy in ways that achieve their objectives (e.g., political power), which are not necessarily consistent with society's.

Modern political economy analyzes the workings of political processes in determining policy, and is a key part of modern economics.[15] This approach explicitly recognizes that the political process is subject to imperfections, either due to attempts by private or public individuals or interest groups to manipulate politics to their own advantage, or due to the inability of any political process to fully represent every individual's preferences.

In particular, the need for political economic analysis arises from the recognition that there is governmental failure as well as market failure. Governmental failure can arise for a number of reasons. One is simply due to the lack of feasible mechanisms to implement optimal collective decisions (e.g., Arrow 1951; Sen 1970). A simple example of this is collective choice of a policy by referendum decided by majority rule. Even if preferences over the policy are distributed such that majority rule results in a unique equilibrium, it can still be a suboptimal collective choice, since the preferences of the minority are not represented (Buchanan and Tullock 1962). Another reason is rent seeking, or attempts at self-aggrandizement. Rent seeking on the part of special interest groups can lead to distortions in policy choices (Tullock 1967; Krueger 1974). Additionally, this process results in costs from attempting to influence policy that are socially wasteful (see Mueller 1989: chap. 13 for a useful survey on rent seeking). Another reason is the failure of government bureaucracy to be responsive to social objectives (e.g., Niskanen 1971).

Evans discusses at length how rent seeking can influence and distort the process of policy making with regard to market reform. However, he entirely neglects any distortions in a public sector–dominated system. This is logically inconsistent. If governments and policy making are susceptible to rent seeking over one policy, this must be true for other policies. In the case of a public sector–dominated health system, the rent-seekers will be those who benefit from such a system, including government employees and private firms and individuals to whom rents flow. This is simply Evans's analysis of rent seeking in market reforms applied to public systems.

Further, as indicated above, there are more potential sources of government failure than rent seeking. Political processes do not necessarily work well even without attempts by special interests to influence policy to their advantage, either because of problems with representation or bureaucratic performance. There is simply no consideration or justification in the paper for focusing on only one potential source of government failure.

The second claim made by Evans is that "much analysis, particularly by economists, misdirects attention by assuming these issues away." We find this statement mysterious. As we stated in the previous section, positive economic analysis is a necessary contribution to a policy decision, regardless of one's policy goals. Further, economics as a discipline can hardly be accused of ignoring issues of political economy. We agree that more rigorous political economic analyses of health policy are called for, but that hardly implies that positive economic analyses of health care are useless or misleading. Quite the opposite is true. Just as analyses of efficiency alone are not sufficient for making policy, neither are analyses of redistribution in isolation.

The third major flaw in the paper is the use of conspiracy theories and ad hominem arguments. In a number of places Evans refers to "covert" motives behind market-oriented reforms (see p. 68, for instance), or pretenses that health can be organized as a market "serves to draw a veil over the activities of those who *do* in fact exercise power, and to screen them from public accountability for its use" (p. 70). This sort of verbiage alleges—without attempting to document, let alone prove—that there is some sort of nefarious conspiracy behind market-oriented reforms. It may be that there is some sort of conspiracy to support Evans's allegations. Nonetheless, conspiracy theories, unless carefully documented, are undesirable methods for logical argumentation, because they cannot be refuted. These allegations are also a form of ad hominem attack, in that they imply that arguments in favor of market-oriented reforms can be (conveniently) dismissed in toto, without any consideration, due to the (unsupported) allegation that anyone making such arguments must be a member of some mysterious cabal.

Evans also divides participants in health policy debates into two groups: fundamentalists and instrumentalists. Fundamentalists are defined as those who hold certain forms of economic organization to be good per se, while instrumentalists are interested in policies as a means to an end. Whether an individual is a fundamentalist or an instrumentalist is as irrelevant to the validity of their argument as is the color of their hair. Surely the sky is no less blue because (pick your favorite villain here) claims it is so. Analyses of health policy must be evaluated by the validity and strength of the analysis, not by the identity of the analysis.

We claim no knowledge with regard to whether market mechanisms are particularly well suited to facilitating and concealing the process of redistribution, as claimed by Evans. However, it is not obvious to us whether this is true, or whether markets or government are more susceptible to such covert actions. Again, this is simply an unsupported assertion, so it is not possible to evaluate the validity of the claim.

The last problem in general is the pervasive use of unsupported assertions. The article is rife with them. We only mention a few here. Figure 2 (p. 74) contains data points from eleven different countries on 1989 per capita health spending and the proportion of survey respondents indicating that the health system works well. There are no statistical tests performed nor any statistics reported other than the country-specific means in the figure. Evans concludes, "More spending leads to more satisfaction. The United States is different—and Americans are not happy about it." These assertions may or may not be true, but they simply cannot be tested with the data reported by Evans in Figure 2. As mentioned previously, it is hard to know what to make of the responses to the questions about how well a country's health system works. There are many alternative interpretations of the observed responses, of which Evans's is only one.

However, even if Evans's interpretation of the satisfaction measure is correct, it seems unlikely that his hypothesis can be tested in any meaningful way with only eleven data points.[16] As an example, we regressed the data for per capita health spending (spending) on the proportion reporting the system works well (satisfaction).[17] The satisfaction level for the United States falls within the *70 percent* prediction interval for the regression, meaning that satisfaction in the United States does not differ in a *statistically* significant way from what we would predict from its level of spending.[18] This does *not* imply that the relationship between health spending and satisfaction is the same for the United States as for the other countries; rather it implies that there is so much noise in the data that *no statistically valid inferences can be drawn from them.* While the pattern in Figure 2 may look interesting, the data simply cannot be examined in a scientifically meaningful way.

On p. 76 Evans asserts, "Nobody pretends that other countries do not have substantial problems with their health care systems. But they are typically problems that most Americans would be very relieved to have to face." Not only is this a completely unsupported assertion, but we find it astounding that Evans claims to know what health care problems "most Americans" would like to face.

On the same page he claims, "The record of the last forty years seems to show that the United States took the wrong road in trying to rely on private action to organize and finance health care. The rest of us groped our way to what now seems to be a reasonably satisfactory road." This amounts to proof by assertion, and in two sentences, no less! These statements reveal Evans's opinions, but nothing more.

In regard to the nature of the market for health care services, Evans states that "supply creates its own demand" (p. 79) and "the direct impact of capacity on use is one of the most solidly grounded empirical relationships in health economics" (pp. 79–80). This is simply Evans's opinion. Whether there is any relationship between capacity and use is in fact the single most controversial topic in health economics. There is a great diversity of opinion among health economists on this matter, and a great deal of evidence claimed as support on both sides of the issue (Fuchs 1996; Feldman and Morrisey 1990; Feldman and Sloan 1988). It is inaccurate and misleading to state this as fact rather than as personal opinion.

In regard to the relation between expenditures on health services and providers' incomes, he states, "more expenditure always yields an increase in incomes" (p. 79). There is no logical requirement that this be true. Simply put, more expenditures on services can lead to greater incomes for providers, or the same or lower incomes, depending on the number of providers and the nature of the market for provider services. A scholarly study of rent seeking and the political economy of health policy must clearly establish that there is self-interest sufficient to generate rent-seeking behavior.

The true, and truly important, question of political economy in health care remains. In an imperfect world, which implies both market failure and government failure, what are optimal health policies? While this question is critical, and subject to careful and honest scholarly analysis, it has not been addressed by Evans's essay. Evans's efforts are useful in raising the general issue of the political economy of health policy, but his analysis is so severely flawed that it can only be regarded as opinion, not as scholarly inquiry.

Summary and Conclusions

We have commented on the attempts in the Evans and Rice essays to discredit the use of economic analysis in health policy. As indicated, we feel that the arguments in both articles are subject to so many factual and logical flaws that they do not advance the debate. This does not mean, however, that we feel the issues raised in the articles are irrelevant or settled. There is much room for improvement in economics and in the application of economics to health care, including developing more comprehensive tools for welfare economics and more extensive research in the political economy of health policy. We welcome a rigorous and informed scholarly discourse on these topics.

Notes

1. In fact, one of the major undergraduate textbooks in health economics (Folland, Goodman, and Stano 1993) devotes an entire chapter to issues in applying welfare economics to health care.

2. These are the First and Second Fundamental Theorems of Welfare Economics. See, for example, Debreu 1979.

3. This does not stop economists from using phrases like *better-off* to describe more complete satisfaction of consumers' preferences. This fact has led to considerable criticism of the normative uses of Pareto optimality as calculated by economists (e.g., Sen 1982). Attempts to overcome this problem have included replacing (in the normative moral theory) observed choices with the choices that would be observed were consumers to be perfectly informed (e.g., Griffin 1986; Arneson 1990; and Hausman and McPherson 1996). The use of Pareto rankings as calculated by economists in practical normative judgments may then be justified on practical grounds. Observed preferences may be the best available guide to fully informed preferences. Or, the more directly practical considerations mentioned elsewhere in the text may dominate.

4. Unless coercion is costless, even a despot must take her subjects' preferences into account in order to secure some degree of cooperation.

5. The attentive reader will see that we go on to speak of an in-kind transfer of health care, whereas Rice speaks of an in-kind transfer of health insurance. The structure of the argument remains the same in either case.

6. Obviously, poverty is not the only characteristic which might make a person prefer to take the money. Someone with an unusually high tolerance for pain, or a lifestyle which does not frequently bring on angina attacks, or a particularly compelling use for the money, or a particularly strong aversion to the substantial risk of death attendant on CABG, or any one of a number of other factors might also induce someone to prefer to take the money.

7. See McClellan 1995 on this point. Some would argue that if the consumer's assessment of the probability of buying a good apple is "wrong," then there is a basis for frustrating his preference.

8. To illustrate the difference between marginal and average utility, consider how much a glass of water is worth to a thirsty man. If he has no water at all, the first glass may be worth a great deal to him, perhaps $10. After having consumed the first glass, his thirst is somewhat reduced and the second glass is worth only $1. If he is consuming two glasses of water currently, their average utility to him is $(\$10 + \$1)/2 = \$5.50$. The marginal benefit of the first glass (relative to nothing) is $10, and the marginal benefit of the second glass (relative to only one) is $1. To see why marginal and not average utility is the right thing to look at, suppose the price of water is $1.50. This is clearly less than the average benefit of two glasses of water, since the average benefit is $5.50. However, the thirsty man will not buy two glasses of water! Why not? Since the second glass is worth only $1 to him, he would be better-off (by $0.50) consuming

only the first glass. The relevance of marginal and not average utility for choosing consumption is a very general proposition in economics, and for one formalization of this distinction in the example of health care demand see Peele 1993 and references therein.

9 Specifically, for purposes of the following discussion, assume that each service contributes some fixed amount of utility for consumption of the first unit, and no utility for consumption of subsequent units.

10 Of thirty-two measures of health status, thirty showed no difference between consumers receiving free care and those paying coinsurance. Only two measures showed significant (at 5 percent) changes due to different health insurance levels. Since we would *expect* between one and two rejections out of thirty-two tests at the 5 percent level, this constitutes no evidence that higher coinsurance causes people to forgo valuable (by these conventional measures) health care services. Also, Newhouse (1993) points out that the effects (or lack thereof) of coinsurance on health status are measured precisely, so that these tests are likely quite powerful.

11 In a previous response to this argument, Rice (1993b) made recourse to the following line of reasoning (which he adopted from Lohr et al. 1986). If the reduction in highly effective services was accompanied by a precisely offsetting decline in the use of *actually harmful* ineffective services, then there might be no effect on health outcomes. Beyond pointing out that this explanation is both speculative and would require an amazing and convenient coincidence, little can be said.

12 The obligatory discussion of Edgeworth's Box, for example, explicitly demonstrates the lack of perfect congruence between competition and Pareto optima and distributional issues.

13 For example, see Feldstein 1988b on the political economy of health legislation; Friedman and Kuznets 1954; Friedman 1962a; Kessel 1958, 1970; Leffler 1978; Rayack 1967; Shaked and Sutton 1981 on physician control of medical education and licensure; and Joskow 1981, Posner 1974, Sloan and Steinwald 1980, and Salkever and Bice 1976 on hospital certificate of need regulation. Evans claims that professional self-regulation has disappeared from the consciousness of most of those who approach health systems from a market perspective. As indicated by the above citations, this is clearly incorrect.

14 Rent seeking means self-aggrandizing attempts to influence policy. The economic gains from such actions are referred to by economists as *economic rents,* hence the term *rent seeking.*

15 See Inman 1987 on Mueller 1989 for surveys of the field. Indeed, two recent Nobel laureates in economics, Kenneth Arrow and James Buchanan, were awarded their prizes largely for fundamental work on political economy.

16 If standard errors of the means had been reported, it would have been possible to test for significant differences and to perform power calculations.

17 The regression results were: Satisfaction $= 0.33$ $(2.37) - 0.0000124$ (-0.12), $R_2 = 0.0016$, $F(1,9) = 0.014$. T-statistics are reported in parentheses.

18 The actual value of satisfaction for the United States is 0.1; the value predicted by the regression is 0.304, and the 70 percent prediction confidence interval is [0.091, 0.52]. The interval gets wider, of course, for greater degrees of confidence. It is $[-0.13, 0.74]$ at the 95 percent confidence level, for example.

Response

A Reply to Gaynor and Vogt, and Pauly

Thomas Rice

This is a reply to the commentaries by Gaynor and Vogt, and by Paul, concerning my essay, "Can Markets Give Us the Health System We Want?"

I will focus my remarks on the commentary by Gaynor and Vogt because I had far more problems with it than with the one by Pauly. Quoting them, my problems with their piece "are too many to enumerate individually in this space." Briefly, here is my "top ten" list:

10. One of their main contentions (which was shared by Pauly) is that my essay offers nothing new, because all economists know that the assumptions of perfect competition are not met in health care (the "straw man" reference). Further, Gaynor and Vogt write that "if [I] were to read almost any major economic textbook" I would find a listing and discussion of the many types of market failure. It turns out that I have read a number of such textbooks and have been struck by how little attention is paid to the assumptions upon which my essay focuses. The essay analyzes seven assumptions of the competitive model, only one of which—good consumer information—has received much attention from the health economics profession. (My noting that assumption, if perhaps unoriginal, was used to illustrate a point that *has* been ignored by the professional: demand curves in health don't mean what we say they do.) The other assumptions—that is, challenging the Pareto principle, considering the implications of endogenous preferences, questioning consumer rationality through the use of cognitive dissonance theory, examining whether consumer choices really reveal their preferences—have received scant attention from health economists. My essay then provided many health applications specific to these particular assumptions. Thus, the arguments can hardly be viewed as knocking down straw men.

I tried to show the important implications that arise for our field when one reexamines assumptions that have heretofore been ignored; I am surprised that the two sets of commentators do not find this to be a worthy inquiry.

9. Although about half of the Gaynor and Vogt commentary devoted to my article criticizes the discussion of the Pareto principle, it completely misses the point, which can be understood by considering a simple illustration. Suppose that all of the assumptions of competition are met, so that the operation of market forces results in Pareto optimality. Further suppose that three-quarters of people do not engage in any form of market transactions and as a result remain at the same level of wealth, but that the remaining one-quarter do engage in such entrepreneurial activities, resulting in a doubling of their own wealth. My point is simply this: If people care about relative as well as absolute wealth, the majority of people (here, 75 percent) might find that competition worsened things because they find themselves farther behind. This point, which is the crux of my argument for the first of the seven assumptions I consider, is left virtually untouched by Gaynor and Vogt. (Rather, they rehash the definition of the Pareto principle and focus on other areas not in dispute, such as the fact that a Pareto optimal outcome is possible when preferences are endogenous, as noted in Point 7, below.) Nor do they attempt to dispute my assertion that people do indeed care deeply about relative status, which forms the basis of the conclusions reached.

8. In making their point about the Pareto principle, Gaynor and Vogt state the following: "It is not clear to us in what way an economist saying 'trade barriers make everything worse-off than' is any more or less normative than an engineer saying 'bridges made out of cardboard will fall down more frequently than'" (p. 113).

This sort of a statement shows, I think, how deeply many economists are entrenched in believing that their discipline is "value free."[1] There are two answers to their question: (a) The assumptions of a competitive marketplace are, to put it mildly, more heroic than those of physics; and (b) empirical testing of cardboard bridges is far easier and less ambiguous than testing who gains and who loses from trade barriers. Gaynor and Vogt's assertion is doubly odd given that they say that the Evans essay doesn't demonstrate the difference between *is* and *ought*. To say that a welfare statement like "trade barriers make everyone worse-off" is not value-laden (not to mention blatantly false, given that there are strong constituencies in support of trade barriers in order to further their own economic interests) is to misunderstand the meaning of normative versus positive statements, and therefore, the limits of economic theory in addressing such questions.

7. The criticism of the section on endogenous preferences also misses the point. Gaynor and Vogt confuse the arguments I make about the Pareto principle with those on the problems of assuming preferences to be exogenously determined. When considering the latter, for convenience it was assumed that fulfilling the Pareto principle was desirable—so that we could consider the importance of the assumption about exogenous preferences in isolation. They are right in saying that one can still get a Pareto optimal outcome when preferences are endogenously determined. But this is completely unrelated to my point: that if preferences are endogenous, individuals are likely to make choices that are not in their best interest. Again, the commentary failed to address the topics considered by my article, and instead disputed others that in actuality I did not raise.

6. In this regard, they bring up the issue of addiction, noting my point that a cigarette addict may be better-off if he or she quits smoking. Gaynor and Vogt object, noting that "it is far from obvious to us that the addict's pain or withdrawal is somehow less valid than any other motive for preference formation." This viewpoint, which seems to be shared by many economists, is curious and, I think, unfortunate. Essentially, what they are saying is that if we don't know *with certainty* that smokers have made a choice that is not in their best interest, then there is no cause for intervention. (An example of such an intervention is government-funded advertisements aimed at getting people to stop smoking.) Their viewpoint represents consumer sovereignty run amok—that people make the best choices *no matter what*. It also allows advertisers to invest in changing consumer tastes (here, toward more smoking) with few if any market incentives for the other (and in this case, medically objective) side of the story. One would hope that such a scenario would not be viewed as optimal by Gaynor and Vogt, but that is the inevitable conclusion one reaches by following their arguments.

5. When discussing cash grants versus providing in-kind services to the poor, Gaynor and Vogt again completely ignore the arguments made in my article. My point was quite simple: If one considers the wishes of donors as well as those of the recipients, then a strong case can be made for the superiority of in-kind transfers (e.g., health care coverage like Medicare and Medicaid) rather than cash grants. I further argue that far less would be donated (either directly, or through willingly paying

higher taxes) if all subsidies took the form of cash grants. It would have been interesting to see how they responded to the crux of the argument, but they avoided it, instead raising an example (about coronary artery surgery) unrelated to the points I was making.

4. In discussing consumer choices under uncertainty, Gaynor and Vogt assume that consumer choices will, *on average,* be correct. They provide no evidence, however, that this is indeed the case with medical care. If people systematically underestimate the value of preventive services, for example, their purchase decisions will not make them best-off. This is a classic case of how markets may not operate to make consumers best off—something that Gaynor and Vogt fail to consider in the commentary.

3. In discussing the results of the RAND Health Insurance Experiment, Gaynor and Vogt raise a number of arguments to bolster the proposition that people's behavior in the wake of higher coinsurance rates—in which they cut back on medically effective services as much as ineffective services—does not violate consumer theory. It's easy to come up with reasons why it is still possible that consumer theory might survive the findings of Lohr et al. (1986). As they note, this issue has been discussed elsewhere; answering all of their points would necessitate yet another full-length article. What is perhaps most noteworthy is that they do not even consider the *possibility* that consumer behavior might be inconsistent with the theory. Nor do they successfully refute the alternative that I presented—that one can better measure social welfare loss by computing the cost of unnecessary medical services.

2. More generally, in reading the commentary, one is struck at how hard Gaynor and Vogt fight to preserve the status quo. If one cannot *prove* that the assumptions of the competitive model are not met in health care, then one cannot dispute its recommendations. (Pauly's essay is much less doctrinaire in this regard.) Needless to say, it is very difficult to reevaluate the role of existing theory, and to open new areas of inquiry into alternatives to such theory, when adherents fight so doggedly against doing so.

1. Finally, my *number one* problem concerns future discourse in our field. Gaynor and Vogt end their commentary by calling for "a rigorous and informed scholarly discourse on these topics." Unfortunately, their method of argument makes it difficult to elevate the debate to the level of scholarly discourse that they purport to desire. A reading of their commentary shows that it is littered with gratuitous remarks that have no place in a scholarly journal. This stifles rather than enhances scholarly

discourse. Much more can be accomplished if one puts aside name-calling and focuses on the issues at hand.

Notes

1 One is reminded of Amartya Sen's (1970: 5) quote, "It must be regarded as somewhat of a mystery that so many notable economists have been involved in debating the prospects of value-free welfare economics."

Coarse Correction—And Way off Target

Robert G. Evans

The comments by Gaynor and Vogt, and Pauly, seem to me to touch my essay at so few points that a detailed response would be as futile as it would be tedious. It is as if, having set out to analyze the role of Islamic fundamentalism in Middle Eastern politics, one were attacked for having misinterpreted the Koran—and blasphemously at that. But my concern, at least in this context, is not with points of economic doctrine.

Gaynor and Vogt assert, however, that a main theme of both essays is the inapplicability of economic analysis to health care. Precisely the reverse is true. (That some such applications are misleading or harmful, however, is something that surely no one would wish to deny.) Their comment indicates a misreading so profound as to explain much of what follows. In fact, my essay interprets debates over the roles of "the state" and "the market" in a way that is solidly rooted in fundamental economic ideas.

I start from perhaps the most basic hypothesis in economics, namely that people, individually and in groups, are strongly motivated by their perceptions of their own interests. And people pursue those interests in a number of ways, in and out of markets. In particular they engage in collective advocacy of public policies that benefit themselves. Such advocacy, whether by formally organized groups or by more loosely defined aggregations ("classes"?) sharing a common interest, may appeal to principle but is also deeply rooted in interest. Gaynor and Vogt refer to "conspiracies" and ad hominem (ad personam?) arguments; a less pejorative description would be political behavior.

Second, the economy as a whole is bound by "adding-up constraints"—accounting relationships—which are matters of logic, not of theory. The income-expenditure identity may be a more or a less helpful way of looking at the framework within which economic behavior takes place, but it is not falsifiable. One person's expenditure *is,* by definition, another's income; and many of the basic conflicts over health care policy flow from that ineluctable fact. (Gaynor and Vogt's comment that more expenditures do *not* necessarily imply greater provider incomes refers to average incomes *per* recipient, and suggests that they may have missed the centrality of the aggregate identity. Greater expenditure increases either the number or the average size of income streams, or both. And people are interested in both.)

One need only add the assumption that the members of a society are not identical in their preferences, risk status, and income sources and levels (i.e., the opposite of Arrow's assumption, as quoted), and one has an economic basis for continuing policy conflict. That assumption seems to me to be empirically undemanding, although it creates more difficulty for theoretical analyses than many economists care to admit.

Economists are not, however, the central focus of the essay. Both Pauly and Gaynor and Vogt seem to miss this point. Rice is fundamentally concerned, and in my view correctly, with the content of economic theory and the behavior of economists; but for me these are side issues. Out in the real world the recurring political advocacy of a greater role for market forces in health care is driven, not by the work of theoretical economists, but by the interests and expectations—more or less well-founded—of the principal categories of advocates that I identified. Rational self-interest—what could be more consistent with conventional economics?

In fact Gaynor and Vogt sum up this idea quite nicely (except that they get it backward) when they say that whether an individual is a fundamentalist or an instrumentalist is irrelevant to the validity of an argument. To an instrumentalist, the *validity* of an argument is irrelevant— that is why the same faulty logic and factual misrepresentations keep coming back over the decades (and why Rice's essay is necessary). The key question is, Does the argument serve a continuing interest? If so, it will recur, not just in the academic literature, but in the policy arena.

And it is the instrumentalists who are politically potent. Economic arguments are just part of their rhetorical armamentarium—"icing on the cake," as I described them. When economists make arguments for which there is no resonance among the major interest groups involved, nothing happens. Pauly illustrates this well with his reference to the regressive effects of the tax expenditure subsidy. Economists have been making this point for at least twenty-five years, and few of us, I think, would disagree. And the result?

More generally, as I noted, there is *no* support among the various advocates of the market, out in the real world, for anything resembling the freely competitive marketplace of the theoretical economist. Even if one believed that such "perfect" markets were a general desideratum—which as Rice points out is not a conclusion that can be derived from economic theory—they have not had and will not have any existence outside the theoretical imagination. What is offered by advocates is always some form of managed and regulated market managed and regulated by and/or in the interests of the advocates.

That is, of course, a generalization about the world of experience that Gaynor and Vogt could quite correctly call an "unsubstantiated statement"—unsubstantiated in the present context, that is. And it is quite true that there are a number of such statements in the essay, as in all essays. One does not constantly reassemble the evidence for the obvious. And what is obvious depends upon the community of interpretation. But an assertion does not become substantiated simply by virtue of being written in mathematical symbols, for communication within a self-referential community. (It may, however, become less recognizable as a bald assertion, not only unsubstantiated but quite possibly implausible or simply erroneous, by those who do not routinely employ such symbols.)

The observation that the American pattern of health care organization and finance is not only unique but uniquely unsatisfactory in the developed world is clearly such an assertion. But the response that both governments and markets may "fail," and that rent seeking is universal, leads one back into the realm of the a priori, where all things are possible and conclusions are reached only by convention (commonly in the form of mathematically phrased assertions).

In the real world the evidence is overwhelming and the verdict has been in for some time. The basic facts are well known to all students of comparative health care systems. Only in the United States does (carefully nurtured) controversy persist. Advocates of the marketplace in all other countries routinely assure their audiences that such proposals will *not* lead to an American-style system.

The effect of capacity on utilization provides another example. Gaynor and Vogt call this a highly controversial proposition, but the controversy is only among a small subset of academic health economists. As Reinhardt (1985) asked, who outside the American economics profession would ever doubt it? There is a much wider community of health researchers and policy practitioners, from a diversity of disciplines, among whom "Roemer's Law" has been accepted for years. These people draw on a more extensive range of empirical information, and their own experience provides regular confirmation. That is why capacity-control policies of various forms are now virtually universal in the developed world. "Health economics" includes what is thought and done in this wider community; it is not restricted to the activities of academics publishing in professional economics journals.

Indeed, a confusion between the subject matter of economics and the interests and activities of a particular subset of health economists may lie at the heart of both comments. Contrary to Gaynor and Vogt's assertion, what both Rice and I identify as inapplicable to health care is not economic analysis, but a certain set of analytic conventions that embody not only implausible and rarely articulated assumptions—for example, Arrow's assumption above—but also the value judgments of the analysts themselves (Reinhardt 1992; Culyer and Evans 1996).

Pauly elsewhere states explicitly that "welfare economics . . . does, [given the acceptance of the assumptions], permit normative conclusions to be drawn" (1994b: 370) because "the assumptions of welfare economics . . . [include] that the distribution of income is accepted as ethically correct" (1996b: 253). This would come as a surprise to most other economists, who labor to communicate to students the distinction between *positive* and *normative*. Theories, economic or otherwise, are made up of positive "if . . . then" propositions. The only way to get value judgments out is to put them in first—"No ethics in, no ethics out," in Archibald's phrase—and that is what Pauly is doing. Any ethical assumptions he uses are *his*, and are given spurious authority when linked to the discipline of welfare economics. The derivation of normative propositions from a priori principles is the province of religion.

The tone of Pauly's comment here is rather different, reflecting upon the range of policy alternatives, political or market-based, that might improve the functioning of different health care systems. Yet elsewhere he finds the process of collective decision making superfluous: "Using economic welfare . . . allows us to avoid the murky area of 'societal decision-making.' . . . no recourse to 'societal values and objectives' is required" (Pauly 1994a: 370; see also 1994b and 1996b).

Is the "sizable" role that he envisions for government in this comment only that of enforcing a closer approximation to the outcomes a hypothetical market might have produced, regardless of people's political choices? But the values implicit in that market outcome, however attractive to Pauly, do not appear to be widely shared (van Doorslaer, Wagstaff, and Rutten 1993). Are the rest of us simply suffering from false consciousness, or has he changed his mind?

In any case Pauly slides far too easily from what is to what might be, if only the responsible proposals of certain economists were followed (*and* implemented as planned!). He would have us focus on the latter, not on the current American reality. But as Culyer (1982) pointed out some time ago, it is misleading to contrast working, real-world systems with untested hypothetical alternatives. When you go for the market, the United States is what you get—or at least it is the only example we have.

Of course Pauly may fairly claim that motives should be judged by (good) intentions, not by (others') expectations of actual outcome. But he makes the same error as Gaynor and Vogt in focusing on the motives of *economists* and attacking the notion of a secret "plot" by certain analysts to promote the market. There may be such a plot—self-referential groups tend to look like conspiracies from the outside—but if so I have no more knowledge of it than Pauly does. Hence my very explicit distinction between fundamentalists ("advocates without predicates") and the instrumentalists identified in the essay. The latter, with an economic interest in private finance, are certainly "plotting" in most countries, both openly and more covertly. And they tend to seize upon any form of analysis that assists their case. But again, we normally refer to this as political behavior.

This misreading may lie behind the vigor, the tone of injured outrage, and indeed the plain offensiveness in the comments of Pauly and particularly Gaynor and Vogt. This tone seems hard to understand from the substance of their critique alone. On the other hand I do quite explicitly (though hardly originally) write off the unique American approach to health care finance as an unfortunate and apparently irremediable mistake. This mistake is linked to a dogged persistence in trying to employ market mechanisms to fund and allocate health care, which in turn is traced to the influence of those who benefit from such mechanisms.

In the process, questions about market functioning, in the United States or in some more abstract environment, are bypassed as largely irrelevant to the better-organized systems of the rest of the developed world. Yet these are questions to which American economists in particular (and understandably) have devoted considerable analytic attention, dominating the international academic journals.

Rice then demonstrates that neither the substantive assumptions behind many of these analyses, nor their conclusions, could be supported from economic theory per se anyway; and I point out that a focus on and advocacy of market-based approaches, however motivated, in practice serves readily identifiable and narrowly based economic interests. A certain amount of unhappiness, and even rudeness, in response is really quite understandable.

But it is necessary to restate the obvious from time to time, lest we be led astray by illusions (whether or not dressed up in mathematical symbols). As Francis Bacon remarked about another who found himself unpopular in certain circles for being too explicit: "We are much beholden to Machiavel and others, that write what men do and not what they ought to do."

The Technocratic Wish: Making Sense and Finding Power in the "Managed" Medical Marketplace

Gary S. Belkin

The exposé of power did not take a history of reason into account.

In the past few decades, scholars of health care were fascinated with the big lie. Physician power was in fact political power, not merely the natural value and effects of exercising the knowledge they had laboriously acquired. Physicians took some knowledge and transformed it into lots of unique political authority and privilege over health matters. "The dream of reason did not take power into account," opened Paul Starr's (1982: 3) emblematic exposé of how knowing a little something led to maintaining political and clinical autonomy over health care. But this analysis could be inverted through the 1980s from Starr's writing *The Social Transformation of American Medicine* to his arriving at the Clinton White House. The power of physicians' reason became appropriated by others, but in doing so a new transformation occurred that would escape the scholarly critique of physician power. The very nature of what counted as reason in health care was rapidly transformed, facilitating new ways of organizing resources. To only be interested in the power of reason leaves reason itself unexamined. Is the eroded power of the physician expert a replacement by better knowledge, or by simply more effective power that uses a claim to objectivity and scientific validity to sustain itself? Does knowledge find legitimacy in what it can reap and explain, or are those very results of subscribing to one way of explaining things the reasons why a claim to knowledge becomes ascendant and certified as objective and scientific? What other connections can we draw between being knowledgeable and being powerful in the politics of the health care marketplace? If we want to explain, change, or benefit from managed care, we need to be curious about a key source of its authority—an appeal to rationality.

Starr's own embrace of a version of managed competition paralleled a national journey of breathtaking speed: from medicine understood as seeing a doctor who implemented decisions based on his or her knowledge, experience, and judgment, to a corporate organization that laid out restrictions and particular decision making, access pathways, and protocols based on the measured experience of large numbers of people. This transformation, from a medicine shaped by the needs and aspirations of numerous individual practitioners to one responding to institutional budgeting and performance assessments in order to predict and control the medical care of huge populations, can be praised or vilified. It commodifies health care as the product of competing companies but it also provides necessary control over uncontrolled resource use. Either characterization reflects the scope of the changed health care marketplace within the last decade.

The flip side to Starr's fashionable exposé of medical muscling became extraordinarily relevant but far less studied. Whereas knowledge brought physicians power, power in turn often relies on a justificatory regime of knowledge. White House endorsement of the power of corporate managers to manage health care hid critical assessment of an associated bag of knowledge claims that made such management plausible. Science gave legitimacy to physician political authority. But now, business using managed care techniques ride the same translation of knowledge into political power. Asserting unique knowledge of medical needs through certain aggregate measures, assumed better able to determine what is important about medical encounters than individual doctors, justifies authority over physicians and shows the changing beneficiaries of Starr's "dream of reason."

We need to examine the important connection between being convincingly scientific and being successfully powerful in health policy. The rapid spread of managed care reflects what I call the *technocratic wish*.[1] This wish is a particular kind of appeal of "scientificness," and is one way that the social and political perception of something being scientific in fact shapes what is regarded as scientific. Seeing managed care as a knowledge claim, as an assertion that we only really know about the proper use of medical resources or the relevant aspects of a medical encounter from aggregate, generalizable data about large population experience, returns study of the new power politics of the medical marketplace to its complexity as a contested site of valid knowledge in culture.

The "reason" managed care specifically tries to offer medicine should itself be subject to scrutiny. Those studying managed care need to have greater acquaintance with work in the history of science and medicine and how accounts of nature or methods for studying it acquire their compelling, authoritative, and "truthful" nature. Reason's powerful empire can best be studied if we also open up to study how contingent social roles, needs, and agendas shape the success of one set of scientific claims or methods over another. We need to look here to understand how one approach (outcomes studies, aggregated behavior) gets preferred to another (individual physician judgment and experience).

Managed care needs to be placed within a history of the close relationship between scientific justification and shifts in power, policy, and politics. In this relationship, the very believability of the scientific claim (and that it is indeed objective and scientific) often relies on the degree to which such a claim can enable and command assent for such political shifts. It is a history of how democratic societies rely on an objectivity of standardized measures, rather than on individual expert judgment to broker disagreement. It is a history of the technocratic wish. Through this wish, otherwise difficult, if not impossible, power shifts can instead be understood by those involved as shifts to "better" knowledge, more scientific and rational practice, but where the very credibility of the new practice as in fact scientific and better is shaped by its social need, use, and source.

This is in contrast to a history of scientific techniques, for example, techniques of measuring and analyzing medical practice, as a progressive, logical development whose position at the end of fruitful refinement of long-standing ideas confirms its scientific credibility and objectivity. I will frustrate this history by detailing the case of early-twentieth-century physician Ernest Amory Codman, often invoked as a precursor to current changes in medical management. I will show his quite different goals and thus offer a much more fruitful lineage of events with which to associate managed care—a history of science literature examining the appeal of objective standarized measures when it enables overcoming political and economic conflict; a history of the technocratic wish.

Along the way I distinguish two meanings of *standardization:* instrumental and epistemological. Although often running one into the other, these terms capture and underscore the selective and varied use of standard measures as authoritative references through which to achieve agreement about the nature of things. The varied meanings for a "standard" measure illustrate my point that debate about the organization of health care services can be seen as part of more contingent and contested struggles over what counts as valid measuring and proof. The rush to see in Codman transcentury affinity around current concepts such as "standardization" and "efficiency" reveals more about our faith in these as hard scientific realities (reveals more about the technocratic wish) than their true stable meaning and purpose historically.

Before turning to Codman and these distinctions as to how his vocabulary about monitoring physicians differs from that on which managed care relies, I will need to expand on two points in the sections that follow. The first point I summarize is the subjectivity of objectivity problem, and is explored in the next section. There is great variability among very capable scientists as to what evidence, techniques, assumptions, and so on, count as "scientific." Scientific work still needs to contend with subjective choices that are debated among scientists themselves and that result in brokered agreement as to norms for the objective isolation of phenomena (Pickering 1992; Knorr-Cetina 1981; Collins 1974). Despite this subjectivity of objectivity, political institutions often act on the belief that their behavior is justified as objectively good or natural based on models of scientific law, practice, or specific knowledge. If what is scientific is clearly so fluid but, and with great consequences, viewed within politics and economic behavior as uncomplicated and stable, we need to explain how a given version of scientific credibility is embraced as such to sustain influence and power in society.

The second point is that managed care is an example of a claim to scientific "obviousness" and reliability, and that this claim is critical to its acceptance and power. The subsequent section explores this claim. Codman is but one small example that instead demonstrates the historically contingent meanings and uses of the presumed scientific objectivity of standards and measures advocated at various times to rationalize medical practice. Managed care's value and success are significantly tied to the degree that it offers an objectivity that is specifically needed to resolve current political and economic tensions around health care. This value, this social and political "fit" with what can count as objective, allows managed care to bypass the subjectivity of objectivity problem.

Politics and the History of Claims to Scientific Authority

To approach science and scientific claims as cultural resources—as conventions of argument, evidence, and authority in society at large—requires confronting the fact that great changes and disagreements in what counts as true scientific theory, methods, or beliefs are often heavily shaped by social interests, needs, and institutions. Examples are abundant and varied. Acceptance of the voltmeter as a valid measure of electricity only occurred when its use and those who used it were reconciled with a prior dignified ideal of class and social status that physicists had of themselves (Wise 1995). Artificially created, apparatus-based experiment and isolation of phenomena vied in the seventeenth century with philosophical debate as a preferred method to obtain knowledge of nature. It succeeded not because it was obvious—indeed, it was vehemently debated—but because it responded to other social and political needs within Britain for a peaceful post-Revolutionary discourse regarding how nature worked that appeared more neutral about theologically charged issues. It conformed to and was purposefully modeled after accepted social norms of gentlemen's behavior that were associated with trust, veracity, and authority (Shapin 1994; Shapin and Schaffer 1985). Tissue typing for transplantation seems like a straightforward laboratory sorting of differences in immunologic patterns (and thus success in transplantation) of organs. But scholarship shows its controversial nature among scientists and the importance of factors like the organizational culture of different medical institutions and social interest in standardized, "blind" distribution practices, in the acceptance and use of typing methods (Hogle 1995; Lowy 1986).

Similarly, techniques that people view as offering uncomplicated objective proof, when more carefully examined, are easily seen to be the result of a multitude of subjective choices (my subjectivity of objectivity problem). Health services research and the foundational practices of managed care that, as I will argue, appear to offer new scientific rigor to medicine are perfect examples of this. Measuring outcomes of medical interventions and paying for, approving, and rewarding those treatments with desirable outcomes seems obvious, straightforward, and long-delayed. But the value-laden nature of what is "desirable," the innumerable choices and disagreements as to outcome variables, interventions, and observed population definitions, make the measuring of outcomes anything but straightforward. The benefits of physician "subjectivity" and the inherent limits of medical knowledge, as well as the similar subjective, value-based decisions that mark the processes of outcomes research, have been explored (Tanenbaum 1993; Gifford 1996; Ashmore, Mulkay, and Pinch 1989; Gorovitz and MacIntyre 1976; Hunter 1991).

Summarizing the responses of many people to constructed measurements in an average so as to ostensibly capture true causal inferences, is fraught with methodological constraints that complicate their easy generalizability. Statistical inference based on standard measures has identified and mobilized critical behaviors and insights to the benefit of mankind. But as just one way of fruitfully understanding and organizing nature and social life, its often dominant power needs to be explained. Transforming seemingly chance events, resistant to prediction and control, into tabulated observations interpreted to reveal not chance but fundamental traits and patterns, was a central event in modern culture. This was a transition from seeing in large, quantified descriptions of society (crime rates, tabulated heights, occupations, disease occurrence) simple descriptive information about the world, to seeing in them lawful regularities offering primary knowledge preferable to individual experience. This transition did not change culture by the sheer force of its logic. To be seen as self-evidently logical, many other things such as a liberal political project that saw an opportunity to reform, manipulate, and improve large populations was necessary. Such changes occurred, as detailed in the European stage, over the nineteenth century (Hacking 1990). New approaches and meanings of tabulated experience confirmed and were themselves reinforced and confirmed by broader developments in political economy.

These events stand at the beginning of a possible history of the technocratic wish. Such a history is not interested in proving or disproving reality, but in investigating how and why circumstances arise such that appeals to one choice for explaining reality—standard, objective, numerical measures—come to be compelling. Especially when they previously were not compelling and supplanted a prior and different tradition, usually individual expert-based judgment, which despite its poverty of aggregate standard measures, accomplished quite a bit in terms of "real" knowledge (e.g., evolution, most causes of most diseases, and the effectiveness and existence of important drugs).

Consider studies of the introduction of cost-benefit ratios for choosing among competing public works projects (a critical entrée for cost-benefit analysis in public policy), pursuit of randomized-control trials by the Food and Drug Administration and advocacy groups as the necessary method for assessing drug efficacy, and the use of a few standard grain grades to capture what had been direct individual inspection of grain quality and diversity by purchasers. These changes were not "obviously" scientific, but acquired their obviousness in order to reliably facilitate other compelling political and economic goals. These events should be understood in the way that they respectively reduced conflict over which town got a bridge, provided a tool for consensus about regulation of pharmaceuticals, enabled groups such as Planned Parenthood to transform a controversial opinion or cause (birth control) into a measurable medical problem that could be studied, and permitted commodity (grain) trading at a location distant from the product and thus the marked expansion of that market. Without such anxieties, suspicions, or ambitions, these decisions to trust in certain kinds of numbers and their compilation would not have taken place the way they did (Meldrum 1996; Porter 1995).

The social nature of scientific change and the subjectivity of objectivity resonate with each other and point to the technocratic wish. The former raises an obvious question: What does it mean to say that there is a social "nature" or "influence" to science? Is a scientific claim merely what people construct nature to be? There is a vast literature exploring the social nature of scientific knowledge and how norms of scientific proof change. It is diverse and wide-ranging in the degree of autonomy versus social construction accorded to science, and is beyond the scope of this article (Bloor [1976] 1991; Fleck [1935] 1981; Latour and Woolgar 1979; Merton 1973; Popper 1972; Kuhn [1962] 1970; Wittgenstein 1956).

The best way to approach these issues and not fall into a trite social constructionism is first not to lump every single scientific discovery together and feel a need to find a single explanation for their acceptance. More important, however, there appears to be a fairly comprehensive notion of the social nature of what counts as objective knowledge which does not paralyze us into accepting that there are no real phenomena out there. The technocratic wish is one historical interpretation of the social aspects of scientific change that powerfully approaches these vexing questions. It is particularly compelling and underscored by events in the medical marketplace.

There are very appealing things in requiring physicians to comply with how a population is observed to respond to different interventions. The point here is that there are many ways to prove causes and effects, to identify events or behaviors we need to worry about and see as a "problem," and many ways to compel faith in the methods to do so. The ones we choose are not exclusive possibilities and are consistent with social and cultural expectations and organization. Social and political life is seen through the technocratic wish not as a simple producer of what is true, but as quite real aspects of our experience whose stable and smooth running requires certain agreed on ways of certifying what is true. This experienced reality of our social and political lives can often preclude or keep noncompelling other possible ways of doing so.

The power of medical treatments or outcomes measures to predict and manipulate things in the world is not being denied here. In fact, this power is what I am trying to explain. To accept such treatments or measures as compelling reveals the investment society is making and the extent to which it is arranged so as to act on and respond to these measures. Psychometric testing, such as IQ testing, is one example of how laboratory techniques were shaped by the needs of certain large organizations (the military, school systems) to accomplish things important to them, such as selecting individuals along a range of abstracted global abilities. The summary result, the IQ, became regarded as a natural phenomenon in its own right, and not only the laboratory but the initially interested social institutions organized their behavior around this measure, reinforcing its "naturalness." IQ testing is not meaningless. It predicts much about how one may function in certain settings. It sorts persons along a dialectic fit between social needs and laboratory abstractions of nature by summing the performance of individuals based on selected variables (Danzinger 1990).

This approach to the social construction of scientific knowledge—more a social "framing" of science (Rosenberg and Golden 1992)—makes the subjectivity of objectivity both expected and particularly illuminating. It directs us to the technocratic wish. For if objectivity can be shown at times to be made of subjective choices, what gives it definitive authority? What offers, for example, a compelling sense of reasonableness to average physician performance along a certain indicator, patient outcomes along a certain parameter, disease severity along a summed measure, and confidence in accurately identifying relevant aspects of medical practice in these ways? More specifically, how are we able to agree to hide the multitude of subjective choices in making any of those claims and agree on the objectivity of the final product?

The answer is because we often need to, so that the ways we organize our social and political life make sense, or can be sensibly changed. Agreement about objectivity sustains our basic political and economic institutions. Indeed, the authority of liberal political and market institutions is barely understood without considering the knowledge claims behind them, barely noticed because they are so ingrained in how we arrange our life so as to be reinforced as palpably and really true. The technocratic wish is a variant of a much broader function that scientific credibility has in sustaining these institutions.

Liberalism regularly struggled to explain how freedom would result in a nonetheless ordered society, and how a free system would still permit certain constraints on liberty that could be seen as moral. A regular aspect of attempts at explanation has been a confidence in scientific paradigms and their applicability to social and political behavior (Ezrahi 1990; Albury 1983). Scientific claims, or at least rhetorical appeals, provide reassuring natural lawfulness that the best outcomes will emerge from laissez-faire competition on the one hand, or on the other, that learned experts can be legitimately delegated political authority to manage complex aspects of our life in a way that will be disinterested and merely technical. The simple faith that representative government remains a process openly visible and accessible to public observation is embedded in seventeenth-century arguments for the superiority of facts known by a shared, standardized form of observation—the experiment—rather than passion, philosophy, or theology.

Generalizing the success of some efforts to manipulate the natural world, models of scientific mechanism and prediction are transposed onto political behavior and offer assurance that democratic institutions will work reliably and altruistically.

> Transposed into the sphere of public action, the presuppositions of representation and the idea that experts can optimize the technical effectiveness or efficiency of public actions imply that the actions of public officials, like the actions of physicians or engineers, can be made sufficiently detachable from the subjective values of their agents to warrant trust in their integrity as functionally representative. . . . The perceived historical role of experiments in the advancement of knowledge, and later machines in the industrial revolution, has socially enhanced the rhetorical power of instruments and technical operations to authorize claims not only in the context of science but also in wider areas of discourse. . . . Science and technology have fulfilled, then, a series of key functions in the ideological construction of modern liberal-democratic politics and, more particularly, in the justification of instrumental paradigms of political action. By furnishing authoritative means to define political action in instrumental impersonal public terms, science and technology facilitated a shift from early liberal-democratic notions of public action as an aspect of involuntary "natural" regularities to notions of public action as the result of deliberate voluntary choices. (Ezrahi 1990: 45, 94–95)

The technocratic wish not only describes the expectation and hope that contentious issues in public life can be resolved by appeal to scientific measures and procedures rather than by the wise judgment of selected individuals; it more particularly appeals to measures that stand on their own as explanations. A cost-benefit ratio, a statistical inference comparing a known and a new drug, or a devised standard system for grading grain quality, are measures asserted to contain in themselves answers as to relative value. The measure is sufficient to know whether something is good or bad, and in a way that is definitive and hard to contest. This incontestability (how do you yell at a number?) is purposeful. These measures allow parties to avoid relying on the judgments of selected individuals, and skirt contentiousness. The histories of many measures reveal their appeal in offering closure to which all contestants will offer assent, or as a method for gaining new credibility with competitors or needed allies for political authority that avoids indicting or relying on the judgment of an individual.

Managed care relies on a similar assertion, or a wish, that standardizing medical practice through knowledge gleaned from aggregated measures, disciplined through the "logic" of the marketplace, will control costs while it maintains quality. By offering a scientific solution, it could finally crack the nut frustrating health policy for the past decades: reconciling global budgeting decisions with individual physician behavior. Only a solution understood as scientific was able to bridge this gap, and in essence, to bridge physicians' unique claim to expertise. But again, it is a scientific solution of a particular sort. The technocratic wish is not mere reliance on standardized practices. Commodification of product and specification of predictable costs and inputs are a staple of routine industrial management practices now taking over health care. Rather, with the technocratic wish, the legitimacy of applying such practices relies on the unique scientific credibility and insights offered by the standards themselves. The very measures they represent ostensibly reveal real fundamental knowledge about disease, health, and medicine.

This distinction reflects a difference between an instrumental and an epistemological standardization. Agreed-on measures, such as age sixteen for driving, conventions for dimensions of industrial parts, or shared reporting formats for law enforcement or other agencies, are diverse examples of how practices (methods of data gathering) are designed to enhance and predict some control over a large range of activity and facilitate large organizations or productions. But the standards in these cases do not in themselves reveal new information. There is no inherent relationship between age sixteen and driving ability. It is a rule-of-thumb intervention to allow a population to have some control over a certain activity. This is an instrumental use of standardization.

In epistemological standardization, the efficacy of certain medical treatments, for example, or the confirmation of adequate severity of illness to justify treatment, is increasingly known or confirmed as true, based on standardized measures. For example, in mental health care, severe depression may be primarily known by a certain score on a depression symptom survey. This instrument, manifested through a summary score, is thought uniquely able and sufficient to identify and conclusively find a real, defined entity, clinical depression. This is a different way of knowing than knowing driving ability from date of birth. The latter sorts persons, but does not assert unique knowledge about them. Epistemological and instrumental uses of standards interact and reinforce each other in a way that smoothes what were highly contested claims to authority, into comfortably predictable routines. The epistemological claims of a standard—what it says, truly, about reality—and debate surrounding it can recede with routine of use, and the standard then becomes habitually enforced and authoritative.

Managed care may represent such a transition from epistemological to instrumental standardization, from using standard measures as tools for more accurate knowledge about disease and treatment, to relying on such scores, protocols, and algorithms for their instrumental convenience in managing the needs of large numbers of people. Acceptance of instrumental standards often relies first on making a successful epistemological argument (e.g., "Let us sort by age because it really directly measures a true ability"). And, in turn, seemingly scientific epistemological claims about a standard are believed and gain credibility because they dovetail nicely, they are comfortably "framed," with other social forces seeking to commodify, control, and/or standardize behavior.

Managed Care as a Claim to Science

The most salient feature of managed care is its assumption of and reliance on an asserted ability to know things through generalizable, aggregate measures (Belkin 1994). Managed care would not be possible without some convincing argument that better knowledge of what is efficacious or appropriate action in a medical, usually doctor-patient encounter, is obtained outside that encounter by individuals with no direct familiarity with the patient. Others can know better by having access to selective summary data about a patient, and it is legitimate to compare such summary data for an individual to that of a population as a way of determining the proper action for a given individual.

The swift ascendancy of this approach to medical decision making needs to be explained. To do so by saying it is obviously correct is to be naive about how other regimes of explanation became successful. But to explain it by saying it is *better* is a real starting point. *Better* demonstrates how understanding medical information some new way enables us to do things we could not do before, and thus invites a more appropriate line of questioning: What needs changed such that organizing ourselves and our knowledge this way was of interest?

It is, and never was, "obvious" that managed care is the answer to cost control in medicine. Political and economic "realities" may not have—because they hadn't—resulted in managed care without the technocratic wish and its fulfillment. Jim Morone and I have argued elsewhere that overcoming physician authority over clinical matters and thus their control of health care dollars has been a decades-long goal. It became successful when a scientific rationale for doing so became available through picking up, and in ways transforming, the claims of health services research (Morone and Belkin 1995). Health services research represented a reductionism long criticized in medicine, but in this way was able to assert scientific superiority and identification (Frankford 1994). Managed care architect Paul Ellwood saw outcomes and other standard measures and research tools for comparing population experience as potential new "technology" capable of supplanting clinical discourse with a more precise and measurable "universal language to communicate hurting, functioning, working, interacting and living" (Ellwood 1988: 1551).

"The role of biomedical science is to generate ideas and technologies; it is the role of the evaluative sciences to provide the necessary clinical information linking treatments to outcomes" (Wennberg 1992: 67–71). Evaluative science could displace clinical judgment because of the latter's newly recognized subjectivity. Health service research allowed replacement of "a matter of great subjectivity ('clinical judgments') to a matter of such objectivity that patient care decisions could be reviewed and affirmed or denied by individuals who did not even see the patient" (Gray 1992: 64).

This eclipse of individual expert clinical judgments by standardized aggregate measures suggests the kinds of questions I have been suggesting. How did subjectivity and objectivity get divided up and parceled along these lines with subjective doctors opposed to objective protocols, algorithms, and standardized care formats? How, even more basically, did objectivity become valued? Why did the famous practice variations of John Wennberg (1992) (where physicians in even closely related geographic areas had wide variation frequencies for performing certain medical procedures that were unexplained by patient characteristics) become a problem? Very respectable and productive medical traditions found variations natural and expected (Howell 1995).

Health services researchers and managed care providers might argue that they became a problem when they were discovered to exist, following the gradual development of powerful objective techniques to study physician practices. But the analysis I have been developing here would tell a different story. The problematic nature of variations was not a problem discovered. Its problematic nature required many other things first in order to present such problems. In particular it required a desire to predict and standardize medical practice and a belief that one could do that with methods and measures felt objective, scientific, and thus fair. The necessity of these measures needed to be sold as they were not obviously necessary or uniquely scientific, nor do they remain uncontentious. Their unique objectivity would not have been convincing without buyers, that is, without people whose goals resonated with such understanding of these methods.

Hence the particular importance and relevance of efforts to portray tumultuous changes in the health care system as historically continuous normality and business as usual. Karen Davis and others in a *Health Affairs* essay saw managed care as part of an interest in capitated systems of care "back to the early 1900's" (Davis, Collins, and Morris 1994: 179). A recent extensive review of managed care and its ethical and legal implications saw managed care as part of a long "prepaid" medical history from 1800s "slave owners . . . contract[ing] with panels of local physicians on a capitated basis" (Zoloth-Dorfman and Rubin 1995: 339). Claims about the historical lineage of effectiveness and outcomes measures reach Codman's work, resurrected to become the father of the new medical marketplace. Bernard Bloom (1986) placed Codman as part of the tradition of prospective controlled trials, although Codman is actually a latecomer in his story. Daniel's argument to Nebuchadnezzar's guards to allow demonstration to show the safety of food he wanted to eat is placed by Bloom at the outset of this apparently continuous tradition. Joel Howell's (1995) important study of technology and standardized practices in hospitals argues that Codman was essentially a John Wennberg without a computer. Codman found affinity with other agendas. Susan Reverby's (1981: 171) review of Codman finds that the "effectiveness and efficiency" associated with the health planning era have Codman as a forefather, and thus legitimator: "If the current moves to undermine most public health planning are successful, we will have a contemporary example of the difficulties Codman faced."

But this risks historical sleight of hand. Is Codman's efficiency what 1970s health planners had in mind? Wennberg? How should we compare efforts to scrutinize medical work? Indeed, Reverby (1981) cited Archie Cochrane's (1971) *Effectiveness and Efficiency* and Alvan Feinstein's (1967) work as part of one twentieth-century thread of interest in measuring medicine, first grabbed by Codman. These writers and others invoked as forebears to the "technology" of health services research, if not managed care, might have shared an interest in how aggregated data clarifies clinical questions. But this can mean, and be motivated by, many things.

What they each responded to, what they each hoped to change about medical practice, what other scientific projects they wished to pursue or answer, what other social interests and actors expected from them, or whom they wished to court, were quite varied (Cochrane 1971; Feinstein 1967; Hill 1962; Meehl 1954).

Codman's story is not just a curiosity. Particularly because he is invoked by supporters and analyzers of changes in the medical marketplace, the easy association of Codman and others to a single tradition of rigorous medical critique, gives credence to the objective, stable, scientifically and logically accumulating nature of medical measuring. It also hides from view the more coherent history within which to place managed care—a history of the technocratic wish, of agreeing to find knowledge in certain standardized and usually quantified measures. When considered in context, the way Codman does not fit the managed care project underscores this analysis. In particular, his is more an instrumental standardization. Codman's case demonstrates the varied meanings and purposes that the idea of standardization can take.

Codman's Science, Codman's Market, Codman's Standards

It is not hard to find in Codman a fellow traveler of managed care executives and market enthusiasts.[2] In a handout entitled, *Fundamental Differences in the Problem of the Management of a Manufacturing Business and That of a Charitable Hospital* (c. 1915), Codman was skeptical of reducing health care to just any commodity transaction. But he clearly wanted to emulate certain tenets of business practice and logic. They resonate throughout his work, including the idea that goods be based on their value to, and sensitive to demand by, others; that products be predictably consistent, that is, by knowing the name or identification of the product one can reliably know what one is going to get; that the *laborer who* gets paid is capable of delivering the finished product—he is not paid for privilege or reputation enhancement. In "A Study in Hospital Efficiency," Codman approvingly saw "Insurance Companies [as] differentiating between one hospital and another, according to the actual service that can be rendered to their client," and assuring that they "conduct their affairs on the basis of actual accomplishment" (Codman 1914: 26).

But do not presume that Codman's agenda was concerned with costs, or that the outcomes that interested him would be about efficiency or measures of the value of certain medical interventions. Codman illustrated how universalizing such terms misleads. He swam in a sea of notions about efficiency and the purpose of standardized measurement that differ from those that occupy our current attention.

Codman's work revolved around his "End Results System." This system essentially involved the completion of an index card that contained information on a patient's symptoms or presenting condition for which he or she sought relief, the doctor's diagnosis, the treatment plan, the complications of that treatment plan prior to hospital discharge, and the patient's condition one year later. Any errors in diagnosis, plan performance, or morbidity from the treatment were also classified according to certain categories such as errors in technical skill, errors due to poor equipment, and patient's refusal of treatment.

In order to characterize this work, several things need to be understood. First, Codman was concerned with hospital-based work and with hospitals as institutions. Codman was a formidable and prominent participant in efforts through the 1920s by the American College of Surgeons (ACS) to detail standards expected of hospital staffing, equipment, facilities, and practices, and which led to the creation of the Joint Commission on the Accreditation of Healthcare Organizations. The ACS work successfully altered expectations of physician training and services in hospitals so as to move away from what ACS Director John G. Bowen described as "institutions that are boarding houses and that . . . are unworthy of the confidence and support of their communities" (Bowman 1918). The hospital was identified as a public space and professional workshop for detailing and enacting those expectations. Physicians were expected to have certain training and available equipment, staff, and record keeping. This role of the hospital as the vehicle for the medical profession consolidated early in the twentieth century. It was where the profession laid out the possibilities of competence and excellence of its professionals and their training. This is how the hospital moved from charitable moral steward to a source of medical knowledge (Stevens 1989; Rosenberg 1987).

The second point is that Codman's work was viewed contemporaneously and by himself as part of (if not seminal for much of) a hospital efficiency literature. This was efficiency of a particular type for a particular purpose: for dedicated, trustworthy professionals to best maximize their brilliance and obvious gifts, and make good on the public trust and resources that they so obviously deserved.

An exploding hospital management literature reflected this. One illustration in the *Boston Dispensary Quarterly* (1913: 16) portrays the concept of hospital efficiency as a spoked paddle wheel churning in a literal "stream of public benevolence." The spokes of this wheel are the hospital's mission, labeled with such items as the teaching of students, the education of the public ("to cooperate with physicians"), the treatment of acute illness, and the provision of aftercare. "If any of the spokes of the paddles are lacking, much of the energy of the stream is wasted." G. Sherman Peterkin (1914), an admiring Codman correspondent and the author of works on medical efficiency, detailed numerous "efficiencies," from the positioning of furniture to white surfaces (allowing for easy glances to check cleanliness and thus conserve physician time) aimed at enhancing the ability of physicians to concentrate easily and effortlessly on their tasks and realize their expert role to relieve humanity. S. S. Goldwater (1916), another Codman correspondent, detailed in the pages of *Modern Hospital* the "efficiencies" of various organizational and administrative practices. The aim again was to offer a predictable, manageable, smooth organization of a small community to limit distractions, and mistakes, and thus enable skilled individuals to perform their best.

Efficiency was explicitly tied to endorsement of the kinds of knowledge and activities physicians claimed that they could perform and that hospitals were being fashioned to provide. In a paper by prominent Massachusetts General Hospital (MGH) physicians (Washburn and Bresnahan 1915), a Codmanesque scheme using an "End Result Card" to track patients is described that contained admission data and one-year follow-up. Also described were efforts to match certain surgical procedures with the practitioners who primarily specialized in them in order to improve their success. The aim of doing all this was not to minimize fiscal risk or open up MGH to consumer scrutiny, or to use such data to establish set algorithms and pathways of patient experience. For these MGH physicians, "efficient" data gathering and patient selection enhanced a science focused on physician-based emerging new technology and subspecialties. When evaluating hospital efficiency, "such an institution does its full duty only when it contributes to the common fund of what may be termed 'hospital knowledge'" (ibid.: 1). These efficiencies included the opportunity for cooperation in one location between disease subspecialists, and the advent of new technologies such as electrocardiography that required hospital resources but could provide new prognostic information for "efficient" care. The hospital was seen as a creative, newly appreciated place for new knowledge; efficiencies assisted brilliant men to realize this potential.

Standards and efficiencies were to enforce behaviors, not learn what they should be. Knowledge of success or failure, good or bad care, was not known from the measure. It was known by unquestioned, professionally based skills. Codman's data collection systems were to ensure that such skills would be performed and physicians held to them. Such standards would help purify and assure a direct connection between those skills and their receipt by patients.

A Standard Is Not a Standard, A Market Is Not a Market

Yes, Codman wished to apply standards, as did much of early-twentieth-century medicine, particularly for the performance of surgery in hospitals. But these were to offer monopoly to certain methods and sources of expertise considered a priori right and good. His was not a claim that certain things were better known by summarizing disparate phenomena and identifying a mean. It was not a claim to the unique powers of inference to characterize medical encounters. His standardization was more traditional: to assure compliance, to use rules or standard practices to promote certain previously preferred behavior, not to learn. It was similar to the use of standardization in large firms or organizations in order to diminish variability and enhance comparability of product or task performance, and predict and control the costs of production, method of distribution, or use of products.

Managed care found in standards new valid knowledge with which to override physician judgment. In this case, standard measures not only implement action, they are the source of relevant knowledge. For example, in mental health care, a symptom checklist score or deviation from an average frequency of visits for a given diagnosis is often treated as sufficient information that enables one to "really" know a patient's condition or needs. The score or number is primary knowledge and sufficient data to characterize what is wrong with someone or the adequacy or excess of their treatment (Belkin in press; Jayaram et al. 1996). This epistemological use of a standard was not Codman's goal.

Implications

Hospital standardization in the early twentieth century operationalized a consensus of the medical elite as to what counted as medical expertise. Managed care is still in the midst of challenging what counts as such expertise. In this light, managed care may very well be at a transition point where the epistemological importance of standardization gives way to the instrumental. Dissent over the validity of basing knowledge claims in summations of patient experience that represent all patient experience may give way to the seemingly settled matter of that question, indeed, amnesia as to its controversial nature, and simple focus on its implementation.[3]

The conflict of subjective judgment versus objective algorithms and standardized formats only appears as an opposition now. It may not remain so. But we can anticipate how and where resolution or further conflict will lie. Changes in the practices and etiologic paradigms in medicine often require accompanying acceptance by physicians of related, changed, social identities. If other changes in medical practice are any guide, such as the acceptance of the hospital as a standardized product, we can expect the success of managed care to rely on either a changed authority and place for physicians as the arbiters of what is scientific in medicine, or physician acceptance of it in ways that reconcile the new practices and related social identity with still having unique scientific expertise.

Nineteenth-century changes in medicine have been particularly well studied to show how this happens. Scientific models and interventions in medicine had strong moral and social meanings. These meanings played a critical role, not only in solidifying certain agendas within medicine such as germ theory or the use of pharmacology such as anesthesia, but in acceptance of and enthusiasm about these developments by others. The consolidation of allopathic medical "orthodoxy," for example, was enabled, if not permitted, by a hotly debated therapeutic and moral identity of the physician that could convincingly address the various problems raised by reliance on drug treatments such as the division of labor between natural and personal intervention (Warner 1986; Pernick 1985). The acceptance of germ theory also demonstrates how crafting an associated and acceptable social identity is critical for deeming beliefs and practices in medicine as scientifically credible. Germ theory diffused among physicians when it could be incorporated into an identity of the physician as the source of evaluation and intervention for individual patients, and where the uniqueness of patients and thus the specifically derived treatments of individual physicians justified centrality of the doctor-patient relationship (Latour 1988).

Newly voguish algorithms and generalized measures may be less easily digested by such an individualized professional identity, but the tumult around these techniques reflects a battle to remake or readjust the social identity of physicians that comes with them (such as the profession's ethical self-understanding, training goals, and the value of its evaluative expertise). A flurry of writing in bioethics around managed care is one example of a discipline trying to grapple with this realignment of scientific and social identity (Belkin in press). The success of that makeover will very much shape the scientific "advance" attributed to these techniques. Physicians may offer a convincing, socially satisfying, and fiscally realistic notion of their judgment as of primary scientific value, or may make over their identity as technicians carrying out and refining aggregate data sets and protocols, or may cede authority to others over what information is really scientifically important for assessing medical encounters.

Aside from what managed care may mean to physicians, it may have appeal to others if it is successfully allied with and understood as a needed rejection of privileged influence, much as Codman's work was. Quantification may have a bad name among many scholars. It is characterized as a tool to manipulate objectified objects and to create an illusory "natural," and too often, oppressive language of normal and abnormal (Hacking 1990). But the frequency and enthusiasm with which it is often seized and embraced by those unempowered is less seriously considered by scholars. The metric system was aggressively advocated by radicals because basing measures in nature substantially undermined the authority of the nobility over commerce and social life (Rusnock 1995). In health care there are many examples of often radical and persecuted advocacy groups finding respectability in identifying their cause as instead a problem of assessment and research. As I mentioned, Planned Parenthood turned contraception from a social cause into a scientific problem and medical question of how to measure fertility, thus altering its place in American politics and culture.

Statistical inference was pursued specifically for its superficiality, its measurement of broad and not individual experience, by a host of thinkers including Auguste Comte, Etienne Condillac, and Karl Pearson. It was precisely this ability to isolate more general variables and phenomena that would permit more open and egalitarian debate about social questions. Claims by elite "experience" would then lack unique authority (Porter 1995). Those who wish to retain physician-based medicine and the ideal of a physician as individual advocate and counselor will need to answer the implications of physician discretion, particularly how it may be understood as threatening to those forces behind managed care.

But inasmuch as standards may serve these purposes, they are then implicitly socially framed and mediated values with a range of implications that can either order and enhance, but also tyrannize, aspects of our lives (Freidson 1986). The metric system was also opposed by rural populations that found their own power and control over their lives better secured in locally based traditions of measurement.

The technocratic wish shows the use of a specific historically contingent notion of objectivity as a tool to reach agreement on how to solve contentious problems, permit inclusion of previously excluded interests, and/or allow social or economic forms of organization to argue to themselves and others that their authority or deployment of capital is guided by objective knowledge, because they can no longer efficiently rely on, or trust, expert judgment. They then seek reassuring, or more advantageous, roots of knowledge elsewhere.

The grasp for what history often shows to be an illusory (or at least not unique) objectivity helps parcel out power in a way that justifies the resulting pattern of winners and losers as naturally "necessary." Engaging managed care means engaging and not further implying transcendent and obvious logic to the claims of scientific uniqueness which enable the new medical marketplace to move on and settle into a routine that could transform our lives.[4] Managed care may be the necessary intervention to manage and save an unwieldy and costly health care system. Making and meeting standardized expectations of health care may very well offer an excellent and consistent level of quality in a predictable and reliable fashion. My point here is that scholars and policy makers should examine how we justify and enter the routine of using these tools. Otherwise, we lose sight of the options we do have, the multiple ways of assessing, intervening in, and organizing health care, and the interests and agendas behind the particular development of the provision of health care, this time.

Notes

An earlier version of this article was presented at the *Journal of Health Politics, Policy and Law* Conference: Health Care into the Next Century: Markets, States, and Communities, Duke University, 3–4 May 1996. I am grateful for the responses of the members of that audience. I also wish to thank the patient and insightful comments on the manuscript by Mark Peterson and Maria Schiller. This article was supported by funds from the Robert Wood Johnson Foundation.

1   Or, "The Science Illusion," which is the title of a paper by James Morone and myself (1995), whose spin on his book title, *The Democratic Wish* (Morone 1990), inspires this label. Our paper argues that the use and behavior of health services researchers is the critical element enabling diverse forces to cohere around the practice of managed care, that is, for this practice to seem sensible and convincing. This interpretation neatly fits the theory of Bruno Latour as to how scientific work allies and mutually transforms social interests (see Morone and Belkin 1995; Latour 1983).

2   For access to Codman's work and associated materials, I wish to thank Dick Wolf and the staff of the Countway Library of Medicine, where the Codman Papers are deposited and cataloged.

3   The result of which could be removing each of Kenneth Arrow's (1963) "special characteristics" of medicine that have been assumed or studied by students of health care for over thirty years. These were the unpredictable nature of demand, the limited self-interest as a motivation of provider decision making, and the uncertainty of outcome when entering a medical transaction.

4   A compelling example of the rapid remaking of routine health care discourse is a recent *Newsweek* cover story that compared and rated HMOs. The article perseverated on what measures assess HMO quality; which HMOs measured their own work most vigorously was a critical part of the rating each was given. Several large insurers that use standards and protocols to evaluate their own providers declined to participate in this survey, citing that the methods *Newsweek* was using to assess *them* were primitive (Spragins 1996). Whether patient or insurer, the dialogue about medicine and where we locate authoritative assessment of it has shifted markedly. Whether it offers assurance to anxious patients, monitors doctors, or negotiates the oversight of payers, talk about medicine is talk about the credibility of certain aggregate measures, and the politics of health care may well be dominated by contest over their derivation and implementation.

The Doctor as Businessman:

The Changing Politics of a Cultural Icon

Deborah A. Stone

Every medical care system is embedded in a culture, a set of ideas about what medicine is and how it ought to be practiced and distributed. The culture of medicine includes ideas about the causes of illness, the nature of healing, responsibility for illness and health, and the role of private and public institutions in providing medical care. One important aspect of the culture of medicine is its understanding of the role of healers and the relations between healers and those who would be healed. Central to these issues is the place of money in healing. How does money influence the mind and practice of the healer, and what role does money play in the relationships between healers and patients?

Over the last two decades in the United States, these aspects of the culture of medicine have radically changed. We have reconfigured the place of money in medicine. We have gone from believing that financial considerations should have no bearing on doctors' clinical judgment to thinking that they should be central to it. From the mid–nineteenth century through the first half of the twentieth century, the cultural figure of the doctor evolved from a businessman to a professional. In the late twentieth century, the doctor has been reconceived as an entrepreneur who is now in the business of insuring patients as well as caring for them. This article describes these transformations, examines their implications for the practice of medicine and the doctor-patient relationship, and explores the political uses of cultural myths in the health care system.

Erecting a Wall between Money and Medicine

Before the mid–nineteenth century, healing was simultaneously a craft and a business, and a healer worked much like a shoemaker or a barber.

(In fact, many barbers were healers.) The healer set up a practice. People came with their problems, or the healer visited them in their homes. The healer sized up the problem and offered remedies, most of which he or she made and sold. The business relationship between the healer and the patient was simple: The patient paid some money in exchange for the healer's advice, skill, and medicines.

As medicine became professionalized, the role of money in the doctor-patient relationship became highly controversial. To be perceived as something more than commercial salesmen, physicians wanted to create an image that their decisions were motivated by something other than profit. Professionalization, the transition from a craft to a profession, required above all that physicians project an image of competence. To assure the public that they were motivated by knowledge and altruism rather than by self-interest, they elaborated a system of lengthy training, examination, credentialing, licensing, and monitoring (Starr 1982: chap. 10). The entire organization and ideology of the profession was meant to show that doctors' decisions and recommendations were dictated by the best interests of the patient and by science—and distinctly not by the pecuniary interests of the doctor.

This is not to say that doctors were not entrepreneurial. After all, the system of credentialing and limiting entry into the profession was constructed quite intentionally to enhance the profitability of doctoring. However, early medical organizations justified these market restrictions as necessary to protect patients' health, not doctors' incomes. The image of being motivated by the public's health, not the profession's business interests, was important to medicine's political claims for powers of self-regulation.

Two campaigns by the American Medical Association (AMA) at the turn of the century illustrate how the medical profession sought to consolidate its authority and distinguish itself from ordinary commercial businesses and quack healers (Starr 1982: 127–134). In a campaign against patent drug manufacturers, the association supported muckraking journalists in revealing how patent drug makers were merely "sharks" after people's money. The AMA established its own department to evaluate patent medicines, and it refused to accept advertisements in its journal from companies who also advertised directly to the general public. A similar campaign was conducted against makers of infant-feeding formulas. "The proper authority for establishing rules for substitute feeding should emanate from the medical profession, and not from non-medical capitalists," declared Thomas Rotch, a prominent pediatrics professor at Harvard Medical School (quoted in Apple 1980: 406). These policies were designed to weaken and eliminate other kinds of healers by per-suading the public that doctors evaluated and prescribed medicines solely on scientific grounds, with no consideration of financial interests. That drug and formula advertising was a main source of revenue for the fledgling professional organization, and that doctors might therefore have some economic motivations for prescribing particular drugs and formulas, was never discussed.[1] The public story was that doctors prac-ticed medicine untainted by the influence of money.

When academic social science began to examine medicine in the 1950s, the problem of motivation—Was it money or was it something else?—was at the heart of its inquiry. Talcott Parsons, the pioneer of medical sociology in the United States, declared that, "unlike the role of the businessman," the role of the medical practitioner is "collectivity oriented, not self-oriented" (Parsons 1951: 434). However, the normative and empirical social science traditions were at odds. The normative claim that physicians (and other professionals) *should* not be motivated by commercial considerations conflicted with empirical knowledge that commercial interests did play a role in medicine. Three years after Par-sons's work became the locus classicus in American social science schol-arship on medicine, the *Yale Law Journal* published an in-depth exam-ination of the American Medical Association, revealing its unionlike and lobby-group activities on behalf of the financial self-interests of its mem-bers (American Medical Association 1954). With few exceptions, though, writing in academic social science, policy circles, and organized medi-cine all danced around the issue of money and motivation. There re-mained an unresolved tension at the heart of medicine, a tension be-tween medicine as a scientific profession and medicine as a business.

To see how a policy elite creates a culture about the relationship be-tween money and medicine, it is useful to consider the following diagram from a West German health policy textbook of the late 1960s (adapted from Herder-Dorneich 1965). This was the first health economics/health policy textbook in West Germany, and its presentation of the West Ger-man national health insurance system captured and then perpetuated a widespread self-understanding about the system (see Figure 1).

The lesson of the picture and the textbook is that the organizational structure of health insurance removes money and money considerations from the doctor-patient relationship. Money and financing *are* important in the health system, the book acknowledges, but clever organizational design protects the core of medicine, the doctor-patient relationship, from the influences of money. Patients belong to sickness funds or pa-tient associations, which handle all financial dealings. Doctors belong

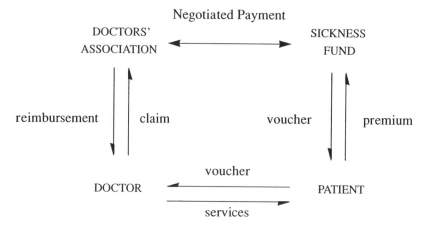

Figure 1.

to doctors' associations that handle all their financial transactions. Sickness funds and doctors' associations negotiate contracts for the method and amount of physician payment. Patients receive an open-ended voucher from the sickness fund, and beyond giving the voucher to their doctor (or doctor's staff), they have no financial discussions or money exchanges.

The point here is not that money doesn't influence behavior in the German system—it does and always did—but rather that German political culture emphasized the moral importance of removing the influence of money from the doctor-patient relationship. The political system created a health insurance system with the express purpose of insulating the doctor-patient relationship from financial motivations, and the intellectual culture that grew around health policy perpetuated the image that the organizational solution worked.[2]

Something similar happened in the United States. No single image comparable to the German diagram represented the American health care system, in part because the United States never had a unified health financing system. However, two stories about the relation between medicine and money evolved, stories that served a similar function: They countered patients' fears that medical decisions might be determined by pecuniary considerations.

The first story was the professional self-discipline story. Accordingly, the medical profession was its own watchdog and policed its members. Doctors who put pecuniary interests before patients' health interests would be driven out or stopped. In this story, organized medicine eliminated commercial motivation by selecting high-minded students for medical school, by socializing them during their training, and by enforcing a code of ethics that put patients' interests first. Talcott Parsons's (1951, 1975) writing exemplifies social science that accepted the profession's claims at face value. Paul Starr's (1982) history of the professionalization of healing exemplifies social science that analyzed the professional story as a political claim.

The AMA's *Principles of Medical Ethics* from 1957 explicitly promised that medical judgment would not be influenced by financial interest: "A physician should not dispose of his services under terms or conditions that tend to interfere with or impair the free and complete exercise of his medical judgment and skill or tend to cause a deterioration of the quality of medical care" (quoted in Rodwin 1993: 270).

In claiming to protect medical care from financial influence, the association implied that separation of clinical judgment and financial interest was possible. The idea that fee-for-service payment, the dominant arrangement (and the only payment method sanctioned by the AMA at the time) might itself "interfere with or impair" medical judgment was not acknowledged by the association.

As with Parson's (1951, 1975) academic writing, the normative claims and empirical realities about self-discipline were at odds. Many studies starting in the 1960s showed that self-disciplinary mechanisms were weak at best and that they rarely, if ever, monitored financial conflicts of interest (Derbyshire 1965, 1969, 1974; Freidson 1975). Other research suggested that different modes of paying physicians influenced the volume and kinds of services they provided. In particular, fee-for-service payment seemed to increase the volume of hospital services compared to capitation or other closed-end payment methods (e.g., Klarman 1963; Donabedian 1969; Perkoff, Kahn, and Haas 1976). The cultural backdrop for these studies expressed a clear moral imperative: Ethical medicine meant money would not be a factor in medical decision making. The new findings about money's influence on medical decision making and about the profession's failure to eliminate money's influence were conveyed with a tone of revelation, even mild shock. Organized medicine's public story, and the story medicine's public wanted to hear, was the story that doctors were not businessmen.

The second story about money and motivation in medicine is the insurance story. As health insurance grew after World War II, especially with the expansion of doctor-controlled Blue Cross and Blue Shield plans for the middle class, insurance was named a "third party" and described as a neutral go-between that handled the money aspects of the doctor-patient relationship. In this story, no money changes hands between doctor and patient, or at least, only small token amounts are collected at the doctor's office. Patients pay premiums to insurers, and insurers reimburse doctors and hospitals. When patient and doctor meet, they talk and think about illness, diagnosis, and treatment—not money.

Private health insurance was promoted to the American middle class on two promises. First, health insurance would free people from worry about financial considerations when and if they needed medical care. The advertising of Blue Cross/Blue Shield, as well as that of commercial insurers from the 1930s through the 1960s, conveyed the idea that hospital care and family doctors were essential to good health but expensive, and that only if people were insured could they be assured of access to this essential and costly care (Rothman 1991). Second, Blue Cross, in particular, promoted its plans to the middle class with the subtle but unmistakable message that health insurance meant not being treated like a poor person, not having to use the public hospital, not crowding oneself into a ward. Access to health care, the advertisements implied between the lines, was indeed connected to money. Quality of care was connected to money as well—whether one had a family doctor who would treat disease early or whether one was in a ward or a private room. Health insurance, whether commercial or nonprofit, was promoted as a way to remove financial considerations from doctors' and hospitals' decisions about how to treat. Insurance was the great equalizer of patients seeking care (Rothman 1991, 1994).

Just as the professional self-discipline story had a rather different face in reality, so did the insurance story. As soon as private health insurance began catching on, doctors began resisting what they plainly understood as the imposition of nonmedical decision makers between them and their patients. In the early decades of the century, professional societies opposed "contract medicine," an early form of employee health insurance in which large companies hired doctors to provide medical care for their employees and often financed it through compulsory payroll deductions. Professional societies especially objected to the control over physician fees exerted by the companies, and their ability to recruit doctors who would accept reduced rates (Starr 1982: 200–204). In 1934, only five years after the start of the first Blue Cross plan, the AMA issued guidelines for what it considered acceptable private insurance arrangements (AMA 1934). These guidelines show just how clearly organized medicine understood that medical insurance would indeed insert financial considerations into clinical judgment, not remove them as the public advertising claimed. The first principle stated: "All features of medical service in any method of medical practice should be under the control of the medical profession." The second held: "No third party must be permitted to come between the patient and his physician in any medical relation." The third insisted that "patients must have absolute freedom to choose a duly qualified doctor of medicine who will serve them from among all those qualified to practice and who are willing to give service." The fourth principle was that a "confidential relation" between patient and physician "must be the fundamental and dominating feature of any system." Finally, the tenth principle declared: "There should be no restrictions on treatment or prescribing not formulated and enforced by the organized medical profession."

One gets the uncanny sense that medical leaders in the 1930s were writing paper shields against what would eventually happen by the 1990s. Both medical leaders and insurance leaders knew all too well that insurance would have exactly the opposite effect of that promised in the public relations story. Instead of guaranteeing patients that their care would not be influenced by financial considerations, insurance would ensure that money would be an unwelcome boss at the bedside. Reading the AMA's 1934 Principles makes one realize just how prescient medical leadership was, and how long the profession was able to resist control by insurers.

There were obviously elements of naïveté or denial that made acceptance of these two stories possible. If the professional leadership believed, as it apparently did, that the selling of medical services distorts medical judgment and deteriorates quality of care, then it had to ignore the fact that medical services were always sold and that the profession had been defending doctors' financial interests all along. If it acknowledged that doctors did (and had to) sell their services to make a living, then it had to pretend, as it did in its *Principles of Medical Ethics,* that at least some financial arrangements and commercial relationships did not distort clinical judgment. A similar kind of denial and naïveté clouded the public mind and minds of policy makers, who delegated authority for self-regulation to the medical profession while ignoring the conflict of interest that self-regulation posed.

The idea that clinical judgment should be completely untainted by financial considerations had been the strong moral norm in American political culture for the last century. Organized medicine maintained the facade, although with increasing difficulty after the mid-1950s. In all its formal principles and regulations on medical ethics, payment arrangements that might distort doctors' clinical decisions were formally forbidden, and by and large "didn't happen." Fee splitting between general practitioners and specialists to whom they referred, physician investment in pharmacies, and any arrangement that enabled doctors to profit from referrals or from sales of remedies they prescribed were all branded as unethical (Rodwin 1993).[3] Any evidence of the existence of these practices was treated as high scandal. "Why Some Doctors Should Be in Jail" was the title of one article about fee splitting in 1953; "Fee splitting was like venereal disease used to be," wrote a New Jersey newspaper. "It existed, but nice people didn't talk about it" (both quotations from Rodwin 1993: 34). According to Marc Rodwin, these practices became so common after the mid-1950s that organized medicine could no longer gain consensus on condemning them in its formal statements on ethics. Nevertheless, throughout the 1980s, findings that physicians were accepting any form of compensation for referring patients, prescribing drugs, or using medical devices were presented with a tone of muckraking horror and treated by news media as well as government agencies as fraudulent and unethical. To be influenced by money in medical judgments was to be immoral, and was sometimes even grounds for dismissal from the profession.

The German and American health financing systems are usually taken as expressions of opposite political values and norms. To Americans, Germany represents belief in the full socialization of health financing and faith in public sector control and operation of insurance. The United States represents the other end of the spectrum: belief in individual responsibility for the costs of illness, distrust of government, full faith in the private sector, and the nearly complete privatization of health insurance, with Medicare and Medicaid as exceptions to the normal pattern. With respect to the deeper political culture about money and medicine, however, the two nations have been very similar. Both operate on a widely shared belief that the practice of medicine should be based as purely as possible on scientific knowledge, and that the influence of money on clinical judgment and clinical practice should be minimized, and even eradicated.

Reconfiguring the Role of Money in Medicine

The theorists of market reform and managed care reversed the traditional norm that medicine, and especially the doctor-patient relationship, should be immune to pecuniary interests. On the contrary, they extolled the power of financial motivations to control medical costs by shaping physician, hospital, and patient behavior. From Clark Havighurst's efforts to apply antitrust law to the medical profession, to Paul Ellwood's advocacy of HMOs, to Alain Enthoven's promotion of managed competition, the proponents of market-driven medicine saw financial motivation as a natural force that could not be resisted but that could be exploited to improve the quality and distribution of medical care (Havighurst 1974, 1977; Ellwood 1970, 1973; Enthoven 1978a, 1978b). The essence of managed markets was to harness commercial motivation as a regulating device. In what is probably the single most important document of the cultural transformation surrounding medical care, Alain Enthoven began his 1978 Shattuck Lecture to the Massachusetts Medical Society with a justification of why he, an economist, should be giving this distinguished lecture instead of a doctor (1978b). He found his answer by redefining the central problem of medicine. It was not simply how doctors could use medical knowledge to make people healthier, but rather, how people could "most effectively use their resources to promote the health of the population" (1229). After dismissing government regulation as ineffective, he offered as the alternative changing "the basic framework of financial incentives within which the health-care industry operates" (ibid.). The key issue in health care costs, he said, was "how to motivate physicians to use hospital and other resources economically" (1230). It was time, he concluded, for physicians to look beyond the physical and biological sciences as they crafted the art of medicine, and to draw on "the decision sciences," by which he meant cost-effectiveness analysis, "a synthesis of economics, statistics, probability and decision theory applied to the complex and uncertain problems of medical decision-making" (1236).

Here was the first bold statement of the great reversal. Medical decisions should no longer be purely clinical. They should be based, at least in part, on economic consequences for society. These economic consequences could be made to influence medical decision making by translating them into financial incentives for physicians and patients. In Enthoven's (1978b) vision, research physicians would help health care plans develop clinical guidelines that incorporated cost-effectiveness analysis, plans would give practicing doctors incentives to follow these guidelines, and if patients were given the opportunity to shop for plans in an open market, the most cost-effective plans would win greater market share.

Alain Enthoven did not originate the idea of using financial incentives to influence clinical decision making. Many prepaid group practices, HMOs, and other new forms of payment were already in operation at the time of his lecture, and he drew on their experience. Enthoven did, however, articulate more clearly and forcefully than anyone else a complete theory of a new moral economics of medicine. His theory promised that medical care could be reorganized to use objective, scientific knowledge about costs and effectiveness and thereby bring about a more efficient and equitable health care system. We could, as the title of his lecture promised, cut costs without cutting quality.

Hand in hand with the cultural reassessment of the role of money in clinical judgment came a change in the way medical care was understood as a social system. Once money became a positive force, medical care could be viewed as a pure market relationship. The patient would become a consumer of services, the doctor a seller. Money, in the form of price signals, would aid buyers and sellers in maximizing their own interests. What could be more benign, even beneficial? There were some potential troubles, Enthoven pointed out. Overly strong cost-control incentives might "lead to inadequate service." Moreover, "a doctor could benefit financially by discouraging high-risk patients from continuing their enrollment with him." But, he reassured, there were safeguards against these problems, "the most important of which is the freedom of the dissatisfied patient to change doctors or health plan" (Enthoven 1978b: 1233).

In market theory, consumer choice was the absolute best source of discipline for producers. The hitch in applying classical market theory to medicine, though, was the assumption that the consumer who paid for a product was the same person who used or consumed it. By the late 1970s, when market theory took hold among health policy analysts, no one could pretend that the patient and the payer were the same person. The language of "third parties" was everywhere. Yet health economists and others promoting free markets in medical care glossed over the separation and talked vaguely of the power of health care consumers to vote with their feet. Market rhetoric was politically appealing because it seemed to reconcile a deep political conflict over who would control medical care—insurers or patients. Market imagery suggested to insurers that, as purchasers of care, they would gain control, while it suggested to patients that they, as consumers of care, would gain control (see Havighurst 1986).

In this light, it is not surprising that the language of consumerism was also adopted and promoted forcefully by a movement that was essentially a patient revolt against professional authority in medicine. Parts of the women's movement and the consumer movement of the 1960s joined in the women's health movement, which self-consciously used the imagery of markets and consumers to symbolize a more equal power relationship between doctors and patients (Dreifus 1977; Ruzek 1978). Thus, the market model offered not only the possibility of controlling costs by turning medical care into a pure business relationship, but also the possibility of improving health by empowering patients to participate in their own care.

In a sense, what ensued was a contest—albeit unequal—between these two very different conceptions of a market in medical care: the neoclassical market theory conception, where the payer was king, and the consumer movement conception, where the patient was king. The consumer movement conception required a "patientry" backed by money. Patient consumers could have power vis-à-vis doctors only if they controlled what economists call demand—the willingness to purchase services backed by the resources to do so. By the time the consumer movement came along, health insurance was the major source of money for purchasing medical care, so what patients really needed was health insurance plus the power to control their insurance. They needed to be able to take their insurance certificates to any doctor and hold out both the possibility of purchase and the possibility of taking their business elsewhere.

The idea that patients, as policyholders, could control the source of payment for their medical services was never realistic. Insurance, after all, is a pooling of funds and a giant collective agreement that the pool will pay for medical care for those who need it. What people didn't understand when they purchased insurance was that they were agreeing to let *their* money be used for other people's medical care as long as they didn't get sick. They were, in effect, giving up control of their money to administrators of the collective insurance arrangement. The appeal of individual medical savings accounts in current policy debates is precisely that they permit individuals to control at least that source of payment for their care.

Indeed, insurance, the sector that controlled the money, was able to prevail with its conception of a market in medicine. Insurance, here, includes not only private, for-profit firms we conventionally think of as insurance companies, but any payer and part controller of an insurance plan: federal and state agencies that operate Medicare, Medicaid, and other health insurance programs; employers who operate self-insurance plans or who control and contribute to other plans for their employees; and, of course, nonprofit plans such as Blue Cross/Blue Shield (several of which are now converting to for-profit). For insurers, the essential purpose of shifting to a market model of medical care was to control costs (or generate more revenues, in part by controlling costs). Since, from payers' point of view, doctors are the ones who generate costs, the market model meant that insurers, not patients, would gain power over doctors.

None of this is to say that, suddenly in the 1970s, commercial motivation entered medicine. Physicians are and have always been paid for their services, and any mode of payment creates financial incentives, willy-nilly. Under the predominantly fee-for-service payment system of yore, the financial incentives were primarily for doctors to provide more services of all kinds. Under the new payment systems of managed care, the incentives are primarily for doctors to provide *fewer* services of all kinds. The existence of incentives is certainly not new, only their direction.

The really dramatic change, though, is not in the fact or even the direction of financial incentives, but in our cultural assessment of them. We have gone from thinking that medicine should not be a commercial enterprise (and pretending that it wasn't) to promoting a system of medical care in which doctors are subordinated to financiers. We have gone from believing financial considerations should not influence medical judgment to thinking that financial considerations should be important, perhaps even sometimes determining, considerations.

What brought about this cultural change? One factor is surely the rise of market-oriented thinking in policy discourse more generally, along with declining faith in the ability of government to solve social problems (see Kuttner 1996; Hodgson 1996). But equally important is the failure on the part of both health institutions and government to discipline the traditional fee-for-service payment system and to bring health care costs under control. With costs for taxpayers and employees skyrocketing and seemingly no end in sight, old cultural beliefs in the sanctity of the doctor-patient relationship gave way to a more tough-minded acceptance of the thing that had always been denied: Doctors' clinical judgments *are* influenced by their business interests, and the incentives they face can be manipulated by payers. For their part, many doctors came to accept the introduction of explicit financial incentives into their clinical practice because they were told it was the only alternative to the bogey of government regulation (see, e.g., Enthoven 1978b: 1237; Moore 1979).

Remaking the Doctor as Entrepreneur

As a cultural figure, the doctor who emerged from the nineteenth century was a professional, above motivation by financial gain. As late as 1957, the AMA's *Principles of Medical Ethics* made it unethical for a physician to sell services under any terms that would "impair the free and complete exercise of his medical judgment" (quoted in Rodwin 1993: 270). In the new syllogism of late-twentieth-century medical economics, the doctor is an economic actor just like everyone else: Scarce resources are a fact of life; medical care is consuming more and more social resources; doctors are the key decision makers about consumption of medical care; ergo, doctors should internalize the costs of their clinical decisions so that medical consumption can be brought under control.

The old payment systems—fee-for-service, salary, and capitation—had been shown to have some apparent influence on doctors' clinical decisions, but they were not enough. Salary and capitation might make each doctor conserve his own time, but unless there was a way to bring *all* the costs generated by a doctor's recommendations and prescriptions back to his doorstep, there could be no serious cost containment.

Sometime in the 1980s, health insurers began a radical change in payment. They no longer paid doctors by one simple method, such as capitation, salary, or fee-for-service. Instead, the doctor's pay was linked to other medical expenditures through a system of multiple accounts, pay withholding, rebates, bonuses, and penalties. There are innumerable variations on the general method, but the main elements are these. Health insurance plans divide up their revenues—the premiums—into funds for different kinds of services. In addition to a fund for primary care doctors' pay, there might be funds for specialists' fees, prescription drugs, emergency room visits, and ancillary services such as physical therapy, laboratory tests, and X-ray and other imaging studies (Physician Payment Review Commission 1995a). Primary care doctors receive some regular pay, which might be based on salary, capitation, or fee-for-service. Crucially, part of their pay is calculated at the end of an accounting period and based on the financial condition of the other funds after all the bills for other services have come in. Typically, the plans also withhold part of each doctor's pay.

The most complete picture of HMO payment methods still comes from Alan Hillman's (1987) survey of all 595 HMOs operating in 1987, of which half responded.[4] Already at that time, fully two-thirds of the HMOs routinely withheld some of each primary care doctor's pay. These "withholds" are the real financial stick, and the mechanism through which plans make doctors share in the financial risk of health insurance. Doctors may eventually receive all, part, or none of the withheld pay. The amount of the withholds varies, but the most typical rate was between 11 percent and 20 percent of pay (used by 45 percent of the plans that withheld). Eleven percent of the plans withheld between 1 and 10 percent of pay; 8 percent of the plans withheld 21 to 30 percent of pay; and 2 percent (seven plans) withheld more than 30 percent of pay.

Withholding doctors' pay might be expected to have a significant impact on their clinical decisions by itself, but 30 percent of the HMOs imposed penalties beyond the withholds for physicians who "overspent" in other accounts. These penalties might be applied by increasing the amount of a doctor's withholding the next year, decreasing a doctor's regular capitation or other rate, reducing the amount of rebate from surpluses in future accounting periods, or even placing liens on a doctor's pay. Another indicator of the strength of financial incentives is how much a doctor's income can vary each year as a result of a plan's financial incentives. According to the Physician Payment Review Commission's (1995: 234) survey in 1994, a doctor's pay could vary by more than 20 percent in one-quarter of all plans and in nearly half (46 percent) of network and IPA-model HMOs.

In some HMOs, the amount of rebate a doctor receives is tied directly and only to his or her own behavior—whether he or she hospitalized too many patients, ordered too many tests, referred too many patients to specialists, or prescribed too many drugs. In other plans, each doctor's rebate is tied to the performance of a larger group of doctors.[5] Forty percent of plans in the Hillman survey made primary care doctors pay for patients' lab tests out of their own fund or a combined primary care-lab test fund. These arrangements all make doctors keenly aware that a significant portion of their pay is linked to their willingness to hold down the amount of care they authorize.

Is it possible for doctors to resist the influence of financial incentives on their clinical judgment? As more patients are insured by HMOs— about 70 million in 1995—doctors virtually must work for HMOs to have access to patients who can pay. As a few insurers gain control of large market shares—and as one or two HMOs come to dominate a local market—doctors may not even have any choice about which HMO to affiliate with.

One might suppose that by keeping some organizational distance from HMOs, though, doctors can preserve a modicum of clinical freedom, some ability to keep their medical judgments unimpaired by the financial terms of service. Perhaps doctors who remain in independent practice and join IPA-type HMOs would have more freedom than those who join a staff-model HMO. The group-practice model (where an HMO contracts with a single group practice to provide services to its members) and the network model (where an HMO contracts with multiple group practices) might provide intermediate levels of clinical freedom. Hillman's (1987) survey, however, suggests otherwise. The looser the organizational relationship between doctors and an HMO, the tighter the financial control: only one of the twenty-nine staff-model plans (3 percent) used withholding; 45 percent of group-model plans, 59 percent of network-model plans, and 83 percent of IPA-model plans used it.

We know that financial incentives are there on paper, but how do they influence doctors as they go about the daily business of evaluating patients and recommending referrals, tests, and treatments? As Himmelstein and Woolhandler (1995) noted, to the extent that doctors' pay is reduced by any referrals they make, the new incentives are the reverse of financial kickbacks. The primary care doctor gets a bonus, a greater rebate, or less of a penalty for *not* referring each patient to a specialist. Similarly, larger rebates or lower penalties for *not* authorizing emergency room visits, diagnostic tests, or procedures are the equivalent of kickbacks for withholding these kinds of care. Of course, the point of medical gatekeeping under managed care is precisely to reduce medically unnecessary specialist and emergency room visits, diagnostic tests, and procedures. However, under managed care, financial as well as clinical considerations now very explicitly enter the primary care doctor's decision about whether a specialist referral, test, procedure, or emergency room visit is "necessary." Under these new payment methods, the criterion for doctors' decision making is changed from *medically necessary* to *medically necessary for the patient and financially tolerable for the primary care doctor.*

In the structured market theory of Enthoven (1978a, 1978b) and others, the new forms of organizing and paying for medical care were *supposed* to change the criteria for medical decision making, but not in the way that the new incentives change them. Instead of asking whether a test, procedure, or referral might have any net benefit for a particular patient, the doctor is supposed to decide on the basis of cost-effectiveness analysis.[6] If cost-effectiveness were to become a criterion of clinical decision making, it would require that doctors consider the probability of "success" as well as the cost of care for each patient.

However, the way the new managed care payment systems are structured, financial incentives do not push doctors to think about cost-effectiveness, but rather to think about the impact on their own income of authorizing care for individual patients. It may be that doctors try to use their knowledge of cost-effectiveness studies to help them make the difficult rationing decisions they are pushed to make, but the financial incentives built into managed care do not in themselves encourage anything but personal income maximization as a decision criterion.[7] Under managed care, doctors are no longer sellers of medical services, but rather something like "negative salespeople" for insurance plans—they are rewarded for selling fewer services, not more.

Because doctors in managed care often bear some of the risk for costs of patient care, they face some of the same incentives that govern commercial health insurance companies—incentives to seek out healthy customers and avoid sick or potentially sick ones (Stone 1993). Sometimes these incentives may come in the form of explicit directives from managers. In California, the chief of a large university hospital told doctors in a memo that their HMO could "no longer tolerate patients with complex and expensive-to-treat conditions being encouraged to transfer to our group" (Parrish and Sloane 1995). The memo went on to explain: "We have experienced a dramatic increase in patients joining our medical group with recently diagnosed conditions that require expensive treatments. We do not receive additional funds from contracting health plans when this occurs. In some cases, we are forced to provide tens of thousands of dollars of care in the course of a single month."

More commonly, the incentives to avoid sick patients are between the lines of physician payment contracts, but are still all too clear. Many doctors have described their acute awareness of a linkage between their pay and the illnesses of particular patients. Here is how David Blumenthal, a doctor who is also a health policy analyst, explained his bonuses one year:

> Last spring I received something completely unexpected: a check for $1200 from a local health maintenance organization (HMO) along with a letter congratulating me for spending less than predicted on their 100 or so patients under my care. I got no bonus the next quarter because several of my patients had elective arthroscopies for knee injuries. Nor did I get a bonus from another HMO, because three of their 130 patients under my care had been hospitalized over the previous six months, driving my actual expenditures above expected for this group. (Blumenthal 1996: 176)

Blumenthal went on to detail the medical conditions of the three patients who accounted for his lack of bonus. This kind of consciousness of a link between specific patients and individual paychecks is not likely to make doctors think that their income depends on how cost-effectively they practice, as market theory would have it. Rather, they are likely to conclude, with some justification, that their income depends on the luck of the draw—how many of their patients happen to be sick in expensive ways.

The payment system thus converts each sick patient, even each illness, into a financial liability for the primary care doctor. Doctors' awareness of the direct link between a patient's problems and their income loss can easily change their attitudes toward sick patients. Many doctors have noted how, under managed care payment plans, they come to resent sick patients and to regard them as financial drains. One doctor described his relationship with an elderly woman who had chosen him as her primary care doctor in a Medicare managed care plan. Shortly after she enrolled, she was diagnosed with inoperable cancer, and her bills drained his bonus account:

> At a time when the doctor-patient relationship should be closest, concerned with the emotions surrounding death and dying, the HMO payment system introduced a divisive factor. I ended up resenting the seemingly unending medical needs of the patient and the continuing demands placed on me by her distraught family. To me, this Medicare beneficiary had effectively become a "charity patient." (Berenson 1987: 12)

The financial incentives under managed care profoundly change doctors' relationships with illness and with people who are ill. Illness becomes something to avoid rather than something to treat. Sick patients become adversaries rather than occasions for compassion and intimacy.

Here is the source of the most profound change wrought by managed care insurance. Health insurance marketing in its early decades (the 1930s to 1950s) promised to keep subscribers out of the wards, to lift them above the base care they could expect as charity patients. Managed care insurance, doctors and patients are beginning to realize, renders all its subscribers charity patients. It lays bare what was always true about health insurance: The kind of care sick people get and whether they get any care at all depends on the generosity of others. All insurance involves redistribution from those who don't incur losses to those who do. Classic indemnity insurance, by pooling risk anonymously, masking redistribution, and making the users of care relatively invisible to the nonusers, created the illusion that care was free and that no one had to be generous for the sick person to be treated. It was a system designed to induce generosity on the part of doctors and fellow citizens. Managed care insurance, to the extent that it exposes and highlights the costs to others of sick people's care, is calculated to dampen generosity.

Putting the Doctor Businessman to Work

The insulation of medical judgment from financial concerns was always a fiction. The ideal of the doctor as free of commercial influence—the moral incompatibility of doctor and businessman—was elaborated by a medical profession that sought to expand its authority and its market. The fiction was maintained by the medical profession through most of the twentieth century, because doctors' public support in policy battles, as well as their economic support in terms of clientele, depended on convincing the public that doctors base their decisions on medical science, not profit.

Now, the opposite ideal—the image of the doctor as ethical businessman whose financial incentives and professional calling mesh perfectly—is promoted in the service of a different effort to expand power and markets. Corporate insurers use this refashioned image of doctor as businessman to recruit doctors and patients. The new image has some appeal to doctors, in part because it acknowledges that they need and want to make money in a way the old ethical codes didn't, and in part because it conveys a sense of independence at a time when clinical autonomy is fast eroding. Through utilization review and prior authorization, insurers are taking clinical decisions out of the hands of physicians, lodging authority instead in their own reviewers, who often are not doctors, or in outside organizations with whom they contract to review records and make clinical decisions in specific cases. Drug formularies (lists of drugs a plan will cover), hospital length-of-stay rules, and exclusive contracts with medical device suppliers are some other ways that insurers remove discretion from clinical doctors.

In contrast to this reality of diminished clinical authority, images of the doctor as an entrepreneur, a risk taker, and as "the 'general manager' of his patient's medical care" (Enthoven 1978b: 1233) convey a symbolic message that clinical doctors are still in control. If they practice wisely, in accord with the dictates of good, cost-effective medicine, they will succeed (to paraphrase Enthoven) in raising income without cutting quality.

A good example of the recruitment function of this rhetoric is an article published in the *New England Journal of Medicine* in 1979 by the medical director of United Health Care. The article was a thinly disguised puff piece aimed at persuading doctors (the primary readership of the magazine) that this new type of network HMO helps them fulfill "their desire to control costs rather than allowing more governmental regulation of the health care industry" (Moore 1979). The article's description of the physician payment system lionizes the independent, sole-proprietor entrepreneur who can manage his business efficiently:

> Incentives encourage the primary-care physician to give serious consideration to his new role as the coordinator and financial manager of all medical care. . . . The purpose of these incentives is to

give the primary-care physician a vested interest in the costs of care so that he will help to co-ordinate care in the most cost-effective way. Because accounts and incentives exist for each primary-care physician, the physician's accountability is not shared by other physicians, even among partners in a group practice. . . . Each physician is solely responsible for the efficiency of his own health-care system. . . . In essence, then, the individual primary-care physician becomes a one-man HMO. (Moore 1979: 1360)

The image of entrepreneur suggests that doctors' success depends on their skill and acumen as managers. It plays down another reality of managed care payment systems—the degree to which doctors' financial success *and* their ability to treat all patients conscientiously depend on the mix of sick and costly patients in their practices and in the practices of other doctors with whom they are made to share risks.

The image of doctor as businessman that was so negative in the past has been recast to appeal to patients as well, as insurers and payers try to persuade them to give up their indemnity insurance and move into managed care insurance. Doctors, the public has been told by all the cost-crisis stories of the past two decades, have been commercially motivated all along. They exploited the fee-for-service system and generous health insurance policies to foist unnecessary and excessive "Cadillac-quality" services onto patients, all to line their own pockets. Patients, the story continues, have been paying much more than necessary in order to obtain adequate, good-quality medical care. Doctors have shown they cannot be trusted, so insurers will take on the role of consumer protectors and medical advisers. By changing the financial incentives facing doctors, insurers and payers will help patients get what they deserve: value for money. Insurers will make sure doctors' financial incentives are perfectly aligned with the imperatives of good-quality, scientifically proven medical care. Under the good auspices of insurers, doctors will be converted from bad businessmen to good businessmen. Thus, to paraphrase Enthoven (1978b) again, managed care offers patients the possibility of cutting costs without cutting quality. With the money they save, they'll even be able to buy more medical care than they were getting before.

If patients knew how much clinical decision-making authority was actually removed from their doctors in managed care plans, they might be more reluctant to join. The marketing materials of managed care plans typically exaggerate the independence and autonomy of primary care doctors. They tell potential subscribers that their primary care doctor has the power to authorize medically necessary services, such as referral to specialists, hospitalization, X-rays, lab tests, and physical therapy. The actual contracts in many cases give the HMO the power to authorize medically necessary services, and more importantly, to define what services fall under the requirements for HMO authorization or approval. But doctors in these marketing materials are portrayed to consumers as the ones who "coordinate" all care, "permit" patients to see specialists, and "decide" what care is medically necessary (Green, Kohn, and Lee 1995).

In the marketing materials of managed care, doctors not only retain their full professional autonomy. Under the tutelage of people with management expertise, they also work a kind of magic with economic resources. Through efficient management and adherence to the principle of cost-effectiveness, they actually increase the value of the medical care dollar. Enthoven promised far less—only that "spending can be reduced with no discernible loss in benefit to the patient" (Enthoven 1978b: 1234). The recruiters for managed care plans promise more: "patients get *better* and *more coordinated* care at a lower cost," as two executives of a managed-care plan put it in an op-ed essay (Paris and Vernick 1995: 21). "Because of our expertise in managing health care," a letter to Medicare beneficiaries from the Oxford Medicare Advantage plan promised, "Oxford is able to give you *100% of your Medicare benefits and much, much more*" (Green, Kohn, and Lee 1995: appendix).

In an era when employers and governments are seeking to reduce their financial commitments to workers and citizens, the image of the doctor as efficient manager is useful, persuasive rhetoric to mollify people who have certain political expectations of benefits. To lower their costs, employers are cutting back on fringe benefits to their workers and shifting jobs to part-time and contract employees, for whom they have no obligation to provide health insurance. The federal government is similarly seeking to modify its legal obligations to citizens in order to cut back the costs of Medicare and Medicaid. The image of doctor as businessman, as an efficient manager who can actually increase the value to patients of the payer's reduced payments, help payers gain beneficiaries' assent to the reduction in their benefits. Thus, the cultural icon of doctor as businessman has become a source of power for employers and governments as they cut back private and public social welfare commitments.

Notes

Thanks to my father, Stephen Stone, for his superb clipping service and for numerous provocative discussions about managed care. Thanks also to Jim Morone, Mark

Peterson, and Mark Schlesinger for their thoughtful comments on earlier drafts of this article.

1 Thomas Rotch was no small medical capitalist himself. From his chair at Harvard Medical School, he promoted a complicated method of prescribing and mixing infant formula. In 1891, he established a company to produce individualized infant formulas according to doctors' prescriptions and to deliver the formula directly to mothers' homes. His company, which he called Walker-Gordon Laboratory, eventually had branches in several major American cities and London (see Apple 1980; Cone 1979: 136–138).

2 West German social science had its clash between empirical and normative traditions, as in the United States. Thus, *Lobby in Weiß* (Rauskolb 1976), an exposé about the pecuniary motivations of the medical profession, became a best-seller.

3 As Rodwin (1993) noted, however, the AMA never did prohibit doctor *ownership* of laboratories and diagnostic facilities, although it was clear that doctors' proprietary interests would and did encourage them to liberally refer patients to their own facilities.

4 All figures on managed care payment methods in this section are from Hillman 1987, unless otherwise stated. Hillman continued to follow up the original survey in 1988, and published a further analysis of data in Hillman, Pauly, and Kerstein 1989. A third report based on a survey of 260 HMOs in 1988 is in Hillman, Welch, and Pauly 1992.

The Physician Payment Review Commission sponsored another survey in 1994, but its information is in many ways less concrete and less precise. It was a telephone survey, rather than a mailed, written questionnaire; it included only 138 HMOs; its questions were more vaguely worded. It often asked respondents to characterize their impressions about how often or how important something was, rather than asking whether or not some method was used, so that much of the information is not very precise and not comparable to the Hillman data. For example, to determine how plans select physicians, it asked respondents whether various kinds of information about doctors had "major value" or "limited value" (see Gold et al. 1995; Physician Payment Review Commission 1995a: chap. 10).

5 Eighteen percent of all plans used this method in Hillman 1987; 15 percent used it in Hillman, Welch, and Pauly 1992.

6 Cost-effectiveness analysis is a technique that can be applied only to large groups. Enthoven (1978b) thought that insurance plans should make use of cost-effectiveness analysis to make broad coverage decisions, but he also meant for doctors to use it in their decisions about individual patients: "The development of cost-effectiveness analysis is needed because of the extreme complexity of medical decision problems. I recognize that these decisions require difficult judgments in the face of uncertainty, with wide variations in the responses of different patients. . . . But I believe that physicians need help from other disciplines in the development of a set of aids to decision comparable to those developed in other fields" (1236). Because cost-effectiveness measures use aggregate outcomes in a large population to calculate the rate of success (effectiveness) of any procedure or intervention, they can tell us the *average* cost per patient of a successful outcome, but not the actual cost for any one patient. Thus, it is not clear how a physician is supposed to apply cost-effectiveness analysis in deciding about individual patients.

7 Most plans make some use of "practice guidelines," which are guidelines for diagnosing and treating specific diseases, and which often are developed using some cost-

benefit analysis (Physician Payment Review Commission 1995a). Most plans also say that they even monitor doctors' compliance with practice guidelines. However, when the Physician Payment Review Commission survey asked plans about the criteria they use to determine physician compensation, compliance with practice guidelines was not even one of the options given by the survey (237). In the absence of different information, it would be hard to argue that managed care payment methods give doctors an incentive to follow practice guidelines.

Part 2   *The Market in Practice*

The Dynamics of Market-Level Change

Paul B. Ginsburg

n Orange County, California, health plans are pressed to lower premiums by powerful purchasing cooperatives and employers' and employees' willingness to switch plans to get a better price. The plans, in turn, are demanding lower prices from hospitals and physicians, who can no longer avoid competing to be included in networks because most of their patients are in some type of managed care. Medical groups are consolidating and organizing themselves to contract with health plans on a capitated basis to deliver care profitably within that rate (Ginsburg and Fasciano 1996).

Though somewhat further along the path toward a competitive health care market than other communities, Orange County exhibits the dynamics that we see in many communities across the country. Health care has not been devoid of competition in the past, but it was less pervasive and took very different forms. Physicians competed for patients on the basis of reputation and referral relationships, hospitals competed for patients by attracting doctors to their staff on the basis of facilities and support, and insurers competed to sell policies on the basis of keeping administrative costs down and building potent sales forces.

But competition in health care today has moved closer to patterns in other service industries. Price is a much more important factor. Entities are larger, both to achieve scale economies that are more important to survival and to gain power to charge higher prices for their services and pay lower prices for the resources they must buy. Vertical integration, whether through ownership or through complex contracts, is increasingly pursued to coordinate care better or to increase market power.

This essay attempts to provide an overview of the dynamics shaping competitive health care markets today. With little research available on the dynamics of health care markets today, this article draws heavily on the trade press and conversations with consultants, leaders of health care organizations, and other researchers. It has been influenced a great deal by the RWJF Community Snapshots Study (Ginsburg and Fasciano 1996). The process of designing a longitudinal study of health care in a sample of communities also contributed by requiring consideration of where changes were likely to occur, and by asking which changes would have relevance for public policy (Kemper et al. 1996).

Overall, these sources were rich in examples of the forces affecting health care market participants and their strategic behavior to deal with those forces. They were less useful in determining the pervasiveness of forces and behaviors, and even less so in documenting the impacts of these organizational changes on care delivered to people. Nevertheless, a synthesis of what is known at this point helps set priorities for research and helps decision makers who must act before more research is available.

This essay begins by outlining a framework for examining markets. Then it describes the forces outside the health care system that are affecting health care markets. These include both forces that motivate action on the part of entities in the health system and developments that provide new tools with which to respond to pressures. A discussion follows on the major components of the health care system, describing the pressures that each experiences and how they are responding. These responses, in turn, pressure other system components, which then respond.

Framework for Examining Markets

Much is made of the blurring of roles of health care organizations today. Some hospitals are providing managed health plans and management services to physicians. Some insurance companies are delivering primary care through ownership of clinics. The organization of health care is best discussed in terms of functions performed and the organizations performing them. For example, one functional component is insurance: accepting responsibility for the cost of care in return for a fixed payment. Whether performed by a traditional insurer or a provider organization, some entity must accept the risk of service use and implement mechanisms to control it. A distinct function is organizing the delivery of health care services.

The organizations that provide each function in the health care system are impacted by an array of forces. For example, insurers or health plans face the prospect that employers or individual purchasers will switch to a competitor that is offering a lower price or a better product. They also face demands by providers for higher prices or changes in practice patterns that involve increased use of new technologies.

Whether to survive or to prosper, each organization devises strategies to respond to these forces. Continuing with the health plans example, organizations might develop managed care products to obtain better prices from providers and to gain some control over the volume of services provided to enrollees. These responses would, in turn, be seen by organizations comprising the other components of the health care system as forces that must be dealt with. The increased role for and evolution of managed care, for example, leaves hospitals to deal with lower unit prices and empty beds. The process is dynamic, in that each organization's responses to external competitive forces changes the environment for other organizations, which in turn react. Although this process may tend toward an equilibrium, continuing influences from outside the system, and the time required to perceive the forces and then to design and implement strategies to respond to them, are likely to make the process seem to be one of continual change.

Although the forces affecting different health care markets are similar, the dynamics of market response are likely to differ across markets. For example, markets with strong hospital systems are more likely to have change led by hospitals. In Portland, Oregon, for example, three major hospital systems have developed organizations that include either a captive insurer or an exclusive arrangement with a large insurer and a network of physicians. But in markets without strong hospitals, the health system may be led by physician groups (Orange County) or by health plans (Minneapolis–St. Paul).

External Forces

Some of the powerful forces that are causing change in health care markets originate outside the health care system. Four seem particularly noteworthy:

- increased pressure on purchasers for cost containment
- development of information technology
- management innovation in service industries
- advances in medical technology

Both private and public purchasers face increased pressures to contain health care costs. Part of these pressures come from the increasing portion of health care costs in their budgets. When health benefits are 12 percent of payroll, there is more motivation to address their costs than when they are 3 percent. But part of these pressures come from outside the health care system.

For private purchasers, increasing competition in the general economy forces more attention to reducing costs. Many markets have been deregulated. Reductions in transportation and communication costs expand the reach of enterprises so that more competitors, including foreign ones, are present in many markets. Threats of takeovers and more aggressive shareholders motivate managers to strive for lower costs even when profits are high.[1]

For public purchasers, increased attention to limiting deficits, combined with strong resistance to tax increases, has increased the urgency to contain costs in the Medicare and Medicaid programs. Local governments encounter similar situations in their support for provision of services to those without health insurance. With tax revenues unlikely to grow more rapidly than incomes, but with health spending traditionally having grown much more rapidly than incomes, the pressures to contain costs in public programs have become more acute. Pressures for change may become particularly intense if the Medicaid entitlement with its matching federal funding should be capped or turned into a block grant. Under either approach, states will gain one dollar for every dollar that spending is reduced, in contrast to thirty to fifty cents under current law.

Developments in technology are a mix of eternal and internal forces affecting health care. External ones include new medical procedures originating from advances in computer technology, materials technology, and basic research in health sciences. Internal ones come from the development of new medical technology taking its cues from the medical marketplace, such as receptivity to improvements that are more costly, and demand for cost-saving innovation. Although it is difficult to monitor whether the external component of medical technology advances are increasing or decreasing in costs, some have argued convincingly that the future direction will be toward increases in costs (Schwartz 1994; Goldsmith 1994).

Developments in information technology are likely to provide new opportunities for cost containment. Current abilities to analyze claims or encounter data inexpensively, development of the computerized patient record, and advances in networking that extend the ability to provide large amounts of information on-line are creating many opportunities to identify effective practice patterns, support clinicians with this information, and motivate them to change practice styles.

Management innovations in other industries are providing the health care industry with new tools to contain costs. For example, total quality management, developed elsewhere, is being applied increasingly in hospitals. Other mechanisms to assure quality in other service industries may find applications in health care. Throughout the economy, new types of complex long-term contracts are being used in order to obtain some of the benefits from vertical integration without its costs. This may have inspired some of the complex contracts among health plans, hospitals, and physician organizations.

Finally, public policy has the potential to cause profound changes in health care. Beyond the pressures on public purchasers outlined here, however, much public policy in health care is not so much an external force as one that is developed in response to demands from health system organizations or consumers of health services. Note the recent attention to regulating the practices of managed care plans—minimum hospital stays for normal childbirth, "gag" rules, physician abilities to join or remain in networks—and to regulating conversions of nonprofit organizations to for-profit status. The initiatives for these policies lie with physicians, consumers, and unions of health care employees.

Components of the Health Care Market: Pressures and Responses

Those organizations subject to the external pressures outlined above are taking steps to respond to them. Many of these actions, in turn, affect other organizations, both their competitors and organizations that they buy from or sell to. For each of the major components of the health care market, this section reviews the pressures that they are experiencing and the strategies that they are pursuing to respond to them. First, it outlines strategies that appear to be relevant to most components of the health care system.

Core strategies

Three strategies for competing in health care markets appear to be important: increasing market share, increasing market power, and achieving efficiencies. In many cases, success in achieving one objective implies success in achieving one or more of the others, although in other cases, trade-offs must be faced.

Increasing market share serves two main purposes in the context of competition: decreasing unit costs by spreading fixed costs, and increasing market power. In addition, market share has implications for prestige, whether staff will be hired or fired, and other considerations perhaps not reflected immediately in the bottom line, but that are nonetheless important motivations.

Market power is the ability to charge high prices for what you produce or pay low prices for what you buy. It is a relative term across a market: If the seller has the market power to charge high prices, then the buyer lacks the market power to pay low prices. Common to all components of the health system is the fact that having fewer competitors leads to market power. This is the foundation of traditional antitrust policy. Differentiation of product leads to market power for sellers, but willingness to buy many variations of the product leads to market power for buyers. A way of characterizing market power is to ask which party in a transaction faces a greater downside if the deal falls through (Miller 1996).

Sometimes, fascination with steps to gain market power detracts attention from the equally important steps to increase efficiency. This essay is not the place to review the various strategies to increase efficiency. But competition has clearly served as a stimulus to take steps to reduce costs. Organizations have taken steps to reduce costs quickly, such as downsizing staff, but have also attempted to put into place processes that will generate efficiencies over time on a continuous basis.

Important trade-offs among these strategies may exist. For example, mergers designed to increase market share and market power may reduce efficiency. After a point, increasing the size of an organization increases unit costs. But this decrease in efficiency may be acceptable to the organization if the increased market power enables charging higher prices. Similarly, increased power to charge high prices will reduce the motivation of management to increase efficiency. Indeed, in the short run, the energy of management required to negotiate and implement mergers makes it less likely that as much attention will be devoted to achieving internal efficiencies unrelated to the merger. These trade-offs increase the importance of antitrust policies.

Private purchasers

As described earlier, some corporate benefit departments are under great pressure to contain the costs of health benefits programs. Because health benefits are a component of employee compensation, eliminating them or shifting the burden to employees makes the compensation package less valuable to employees. Except for those employers seeking to reduce overall compensation, emphasis is likely to be placed on containing costs so that employees do not perceive a proportionate reduction in the value of their health benefits. In the language of the field, the focus is on "value."

Many private purchasers are seeking to accomplish this by replacing their traditional indemnity insurance plans with managed care plans. Willingness to change plans can often lead to lower premiums. In markets with a large number of managed care plans, purchasers can exercise market power simply by being willing to change plans. Regardless of the degree of concentration in health plans, purchasers have the potential to increase their market power through the formation of cooperatives (Lipson and De Sa 1996).

Activities of organizations formed by purchasers vary according to the objectives of the sponsoring employers, their sophistication, and the structure of the health plan market. Some only standardize benefit structures so that employers can more effectively compare premium differences. Some develop requirements for data on quality that health plans must provide and require that new products be developed. Some pursue joint purchasing on behalf of the sponsoring employers. Others operate as preferred provider organizations (PPOs) to obtain provider discounts for self-insured employer plans.

The nature of private purchaser activity depends a great deal on the size distribution of employers and the extent to which large establishments are parts of multilocation firms. Many purchasers have not been very active. Union agreements, downsizing the benefits department, the importance of standardization for firms with employees in many locations, and employee resistance to managed care are some of the factors that discourage initiatives in this area.

Public purchasers

Public purchasers are under intense pressure to keep growth in spending more in line with growth in the tax base. They appear to be in transition between strategies to contain their costs. Until recently, the focus of Medicare and Medicaid was on provider payment methods and rates—areas in which public purchasers have substantial market power. But perceiving that additional provider payment cuts that do not involve more sacrifices in access to care are limited, focus has shifted toward managed care.

In shifting their beneficiary populations to managed care, the two programs have, until recently, pursued very different courses. Medicare's course has been passive and voluntary. Its only exercise of market power is the rule that plans cannot charge more for the basic Medicare benefit than the payment from the program—a rule that is very difficult to enforce. The result has been that the savings from managed care have gone entirely to beneficiaries and health plans, principally in localities where the Medicare payment rate is highest.[2] Also, despite a recent surge in interest, only 14 percent of Medicare beneficiaries were enrolled in HMOs in June 1997.

The Balanced Budget Amendments of 1997 included many important changes in Medicare policy toward managed care. The range of options for beneficiaries has been expanded a great deal and the payment formula has been revised. But the characterization of the program as passive and voluntary remains the same.

Medicaid programs are pursuing managed care much more aggressively. They have obtained Section 1115 waivers from the Health Care Financing Administration to enroll large numbers of beneficiaries in HMOs. Although beneficiaries have a choice of HMO, they usually do not have the option of remaining in the traditional Medicaid program. In this way, the programs have a better chance of capturing the savings from HMO enrollment because they are not at risk for adverse selection.

Health plans

Health plans face pressures from purchasers to provide less costly plans that still provide an extensive choice of providers, and are accountable for quality. The most common response to these pressures has been the development of managed care plans and the incorporation of management features into traditional insurance plans.

Managed care plans have pursued a number of strategies. One has been horizontal integration. Plans have merged with others to improve geographic coverage (making them more attractive to employers seeking to offer a limited number of managed care plans), to increase market share, to take advantage of scale economies in marketing and administration, and to increase market power in relation to both purchasers and providers.

Some plans have entered new markets. This holds the potential to spread some of the fixed costs of development of data systems and management systems across more enrollees. In addition, it provides an opportunity for an organization to employ its skills in markets that are less competitive. Some analysts believe that expansion into new markets should await exhaustion of opportunities to expand in existing markets (Ginsburg and Grossman 1995).

Health plans have taken other steps to broaden their networks. Responding to consumer demands for a wider choice of providers, group- and staff-model HMOs have sought to add networks of small groups and individual physicians. Network HMOs have invited more providers into their networks. Whereas broader networks make plans more attractive to consumers, they are at odds with strategies to increase market power through product differentiation. HMOs have also sought to respond to consumers' demand for additional choice by developing point-of-service

(POS) options. The prospect of Medicaid managed care has led HMOs to contract with community health centers and other providers that serve the low-income populations that they seek to add.

Pressure on premiums has motivated plans to increase efficiency through stronger management of care. This has, in turn, led health plans increasingly to delegate this function to physician organizations. Plans contract with multispecialty group practices on the basis of capitation. Some have encouraged the development of independent practice associations (discussed in the following section) to serve as intermediaries between physicians and health plans, essentially outsourcing the function of managing utilization. In addition, plans are investing in the development of data systems to monitor practice and to support clinicians' attempts to practice more effectively. Information systems are also central to the increasing use of preventive services. Plans have also expanded the role of primary care physicians, expecting them to handle a larger scope of practice before referring patients to specialists. In some areas of the country, HMOs have contracted with organizations to provide services in a specific specialty, for example, oncology, on a capitated basis. But this has not happened in areas in which multispecialty group practices are strong. These organizations have long emphasized the synergies of having different specialties in the same organization.

Many of the responses of health plans to the pressures in the marketplace are very demanding of capital resources, at least at the organizational level. For investor-owned plans, equity markets have been receptive to demands for capital. But nonprofit Blue Cross and Blue Shield plans are limited to internal resources and debt. This has led a number of them to create subsidiaries to share ownership with investors or to convert the entire plan to for-profit status. This is consistent with historical patterns in health care, in which nonprofit status is retained unless capital requirements are too large.

Hospitals

Hospitals have had to confront market pressures for lower prices, to accept risk for the volume of services delivered per patient, and to deal with declining rates of use of inpatient services. They have responded by taking steps to cut costs and increase their market power.

Hospitals are cutting costs in ways similar to other service industries. Staffs are being cut, and remaining personnel are expected to be more productive. Total quality management programs seek to change processes of service delivery and cut staff requirements while increasing quality.

Hospital management is playing a more active role in physician decisions on care that is delivered in the hospital. This enables institutions to provide care under payment mechanisms, such as capitation or DRG payment, that shift risk to them. Hospitals are active in developing clinical pathways and profiling systems to support efforts by staff physicians to practice more effectively.

Hospitals have sought to increase both market share and market power by horizontal and vertical integration. Mergers have increased concentration in local hospital markets and provided opportunities to reduce administrative costs. They have also served as a mechanism to reduce duplication of services. When hospital systems become large, they gain market power because health plans cannot risk excluding them from their network of providers. Developing a reputation for quality can increase market power through product differentiation.

Hospitals have pursued numerous mechanisms to align more closely with physicians who practice in them. The traditional motivation—inducing physicians to admit their patients to the hospital—continues, but the bonds are potentially more complex as hospitals and physicians jointly accept risk in contracting with health plans. One mechanism is the formation of physician-hospital organizations (PHOs), which can negotiate with managed care plans to take responsibility for all services. Hospitals have also purchased practices of primary care physicians. This not only captures patients whom the primary care physician hospitalizes, but also directs referrals to specialists on the hospital staff. It also increases the attractiveness of the hospital's PHO in contracting with health plans.

Some hospitals have sought to displace the health plan as the "general contractor" for health services delivery. Today, it is the health plan that contracts with the purchaser for a fixed payment and in turn subcontracts with physicians, hospitals, and other providers. However, because many of these subcontracts require providers to accept capitation risk and take the initiative for management of care, hospitals and physician organizations have begun to experiment with assuming the general contractor role, either through vertical integration or by purchasing administrative services. Some hospitals have created HMO subsidiaries. Others are approaching large employers about direct contracting. Although seen principally as a strategy to gain market power (a mechanism to capture some of the portion of the premium retained by HMOs), the viability of this approach over the long term will depend on whether providers or health plans can best perform the function of organizing the delivery of care efficiently. This judgment will be made by the marketplace, with the weights given to costs versus quality, dependent on the priorities of purchasers and consumers and their ability to measure the latter.

Access to capital is important in hospital responses to the competitive market. It makes some institutions attractive partners for physicians, who tend to have less access to capital. In contrast with the 1970s, the share of hospitals that are investor owned has been relatively stable. This implies that nonprofit hospitals, which tend to have lower costs of capital, have found the capital resources available to them to be adequate for their needs.

Physicians

Physicians are facing numerous pressures from various components of the health system. Managed care plans have pressed for reductions in payment levels and for physicians to assume risk for service use. The former has affected specialists most severely due to their current excess supply. In addition, managed care plans encourage primary care physicians to expand the scope of their practice by making fewer referrals to specialists.

Physicians are responding, both as individual practitioners and as physician organizations. As individuals, departures from fee-for-service payment may lead to different practice styles, involving less intensity in the performance or prescribing of services. I am not aware of any research that tests this hypothesis, however.[3] Lower fee levels may be leading to more scrutiny of practice expenses on the part of physicians in an attempt to preserve net income.

Physicians are forming organizations both to increase market power in dealing with health plans and to increase their ability to contract on a capitated basis. They see the latter as a mechanism to offset lower fees with savings from reductions in utilization. Some physicians are joining group practices; the practices are in turn merging with others to achieve sufficient size to accept capitation risk and to gain market power. Some are forming independent practice associations (IPAs) to serve as intermediaries between themselves and health plans. These organizations, formed by medical societies or entrepreneurs, commonly accept capitation payments from health plans and pay physicians on a fee-for-service basis with withholds and bonuses. Physician management companies, such as PhyCor, either purchase practices or contract to manage the physician's practice. Some are taking on the role of IPAs as well.

Other physicians are pursuing similar ends by aligning with hospitals. This is accomplished either through contracts with PHOs or by selling their practice to the hospital. The recent Medicare legislation allows provider service networks (such as PHOs) to accept capitation payments directly from Medicare.

Safety-net providers

Providers that serve predominantly low-income patients, such as community health centers and public hospitals, face their own challenges from actions by purchasers and by health plans. Most important is the growth of Medicaid managed care. These providers are going from a world in which they are reimbursed on the basis of costs for services to Medicaid beneficiaries to one where this population can be accessed only through contracts with health plans and at prices that are determined by the market. Safety-net providers will also be affected by changes in Medicaid eligibility that result from the recent welfare reform legislation.

These providers are taking a variety of steps to respond to these changes. Many are merging or affiliating with like organizations, both to strengthen management and gain efficiencies and to increase their clout with health plans. Some are contracting with managed care plans that have Medicaid contracts, and others are vertically integrating into the health plan business and seeking contracts with Medicaid programs.

Consumers

In this rapidly changing health system, the implications for consumers are quite variable. For example, take the employees of a company that has replaced a traditional insurance plan with POS plans: For those who are comfortable using the providers in the network, the switch means lower out-of-pocket costs; but for those with strong attachments to existing providers who are not included in the network or whose needs are very specialized, the shift means higher out-of-pocket costs.

Much of what is known about the behavior of consumers in competitive health care markets comes from knowledge about steps taken by the organizations described previously. Employers are reducing choices of health plans and are more willing to switch health plans. But they are also pressing the plans to broaden their provider networks. For some consumers in managed care, this has led to more frequent changes in providers, but others have been protected from this due to extensive overlap in provider networks. Employer surveys show a shift in responsibilities for premiums from employers to employees (Ginsburg and Pickreign 1996). Medicaid beneficiaries have been required to enroll in an HMO in many states, but often do have a choice of plan. The uninsured may face a reduction in access from pressures on providers that traditionally serve them. Research is needed to gauge the magnitude of these pressures and the impact on access to care for the uninsured.

Consumers are responding to rising costs by enrolling in managed care plans, or by switching from PPOs to HMOs or POS plans. For those with employment-based health insurance, the proportion enrolled in conventional insurance plans dropped from 71 percent in 1988 to 18 percent in 1997, whereas the proportion enrolled in HMO or POS plans increased from 18 percent to 50 percent (KPMG Peat Marwick 1997: 28). Purchasers and health plans indicate that consumers are demanding a broad choice of providers when they choose among health plans, and that plans are broadening their networks in response, despite the potential for reduction in plans' abilities to manage care. A recent survey of consumers conducted as part of the Community Snapshot study reported a positive view of the trend toward managed care, and an expectation that managed care would reduce costs (Knickman et al. 1996). Both this study and an earlier one by Davis et al. (1995) indicated that satisfaction with managed care varies a great deal by market.

Public policy
Federal policy is often mentioned as an important force behind increasingly competitive health care markets. But in recent years, more has been due to market participants taking anticipatory steps to prepare for policies that might be enacted than to actual policies that have been implemented. Many leaders of health care organizations have reported that the Clinton health reform initiative was a catalyst for organizational change in their communities (Ginsburg 1996). Because the vision of managed competition in this proposal was consistent with the direction of market forces, organizations felt both compelled, and safe, to take initiatives to prepare for the proposed legislation. Despite the failure of the Clinton initiative, actions by other market participants validated the steps taken in anticipation of policy change.

A similar process may have taken place in response to the Republican initiatives for Medicare and Medicaid in 1995. Providers feared sharp cuts in payment rates from Medicare and a block grant from Medicaid that would reduce eligibility and increase the proportion of Medicaid beneficiaries served by managed care. Again, these initiatives were enacted in that year (though many were ultimately enacted two years later), but health care organizations took steps to prepare for managed care becoming the dominant mode of delivery for beneficiaries of public financing programs.

Perhaps the most important public policy initiative came from government's role as purchaser. Through the Section 1115 waiver program, many states have transferred large numbers of Medicaid beneficiaries from fee-for-service plans to managed care. Many anticipate that the Medicare provisions enacted in 1997 will have profound effects as well. For example, the end of the requirement that Medicare and Medicaid beneficiaries comprise a minority of health plan enrollees creates intriguing opportunities for provider organizations to offer products in a narrow geographic area (e.g., around a hospital or clinic).

An increasingly important part of public policy can be seen as a response to the developments in the marketplace. Recalling the Clinton administration's initiative for managed competition, one could say that the competition has already come to the marketplace, stimulated by the actions of both private and public purchasers. Today's policy issues are focusing on the management of competition, with government being mostly reactive to pressures being brought to bear by constituencies that have been injured by, or fear injury from, competition.

One result of market developments has been a revamping of antitrust policy. Hospitals and physicians have complained to the federal government that current policies have precluded them from developing organizations that have the potential to deliver care more efficiently and can compete with health plans. Although specific legislation has not been enacted, the Department of Justice and the Federal Trade Commission have taken the initiative to issue statements that guide hospitals and physicians on what types of ventures will not be challenged (U.S. Department of Justice and the Federal Trade Commission 1996).

Physicians and consumers have pressed governments to ameliorate what they see as excesses of managed care. These initiatives have focused on setting minimum hospital stays for childbirth and prohibition of "gag rules," which limit what physicians can tell their patients about restrictions on their practice patterns imposed by health plans. Much of this activity has occurred at the state level, but in 1996 the federal government enacted restrictions on early discharges of maternity patients. The following year, the president created a commission on quality to attempt to deal with these issues on a more comprehensive basis.

Some states have enacted other restrictions sought by physicians on managed care plans. These give physicians the right to be included in a network if they agree to its terms ("any willing provider"), or place restrictions on the ability of plans to drop physicians from networks. These initiatives have been opposed not only by health plans, but by purchasers, who are sensitive to restrictions on health plans' ability to contain costs.

Small employers and health care providers have pressed for reform of the small-group insurance market. The increasing competitiveness of insurance markets—with additional medical underwriting—may have contributed to these pressures. Many states have enacted reforms, but have been limited because their initiatives cannot apply to self-insured employers. This has changed with the passage of the Health Insurance Portability and Accountability Act of 1996 that applies rules on the portability of coverage and limits on medical underwriting to self-insured employers as well as insured products.

The health care system has long run on cross-subsidies. Hospitals have provided some degree of care to the indigent, subsidized medical education and research, and provided some services (e.g., trauma units) below cost. Some funds for these subsidies have come from grants, but in recent years, an important part has come from setting prices paid by insured patients above costs. Similarly, many Blue Cross and Blue Shield plans have served as "insurers of last resort," offering coverage to those rejected by other insurers at premiums that do not reflect the medical problems faced by these individuals. These subsidies tended to be paid for by exemptions from taxes, including state premium taxes.

But as health care markets have become more competitive, this pattern of cross-subsidies has been disturbed. Governments have begun to address how to direct resources to services that are judged worthy of additional support. With budgets tight, the approaches have tended to work through regulation of private organizations rather than subsidies with public dollars.

Academic medical centers have had some success in advocating explicit pools that are funded by assessments on either insurers or providers and are used to subsidize graduate medical education. New York State has done this in conjunction with the repeal of its rate-setting system. The federal government has debated this in a number of contexts. Creation of a pool was a provision in the Clinton health reform initiative. In the context of Medicare, the 1997 legislation directs a portion of Medicare risk payments to HMOs (the equivalent of the additional payments for graduate medical education that go directly to teaching hospitals under the traditional Medicare program) to be paid directly to teaching hospitals on the basis of their treatment of beneficiaries enrolled in HMOs.

Governments have been engaged as referees in the battles between providers (hospitals and physicians) and health plans over the role of "general contractor" (see above). When providers have contracted directly with purchasers, health plans have sought to have them regulated as insurers. Providers, in turn, have sought to be regulated in a manner different from insurers on the basis that many of the services that they are at risk to deliver will be provided by the hospitals or physicians that own the organization contracting to provide services.

Conversion of hospitals and health plans from nonprofit to for-profit status, spurred by requirements for capital and by financial stress experienced in some organizations has also engaged state governments. States have become active in developing rules to insure that charitable assets are protected and that conflicts of interest by officials of nonprofit organizations are avoided. Some of the opposition to conversions comes from those feeling vulnerable to the rapid pace of change in competitive markets, such as hospital employees and physicians.

As a result of increased attention to the implications of ownership form, the question of whether communities are receiving sufficient benefit from the tax-exempt status that is conferred on many nonprofit organizations is now being examined. Some states have developed guidelines for expected community benefits.

Differences across Communities

Although the forces that motivate components of the health system to change are similar across communities, the responses are likely to differ. Not only will some markets move more rapidly toward more competition, but the roles played by different components are likely to differ. Differences are likely in the locus of care management responsibility and the relative market power among components. Factors explaining these differences include the history of the health system, the presence of change agents, the business culture and attitudes toward community needs, and the degree of concentration in different components of the health care system.

The infrastructure to manage care may exist in health plans, physician organizations, or hospitals. In some markets, health plans are investing in the infrastructure to manage care, such as information systems and the development of clinical pathways. In other markets, health plans have not made these investments, and instead, have focused on payment mechanisms that shift risk to providers. In some of these markets, providers are managing care under capitation. Orange County is known for the efforts by large physician practices to accept capitation risk and to take responsibility for managing care. In other communities, such as Portland, large hospital systems have taken the lead in the management of care. In others, managed care plans are playing this role.

Whether health plans or providers will play this key role often depends on the history of the local health system. The long-time presence of large physician groups appears to be important to physician leadership in the management of care. Even if the static economics calls for the formation of groups, doing it takes a great deal of time, capital, and leadership. The advantages of large groups may not be great enough to overcome the lack of an established infrastructure.

For a hospital system to be in a position to play a central role in organizing the delivery of care, it needs to have developed the size and management resources over a long period of time. The difference in capabilities between systems that have been established for many years and have been working to alter practice patterns and those newly formed or that have not been addressing clinical practice is likely to determine whether hospital systems succeed in taking on this role.

Distinct from which component is taking the lead in managing care, communities differ in which components of the health care system have market power. For example, purchasers are better able to demand lower premiums in markets in which they are organized. These differences across markets are likely to persist over time, as they are due to the types of large employers in a community and the presence of leadership. Where purchasers are organized, the culture will determine whether this clout will be focused on lower prices for members of the coalition or for the entire community.

Notwithstanding the preceding discussion, some differences across communities may erode over time. Rapid communication means that the tools and techniques for managing care are available nationwide. Community leaders are aware of the experiences in other markets and learn from them. Medical and business cultures may become more similar. Health plans that operate in many distinct markets will attempt to use similar techniques where possible, as will national employers. However, success on the part of health plans or purchasers that operate in multiple markets may depend on an understanding of their differences. My prediction is that heterogeneity among markets will continue for some time.

Conclusions

Having sketched out what is known about the forces influencing health care markets and the responses and strategies of organizations, we need to emphasize what we do not know. We do not know how successful organizations will be in pursuing their strategies: Will the mergers, alliances, and affiliations accomplish more than merely redirecting the flow of patients? Will they succeed in making care more efficient? How will the excess capacity in inpatient facilities and specialist physicians be eliminated from the system? How costly will it be to health plans to maintain a broad choice of providers for most patients? And finally, how will all of these changes affect access to care, its quality, its cost, and patient satisfaction with it?

The dynamics of market forces are likely to have striking effects on the development of federal and state policies. The erosion of cross-subsidies in health care is likely to force policy makers to assess which subsidies are really important, and to devise ways to replace them with either public funds or regulated private funds. In addition, the system of *unmanaged* competition that has developed is not the one that theorists have advocated as an alternative to a regulated system. Although a system of public management of medical care markets is unlikely to be implemented as part of a grand scheme, as in the Clinton proposal, it is likely to come about piecemeal as various constituencies advocate specific remedies for problems they encounter, which they can successfully portray as affecting an important segment of the public. The result, ironically, may be much more extensive public management than had been proposed in the Clinton initiative.

Notes

This work was supported by The Robert Wood Johnson Foundation. An earlier version of this chapter was presented at "The New Competition: Dynamics Shaping the Health Care Market" conference conducted by the Alpha Center in Washington, DC, on 9 November 1995. I am grateful to Anne Gauthier of the Alpha Center, Peter Kemper of the Center for Studying Health System Change, and Mark Peterson for valuable comments.

1 Many economists believe that higher health benefits costs come from other compensation. If this is the case, then the main motivation for employers to economize on health benefits costs would be to increase the value of the compensation package without spending more on it. But in an economy in which wage increases are small but wage decreases are not seen as an option, economizing on health benefits is nevertheless linked to profits in the short run.

2 Medicare's risk-contracting program was designed to save 5 percent for Medicare by paying 95 percent of an estimate of what would have been paid if the beneficiaries had remained in the regular Medicare program. But studies show that the effects of enrollee selection—those enrolling in managed care plans have been healthier than average—has overwhelmed the planned 5 percent savings. Thus, offering a managed care option has, to date, cost the program money. The seminal study was published by Brown et al. (1993); recent studies have largely corroborated their results (Center for Studying Health System Change 1996b).

3 Such research would require data on physician contracts with health plans and on practice styles. The physician survey being conducted by the Center for Studying Health System Change (1996a) includes direct questions about the former and vignettes on the latter.

The Health System in Transition:

Care, Cost, and Coverage

Kenneth E. Thorpe

Introduction

Despite the recent failure of Congress and the Administration to reach agreement on broad-based health care reform, few periods in recent history have witnessed a more dramatic transformation of the health care system. Over the past decade, regulatory approaches for controlling costs used in several large states, as well as the Medicare and Medicaid programs, have gradually been replaced by market-driven approach. to health care. "Managed" care has replaced more passive models of pure indemnity-style coverage in the private sector. Rate-setting systems pioneered in many of the northeastern states have been replaced by more competitive models in New Jersey and Massachusetts. Dramatic changes have even transpired in states historically wed to rate setting. New York recently passed legislation that replaces its hospital rate-setting system with a competitive model. Under the new law, private payers are no longer locked into regulated rates; instead, they may negotiate their payments with hospitals. This approach represents a major sea change in the philosophy of hospital payments for patient care, graduate medical education, and the uninsured in New York.

Moreover, there is increasing evidence that the Medicare and Medicaid programs are following the lead of the private sector. Managed care in the Medicaid program continues to expand rapidly, accounting for 40 percent of all beneficiaries in 1996. Although Medicare has lagged behind the trend, the Balanced Budget Act (BBA) of 1997 could, according to the Congressional Budget Office (CBO), increase the number of Medicare beneficiaries enrolled in managed care to over 30 percent by 2002 (CBO 1997).

The explosion of market forces has produced substantial changes in the delivery of health care. Many sectors of the health care industry have posted record low rates of expenditure growth. The health care delivery system, responding to changing signals and incentives, has seen large-scale mergers on both the purchasing and supply sides of the market. Both moves are touted as efforts at generating economies of scale, as well as enhanced bargaining power on the demand side: moves that ostensibly are associated with increased "efficiency." On the other hand, other indicators of performance are less encouraging. Although competitive forces appear ready to slow the growth in expenditures, an intricate web of pricing cross-subsidies used by providers to finance care for the uninsured as well as graduate medical education has also been exposed. The potential elimination of these cross-subsidies has raised concerns that levels of care for the uninsured and funds for financing graduate medical education could erode.

The growth in competitive contracting has placed tremendous financial pressure on providers, who have traditionally included the costs of caring for the uninsured and training young physicians in their charges to patients with insurance. Unleashing market forces apparently has slowed the growth in patient care expenses for those with insurance; at the same time, it has the potential for reducing care to the uninsured and revenue available for medical training for resident physicians. Competition may be well suited to continue to slow the growth in health care spending: This remains an empirical question. It seems less well suited to address the other major issues in public importance: caring for the uninsured and financing graduate medical education. This article outlines the growth in competitive forces, comments on its initial impacts on patient care costs, and discusses the broader social issues of caring for the uninsured and providing graduate medical education.

Trends in the Private and Public Health Care Delivery System: The Rise in Competitive Contracting and Managed Care

Rising interest among large health care purchasers in reducing the growth in health care spending has sparked several fundamental changes in the health care delivery system.[1] The tool of choice for employers to control costs is managed care. As of 1996, an estimated 75 percent of employees were enrolled in some form of managed care (KPMG, Peat Marwick 1996), compared with 55 percent enrolled in managed care during 1994. In general, large health care purchasers have relied on health care "plans" (here, broadly meant to include commercial insurers as well as Blue Cross plans) to develop networks of hospitals and physicians, and at the same time, negotiate price discounts with them. In its most general construction, health plans employ several tools to reduce medical care spending. In contrast to the original models of managed care (which largely worked from an indemnity base, and simply included some form of management of high-cost and discretionary cases), health plans in the 1990s are selectively contracting with providers on a capitated basis. Purchasers are also using several strategies, such as increasing the price of fee-for-service plans relative to managed care plans, to move their employees out of fee-for-service plans into managed care plans.

The most fundamental change accompanying the rise in competitive managed care contracting over the past several years is the transfer of risk within the health care system. Under fee-for-service medicine, purchasers of health care (and their employees) largely financed yearly increases in health care costs. Higher health care costs resulted in higher health insurance premiums. To control their health care spending, purchasers have increasingly shifted financial risk to health plans by moving away from fee-for-service payments toward capitation. Health plans that receive these fixed-price contracts often negotiate capitated arrangements (e.g., a fixed payment per member per month) with hospitals and physician groups, thus moving their financial risk downstream to provider groups.

Increased use of risk-based contracting with health plans has raised several issues and market responses. One of the more interesting trends is the broader set of economic actors accepting risk-based contracts. These groups now include not only traditional health plans but also physician and hospital groups, as well as pharmaceutical firms. As a result, one of the major ongoing battles in the delivery system is over who contracts (i.e., an individual firm, or a provider group) with the purchaser to organize and control the network of providers. Use of selective contracting has also raised a more fundamental set of issues concerning providers excluded from the networks, as well as concerns from some consumer groups about the quality of care.

The shift of financial risk to health plans, and subsequently to providers, has increased the number and variety of entities interested in competing for such contracts. It has also raised the stakes among health care plans to become even more vigilant in their ability to produce year-to-year savings for their purchaser clients. Several signs are pointing to an expanding set of competitors to traditional health plans. Traditionally, purchasers have contracted with health insurance companies (now more broadly referred to as *health plans*). Several other groups have expressed interest in contracting with health plans on a capitated basis. These range from prescription drug companies that sell "disease management" services either directly to a purchaser or often to a health plan, or to a provider-based group. Indeed, several vendors, including drug companies, are selling disease management services to health plans, and in some cases, directly to purchasers. These services include the management of asthma, diabetes, hypertension, depression, AIDS, and cancer, among other diseases. The pace of consolidation has been impressive, involving over $77 billion worth of transactions during 1996 (Health 1997).

The increased purchasing power exerted by health plans in response to demands for slower growth in health care costs by purchasers has also rearranged the supply side of the health care market. The new purchasing muscle exhibited by payers has generated incentives for both providers and managed care firms to consolidate, enhancing their ability to negotiate. Managed care firms will continue to consolidate to increase their bargaining power with hospitals, physicians, and drug companies. Providers will continue to respond through their own consolidations to enhance their negotiations with health plans. Among the more notable mergers on the supply side is the growth of the Columbia health care system. This national chain of hospitals has grown rapidly over the past several years, and now owns over 330 hospitals. Most recently, the Columbia system has moved into the insurance industry through its acquisition (pending approval in Ohio) of Blue Cross and Blue Shield of Ohio. This growth has created a substantial national presence which increases its bargaining power with suppliers of health care. Columbia is also active in developing health care networks in local markets through its ownership of local hospitals and, increasingly, through the purchase of physician practices. This strategy provides a single point of entry for patients in the system. Though systems such as Columbia are not "risk-bearing" entities (i.e., they are not licensed by various states as HMOs), this strategy enhances their bargaining power with health plans.

Several other important mergers on the supply side have also transpired. Glaxo recently acquired Wellcome PLC in the pharmaceutical industry. In the hospital industry, Columbia Health Corporation purchased the Hospital Corporation of America, and the merger of National Medical Enterprises and American Medical Holdings created Tenet Health Care. Of particular note is the continued consolidation in the managed care marketplace. The most notable and most recent example of this trend is Aetna's $8.8 billion acquisition of U.S. Healthcare. As a result of that merger, the top four managed care firms in the country now control

Table 1. Managed Care Enrollment of the Ten Largest Plans, 1995

Plan	Enrollment (millions)	Cumulative Enrollment (%)
Blue Cross	8.5	15.7
United Healthcare	6.7	28.1
Kaiser Permanente	6.7	40.6
Aetna/U.S. Healthcare	5.7	51.1
Prudential	4.7	59.8
Cigna	3.9	67.0
PacifiCare/FHP[a]	3.6	73.7
Humana	2.1	77.6
Health Systems[b]	1.8	80.9
All Other Plans	10.3	100.0
Total All Plans	54.0	100.0

[a]Data reflect PacifiCare's buyout of FHP; prior to acquisition, each plan enrolled approximately 1.8 million subscribers.
[b]Health Systems is involved in merger discussions with Foundation Health Plan.
Source. Sanford C. Bernstein and Co. 1996 and InterStudy 1996.

over 50 percent of total enrollment in HMOs (see Table 1). Market consolidation is not limited to horizontal mergers; vertical mergers have also picked up pace (e.g., the Merck/Medco and Caremark/Friendly Hills mergers). Vertical consolidations—where providers of care such as drug companies purchase "managed care" vendors—raise concern among purchasers over the potential conflicts of interest generated by the new entity.

Changes in the Public Health Insurance Marketplace

The changes in the delivery system just outlined have not been limited to private sector purchasers, as both Medicare and Medicaid are following the lead of large purchasers in their approach to cost containment. Moreover, the changes in the health care delivery system outlined here have been reinforced by both federal and state government actions. Several states have requested, and been granted, waivers from federal Medicaid law to expand enrollment in managed care plans. Since President Clinton assumed office, several states have been granted federal Medicaid waivers (known as Section 1115 research and demonstration waivers) allowing states to adopt new purchasing tools commonly used in the private sector.[2] A common approach is states receiving the Section 1115 waivers in the mandatory enrollment of Medicaid beneficiaries in managed care plans. Tennessee is perhaps the most notable, and controversial, example of this approach. As part of its waiver, the state enrolled its Medicaid population in privately administered managed care plans, reducing substantially (largely by setting capitation rates of payment to such plans 25 percent below what was paid to providers on a fee-for-service basis) their costs, and directing the savings toward covering the uninsured.[3] The Tennessee experience has provided substantial lessons concerning the implementation of such approaches, as well as how providers respond to substantially lower (and many would argue too low) rates of payment to care for low-income patients (see Gold's essay in this volume, pp. 284–315).

Although the Tennessee experience has generated mixed results, other states are keenly anticipating the prospect of moving large segments of their Medicaid (and in some circumstances, their uninsured) populations into managed care plans. At issue is whether Congress will pass and the president will sign Medicaid reforms allowing states enough flexibility to rely on managed care as the delivery system of choice. Although the prospects of congressional reforms remain largely unknown, the lure of substantial cost savings linked to moving away from fee-for-service toward managed care will prove too powerful to ignore. Recent studies conducted by the American Academy of Actuaries (1996) place the potential savings of managed care among Medicaid beneficiaries at a range of 14 percent to 30 percent per capita for those enrolled in the Aid to Families with Dependent Children program, and slightly lower levels for other types of Medicaid recipients (i.e., the aged, blind, and disabled). Savings of this magnitude for fiscally strapped state and local governments could be too hard to bypass during the next several years. In short, depending on the nature and timing of congressional action on Medicaid reform, we can expect to see a continued rapid escalation of Medicaid beneficiaries enrolled in managed care plans.

The Medicare program has also indicated its desire to explore the managed care concept. The Health Care Financing Administration (HCFA) has recently indicated its desire to use managed care plans to deliver care to those with end-stage renal disease. Although the number of Medicare beneficiaries enrolled in managed care plans has lagged behind enrollment in both the private sector and the Medicaid program (it currently stands at 4.4 million, some 12 percent of Medicare beneficiaries), both Congress and the president (although their approaches differ substantially) have advanced proposals that would increase Medicare enrollment in such plans. These proposals would increase the types of managed care plans available, such as point-of-service plans, to Medicare beneficiaries.

A final indicator of the shifting attitude of public officials toward public insurance and subsidy programs concerns the important changes in public safety-net hospitals, which provide the bulk of care to the uninsured. Over the past several years, several municipalities have changed the governance of their public hospitals from public to private. The number of public hospitals has decreased from 31 percent of all community hospital beds in 1980 to under 27 percent of all beds by 1994 (American Hospital Association 1981, 1995). There are several indications that these trends are not likely to abate. Recent proposals by New York City mayor Rudolph Guiliani to privatize the eleven acute care hospitals that operate as the city's public health and hospitals corporation have received significant national attention. Similar interest in examining the privatization option has been expressed in other major cities as well.

In short, the market-driven reforms aimed at slowing the growth in health care costs—and in concept, attempting to improve the quality of care—have produced several ramifications for the delivery of health care. The following section examines the impacts of these changes on the performance of the health care industry. As a primary focus of the market-based approach is to slow the growth in health care costs, the discussion starts with recent trends in health care spending. I also address changes in the issues concerning the uninsured, as well as graduate medical education.

Recent Trends in the Growth of Health Care Spending

Several ongoing surveys are attempting to measure the growth in health care spending and costs (Ginsburg and Pickreign 1996). Despite these efforts, developing a comprehensive measure of financial activity in the health care sector remains elusive. Several factors contribute to these difficulties. For instance, whereas economists would prefer to measure the growth in health care costs, purchasers are more interested in the growth in health care spending.[4] Most, though not all, surveys that focus on financial activity in the sector are undertaken by private benefit consulting firms that tend to focus on health care spending (i.e., spending per employee or changes in premiums). Thus, the discussion over the growth in *health care costs* usually focuses on the growth in *health care spending* by purchasers. Second, the surveys usually focus on a small portion of total health care spending: private insurance premiums by small and large firms. This excludes out-of-pocket spending, as well as premium payments by the self-employed and workers in very small firms (fewer than ten employees). Despite these shortcomings, there is growing evidence that the explosive growth of managed care and of network-based health care systems has slowed the growth in some components of health care costs and spending. At issue is the scope of such changes: Have they reduced employer spending, employee spending, or spending for those purchasing coverage in the individual (nongroup) market? And what about broader measures, such as national health care expenditures? Unfortunately, there is no ongoing data-collection capacity to monitor the level and change in spending at this level of detail. Instead, analysis must rely on stringing together studies from several sources, each addressing different sectors of the health care industry.

Although several studies attempt to comment on changes in the level and growth in health care spending, none are nationally representative surveys of all employers or employees. Some surveys collect information solely on employer costs. The most notable survey in this respect is collected by the Department of Labor's employer cost index (ECI; e.g., U.S. Department of Labor 1995). On the other side of the equation, the Department of Labor also collects data on consumer expenditures, including health care, as part of its Consumer Expenditure Survey (e.g., U.S. Department of Labor 1994). Several national employee benefit consulting firms conduct annual surveys asking employers about total health benefit costs for active workers and retirees. Although widely cited, little is known about how representative such surveys are. Finally, the Office of the Actuary in the Department of Health and Human Services routinely collects information on private health insurance and out-of-pocket spending from various sources to estimate national health spending.

As each of these sources relies on different methods and a different sampling framework, their results and conclusions concerning the growth in health care spending differs. As noted previously, data collected from the ECI and various private benefit consulting firms focus exclusively on private health insurance spending. The actuaries at HCFA present a broader view of health care costs, focusing on national health expenditures (such data have also been collected by the Department of Commerce in its annual Industrial Outlook reports. The CBO also generates reports of national health spending [CBO 1997]).

Perhaps the most widely cited studies are those annually released by major employee benefit consulting firms such as Foster Higgins and Peat Marwick. According to its most recent results from Foster Higgins, the growth in total spending per employee increased 2.1 percent between 1994 and 1995. The Peat Marwick survey estimates an even lower rate of growth between 1995 and 1996, less than 1 percent (KPMG, Peat Marwick 1996). The report indicated even lower rates of growth from the year before. These totals reflect the migration of employees from higher-cost fee-for-service plans into lower-cost managed care plans (Foster Higgins 1994, 1995).[5] Results from other major surveys have generated similar findings. Ginsburg and Pickreign (1996) summarized these surveys, and concluded that growth in private insurance premiums has slowed substantially since 1992.

Although most of the news from the employee benefit surveys is encouraging, not all the news is good. As noted before, the surveys do not indicate changes in the very small group (fewer than ten employees) or the individual market. The individual market, in particular, is vulnerable to continued cost escalation given the lack of large-scale purchasing power and less sophisticated approaches to managed care contracting. Moreover, the survey results also noted that the growth in private insurance costs for retirees increased 10.5 percent between 1994 and 1995. This growth largely mirrors the yearly growth in Medicare spending as well. Of course, this is not especially surprising, as most employers use some form of indemnity-based coverage in their coordination with Medicare benefits. (That is, employers often pay the Medicare fee-for-service deductibles and copayments facing their retirees, rather than paying a fixed amount per retiree per year to devote toward health care expenses. As a result, private retiree spending generally mirrors the growth in Medicare spending.) However, as in other areas, employers are increasingly examining new approaches for their retirees, including the establishment of defined contribution plans as well as incentives to join HMOs that contract with the Medicare program.

Although surveys by employee benefit firms miss significant aspects of the private insurance market (i.e., the individual market and for very small groups), the results are still encouraging. Recent surveys conducted by the Department of Labor have produced similar findings, though their results pertain solely to compensation costs facing employers. Nonetheless, these results remain instructive. Indeed, the growth in employer spending on health care benefits has moderated even more than the figures cited here. According to recent U.S. Department of Labor (1995) data, employer spending on health insurance benefits per hour worked actually declined 7 percent between 1994 and 1995. Whereas wages and salaries increased 11¢ per year, this decline in health insurance benefits payments kept total compensation nearly constant during these years. The recent trends in health insurance benefit costs facing employers contrasts with an average annual increase in such costs of 7.4 percent between 1991 and 1994 (see Table 2).

Although the cost growth results for employers seem quite favorable,

Table 2. Employer Costs per Hour Worked for Employee Compensation
and Health Insurance Benefits, 1991–1995 (in Dollars)

Year	Total compensation	Wages and salary	Health insurance	Other benefits
1995	17.10	12.25	1.06	3.79
1994	17.08	12.14	1.14	3.80
1993	16.70	11.90	1.10	3.70
1992	16.14	11.58	1.02	3.53
1991	15.40	11.14	0.92	3.35

Source. U.S. Department of Labor 1995.

Table 3. Annual Pretax Income and Expenditures
for Consumers, 1991–1994

Item	1991	1992	1993	1994	Annual Change
Pretax income	$33,901	$33,854	$34,868	$36,838	2.8%
Average annual expenditures	$29,614	$29,846	$30,692	$31,751	2.3%
Health care	$ 1,554	$ 1,634	$ 1,776	$ 1,755	4.1%
Health as % of pretax income	4.6%	4.8%	5.1%	4.8%	
Health as % of expenditures	5.2%	5.5%	5.8%	5.5%	

Source. U.S. Department of Labor 1994.

data tracking consumer spending on health care present a different picture, at least through 1993 (see Table 3). Whereas reported out-of-pocket spending (both for health insurance premiums and direct payments for health care services) decreased between 1993 and 1994, it has increased faster than pretax income between 1991 and 1994. During this time, the average annual growth in pretax income (per "consumer unit") increased 2.8 percent, with consumer spending rising an average of 2.3 percent per year. During this same period, consumer spending on health care (premiums and out-of-pocket expenses) increased by over 4 percent per year. As a result, for a typical consumer household, health care spending continued to account for a growing portion of both pretax income and share of expenditures. With respect to spending, health care spending increased from 5.2 percent of total expenditures to 5.5 percent during this short time period. In sum, although the managed care revolution appears to have slowed the growth in health insurance premiums, the ultimate impact on consumers appears mixed. Table 3 notes the continued high rate of increase in consumer out-of-pocket spending. The growth in managed care also means that consumers are less able to directly choose their physicians and hospitals. These potentially deleterious impacts on consumers have already resulted in legislation that seeks to expand consumer choices (e.g., mandating that all plans offer at least two health care plans). Building on these concerns, President Clinton recently announced plans to create an Advisory Commission on Consumer Protection and Quality designed to address issues of consumer information and choice of health care plans. The growing anti–managed care sentiment voiced by many consumers may be on a political collision course with both public and private purchasers seeking sustained savings in health spending generated through managed care.

The broadest examination of health care expenditures is that developed by HCFA. Although its survey results reveal a similar downward trend in health care spending over the past couple of years, its results are not as dramatic as those reported in Table 3 (see Table 4). According to these data, the growth in private health insurance increased 5.8 percent per year between 1993 and 1995. This is substantially lower than the annual growth in private health insurance payments reported in earlier years (during the 1980s, the average annual growth in private insurance spending was 11.1 percent). This is the broadest view of private spending, because it is intended to capture all private insurance spending (i.e., retiree spending, active workers across all firm sizes, and the individual market). As a result, it measures the growth in both the individual and group markets, which generates higher estimated cost growth than that reported from surveys that focus on different market segments, or that focus solely on the growth in employer health care spending.

Whereas these results provide some indication of the trends to date in private insurance costs, there is considerable uncertainty about the fu-

Table 4. National Health Expenditures by Source of Payment, 1995–2005 (Billions of Dollars)

Year	Private Insurance	Private Out-of-Pocket	Government	Total
1993	296.1	157.5	387.8	884.2
1995	331.3	175.2	454.9	1007.6
2000	486.7	256.4	673.7	1481.7
2005	709.6	370.6	1002.4	2173.7

Source. Burner and Waldo 1995.

ture rate of growth in private health insurance spending. At issue is whether the substantial slowdown reflected in most survey data represents a one-time savings, or will be reflected in continued reductions in spending. Actuaries from HCFA responsible for health care spending projections believe that the reduction in private sector spending reflects a one-time savings spread over several years.[6] As a result, they project a slightly higher increase in total private insurance spending between 1995 and 2005, on the order of 7.9 percent per year. This growth, however, remains significantly below the double-digit rates of growth observed in the 1980s.

Changes in Access to Care, the Number of Uninsured, and the Financing of Graduate Medical Education

Another measure of system performance concerns the number of uninsured individuals and the level of health care services they receive. Counts of the number of Americans without health insurance are important for several reasons. The first concerns the type of health care they receive compared to those with health insurance. Several studies have noted that the uninsured generally receive less care compared with those with insurance (Marquis and Long 1994–95). In some cases, this care is not appropriate or timely, and results in poor health outcomes. The uninsured also generate uncompensated care.

According to the most recent data (U.S. Bureau of the Census 1997), approximately 41.7 million Americans were uninsured throughout 1996. This represents approximately 1.1 million more uninsured Americans than estimated during 1995. Indeed, despite the prolonged economic expansion between 1993 and 1996, the share of Americans without insurance continues to rise. Based on this experience, the problems facing uninsured do not appear that they will be solved solely through economic expansion and rising employment.

An equally important indicator of system performance concerns the amount and distribution of uncompensated care provided to the uninsured. Changes in the medical care marketplace outlined previously could have a substantial impact on both of these critical indicators of performance. In particular, competition, by its nature, eliminates cross-subsidies built into any pricing system. Consider the method used to finance graduate medical education and care for the uninsured and underinsured. Historically, teaching and safety-net hospitals have included the joint costs of patient care, teaching, and care for the uninsured in their patient care cost structure. This has increased substantially the costs of teaching versus nonteaching hospitals, and may have led to higher charges relative to costs for hospitals treating large volumes of uninsured patients. Traditionally, these higher costs were largely paid by private health plans as well as public payers. The pressure placed on managed care firms by purchasers to extract discounts from all hospitals has begun to erode (and many would argue already has eroded) the higher payments used to subsidize the costs of medical education and treating the uninsured. The elimination of these cross-subsidies in our delivery system highlights an important public policy issue. The nature of these cross-subsidies, and the implications of competitive pricing on them are explored in the following.

Impacts on teaching hospitals and graduate medical education

The impacts of the competitive trends outlined here have important implications for teaching hospitals, because of both their higher costs linked to their teaching mission, and the substantial volume of uncompensated care they provide. As a result, costs in teaching hospitals are substantially higher than in nonteaching hospitals. These differences remain even after accounting for differences in case mix, location, and wages. The residual difference is, in part, traced to the higher costs of training physicians and a large volume of uncompensated care. Traditionally, Medicare has recognized these higher costs through the additional payments made to such hospitals by their indirect teaching adjustment. Medicaid has used a similar approach through its use of disproportionate share payments to such hospitals. Private payers have also recognized these cost differences through higher rates of payment to teaching hospitals. However, as part of the attempt to balance the federal budget, several proposals have been advanced to reduce Medicare's indirect teaching costs. Moreover, managed care networks, in their attempt to negotiate the "best" price, are less willing to recognize this teaching differential in their managed care networks. Both trends raise serious issues for teaching hospitals.

Perhaps the most serious trend involves the new pricing strategies employed by private payers concerning teaching and nonteaching hospitals. According to data from the American Hospital Association, major teaching hospitals receive approximately 38 percent of their revenue from private health insurers. Paying teaching hospitals at rates similar to those paid to nonteaching hospitals would have a substantial financial impact. For example, teaching hospitals have costs (after accounting for differences in case mix, labor costs, and location) that are approximately 25 percent higher than those of nonteaching hospitals (shown in Table 5

Table 5. Ratio of Private Health Insurance Payments to Costs Today
and under Simulated Managed Care Payment Levels, 1993

Type of hospital	Relative costs	Ratio of payments to hospital costs today	Ratio of payments to nonteaching costs under "parity"
Major nonpublic teaching hospitals	1.0	1.19	1.096
Nonteaching hospitals	0.8	1.096	1.096

Source. American Hospital Association 1993 and Prospective Payment Assessment Commission 1996.

as the index of relative costs in teaching and nonteaching hospitals of 1.0:.08). Data from the American Hospital Association *Annual Survey of Hospitals* (1993) indicate that private health plans pay major teaching hospitals an average of 119 percent of their "costs," whereas nonteaching hospitals are paid 137 percent of their costs (see Table 5).

If teaching hospitals were paid rates similar to those received by nonteaching hospitals (and if private health plans largely ignored the higher costs associated with their teaching functions), their private insurance payment to cost ratios would fall nearly ten percentage points, from 119 percent to 109.6 percent of costs. This would reduce private insurance revenues flowing into major teaching hospitals by $1.5 billion per year, reducing their total margins from 2.7 percent today to 20.6 percent under this approach. Of course, many private health plans have targeted their cost-containment strategy simply to pay for "costs," thus, even the 109.6 percent ratio of payments to costs may be seen as too generous. There seems little question that, over the next several years, many of the nation's teaching hospitals will consolidate, or even close.

Although the future for some teaching hospitals is stark, some may be less concerned about the prospect of a reduction in teaching capacity. Recent studies of the medical education marketplace continue to note the abundant supply of physicians and the potential for a growing oversupply (Institute of Medicine 1996). Even the most modest set of policy guidelines has recommended that no new schools of medicine be opened, and that existing class sizes should not expand. Others have called for more aggressive measures.

**Impacts on the number of uninsured
individuals and access to care**

As noted previously, approximately 41.7 million Americans (15.6 percent of the population) were uninsured throughout 1996. Projections of the number of uninsured by the year 2002 range from 15.6 percent of the population to an upper, extreme case of 24 percent (Thorpe et al. 1995). Whereas the uninsured contribute toward the costs of their care when seeking services, such payments account for less than 10 percent of uncompensated care costs in private hospitals (American Hospital Association 1994). Costs that are truly uncompensated (noted here as *unsponsored*) must be financed through revenues from another source. In general, these costs have been cross-subsidized by profits made from nonpatient care revenues as well as from private payers (see Table 6). As noted earlier, such profits have become increasingly difficult to generate.

The results displayed in Table 6 highlight five important trends. First, hospital profits continue to grow, rising from 4.4 percent of costs in 1991 to 5 percent by 1994. Second, whereas total (inpatient and outpatient) Medicare payments to hospitals remain below reported Medicare costs, the extent of these reported losses have dropped sharply, from 4.6 percent of total costs in 1991 to 2.7 percent by 1994. Third, Medicaid payments (which include disproportionate share payments) to hospitals, at least through 1993, have become aligned with reported costs. This reflects, in part, the important role disproportionate share payments in the program assumed during the early 1990s. However, recent changes in federal Medicaid policy limiting disproportionate share payment levels to individual hospitals (P.L. 103-66 as outlined in the Omnibus Reconciliation Act of 1993) reversed this trend by 1994. Fourth, hospital profits derived from private health insurance continue to erode. In 1991, surplus payments by private health insurers to hospitals resulted in a gain of 12.1 percent of total hospital costs (i.e., private insurance profits [payments less cost] divided by total costs). By 1994, these surplus payments had declined, as had their contribution to the bottom line, falling to 10.7 percent of total costs.

A final trend concerns the growth in unsponsored care provided by

Table 6. Community Hospital Gains and Losses as a Percentage of Total Costs, 1991–1994

	1994	1993	1991
Aggregate total gain	5.0	4.5	4.4
Medicare	−2.7	−4.3	−4.6
Medicaid	−1.6	−0.1	−2.0
Private insurance	10.7	11.2	12.1
Uncompensated care	−4.8	−4.6	−4.7
Other	3.4	2.4	3.6

Source. Calculations based on American Hospital Association 1994 and derived from Prospective Payment Assessment Commission 1996: 84.

hospitals. Despite a rising proportion of the nonelderly without health insurance during this period—from 16.6 percent to 17.8 percent of the population—the volume of uncompensated care provided by hospitals remained at approximately 6 percent, with unsponsored care remaining at 4.8 percent of total costs. If hospitals had provided the same level of uncompensated care per capita in 1993 as provided in 1991, total care would have risen from the level observed in 1993: 6 percent (16 billion) to 6.3 percent of hospital costs ($16.8 billion). Whether this difference represents changes in the underlying demand for uncompensated hospital care, or a reduction in supply traced to changing financial conditions, is not known.

This broad view masks significant changes in the distribution of uncompensated care provided by hospitals over time. As noted previously, surplus payments from private health plans to hospitals have decreased rapidly over time. This represents both a reduced share of total costs traced to patients with private insurance (a decrease from 39.3 percent in 1991 to 37 percent in 1993), as well as a reduction in the payment-to-cost ratio. These reductions have disproportionately affected certain types of hospitals (see Table 7).

Losses generated by unsponsored care (uncompensated care net of direct payments either from patients or state and local tax levy support to public hospitals) have remained relatively constant. However, this masks significant variation across hospitals. Losses from unsponsored care have decreased substantially among private hospitals while increasing among major public teaching hospitals. The reduction in unsponsored care provided in private teaching hospitals may be associated with the reduction in profits available from those with private insurance. For instance, in major private teaching hospitals, private health insurance contributed a surplus of 7.8 percent of total costs in 1991, and only 7.3 percent by 1994. Thus, whether the changing level and mix of unsponsored care provided by hospitals reflects a decreased financial capacity to provide such care, or simply that the underlying per capita demand for care has stabilized, is not known. However, the results displayed in Table 7 certainly demand additional and more detailed inspection.

These results highlight two critical issues for the future of major teaching hospitals and other hospitals that provide a disproportionate share of care to the uninsured. Traditionally, private health insurance payments to urban teaching hospitals have been substantially higher than payments to other hospitals for two reasons. The first concerns their higher costs traced, in part, to their teaching mission. The second concerns the relatively higher losses sustained by such hospitals in treat-

Table 7. Community Hospital Gains and Losses as Percentages of
Total Costs, by Source of Payment and Hospital Type, 1991–1994

Type of Hospital	1994		1991	
	Private insurance	Unsponsored care	Private insurance	Unsponsored care
Major public teaching	6.5	−8.0	4.8	−4.4
Major private teaching	7.3	−4.7	7.8	−4.9
Other teaching	10.8	−4.6	11.6	−4.7
Nonteaching	13.1	−4.5	14.3	−4.6
Total	10.7	−4.8	12.1	−4.7

Source. American Hospital Association 1995 and Prospective Payment Assessment Commission 1996.

ing the uninsured. Both of these factors have generated higher charges in teaching hospitals relative to nonteaching hospitals. However, as noted throughout this discussion, the competitive pressures for cost containment in both the public and private sectors will continue to place pressure on teaching hospitals to reduce, if not eliminate, these cross-subsidies built into their pricing systems. Failure to do so will mean some teaching hospitals and safety-net providers will close. On the other hand, accommodating these competitive pressures could result in less care to the uninsured, and a retrenchment of teaching hospitals' mission.

In addition to the analysis presented here, several other indicators already point to the tension facing the move of the system toward competition. Until 1992, New Jersey used an all-payer rate-setting system to reimburse hospitals. The all-payer rate-setting approach in New Jersey, like the ones used in New York, Massachusetts, and Maryland, incorporated several goals: cost containment and an explicit approach for financing uncompensated care, as well as the higher costs traced to graduate medical education in teaching hospitals. The desire to embrace competition in New Jersey, Massachusetts, and New York led to the dissolution of the all-payer approach. It also eliminated the formal mechanism used to finance uncompensated care and the higher costs of teaching hospitals (although New York has retained a portion of its uncompensated care pool). The elimination of these cross-subsidies, a key ingredient in the rate-setting approach, coincidental with the move toward competition, has left hospitals in the undesirable situation of attempting to recover $100 million in "unpaid" uncompensated care for the calendar year 1996 alone. Whether competition will be more effective in controlling total hospital costs in the former rate-setting states remains an empirical issue.

Recent empirical studies have also detailed the difficult choices facing hospitals in states with aggressive, competitive, and selective contracting. California is an excellent example; it has been a leader in developing managed care and aggressive purchasing for employers of all sizes. Its Medi-Cal program was a leader in initiating selective contracting among hospitals in the state for the Medi-Cal program. The competitive pressures and large-scale purchasing power brought to bear in the state have generated an impressive record of cost containment. Several studies have documented the cost savings associated with selective contracting in the Medi-Cal program and competitive contracting in the private sector (e.g., see Zwanziger, Melnick, and Bamezai 1994). At the same time, studies have placed the spotlight on the dysfunctional social side effects of this approach: the reduction in uncompensated care provided to the uninsured, and a public hospital system in deep distress (Mann et al. 1995).

Conclusions

The trends identified here are likely to intensify in the near future. Congress has expressed a desire to slow the growth in Medicare and Medicaid spending as part of its overall strategy to balance the federal budget. Although an agreement has yet to materialize, early proposals would have reduced Medicare payments to hospitals by $80 billion over the next six years. The private sector, armed with a new set of quantitative tools used to measure cost and quality differences across hospitals, will continue its quest to slow the growth in payments. Whether the growing consolidation of power on the supply side will withstand this quest through enhanced bargaining power remains to be seen. It seems apparent that payments made by private health insurers to hospitals will continue to converge toward costs. On average, the private insurance industry currently pays hospitals an average of 24 percent above costs. The alignment of private insurance payments and costs will force hospitals to reduce their volume of uncompensated care, scale back their missions not directly related to patient care, reduce costs associated with insured patients, or all of these. Although it is possible for hospitals to continue to reduce the level and growth of their costs, the rate of cost growth this past year hit a historic low, growing at a negative real rate of growth. This rate of growth does not seem to be a realistic long-term possibility. What seems clear is that the alignment of private insurance payments and costs, combined with substantial reductions in the growth in Medicare and Medicaid payments, will increasingly expose the complex cross-subsidies built into providers' prices. Those services valued by the market, largely patient care services for patients with private insurance, Medicare, and Medicaid, will be produced. Those services not explicitly valued by the market, such as uncompensated care and graduate training, may not.

Although the diffusion of competitive purchasing and demand- and supply-side mergers and acquisitions has produced (to date) impressive reductions in the growth of health care expenditures, it has exposed the intricate cross-subsidies built into providers' prices. Unless some market (or nonmarket) mechanism is used explicitly to finance uncompensated care and graduate medical education, fewer of these services will be provided. Several recent proposals have been advanced that would provide a separate mechanism for financing graduate medical education in our nation's hospitals. This would allow teaching hospitals to compete directly with nonteaching hospitals without having to recover the additional costs of graduate medical education as part of their patient care revenues. The separate pooling approach has substantial merit. It does, however, raise several critical design issues, including the level of funding, distribution across hospitals and other provider settings, and means of financing (i.e., general revenues, or some form of provider tax). What remains unclear is the means for financing care for the uninsured. Whereas the recent growth in the economy and the expansion of Medicaid have, in the near term, slowed the growth in the uninsured, their ranks will clearly increase with the next recession. Even before this occurs, substantial evidence is starting to mount that our makeshift means of financing such care has started to erode. One approach would be to develop a separate national (or state) pool for financing care for the uninsured to accompany any potential dedicated funding for graduate medical education. Another approach is to continue efforts at both the state and national levels to reduce the number of uninsured. Although both approaches raise vexing issues concerning the level of funding, means of financing, and distribution of funds that have stymied most state and national efforts to address these issues, direct subsidies to providers to finance care for the uninsured and graduate medical education may represent the more politically appealing route.

Notes

1   It remains unclear, at least to me, why employers would be concerned with health care benefit costs. According to economic theory, as well as a substantial body of empirical evidence, increases or decreases in health care costs facing employers are

translated into compensating changes in wages and other fringe benefits. As a result, total compensation facing the employer remains constant. The "fixed compensation" maxim dominates the economics literature, and is a fundamental constant in revenue estimates undertaken by the Joint Committee on Taxation as well as the Treasury Department. Either the theory is more complicated (i.e., there are transitory changes that occur in the timing of how the adjustment occurs), or the employer (through its workers) is concerned with the composition of the compensation package.

2   The more common approach used by nearly every state to increase managed care enrollment is the use of Section 1915(B) waivers. These waivers are more limited than Section 1115 waivers; that is, they are usually programs for a limited geographic area within a state, and do not by themselves allow the state to expand coverage to currently uninsured persons (as is typically found in Section 1115 waivers).

3   The use of managed care in most states, with the notable exception of Arizona, has focused on acute care services. That is, most states that have expanded managed care for their Medicaid population have enrolled women and children in managed care plans for a subset of Medicaid benefits. Generally excluded from these demonstrations are long-term care services and the aged, blind, and disabled. Although managed care appears to generate substantial savings for enrolled populations, the savings as a percentage of total Medicaid savings are relatively small.

4   Economists are interested in examining resources devoted to a particular sector. These resources have "costs" in that they are not employed in alternative uses. Purchasers of health care, although interested in costs, are particularly interested in what they pay for health care. As a result, the information on financial activity in the sector represents a mix of measures focusing on both costs and revenues.

5   It is important to note, however, that the underlying growth in point-of-service, indemnity plans, and health maintenance organizations ranged from 2.1 percent to over 10 percent. Thus, the reported decline in spending per employee in the 1994 data simply reflects the migration of workers from higher- to lower-cost plans.

6   This results from the belief that the recent slowdown in private insurance premiums stems from a shift of enrollees across plans, rather than a reduction in the underlying rate of cost growth across all types of plans.

Markets, Medicare, and Making Do: Business Strategies after National Health Care Reform

Cathie Jo Martin

Introduction

Health care is a favorite example of market failure in Economics 101, and every freshman econ major can rattle off the reasons.[1] Third party insurers interrupt the natural balance between providers and patients or supply and demand. Health is (often literally) a life-and-death issue where rational decision making is at its most problematic. As a society we are unwilling to forget about the sick patient who is unable to meet the costs of his or her amelioration; therefore, we must come up with collective mechanisms for financing the uninsured.[2]

Yet markets seem to be omnipotent in the world of health today; indeed, managed care is revolutionizing health care delivery. At the firm level, employers are purchasing increasingly from medical delivery systems that compete on the basis of both cost and quality. Even states such as Massachusetts and New Jersey, the traditional stalwarts of rate regulation, have adopted market reforms (Thorpe, this volume). The past few years have seen an ideological sea change in national health policy: regulatory play-or-pay proposals were replaced with market-based health alliances in Democratic health plans. Finally, as Jonathan Oberlander (this volume) notes, in the post-1994 era markets are making such inroads into our collective political psyche that they are colonizing traditionally public sector arenas such as Medicare.

The market-defying aspects of health care delivery leave us with a puzzle: Why have private market solutions exercised such a grip on the health financing system when medical intervention seems to reject market rationality? Of course some believe that markets and health care can be compatible under the right circumstances; yet the ability of markets to solve health problems has been so widely debated that one wonders how market measures have achieved their current hegemony. This paper explores the contribution of employers to this puzzle, looking at the role business purchasers of health have played in keeping market solutions at the center of the health system. Most analysts agree that in the absence of a well-organized working class, business exercises extraordinary influence in matters of public policy. Therefore, it makes sense to investigate the corporate contribution to our conundrum.

It is easy to imagine that business managers would exercise a preference for market-based solutions to cost containment based both on ideology and interests. In America it is often useful to follow the dollar signs, and indeed, health care is big business. Providers and insurers prefer to be left to their own devices and resist undue regulation. But the history of corporate *purchaser's* engagement, both with companies' own health costs and with the policy arena, suggests a far more nuanced rendering: Big business managers at least are ambivalent about market interventions both at the firm level and at the level of public policy. Big corporate purchasers of health care have been rather inconsistent in their enthusiasm for firm-level market interventions in the past two decades. As primary organizers of health financing, big companies have a bureaucratic interest in retaining the employer-based system that prevents their acceptance of a single-payer plan. As health care administrators they are prone to resist what they view as troublesome and often expensive government regulations. But as consumers and major purchasers of health care, they also have every reason to support any intervention that might stop the relentless escalation of health costs. Although they might be drawn to the market fix for ideological reasons, they will be driven away when they believe that market interventions have done them a disservice. Indeed, Linda Bergthold (1990) has argued that the regulatory versus market debate is less relevant to business purchasers than we might believe. A snapshot view of large employers at the moment finds most expanding into managed competition (if they have not already made the transition) and guardedly hopeful that this new technique will solve their woes.

The public policy arena presents another story. The business community was deeply divided during the national health reform saga, and big business managers were dubious about the Republican initiatives in 1995 to bring private sector market initiatives into the traditionally public domain of Medicare and Medicaid. Large employers doubted that market controls would benefit these public policy areas, fearing that the bone-cutting Medicare proposals would accelerate cost shifting to private business payers. The Republican cause célèbre was a new federalism that devolves regulatory power to the states, eliminates unfunded mandates, and ends intergovernmental relations as we know them. But big-business managers much prefer national standards to state experimentation: "Protect ERISA preemption" is a battle cry on the order of magnitude of "remember the Alamo." The big business voice, however, has been muted. The same organizational weakness that prevented large employers from getting what they wanted in the effort to legislate health reform interfered with their exercising a strong political presence after the reform bill's demise. Thus, the political struggles of the 1990s found large employers largely absent from the inner circles of power.

By comparison, the small business community, a proven political juggernaut in the Republican assault on national health reform, continued to prefer a market strategy and worked closely with the GOP party in the Medicare campaign. Energized by the defeat of national health reform, the small-business Davids (with their big-business fast food and insurance allies) engineered an impressive show of force in the early days of the Medicare campaign, resulting in the quick passage of the bill in both houses. Clinton's veto pen ultimately defeated the 1995 legislation, yet the Republicans were able to secure much of their Medicare agenda in 1997. The omnibus budget reconciliation process allowed the GOP to secure its tax and Medicare goals in exchange for cooperation on budget items desired by the Democrats.

Market Reform and Company Efforts to Control Health Costs

A primary reason for the importance of market solutions to health care cost containment reflects the nature of medical financing in America and the role of employers in this process. The centrality of the privatized, employer-based system means that predominantly public arrangements challenging the employer role, such as the single-payer system, are not even considered most of the time.

For years corporate America has been a major provider of social benefits, filling the vacuum left by the very limited government welfare state (Stevens 1986: 13–19). Employers began developing employee benefits in the late nineteenth century to deal with labor unrest and a tighter labor market. Initially hostile to these company plans, unions viewed benefits as weapons to halt the advance of collective bargaining and to trap workers in onerous jobs. But the onset of World War II and the creation of the National War Labor Board (NWLB) precipitated a dramatic expansion of the employee benefit system. Anxious to prevent inflation, the NWLB specified acceptable wage increases but allowed benefits to be calculated separately. Thus workers and employers negotiated benefit increases as a way of expanding the total compensation package. The excise profits tax also pushed the growth of benefits, because companies could pay for benefits with pretax dollars. Shortly after the war the labor movement expanded its earlier campaign for greater government social provision to include private sector benefits as well (ibid.).

Today, while other countries have public health insurance, training programs, child allowances, and pensions, we have a patchwork system of benefits largely provided through our jobs. Employers have been at the heart of the health care system in this country: almost two-thirds of our nonelderly population are covered through employers (Field and Shapiro 1993). Where health care claimed only 2.2 percent of salaries and wages in 1965, it climbed to 8.3 percent by 1989 (Levit et al. 1991: 117, 127–129). Companies spent $50.6 billion training their workers in 1994 (Industry Report 1994: 30). Even the biggest government benefit program, Social Security, has enormous help from the private sector in funding retirement income: in 1993 Social Security old-age benefits (combined with disability insurance) paid individuals $297.9 billion, and private employer pensions paid out $192.6 billion (Pemberton and Holmes 1995: 14). All this has taken a toll on wages: in 1951 benefits devoured 18.7 percent of payroll; by 1980 this had doubled to 37 percent (Stevens 1986: 24).

Just as market solutions are natural in a system where much of the provision of health occurs through the private sector, market fixes are ideologically attractive to firms, and many health system innovations at the company level have aimed to restructure markets. But this does not mean that large employers are antithetical to regulation or that they are entirely satisfied with innovations to alter market dynamics. Government regulations that are market-conforming, or that do not challenge the dominance of the employer-based health system, have been explored by business managers at different points in time. Indeed, the history of firm-level experiments displays something of a pendulum swinging between alternative avenues of hope. Employers turn to regulatory interventions when they become disillusioned with market efforts and vice versa. Cost controls at the company level today reflect two decades of experimentation.

Firm-Level Market Interventions

When medical costs first emerged as an irritant, large firms eliminated the middlemen by self-insuring or by using insurance companies to administer their plans but not to bear the risk. Companies reasoned that eliminating the insurers' cut would be an immediate cost-saving device.

An additional reason for self-insuring was the Employment Retirement Income Security Act (ERISA): ERISA specified that companies which self-insured would not be made to comply with state regulations in areas such as pensions and health care.

By self-insuring, companies became directly responsible for searching for ways to keep costs down. To this end they introduced cost controls that changed the incentives of both providers and consumers in the health care marketplace (or, as many would argue, the lack thereof). Employers tried to alter the *demand* for health care by changing consumer incentives; for example, cost shifting required workers to bear a greater share through increased premiums, deductibles, or copayments. Firms introduced flex benefits, which give workers financial incentives to choose less comprehensive health coverage and, thereby, to assume some of the risks of illness. Typically, flex benefits allocate a fixed sum that workers can distribute among competing social needs: day care, health insurance, and sometimes ready cash. The approach rested on a betting person's logic: Since healthy individuals use the health system less, they should pay less up front and put their money where they need it more. For example, an innovator of this technique, Quaker Oats, offered all employees $400, which they could contribute to a premium for an expensive plan, keep in a tax-sheltered account for out-of-pocket health expenses, or take as added taxable income. The company bragged that its costs increased only 6 percent a year from 1983 until the early 1990s, a figure considerably below the industry average (Stern 1991: 14–21).

Flex benefits offer savings by giving employees an incentive to join more cost-effective plans, but they have a darker side as well. Flex benefits narrow the scope of the risk pool and alter the previously understood nature of insurance. By definition, insurance offers a mechanism for equalizing pain, by using healthy people's resources to aid the sick and injured. Flex plans by design remove healthy people from the pools, thus reducing the resources available to the less fortunate and returning the risk to the individual for his or her own future ailments. In addition, flex plans, like block grants, have often been used to disguise a real reduction in benefits: If I need day care and you need health care, a reduction in our total benefits through a flex plan means that we can take the hit where we are least likely to feel the pain.

Another cost-saving device aimed at changing individual incentives and behavior was the wellness movement. Wellness programs rest on an obvious assumption: Medical costs go down if health improves. Reflecting the general physical fitness craze of the late eighties, some companies decided to give their employees incentives to lead healthy lives. Since smoking, exercise, and diet have well-confirmed impacts on general health, firms began with incentives for changing individual behavior in these areas. Hershey Foods, for example, developed a complicated formula to reward exercise, nonsmoking, and weight maintenance with deductions from monthly premiums; bad behavior resulted in penalty surcharges. Some employees endorsed this approach energetically; others felt it smacked of social control (Frieden 1991: 56–60).

Firms also experimented with *supply-side* techniques to change provider incentives, to limit excessive medical intervention, and to ensure appropriate care. During the 1980s, systems of utilization review were put into place in which independent physicians randomly monitored medical decisions and identified excessive interventions. In some systems patients were required to seek prior authorization from a "patient advocate" for all but the most emergent interventions. Employees were asked to seek a second opinion for planned surgical procedures. From 1983 to 1985 a sample of large companies with utilization review programs in place jumped from 17 to 45 percent (Friedland 1987: 15). By 1990, 82 percent of a sample of large- and medium-sized firms were using the technique (Grobman 1993: 21–30). Utilization review techniques initially seemed promising; yet, over time, doctors found ways to avoid the constraints imposed by the procedure.[3]

Recently, managed care has swept through the corporate world. The story of managed care, of course, begins with HMOs, first as a Kaiser company innovation and West Coast cooperative movement in the 1930s and then as a matter of public policy in the 1970s. HMOs (in their purest form) pay doctors' salaries; by doing away with the piecework payment of fee-for-service, the physician has no incentive to offer inappropriate care. In addition, doctors often receive a share of the yearly profits as further incentive to restrain unnecessary intervention. HMOs seek to limit hospitalizations with preventive care, thus keeping patients healthier and restraining inpatient costs. Studies report that HMOs have lower hospitalization rates, although these may reflect relatively healthier populations (Herzlinger 1985: 108–120).[4]

Next Preferred Provider Organizations (PPOs) were created that offered special discounts to firms when employees sought treatment from the physicians in the network. But health costs seemed to escalate just as rapidly.[5] After initial enthusiasm, only 20 percent of one sample of companies in 1991 found the PPOs to be very effective (1991 National Executive Poll 1991: 61–71).[6]

Managed care went through another important permutation in the mid-1980s when the major insurers began to reinvent themselves as organizers of medical services. Although Prudential and Cigna had offered HMO options since the 1970s, most other insurers remained restricted to traditional indemnity plans. In the mid-1980s, however, insurers began to offer a new managed care option, the point-of-service (POS) plan. Halfway between HMOs and PPOs, the point-of-service plan assigns patients to a family practitioner who acts as a gatekeeper for other services and often has financial incentives to restrict inappropriate health care.[7]

Corporate providers of health have flocked to managed care in droves since the 1980s. In 1992 Foster Higgins found nearly three-fourths of its sampled companies offering a managed care option (either POS or HMO) (Foster Higgins 1992: 5). HMO enrollment alone went from 2 million in 1970 to 51 million in 1995 (Findlay 1995a). A Foster Higgins survey found that by 1995, managed care networks had come to cover 71 percent of workers who received health benefits through their jobs (Freudenheim 1995b: D1).

Three phenomena contributed to the expansion of managed care. First, corporate America was becoming more desperate about the price of health. Bergthold (1990: 26–30) points out that beginning in the late 1970s, when companies began to make the connection between plunging corporate profits and rising health costs, the term crisis was increasingly applied to health care delivery. Managed care forms (first HMOs and then point-of-service plans) were important forms of experimentation in cost control.

Managed care appealed instinctively to big companies as market-shaping reforms, but as Bergthold (ibid.: 27) points out, it also conveyed the ideology of corporate rationalization. In addition, managed care mirrored what was happening in manufacturing processes during this period. Cognizant of superior Japanese production techniques, American firms became interested in quality and in longer-term relations with suppliers and customers. Where traditional indemnity plans resembled arms-length contractual relations in manufacturing, managed care arrangements operated much like the closer relations between suppliers and purchasers that were becoming popular at that time (Robinson 1995: 117–130). As one manager explained it:

> [The company] started focusing on emphasizing quality in manufacturing processes. Around this time there was a major manufacturing effort to reduce the number of suppliers in the manufacturing process: it went from roughly 4,500 suppliers to about 10

percent of that number. . . . The benefits people thought that this was an interesting parallel to our situation. We also wanted to reduce suppliers and emphasize quality. We felt that the HMOs were the right vehicle for changing the delivery system and getting an organized system of care. . . . A lot of alliances were being formed in manufacturing at this point. These cooperative alliances coexisted with competitive behavior because they were in the best interests of all parties. . . . So benefits said, "Let's apply the same principle in health."[8]

Second, large insurers felt increasingly shut out of their traditional industry by the self-insure movement among large companies and realized that they could reinvent themselves as organizers of medical services. The health insurance industry in the 1980s was in financial turmoil: managed care offered a way to regain profit margins (Kosterlitz 1987: 936). Large insurers launched a major sales drive to advertise their new quick fix for escalating health costs, and big business was impressed. Small insurers were badly hurt by the decline of the fee-for-service market; therefore, managed care served to enhance the power and market share of its big-insurer proponents.

A few of the early innovators in managed care attracted considerable publicity, making it easier for others to follow suit. For example, Southwestern Bell and Allied Signal were among the first to move into managed care. Southwestern Bell claimed that with its managed care plan, company costs increased less than 10 percent from 1988 to 1989, compared with a national average of 20 to 24 percent (Bell 1991: 20). Allied Signal hired Cigna to develop a national HMO network called Health Care Connection (HCC). By 1992 Allied Signal claimed that HCC was 35 percent over previous costs (Bell 1992: 34).

Third, the corporate purchaser coalition movement, to which I will now turn, also made managers more favorably disposed to managed care arrangements. Although the coalition movement primarily attempted to change market dynamics by aggregating consumers on the demand side and thereby increasing purchaser power, the coalitions also considered arguments for improving market performance by restructuring the supply of health care.

Restructuring Markets at the Community Level

The story of efforts to restructure markets would not be complete without reference to the regional coalitions that exercise leverage on markets at the community level. Groups and networks in general were important in sensitizing large employers to issues of cost control, but the purchaser coalitions were most important to the burgeoning managed care movement.[9] Alain Enthoven developed the concept of community-based purchaser coalitions to reinstate market rationality into the health system. By banding together in purchasing coalitions, firms can leverage lower health rates with their greater market power (Cronin 1988: 4–7; Jaeger 1985).

Gradually coalitions targeted quality of outcomes as well as costs. Walter McClure, the Moses of quality, preached productivity in health care to his corporate following. The heart of his message was simple: Too many health dollars are wasted in unsuccessful treatments. If we can identify and implement successful interventions, cost containment will follow. This focus on quality was politically appealing because it suggested that the productivity of health care can be improved and costs lowered without sacrificing benefit levels. One benefits manager recalled this attraction for CEOs:

> The CEOs were in a very uncomfortable position. They were between three rocks: health care costs . . . significant employee relations problems, and the medical people or doctor problem. . . . The CEOs did nothing about the health problem because they got beaten up any way they went. Quality gave them a way out. First, it clearly had appeal and had a chance of actually working. Second, it didn't cost them anything financially. Third, it gave them a good guy position in the community. People thought about how it would play in the papers.[10]

The coalition movement was helped enormously by the efforts of McClure disciple, Dale Shaller. Shaller brought a background in community action to the task of organizing a backyard revolution in the corporate world. Shaller believed that business must be mobilized the same way that others in society are propelled to political action: Systemic change begins in the community. As a consultant to many regional coalitions, Shaller offered his organizing skills to help employers overcome the limits of collective action.

The coalition movement received early seed money from several sources. The Washington Business Group on Health helped to set up local coalitions in a number of regions, as did the National Chamber of Commerce. The Robert Wood Johnson Foundation invested in the coalition movement (Craig 1985). In 1992 the Hartford Foundation gave $2.25 million in a three-year grant to the National Business Coalition Forum on Health, an organization that represents forty-eight member coalitions and was quite active in protecting the community approach in the legislative cycle (Health Action Council n.d.).

But the true stories of coalitions are local, just like the politics that describes them. In some communities coalitions quickly gained a position of prominence among employers; in others the coalitions were dissolved. Some regional groups moved quickly into collective purchasing arrangements; others remained informational in function. The coalition movement seemed to be strongest in the Midwest and West, perhaps because regulatory solutions were more popular in eastern states. But even within the heartland, success varied greatly and seemed to depend on the dynamics of local business movements.

The Cleveland Health Quality Choice Coalition has been a poster child of the coalition movement with a joint purchaser-provider effort to produce outcome measurement techniques for sixty diagnosis-related groups (DRGs).[11] Hospitals are evaluated in terms of their performance in each group; employers can use this outcomes data to steer their employees to the best providers.

The Cleveland case is interesting both because of the high level of cooperation between business and providers and because the business community took the initiative in trying to change the health care delivery system. The story began with a coalition of employers called the Health Action Council of Northeast Ohio (HAC), which covered 350,000 lives and had been meeting since 1982 to try to reduce health costs. According to Executive Director Pat Casey, participants tried the full gambit of usual interventions to restrain costs, but nothing worked. HAC member Don Flagg, the vice president for human resources at the Nestle Corporation and "a good egg breaker," began railing against rising health costs and the hospitals' role in this escalation. Flagg aroused provider ire but drew considerable attention to his aggressive campaign. One participant believes that Flagg "may have pre-softened" hospitals with this early attack.

When Flagg left Nestle's, he was replaced by Powell Woods, a born mediator with a peaceful, humorous manner who ultimately left the corporate world and went to seminary school. In 1988 Woods and the HAC met Walter McClure and were "blown away" by his philosophy. McClure had been working to develop a statewide data collection system in Pennsylvania; however, providers had stonewalled the effort. Therefore, the Cleveland employers decided to limit the scope of their ambitions to the community level.[12]

Woods, Casey, and the HAC set out to sell Cleveland's CEOs on a

McClure approach to cost containment, armed with information and the spirit of true believers. The HAC commissioned a study which found Cleveland's per capita hospital costs to be 50 percent higher than those at the Mayo Clinic. Woods recruited his former CEO John Morley (Reliance) to agitate at the chief executive level, and Morley invited the HAC to present its findings to Cleveland Tomorrow, a group of fifty CEOs that had sponsored reforms in a variety of policy spheres since the city nearly went bankrupt in the 1970s. One CEO wag remarked, "We could send our people to the Mayo Clinic with their families and still pay less." Woods remembers that the model had an enormous impact on the CEOs, because it allowed them to be the "good guy on a social issue of immense importance. . . . They could be the white knights on this issue."

Cleveland Tomorrow and the HAC joined with prominent small business organizations and local hospital and physician associations in setting up the Cleveland Health Quality Choice Coalition. Hospitals devoted $80,000 apiece to the effort, and participating businesses came up with an additional $600,000 (Kisner 1992: 20–27). The employers decided that providers had to be involved from the beginning "so that they couldn't just say that the system stinks." Hospitals were adamant that the data on which they were to be judged had to be correct and different from Medicare's HCVA data. Hospitals also demanded that the data be provided only to employers trained to interpret them. Employers responded with a velvet-glove ultimatum: Either the hospitals must generate acceptable data, or employers would base purchasing decisions on cost.[13] Pat Casey attributed Cleveland employers' success in negotiating with hospitals to the focus on quality over cost. Cost-based negotiations suggest zero-sum dynamics, whereas quality suggests a win-win situation. Woods agreed that the logic was hard to deny: "The CEOs could say to the hospital, 'Everyone knows that these are the best hospitals in Cleveland, so isn't it time to let everyone know it? If they are not, we need to be the first to know.' The hospitals couldn't disagree."

But the other realpolitik ingredient in Cleveland's success was the extreme unity of the business community. The top ten companies were members of the coalition, as were small-business managers. As one hospital executive put it, "These guys are all over my board."

Although the Cleveland effort to control health costs was exceptional, it was not unique. Like Ohio, Minnesota has a strongly unified business community and a coalition committed to quality of care. Minnesota has a progressive history dating back to the Democratic Farmer Labor party; the spirit of cooperation among business managers is powerful in the state. The Business Health Care Action Group was formed by fourteen of the Twin Cities' largest firms in order to collectively purchase health benefits from a network of doctors called the GroupCare Consortium.[14] But the group was not content to negotiate merely about price; it also decided that it wanted to play a role in actively changing the health care market and in improving the quality of care. Like the Cleveland effort, the group sought to ensure quality, but in this case it did so by developing clinical practice guidelines. According to Fred Hammacher (Dayton Hudson), "People don't understand the health care marketplace—it's a dumb market. . . . The mission statement of our group is to change the health care marketplace [in Minnesota] for the benefit of everyone." The group has already developed approximately forty best practices and hopes to complete eighty in all. Each has been developed by a subcommittee made up of business managers, physicians, and hospital representatives. As Hammacher puts it, "You need to develop them at the grass roots so that you can get ownership."

St. Louis also has a well-organized business community with an activist coalition, but the balance of power between purchasers and providers of health is quite different, and early efforts to control health costs collectively failed. Hospitals and medical schools in the city were very strong, and employers were essentially outflanked. One business manager estimates that the greater metropolitan area has about 2,669 extra beds—a powerful testimony to provider power. Thus the backdrop for regional reform differed greatly from that in Cleveland or Minneapolis.

Undaunted by this impressive medical-industrial complex, corporate purchasers of health care decided in the late 1980s to reduce health costs by publishing hospital prices for selected inpatient services, a system they called the Prospective Pricing Initiative (PPI). The St. Louis Area Business Health Coalition led the effort with a CEO group called Civic Progress, representing the twenty-nine largest companies in St. Louis. St. Louis employers had been pooling claims data organized by DRGs since 1983, but now they were going public with the prices.[15] Employers also had hoped to interest managed care administrators, but the latter showed little interest. One administrator responded, "I've already picked my providers, and have already gotten my discounts from them." Employers took this as a sign that the current discounts meant little.

The coalition began by surveying outpatient hospital rates and found a wide gap between the highest and lowest priced provider. Next the employers moved on to inpatient care, asking thirty-six hospitals to give them "real live market prices" on 250 DRGs.[16] Although participants felt that they had cultivated provider support, on the day of delivery only three out of thirty-six hospitals complied entirely; another five offered partial information. The employer coalition spent the next five months trying to persuade the top hospitals to comply, and the coalition's executive director, Jim Stutts, even approached the Federal Trade Commission, but the resistance was unified and immutable.

Despite the failure of the PPI initiative, St. Louis employers later reorganized as the St. Louis Quality Alliance and began a project to measure outcomes data.[17] Learning a lesson from their past failure, employers began to build alliances with other interests and moved away from their past strategies of conflict. Stutts reflected on the newfound spirit of cooperation:

> In the old days business would have tried to take on the hospitals by themselves to get them to scale back their beds. But more recently the major employers have discovered that they must work with a lot of other people. So they got six other organizations to be involved in the project: the Blues, Cigna, Association of Insurance Brokers, City Health Dept., United Auto Workers. All participated at public testimony at the hearings. For the community this was quite important.

Unlike in Cleveland where the business efforts remained private, in St. Louis, employers worked closely with state government. For example, the public and private sectors worked together to pass a health care data disclosure law in 1992. Stutts felt that regulation was a natural outcome of providers' resistance to a voluntary data project:

> Prospective pricing was employers' last chance to say, "This can be done voluntarily." We did all we could do to do it voluntarily and the providers said "No." So we finally said [to state government], "Go do what you want to do." Odd bedfellows have developed in health care in Missouri. Business and labor have a lot in common on this issue. Some of our most conservative members were thrilled at state regulation for data disclosure even though it entailed a lot of government intervention.

Firm Efforts to Control Costs after National Health Reform

Despite some successes in controlling health costs, by the late 1980s many employers felt frustrated with firm-level and community market interventions and began to contemplate systemic regulatory change at the national level. The Clinton national health reform plan reflected the growing frustration with market mechanisms, although in reality it constituted a blend of regulatory and market concepts. Theda Skocpol and Jacob Hacker (1997) argue that managed competition won out over play-

or-pay in part because corporate America had moved into the managed care market. Important corporate forums such as the Jackson Hole group and the Managed Health Care Association pushed policy makers to build reform around the managed care concept (Traska 1990: 12).

Components of the Clinton health plan initially attracted considerable corporate support. In my study of high-level managers from randomly sampled Fortune 200 companies, over half of the business respondents (54 percent) supported mandates and another 19 percent were mixed on the subject. Forty-one percent of the companies had already either developed a supportive position on employer mandates or were about to take a position, and another 13 percent found top management divided and deliberating over whether to become involved. Cantor et al. (1991: 99–101) found that 80 percent of the Fortune 500 executives in their study believed that "fundamental changes are needed to make it [the health system] better," and 53 percent supported employer mandates. A National Association of Manufacturers (NAM) survey in the late summer of 1993 found a clear majority of its members supporting mandates and health alliances for firms of over five hundred employees.[18] A 1994 Washington Business Group on Health survey of large firms showed 72 percent supported requiring all companies to offer insurance, 59 percent wanted firms to pay a portion, and 71 percent objected to an arrangement that allowed small business to escape the mandate.[19]

Managers have described their path to systemic reform as one of increasing frustration with firm-level efforts to change provider behavior. One person told me that her support for a single-payer system emerged in a survey to identify the solution to the U.S. health crisis: "I realized at that moment that the only thing that would make a difference was to have a national solution." Another manager explained, "Most of us recognize that the things we did in the mid-1980s didn't really work." But although national health reform was a response to the legacy of failed market interventions, company attitudes today are shaped by the legacy of failed government policy. In the wake of the downfall of national health reform, firms have returned to private and community efforts as the mainstay of their efforts to curb costs. Are they more satisfied with these efforts than they were in the period before health reform? The evidence is mixed.

On an optimistic note, the growth in company health costs seems to have dropped off. Katharine Levit et al. (1994: 14–31) found that total health spending grew by only 7.8 percent from 1992 to 1993, the lowest since 1987, and that much of this growth was concentrated in the public sector. In 1992 companies using managed care in a Towers Perrin (1992) study reported that their growth rate decreased from 18 percent to 12 percent. Towers Perrin consultants found health costs for employees (in their sample firms) increased only 6 percent in 1994 and 2 percent in 1995, as opposed to 14 percent in 1991 (Towers Perrin 1996). A Foster Higgins study found health costs in 1994 actually declining by 1.1 percent for the first time in a decade (Freudenheim 1995a). A large employer study of employees' feelings about health plans found the greatest proportion (86 percent) pleased with HMOs. The authors surmised that this reflected the low cost sharing inherent in the managed care plans (Jones 1995: 33).

But all is not peaceful on the western front. Huskamp and Newhouse (1994) have cast doubt on the aggregate health spending figures. Using National Income and Product Accounts data instead of Health Care Financing Administration data, and employing a different deflator for inflation adjustment, the authors concluded that the health care spending slowdown "is modest at best" (ibid.: 32–38).

Many employers fear that costs were artificially restrained during the health reform political cycle (in an effort by providers to demonstrate that national legislation was not necessary to curb increases) and are again on the rise. Foster Higgins found a 2.1 percent increase in 1995, although the increase was concentrated in traditional indemnity plans. The cost of benefits in managed care plans continued to decline (Freudenheim 1995b). Towers Perrin (1996) found health costs for employers up 4 percent in 1996, a modest growth rate but still above the 1995 figures.

Some analysts believe that the declining growth rate in health care costs simply reflects a movement out of fee-for-service plans: When this process is completed, health costs will continue to rise (Donlon and Benson 1996: 52). In addition, business managers fear that the initial savings from moving into managed care will not be sustained over time. An early innovator in point-of-service plans reported that after the first few years the plans began to engage in shadow-pricing; the POS plan prices rose at the same rate as the traditional indemnity plans, albeit at a slightly lower level. Administrative costs for point-of-service plans also seem to be higher than those for traditional indemnity plans. There is also the problem of adverse selection—only the healthiest may be willing to join managed care (Bell 1992: 32–38).

Fears about the future of managed care price restraints have been exacerbated by the current wave of mergers and acquisitions within this field. Managed care became predominantly a for-profit enterprise in the mid-1980s (Davis, Collins, and Morris 1994: 178–185). The future of health care provision increasingly looks like "the battle of the Titans" and one wonders what this will mean for cost controls. For example,

Aetna recently acquired U.S. Healthcare for $8.8 billion (Freudenheim 1995b). The managed care industry had 1,100 mergers and acquisitions in 1994 totaling $60 billion (Donlon and Benson 1996).

Some believe that increasingly larger units could give an oligopolistic structure to the industry. Reducing the number of competitors may eventually allow premium prices to rise. Profits in the for-profit HMO sector increased by 40 percent from 1992 to 1994 (Findlay 1995b). Others disagree, arguing that the increasing competition among managed care providers is further reducing price increases (West 1995). For example, James Robinson (1995) suggests that the Pacific Business Group on Health's collective bargaining for its members has contributed to a 9 percent decline in HMO premiums. The Pacific Business firms have found that they do not need to offer many different plans in order to push down costs; rather they can negotiate good prices with a small select group of providers.

Big business managers are also very concerned about the "any willing provider" legislation now being considered in many states in response to aggressive lobbying by the medical profession. These laws could stop employers from having exclusive contracts. As one employer humorously put it, the "any billing provider" legislation could effectively prevent firms from controlling costs at the state level.

Business Involvement in Public Policy: Medicare Reform

Meanwhile, market solutions are making inroads in the public policy arena, and large purchasers of health care are much more ambivalent about this occurrence, as witnessed by the 1995–96 Medicare reform episode. The Republicans came to power with far-reaching legislation that combined tax reduction, spending reduction, and budget balancing, all in one ambitious package. An essential part of the Republican plan was to secure savings from the Medicare program: a big-ticket item in the budget, and due to its entitlement status, one that is usually considered off-limits to deficit reduction. Medicare provides universal coverage for 37 million citizens over sixty-five, at a cost that totaled $159.5 billion in 1994 and that rises 10 percent per annum (Toner and Pear 1995).

The Republicans proposed to cut $270 billion from the Medicare budget over a seven-year period, by reducing Medicare spending by 14 percent in the next seven years (ibid.). The Republicans would glean these savings from a variety of sources. First, Medicare premiums would double from the current rate of $46.10 to $87.60 by 2002. Second, the Republicans would encourage recipients to move into managed care systems, by offering benefits to managed care patients that fee-for-service systems do not currently cover. Originally the Republicans had hoped to use strong financial incentives to pressure more elderly people into managed care arrangements by offering rebates for lower-cost plans. But they ultimately bowed to public pressure and moved away from this more radical stance (Overheard 1995).

Behind the Republican desire to "save" Medicare seemed to be broad goals to restructure social provision in the health area and to reduce the size of government. First, many felt that the Republican proposal was designed less to save Medicare than to reduce overall government spending and to pay for huge tax cuts. Because only about one-fifth of the national budget is discretionary domestic spending (the remainder represents military expenditures and entitlements), the GOP ambitions could not easily be realized. Entitlements were an obvious area of expansion and Medicare was an obvious entitlement to begin with, since the immensely popular social security program is out of bonds. In fact, the *New York Times* claimed that the magic number of $270 billion was actually calculated simply because that was how much was needed. The Republicans figured out what it would cost to balance the budget by 2002 and to cut taxes by $245 billion, and what they could get out of other government programs; the shortfall was $270 billion (Rosenbaum 1995a: A26). The Republican portrayal of Medicare's trajectory toward bankruptcy gave weight to this cynical view. In reality, the Medicare trustees have predicted insolvency since 1980, but Congress has always increased taxes or changed benefit levels to meet new revenue demands. The real problem is that medical inflation is increasing faster than prices in the rest of the economy; therefore, Medicare is commanding an ever greater share of the federal budget. The Democrats argued in 1993 (and continue to argue) that the solution to rising health costs should not be limited to Medicare, but should address the total health system (Rosenbaum 1995a: 18).

Second, some believed that the Republicans were trying to challenge the social right to health care for the elderly and the poor. As Judith Feder (1995) argued in the *Washington Post,* the proposed caps on Medicare spending would change the program from one offering a defined benefit to one offering a defined contribution, a change that was even more explicit in the original Republican plan. Under a defined benefit plan (one that promises to pay beneficiaries' health care premium every month) an elderly person is assured of having his or her health care covered. Under a defined contribution approach, beneficiaries would be given a dollar limit for health care, but would have to come up with the remainder themselves. The obvious advantage of the second approach for government payers is that public funds would cover smaller future increases and would give budget predictability and control that are now lacking. Once a dollar commitment was made, the government could announce that it had done its part and the problems of coping with rising costs would be passed on to the elderly consumer. Republicans defended this defined contribution system as a measure to encourage consumers to make more fiscally responsible decisions and to quicken the move out of costly fee-for-service plans and into more efficient managed care arrangements. The leadership moved away from explicitly endorsing a defined contribution system, but Feder and others argued that the cap pushed the program in that direction. Feder also worried that providers would have incentive to limit the number of Medicare patients that they would accept (ibid.).

The Republicans' proposed changes in Medicaid further eroded the social right to health care. Medicaid was originally set up as an entitlement, or a guaranteed benefit not subject to annual budgetary allocations. The Republicans, however, wanted to include Medicaid in a broad block grant to the states, thereby allowing individual jurisdictions to decide where to use their money and ending the right of the poor to medical assistance.

Third, the Republicans wanted to end Medicare as a universal financing scheme for elderly persons' health insurance by allowing recipients to opt out of the public program and into the private insurance market. Recipients would be allowed to buy into private HMO and Provider Service Network plans with Medicare dollars or to set up medical savings accounts. In medical savings account plans, patients pay very low premiums but very high deductibles; the dollars saved from the premiums could go into a fund to cover the deductibles or could be applied to other life needs. Critics charge that medical savings accounts will fracture the pool of Medicare patients, giving incentives for healthy patients to opt out, thereby driving up costs for those who choose to stay in the plans (McIlrath 1995a). The plan thus alters the incentive structure and logic of insurance: "save for a rainy day" becomes "take the best right now." Because the elderly by definition get sicker (and often poorer) over time, such logic is questionable for this group.

The Congressional Budget Office (CBO) was skeptical about this privatization plan. The CBO estimated that only 21 percent of Medicare recipients would be in HMOs by 2002, as opposed to 14 percent currently (Pear 1995a). It estimated that the Republican bill would mainly save money by increasing costs to the beneficiaries (saving $71 billion out of

$270 billion) and by decreasing reimbursements to providers (saving $152 billion out of $270 billion). The CBO also blasted medical savings accounts, predicting that they would increase total Medicare costs by $2.3 billion over seven years, rather than cutting costs (Pear 1995b).

Republican Allies: Providers and Small Business

In addition to broad spending cuts, the Republican Medicare proposal also contained a number of specific provisions to restructure the health care system. Critics charged that these provisions were designed to attract support from key interest groups.

Doctors were an essential source of political support, and given the huge scope of the intended cuts, a surprising one as well. To some extent the Republicans assuaged physicians' fears about the cuts by promising that Medicare fees would not be reduced for seven years; indeed, because current law was to have lowered physician reimbursement, this represented an actual savings.[20] But the bill also provided for added controls on doctors' fees, should the requisite savings not materialize (Clymer 1995a).

But much more attractive to the doctors was the provider-sponsored network proposal that enabled physicians to form their own provider groups without an HMO license and to cut out insurance middlemen. Currently doctors cannot refer patients to facilities with which they are financially involved; the Republicans wanted to change this practice. The Republican bill would eliminate regulations of medical laboratories and nursing homes, and would require Medicare to reimburse for-profit hospitals for local property taxes.[21] Thus, although the American Medical Association calculated that the biggest savings in the Republican House plan would come from providers (53 percent), it endorsed the measure, drawn to provider networks and tort reform (McIlrath 1995b). Many doctors viewed with alarm the Republican decision to roll Medicaid into block grants. Although the American Medical Association did not officially oppose this decision (since it was told that the block grant goal was nonnegotiable), it did suggest that uniform standards of care be recommended to the states and that the Medicaid budget reductions be softened (Pear 1995c).

For-profit hospitals were with the Republicans from the beginning, drawn to the many special benefits. The American Hospital Association, representing mostly public hospitals, was much more skeptical of the Republican House and Senate plans, feeling that the enormous cuts in Medicare offset any special incentives (Weissenstein 1995). But the Republicans made a series of concessions, especially in the Senate, to assuage the concerns of the big teaching hospitals.

Insurers were attracted to the Republican Medicare concept because they liked the party's efforts to move the elderly into the private insurance market. Most of the largest managed care programs are run by the large insurers. Senator Edward Kennedy (D-MA) charged that this represented a "conspiracy between the insurance industry and the Republicans" to kill Medicare. If all seniors traded Medicare for private insurance options, the industry premium revenue would balloon by $1.25 trillion over seven years (Fisher 1995a). Private health plans received progressively larger concessions throughout the legislative process, culminating in major giveaways in the joint conference committee. In the final bill (vetoed by Clinton) these plans were to receive an 8 percent annual increase in Medicare reimbursement in the near term. Private plans would also be eligible for Medicare money for medical education and treatment of the uninsured, even if those plans did not send members to teaching hospitals or treat the uninsured. These concessions were largely responsible for the erosion of revenue savings in the Medicare bill.[22]

Small business groups were energized by their political success in the fight against national health reform. In the post-reform era these groups have continued to work closely with the Republican party in the budget and Medicare campaigns. Small business groups supported the Medicare changes both because they were part of the larger budget package and because they saw the reforms as a way to restrain the rise in payroll taxes. The Chamber of Commerce publication, *Nation's Business,* suggested that the Medicare Trust Fund was considering raising payroll taxes from 2.9 percent to 4.23 percent to pay for Medicare hospital insurance. To make Medicare solvent for seventy-five years, according to the Chamber, the payroll tax would be increased to 6.42 percent, and 3.2 million jobs would be lost in the process (Warner 1995: 8).

Efforts to satisfy different interests were not entirely congruous. For example, the Health Insurance Association of America (HIAA) objected to the provision making it easier for physicians to form managed care arrangements (Clymer 1995b). The leadership added subsidies for recipients in rural areas shortly before the House vote, but took this money away from big city hospitals, already hit hard by provisions that reduced Medicare subsidies for teaching and for giving assistance to the poor. This prompted four Republican legislators from New Jersey to vote against the House bill (Fein 1995: 1, 8).

Large Employers and Medicare Reform

The subtext for big-business involvement in health policy is the lack of an effective political organization to represent large employers' collective concerns. Despite the widely held myth of big-business power, large employers are so politically fragmented that associations representing their interests engage only in the most reactive political activities. Companies are extremely effective at stopping what they perceive to be hostile regulation and in gaining narrowly concentrated public benefits. But the organizational structure and rules of American trade associations make it very difficult for large employers to pursue their self-defined, long-term collective goals.

Democrats disdained the many concessions to special interests in the Republican proposal; for example, suggesting that the concessions to doctors only encouraged greater incidents of medical waste, fraud, and abuse. The Republicans responded that they preferred to worry about catching all the real criminals out there menacing society, and ridiculed the Democratic concern about Medicare crooks. Pete Stark responded, "To put O. J. Simpson, the Menendez brothers, and Claus von Bulow in the same category as physicians who get kickbacks and who steal from the government is not the issue."

Thus large employers were quite concerned about the general thrust of the proposed Medicare changes, but did little to influence the legislative course beyond damage control—what large employers do best. Large corporate purchasers' single largest objection was to a program for keeping employees in private health plans (as yet voluntary). As the Business Roundtable put it, the government had an obligation to cover Medicare recipients and should not transfer this responsibility to business (McIlrath 1995b: 1). Large employers disliked the proposal to increase the age of Medicare eligibility; to this end the Corporate Health Care Coalition attacked the Republican plan (although the CHCC likes some of the managed care provisions) (Pear 1995d: A22). Some managers also feared that the radical Right would try to slowly phase out the employer-based system altogether and to return health care to individual responsibility.[23] In addition, big-business managers felt threatened by the broad Republican goal of turning policy back to the states, because they worried that these efforts might ultimately threaten the ERISA preemption. A representative of a large food-products firm explained, "Gingrich is scary to business on many fronts, especially the ERISA issue. We'd hate to be at the mercy of 50 different bodies."

Large employers had been alarmed when the Clinton administration proposed cutting Medicare to pay for expanded access, and they continued to worry that the Republicans wanted Medicare reductions to balance the budget (and pay for the tax cut). Large employers worried (and not without reason) that the Medicare cuts would result in greater cost shifting by hospitals to private payers. Many noted that the Republican plan had no incentives to move beneficiaries into more cost-efficient plans from fee-for-service arrangements (Freudenheim 1995b: 49). Thus the benefits manager for a large food-manufacturing company observed, "The Contract with America's attempts to cut Medicare are cost-shifting back to the business community." Business managers also worried that the Republican's proposal to turn Medicaid into a block grant would result in greater cost shifting to private employers. Seeking to reduce cost shifting onto private insurance, employers for some time had argued that government should pay its full share of the health care burden by fully funding programs for the poor. Now they sought to prevent actual cuts in government financing. *Business and Health* warned,

> To the extent that states have been able to control Medicaid spending, they have done so by sharply limiting payments to providers. . . . And guess who makes up the difference? Employers and private insurers. This Medicaid cost shift has been estimated to add between 5 and 10 percent to the cost of health care for private payers. With less money from the federal government under a block grant program, the pressure to ratchet down payments to providers will be even greater. . . . The business community has a strong vested interest in seeing that the Medicaid program gets overhauled carefully. One way or another, it ends up paying the bills. (Findlay 1995: 55)

As in the battles over the Clinton plan, large employers did relatively little to resist the Republican Medicare plan. To some extent big business contributed little to the Medicare discussion because it was busy with more urgent issues, such as deficit reduction, taxes, and regulatory relief. The Business Roundtable group, Coalition for Change, planned to spend $10 million in advertising to support nonpartisan deficit reduction (Stone 1995a).

Large employers were also wooed by the Republican leadership during the period of Medicare proposal development. The Thursday Group pondered how to get large employers to board the Medicare reduction bandwagon. They surmised that if they could shift as many Medicare recipients into HMOs as possible, large employers would be reassured that they would not be subjected to more cost shifting. Early on, the leadership moved away from trying to keep retirees in company plans. Gingrich also personally reached out to some of the large corporations that had been supportive of the Clinton efforts in order to convey the message that he was concerned about the big employers' issues on Medicare. To some extent, the Republicans' dealings with these very specific fears of large employers diminished their expression of broader concerns about the impact of the Medicare cuts.

Large employers were also coerced by the Republicans. The Republican leadership felt that many in the corporate lobby were Democrats with a pernicious influence within the firm. Republicans sought to change the positions and composition of business groups and company government affairs offices by demanding that these groups and firms support the contract and hire more GOP lobbyists. For example, the American Insurance Association approached Vin Weber, former Republican Minnesotan legislator, to supplant its Democratic lobbyist Beryl Anthony (Moore 1994: 2912). Gingrich aide Ed Cutler warned a lobbyist who had worked on the Clinton health plan, "You better be on the right side this year." The leadership circulated information to legislators about the party affiliation of individual lobbyists. Bill Paxton (R-NY) circulated to House Republicans a detailed inventory of contributions from the four hundred largest PACs that "reminds Members who our friends are." Although the Republicans denied that they were planning to blackball Democratic lobbyists, some admitted that access to the leadership at least required the correct political credentials (Moore, Cohen, and Stone 1995: 1341–1343). John Boehner complained: "For years, CEOs have hired liberals for their Washington offices who've kept them in the dark on many things. There's been little change since the election, and that's widened the disconnect between Republicans and the business community" (Big Business 1995: A14).

When large employers did intervene, they felt that the Republicans (like the Democrats before them) paid little attention to their complaints. Some business managers blamed the politicians; for example, one complained that the Republican party was not interested in input from large firms. A representative of a big midwestern office-supplies company remembered working hard to convince the Republicans that "business wasn't as bad as they thought." Another recalled:

> I was very surprised that big business had no stature or weight with the Democrats and now I feel that it is equally true with the Republicans. We're not saints but we have been in the benefits area for

years. We were ignored by Clinton and have been ignored by the GOP. The message is not getting through that we have something to offer. It is startling how poor a job we have done in establishing credibility.

Other managers realized that their inability to influence the Medicare debate reflected the same organizational weakness that prevented large employers from getting what they wanted in the effort to legislate health reform. As a manager from a large northeastern manufacturing firm observed, "Corporate America is preoccupied with short-term issues and now we don't have short-term health care problems." A manager from a utility reflected, "Business did itself a disservice by not taking a cohesive position on it [Medicare]." An oil company manager explained: "We are not going to put our nose up on Medicare at this point. . . . I don't think that large employers have the clout to rein in the Republican agenda—especially in the House, where many first and second termers have no affinity for big business."

National health reform exacerbated the underlying weakness of big business, because some managers had tried to engage their peers and failed. At the height of the battle over national health reform, one had a sense of history in the making, of a defining moment that once passed could never be reversed or forgotten. For the various parts of the business community, health reform was also a critical juncture, at once a lesson in the politics of the possible and a snapshot view of the balance of power among the producing classes. Those big-business managers who had ventured timid support for health system overhaul went away as chastised and enfeebled political actors with renewed atheism about the power of public policy. Business leaders were reluctant to expose themselves to such glaring defeat again. A Washington lobbyist put it baldly:

> Business got a little embarrassed by its association with Clinton. Old manufacturing industries were quick to jump on a Clinton bandwagon. But it divided the business community and embarrassed those like the automobile industry that were too close to the Clinton process. The ARCO CEO (Cook) got a nasty piece written about him in the *Wall Street Journal*. Other CEOs were made to feel like they had knifed business in the back.

The Republican Business Mobilization Strategy

An interest group strategy was central to the Republican efforts to pass the Contract with America, and the small-business groups that nixed health reform were the House Republicans' best friends. The Monday health care strategy meetings between the House Republicans and their small-employer allies were moved to Thursday, but otherwise business continued as usual. Business participants were organized into committees and given responsibility for different parts of the contract. The House leadership asked an old ally to run each coalition. Some individuals were obvious candidates for the job; for example, Dirk van Dongen (National Association of Wholesaler-Distributors) had been fighting product liability for a long time; Paul Beckner (Citizens for a Sound Economy) had a special interest in the tax committee; and Pamela Bailey (Healthcare Leadership Council) had been a central player in the Republican battle to defeat national health care reform.

But the new Republican majority broke with past interest-mobilization strategies in building interest group support. Rather than developing one broad policy coalition to push forward the budget battle, as Ronald Reagan did in 1981, the leadership formed separate coalitions to address general budgetary concerns, taxes, and Medicare. Some participants felt that the leadership's coalition structure served to fragment support and would have preferred a more cohesive strategy with all in a single coalition. They believed that Gingrich designed separate coalitions in order to dissociate tax reductions from the Medicare spending cuts. One business insider felt that the Congressional leaders were "fooling themselves" in trying to keep these two issues apart and feared that the multiple coalition approach produced too many messages: "The problem was when you had all these coalitions, you divided up your resources so that no single coalition could have the punch that you could have had if they were all joined together."

The Coalition to Save Medicare was composed of ninety-nine associations, including insurers, providers, small-business groups, seniors, and right-wing citizen activists. The coalition was cochaired by Bailey and Jake Hansen (Seniors Coalition) (Miller 1995: 82). The Healthcare Leadership Council consisted of players from for-profit hospitals, insurance companies, and drug companies and was a leader in the campaign against the Clinton bill. The Seniors Coalition was begun by Richard Vigurie as a rightist counterpart to the American Association of Retired Persons, and now (with two other right-wing senior groups) raises about $18 million a year for Republican causes. According to Molly Ivins (1995: 136), the group has been investigated by both the New York and Pennsylvania offices of the attorney general.

The Republican interest group strategy was to offer specific benefits to small-business and conservative-right allies in exchange for their commitment to support all parts of the contract. Thus business participants were promised full consideration on the issues near and dear to their hearts, but they had to promise to support the entire agenda of the party. To belong to the Thursday group, members had to take a blood oath to support the contract in its entirety and to restrain individual issues in favor of the broad legislative agenda. Van Dongen explains that the guiding principle for his product liability coalition was, "We have no independent goals; all goals come from the leadership. We will do whatever the leadership feels we should do." Another participant explained, "You're constantly having to pull people back into fighting for the collective good when their impulse is to fight for the particular good."

The Coalition to Save Medicare provided critical help in the early days of the Republican Medicare campaign. First, private interests generated a seemingly endless source of money. In the past decade the health insurance industry gave more to Republicans than to Democrats by a factor of 3.5 to 1 (Marcus 1995: A25). Groups connected to the Republicans spent much more money attacking Clinton's health reform than the Democratic groups spent criticizing the Republican's Medicare campaign. For example, the HIAA spent $15 million on advertising attacking Clinton in 1994; the American Hospital Association spent only $350,000, and the AFL-CIO spent $1 million criticizing the Republicans in the first part of 1995 (Serafini 1995). Supporters of the Medicare changes used public opinion polls to package their message to the public and developed an extensive advertising campaign.

Second, private-sector allies helped the Republicans to define the Medicare issue in a manner that was appealing to the general public. The Republicans realized that the American public would not sacrifice Medicare for a balanced budget or tax reduction; therefore, the case had to be made that Medicare needed saving in its own right. For example, political scientist Bob Blendon found that 73 percent of his sample supported reducing the growth in Medicare spending but that only 44 percent supported cuts to balance the budget, and 28 percent supported cuts to finance tax reduction (ibid.). During the problem-definition stage, the Republicans and their business allies did a full-scale media blitz to convince the public that Medicare was going bankrupt and to establish the legitimacy of the problem. The Republican National Committee started a $300,000 television campaign at the beginning of October to saturate the air waves with positive vibes toward Medicare reform at the critical point of legislation (Jasperse 1995: 4). The Coalition to Save Medicare held a series of "Medicare University" sessions to educate congressional staffers and journalists on topics such as the virtues of choice and the dangers of waste, fraud, and abuse in Medicare (Fisher 1995b: 36). The group, working in tandem with coalition whip Paul Coverdell (R-GA), persuaded Republican senators to put forth radio commentaries on Medicare reform (Stone 1995b: 2152).

Allies of the party initially claimed that this campaign was wildly successful. For example, the Citizens for a Sound Economy's initial focus groups showed a public largely convinced that there was no problem with the Medicare system; yet follow-up focus groups a few months later showed a public largely accepting of the Republican line.[24] Later, however, public opinion shifted against the Republican plan.

Third, business allies worked with the leadership to offer the appearance of overwhelming public support for the Medicare legislation. Shortly before Congress broke for its August recess, the Coalition to Save Medicare held a "Mobilization Event," offering legislators stirring testimonials to take back to the districts (Fisher 1995c: 8). The coalition also offered the occasional grassroots show of force, as when thirty seniors arrived at Congress with 100,000 "message-grams." Bailey described this as a full-scale war.

The Republican leadership learned much from the Clinton administration's experiences with health reform. The administration got bashed for too much secrecy, but the lesson for the Republicans was that too many leaks was a bad thing. The Clinton bill was scrutinized and picked apart for months before members of Congress actually had an opportunity to vote on the measure.[25] Learning from Clinton's errors, the Republicans were careful not to unveil their proposal until they were ready to legislate, and rushed the bill through Congress. The Clinton administration was criticized for being too partisan and for shutting Republicans out of the bill-writing process; the GOP pursued this tactic in earnest. By putting Medicare reform in the reconciliation bill, they could avoid the threat of a filibuster in the Senate. This removed incentives for real bipartisan cooperation; as long as the leadership could keep the Republican ducks in a line, they had little need to cross over to the other side of the aisle. At one point the Democrats held protest hearings in the rain on the front lawn of the capitol to illustrate their feelings of being shut out (Toner 1995: A26). It was not their finest hour.

Although the administration was slammed in the press for being obsessed with policy over politics, it had in fact made many concessions to special interests. The problem was that these concessions were made without sufficiently firm commitments and at a premature stage in the process. The Republicans also made many concessions to special interests but were able to secure firmer commitments in return.

At first the GOP strategy seemed to pay off. The House Republican members finally introduced the Medicare Preservation Act on Friday, 29 September; by the following Thursday the bill had been marked up by both the Ways and Means and the Commerce Committees. Formal Commerce Committee hearings were initially scheduled for only one day; each member was to be given five minutes to comment on the act. The urgency was emphasized with an electronic clock hanging on the wall, counting down the 197 million seconds until Medicare bankruptcy. Both the House and Senate Passed the Medicare legislation with nearly unanimous Republican support and almost no Democratic backing.

The rapid congressional action on Medicare was to no avail when President Clinton put a halt to the process with his office's ultimate weapon. The president vetoed the reconciliation bill that included Medicare reform, signing it with the pen that LBJ had used to make Medicare law in 1965. The Republicans argued that this symbolic gesture was a "cheap trick." Richard Armey (R-TX) wondered publicly if Clinton would authorize troops to be sent to Bosnia with "the same pen that LBJ used to sign the Gulf of Tonkin resolution."

The Republicans tried to play hardball with the president by refusing to pass legislation to fund government during the budgetary impasse. But with a forbearance surprising to even his ardent supporters, the president refused to cave in to Republican demands and to acquiesce on Medicare and other issues. In part the president was emboldened by the shift in public opinion. By a ratio of two to one, Americans criticized the Republican Medicare plan, and only one out of every four approved of the tax cut (Clymer 1995d: A1, D23). Ultimately the Medicare reform plan simply died.

The budget stalemate deeply frustrated the small-business groups who had worked so hard to enact the Contract with America. Employers blamed the Republicans for a lack of leadership and focus. Thus one participant remembered, "The leadership was too busy focusing on the numbers, daily sound bites, and on today's polls [to mobilize business]. . . . There was not much clarity of what they [the Republicans] were looking for from them [business]." Another explained, "There was a real loss in momentum because the original game plan didn't work and they didn't know what to do." Many felt that the Republicans tried for too much too soon and set a priority on taking credit for political victories over securing policy goals. A lobbyist for a large group of small businesses reflected: "Republicans have taken self-destruction to new heights. We all love amateurs, still, some [of the current congressional freshmen] are close to violating their oath of office in trying to shut the government down. They have been overreaching to such a large extent that they are likely to lose everything."[26]

Chastened by the frustrations of the 1995–96 budget battle, the two parties pursued Medicare reform in a spirit of bipartisan cooperation in the 1996–97 legislative cycle. Opinion polls demonstrated a real public concern about possible future Medicare fund insolvency and both parties wanted to address this pressing concern (Yang 1997). Weaver suggests that unpopular political tasks often motivate bipartisan cooperation, as parties mutually engage in blame avoidance, and the Medicare case seems to support this observation (Weaver 1988).

Medicare provisions were considered in the context of the larger ambition to legislate what the president referred to as "the first balanced budget in a generation" (Harris 1997). Ironically, the Republicans were now able to secure with collaboration much of what they failed to gain by intimidation in 1995–96. The bill cut the projected five-year Medicare growth by $116 billion, greatly expanded managed care options for Medicare patients, and created a pilot group eligible for Medical Savings Accounts (Goldstein 1997).

Bipartisan cooperation was eased by the economic boom. Adjustments in economic assumptions, such as the CEO's budget deficit predictions and anticipated tax revenues, enabled legislators to avoid conflict by trading treasured goals in something like the old pork barrel style of politics (Kosterlitz 1997). Thus the Democrats were able to secure a big new health program for uninsured children, greatly expanded education tax credits, and corrections to what they considered the more egregious aspects of welfare reform. In addition to the Medicare changes, the Republicans won a major change in capital gains taxation and the child tax credit desperately desired by the religious right (Pianin 1997).

The disenchantment business felt for the Republican leadership after the failures of 1995–96 also increased the attraction of a bipartisan strategy to the GOP. As mentioned earlier, many groups felt that the party had set a higher priority on politics over policy. Declining approval ratings among the public also hurt Gingrich's ability to mobilize the kind of committed fervor from business during the 105th Congress that he commanded during the 104th. The discrediting of the Republican leadership during the government shutdowns exacerbated the fault lines in the party's core coalition. Major business supporters were never entirely comfortable with the social agenda of the conservative religious groups and time only heightened this mutual antagonism (Garret 1997: 20). In retrospect, many business supporters felt that Medicare reform had been a powderkeg in 1996 and preferred instead to concentrate their energies on much desired tax changes in 1996–97.

Conclusion

The story told here leaves us in an odd state of affairs, one we normally do not associate with big-business attitudes toward markets. Although a current snapshot view shows large employers fairly optimistic about market solutions, history suggests that this may be a high point in a cycle of ambivalence. Large employers may be rushing into managed care and regional coalitions to keep costs down, and many now seem to be rather more sanguine than they have been in recent years. Yet many managers remember failed cost-containment efforts in the past and fear that this rosy scenario is unlikely to continue forever. As the large-scale move into managed care is completed, costs may once again resume a more rapid rate of change.

In the area of public policy, large employers have been more skeptical about market measures. Big business greeted with consternation the Republicans' 1995 proposal to bring private-sector market initiatives into the traditionally public domain of Medicare and Medicaid, fearing that these measures would only increase the big-business burden of health costs for government populations. But large employers did little to protect their interests during the Medicare reform cycle, and ultimately the legislation was stopped only by President Clinton's veto. In a strange turn of events, many of the Republicans' ambitions were realized in 1997, not because business lent its powerful endorsement to these initiatives but because Democratic cooperation was secured by action on other fronts in the budget reconciliation process.

In the long term, then, the sphere of public policy may be where large employers' interests are most at risk, not because liberal Democrats add to their regulatory burden but because conservative Republicans seek to alter the policy landscape. Large and small firms have very different interests in the zero-sum cost shifting of today's health world. Health reform and its aftermath vividly illustrate that the power balance within the business community is shifting: What the little guys lack in size, they make up for in organization. Republicans seem to be much more interested in gratifying their small-business allies than in addressing the concerns of large employers, whom they view with unease and often with downright hostility. In the post-national-health-care-reform era, Republicans and their small-business allies are the new Washington political elite.

Notes

An earlier version of this essay was presented at the *Journal of Health Politics, Policy and Law* Conference: Health Care into the Next Century: Markets, States, and Communities, Duke University, 3–4 May 1996. The author wishes to thank the conference participants and especially Mark Peterson, the Robert Wood Johnson Foundation, and the Russell Sage Foundation.

1 All uncited quotes in this article are from personal interviews conducted by the author.

2 See Rice (this volume) for a lively discussion of market forces in health care.

3 For example, the Houston Area Health Care Coalition provided the Employee Benefits Research Institute (EBRI) with two years' worth of inpatient claims in which 55 percent were subject to utilization review. EBRI found that the inpatient charges for those covered by utilization review were 15 percent lower than for those without (Vibbert 1990: 40, 37–46).

4 In addition, some companies believe that HMOs engage in shadow pricing: their rate increases follow those of traditional fee-for-service plans (Odynocki 1988).

5 A *Health Affairs* study found that premiums for conventional fee-for-service plans increased by 20 percent from 1988–89, and PPO premiums increased by 18 percent (Gqabel et al. 1990).

6 Some companies contracted with centers of excellence for high-priced interventions such as organ transplants. These special arrangements often offered both somewhat lower prices for interventions and much better medical outcomes (Christensen 1991).

7 But like the looser PPO, there tends to be greater freedom of physician choice in the point of service plan.

8 Interview with industry representative, June 1993.

9 For discussions of the role of groups see Martin 1995 and Bergthold 1990.

10 Interview with business participant, May 1993.

11 Employers and thirty-two hospitals participated in the effort.

12 Interview, April 1993.

13 Data had to have adequate risk adjustment, to cover the high cost/high volume procedures, and to look at the patient's evaluation of care.

14 The firms included Bemis, Cargill, Carlson Companies, Ceridan, Dayton Hudson, First Bank System, General Mills, Honeywell, IDS, Norwest, Pillsbury, Rosemount, Supervalu, and Tennant (Power in Numbers 1992: 73).

15 Wyatt Company in DC processed the data for thirty-nine companies for $150,000 a year.

16 The coalition hired a consultant, Mediqual, and Civic Project donated $250,000 to the four-year initiative (1987–1991). They risk-adjusted by DRGs. The project made an effort to pick high-volume DRGs with the least variation in terms of severity of illness, and used generous outliers.

17 Some participants feel that physicians may be more progressive than hospitals. One aspect of the project is to form user groups to discipline managed care vendors. Employers and doctors meet to discuss quality and credible data.

18 Unpublished survey provided by the administration.

19 The NAM survey is described in an interview with Ira Magaziner; Washington Business Group on Health 1994.

20 This has to do with the dollar conversion factor. Each procedure has a value. To

determine the actual reimbursement, this value is multiplied by a fixed monetary amount, called the dollar conversion factor. Current law has the dollar conversion factor going down in the next seven years; however, the Republicans promised that this would not occur. As a result some estimates suggest that Medicare spending could actually increase under the Republican's plan (Pear 1995a: A1).

21 Drug companies liked the end of a regulation requiring them to give discounts to public hospitals and AIDS clinics, and were wooed with a provision banning punitive damages in a lawsuit if the drug in question had been approved by the Food and Drug Administration (Gottlieb and Pear 1995: A1, 20).

22 Originally, the House bill was to save $33.6 billion in seven years, and the Senate would save about $10 billion more; by comparison, the final bill's savings dropped to $26.9 billion with the extra concessions to the private plan (Gottlieb 1995: A1, 26).

23 Interview, 10 May 1995.

24 Interview with Paul Beckner, 14 September 1995.

25 On the many ironies of the two bills see Priest 1995: C3.

26 Interview with industry lobbyist, 23 February 1996.

Managed Care and Medicare Reform

Jonathan B. Oberlander

Thehe changes that have been sweeping through private-sector medical care in the United States are now reverberating in Medicare. Since the demise of the Clinton health plan and comprehensive health reform in 1994, there have been growing calls to restructure Medicare more in line with the health care practices of the market. Advocates of market-based health reform assert that the recent success of private-sector employers in holding down their health insurance costs demonstrates the effectiveness of new cost containment instruments and medical delivery arrangements: managed care organizations, utilization review, capitation, and selective contracting. Expenditures on Medicare during the past few years have grown faster than private-sector health spending, and, these advocates contend, can be restrained only if the federal government embraces market strategies for cost control (Findlay and Meyeroff 1996; Thomas 1995; Wilensky 1995a, 1995b).

To be sure, the line between market and government health policy is blurry. For all the rhetoric of restructuring and innovation, much of the slowdown in private-sector spending on medical insurance has been achieved by aggressively holding down the fees paid to hospitals and physicians—which is exactly what Medicare has been doing since the early 1980s. Moreover, as Marilyn Moon has noted, for most of the past decade Medicare has outperformed the private sector in cost control, and while that situation has reversed recently, the relative success of the private sector has been exaggerated by many observers (Moon and Zuckerman 1995). One need not accept the claims of market rhetoric, however, to recognize its political influence. And the influence on Medicare policy is now substantial, in part due to the ascendancy of conservative politicians intent on promoting market ideology in federal health programs.

The Balanced Budget Act (BBA) of 1997 embodies the expanded pull of the changing health care market on public policy. The BBA legislates a broad series of reforms in Medicare, including: (1) establishment of a Medicare+Choice option that would open up the program to a wide array of private health insurance plans; (2) changed payment policies for contracting health maintenance organizations (HMOs) intended to increase their Medicare enrollments in rural areas and redress geographic disparities; (3) a demonstration project for medical savings accounts; (4) new payment methodologies for skilled nursing and home health services; (5) creation of a bipartisan commission to consider reform options to meet the long-term financing pressures generated by the retirement of the baby boomers; and (6) cuts in the rate of growth in program payments to hospitals, physicians, and other providers. Those cuts are expected to produce a substantial slowdown in Medicare expenditures. The Congressional Research Service estimates that from 1997–2002, Medicare spending will grow at an average annual rate of around 6 percent under the provisions of the BBA, compared to the 8.5 percent growth rate that had been projected under prior law (CRS 1977). Per capita expenditures on Medicare beneficiaries during this period will similarly decline from 7.16 percent to 4.67 percent. In addition to fiscal changes, the legislation may also alter the programmatic character of Medicare. The expansion of insurance options in the program is expected to increase the proportion of beneficiaries who use their federal coverage to enroll in private insurance plans, with the Congressional Budget Office predicting Medicare enrollment in private capitated plans will reach 27 percent by 2002 (CBO 1997).

These changes in Medicare represent a triumph of the agenda of the Republican congressional leadership. The leadership's initial 1995 Medicare reform plan, pushed by Speaker of the House Newt Gingrich, met fierce resistance from President Clinton and congressional Democrats. The ensuing Medicare debate—with Republicans frequently cast as enemies of the elderly and ideological extremists—played a crucial role in rehabilitating the president's political stature and ultimately, in helping to secure his reelection in 1996 against Bob Dole.[1] As the electoral spotlight receded, however, and in the context of persistent concerns about the program's budgetary impact as well as the solvency of its trust fund, bipartisan agreement emerged on Medicare reform that tracked much of the Republicans' original plan.

At the heart of this new consensus is the belief that Medicare should substantially increase the enrollment of program beneficiaries in managed care plans. Expanding the role of managed care plans in Medicare is endorsed by many health policy makers and analysts as the means to controlling program costs, enhancing beneficiaries' choice of health coverage, improving the quality and efficiency of medical services, and bringing Medicare in line with private-sector developments. Managed care is not a new idea in Medicare policy (Butler and Moffit 1995; Ellwood and Enthoven 1995; Aaron and Reischauer 1995; Thomas 1995; Wilensky 1995a, 1995b). Proposals to enroll Medicare beneficiaries in prepaid plans date back to 1970, and in fact, Medicare already permits beneficiaries to join HMOs that are paid by the government on a capitated basis. But rates of Medicare managed care enrollment are far lower than in the private sector or Medicaid. By broadening the range of managed care plan choices available in the program and by increasing payment rates in areas with low Medicare HMO penetration, the 1997 reforms are intended to reduce that disparity.

This chapter explores the implications of Medicare's move toward managed care. The 1997 reforms raise important issues for both the Medicare program and beneficiaries. Are these policy changes likely to produce the outcomes in cost containment, quality improvement, and benefit expansion that advocates anticipate? What does Medicare's historical experience with managed care tell us about future prospects? What changes in program administration and operations lie ahead as more beneficiaries opt out of public Medicare in favor of private managed care insurance? I address these issues by first reviewing the claims that are made for and against promoting managed care in Medicare. Next, I summarize evidence from Medicare's experiences with HMOs since 1982. The chapter concludes by discussing the challenges that will shape the future of managed care in Medicare and options for program reform.

Managed Care in Medicare: Past and Present

Medicare was modeled after the indemnity insurance plans that predominated in 1965. Prepaid group plans, which at the time held only a small share of the private insurance market, tried to obtain authorization to serve Medicare patients on a capitated basis instead of the conventional practice (adopted by Medicare) of fee-for-service (FFS) reimbursement. The medical profession, though, opposed prepaid group practice as a threat to their professional sovereignty; Medicare administrators, fearful of antagonizing doctors during the program's implementation, rejected requests for capitated payment. If prepaid plans wished to participate in Medicare, they had to accept FFS reimbursement, a requirement they regarded as administratively burdensome and incompatible with their organizational principles (Feder 1977).

The 1972 Social Security amendments revised program policy by authorizing Medicare to contract with HMOs on a capitated or "risk" basis. However, only older, established HMOs could receive Medicare risk contracts, and even these plans were subject to retrospective cost adjustments to their capitation payments and to restrictions on their profits (but not losses) on Medicare patients. As a result, the 1972 legislation did not substantially reduce the barriers to HMOs participating in Medicare. By 1979, only one plan had contracted with Medicare on a risk basis (Langwell and Hadley 1989; Brown 1983).

The success of Health Care Financing Administration (HCFA)–sponsored demonstration projects (initiated in the mid-1970s), which placed elderly enrollees in prepaid plans on the same terms as younger members, and the persistently high rates of growth in Medicare program expenditures, stoked policy makers' enthusiasm for increasing the role of HMOs in Medicare. In 1982, Congress, supported by the Reagan administration, passed a provision in the Tax Equity and Fiscal Responsibility Act (TEFRA) aimed at encouraging Medicare HMO enrollment (Schlesinger and Drumheller 1988; Iglehart 1985). TEFRA permitted HMOs, for the first time, to join Medicare on a risk basis without retrospective cost adjustment. The TEFRA risk program began with demonstrations in 1982 and was fully implemented in 1985.

In 1997, 13 percent of Medicare beneficiaries were enrolled in managed care plans.[2] Seventy-five percent of Medicare beneficiaries in managed care are in TEFRA risk plans that receive prospective, monthly capitation payments (per member per month) from Medicare to provide comprehensive medical services to enrollees (Kaiser Family Foundation 1995). Capitation fees are set at 95 percent of the adjusted average per capita cost (AAPCC) of medical expenditures for FFS Medicare beneficiaries, varying with the enrollee's age, gender, entitlement (age or disability), institutional status (residing in a nursing home or not), Medicaid eligibility, and location by county (Brown et al. 1993). If capitation payments exceed HMOs' adjusted cost of providing care to Medicare enrollees, plans must either return the surplus to the government or to beneficiaries by reducing premiums—HMOs may charge premiums for providing benefits beyond the basic Medicare package—and broadening benefits (Zarbozo and LeMasurier 1995).[3]

As Table 1 shows, enrollment in Medicare risk plans has grown rapidly in recent years, averaging 22 percent annually from 1992–1995. During that same period, the number of risk plans contracting with Medicare increased from 96 to 171. Medicare HMO enrollment, though, has remained highly concentrated geographically and by health plan. In 1995, 55 percent of Medicare risk enrollees lived in just two states, Florida and

Table 1. Medicare Beneficiary Enrollment in Managed Care, 1985–1995

Year	Enrollment (millions)
1985	1.2
1987	1.7
1989	1.8
1991	2.2
1993	2.6
1995	3.9

Source. Office of Managed Care, HCFA, and *Medicare Chart Book* (Kaiser Family Foundation 1995).

Note. The 1995 figure was for December 1995; enrollment figures include risk plans, cost plans, and health care prepayment plans.

California, whereas ten HMOs accounted for 44 percent of total Medicare risk enrollment (U.S. GAO 1996a; McMillan 1993).

Risk contracts are not the only option for HMO participation in Medicare. Plans can also sign up for a cost contract or as health care prepayment plans (HCPPs). Cost plans are reimbursed for physician and hospital services under the same rules as Medicare FFS providers. HCPPs, which are often sponsored by labor unions or employers, receive capitated payments for Medicare physician services (Zarbozo and LeMasurier 1995). Together, HCPPs and cost plans account for about 25 percent of Medicare managed care enrollment, with HCPPs representing 18 percent of the total (ProPAC 1995).

The Case for Managed Care

Despite the recent growth, Medicare enrollment in managed care still trails far behind that in the private sector (ProPAC 1995).[4] In 1995, an estimated 71 percent of employees in firms with at least ten workers obtained health insurance from managed care plans, including 27 percent in HMOs, in contrast to the 10 percent of Medicare beneficiaries in such plans (Findlay and Meyeroff 1996). Recent reforms seek to bring Medicare's use of managed care in line with that of the private sector by broadening the range of managed care plans that Medicare contracts with and by increasing the financial incentives for plans to enroll Medicare beneficiaries in areas with historically low HMO penetration. Medicare has traditionally contracted only with closed-panel HMOs and not with preferred provider organizations (PPOs) and point-of-service plans (POS), which are widely used in the private sector (Medicare POS contracting was initiated in 1995). These plans offer a wider choice of physicians and fewer limitations on care than closed-panel HMOs, making them potentially attractive to many beneficiaries. In addition to extending program coverage to PPOs, the 1997 BBA permits providers to form their own health care delivery systems—provider-sponsored organizations or PSOs—to contract for Medicare patients. PSOs may have an important impact in rural areas which do not have the population base or health care infrastructure to support traditional HMOs. Including a wider variety of options could therefore increase the proportion of Medicare enrollees willing to join managed care plans as well as the number of plans that participate in the program. Finally, certain payment changes may also boost Medicare managed care enrollment. Since Medicare HMOs are paid on the basis of local FFS costs, managed care enrollment has been low where Medicare costs are below average. The 1997 legislation increases payments to managed care plans in rural areas in order to reduce the geographic disparities in payment levels and to boost managed care enrollment in these areas.

While the 1997 BBA broadens the range of managed care plans available in Medicare, HMOs remain the focus of attention for both policy makers and the press (Eckholm 1996). The promise of HMOs, with their emphasis on prepayment and fixed budgets, primary care, integration of health services, and risk-bearing providers, is widely thought to be greater for Medicare than other managed care plans. Moreover, the arguments that are made in favor of expanding the role of managed care in Medicare are usually based on the experience and potential of HMOs (Wilensky 1995b; Thomas 1995; Ellwood and Enthoven 1995). The following analysis of issues relating to managed care and Medicare therefore concentrates on HMOs; issues raised by other types of managed care plans are discussed in subsequent sections.

HMOs are believed to have four advantages over traditional Medicare insurance. First, it is argued that they can provide medical care at a substantially lower cost than FFS plans (McCombs, Kaspar, and Riley 1990; Manning et al. 1984). Medical providers in a FFS system have few incentives to restrain the amount and complexity of medical care they deliver; the more services they provide, the more income they receive. In contrast, HMOs are prepaid a premium to provide a range of medical services; providing more services costs, rather than generates, HMOs' income. Prepayment forces HMOs to work within a fixed budget and creates financial incentives to reduce utilization of medical services and deliver cost-effective care (Luft 1981). Prepayment through prospective capitation is also attractive to policy makers because it offers the federal government the prospect of budgetary certainty, in contrast to FFS insurance, whose costs are a function of the medical services provided to beneficiaries.

Medicare regulates the price it pays for medical care, but exercises weaker controls over the volume and intensity of services provided to its beneficiaries. It is HMOs' ability to control service volume and intensity that is believed to produce tighter cost controls than in FFS Medicare. HMOs use primary care gatekeepers and waiting times for appointments to restrict access to more expensive specialists (Luft 1982). HMO physicians are typically put at financial risk for the care they provide through bonuses, shared income, or as is increasingly the case, individual capitation, and their clinical decisions are subject to review. HMOs perform fewer high-cost medical services, such as diagnostic procedures, instead substituting lower-cost alternatives (Miller and Luft 1994a). Because hospital care is the largest component of medical costs, HMOs place a particular priority on reducing utilization of inpatient services (Brown 1983; Luft 1981). Finally, HMOs may buy services they do not "make" themselves, such as hospital care, at reduced rates from other health care providers.[5]

Early studies of HMOs found their costs to be 10 to 40 percent lower than FFS plans, and more recent data have revealed slower growth in employer premiums for HMOs than for indemnity plans (Findlay and Meyeroff 1996; Miller and Luft 1994b; Luft 1981). These savings could translate into lower Medicare expenditures, as well as into reduced out-of-pocket expenses for program beneficiaries. Moving Medicare beneficiaries into HMOs may also save the program money through "spillover effects" (Welch 1994; Zwanziger and Melnick 1993). In areas with high Medicare HMO penetration, competitive pressures may induce FFS providers treating Medicare patients to reduce their prices. Alternatively, the cost-effective treatment practices of HMOs may influence the care given to Medicare FFS patients by physicians who also see Medicare HMO patients. Studies of hospital costs in California suggest that HMOs can impact the rate of growth in system-wide health costs (Robinson 1991).

The second advantage of HMOs is their potential to provide broader benefits than traditional Medicare. Medicare benefits are quite limited compared to commercial insurance plans, with no coverage for outpatient prescription drugs, dental care, and hearing and eye exams, and only limited coverage for preventive services and mental health care (Moon 1993; Schlesinger and Wetle 1988). Even Medicare's most generous benefit—hospitalization insurance—restricts the number of days of coverage and provides no stop-loss limit on beneficiaries' expenses. Medicare provides coverage for short-term, posthospitalization nursing home stays, but no coverage for the long-term stays that represent a sizable proportion of out-of-pocket health costs for the elderly (Wiener, Illston, and Hanley 1994). Moreover, beneficiaries face substantial cost sharing in the form of a deductible for hospitalization ($736 in 1996), 20 percent coinsurance for physician services, and copayments for hospital and skilled-nursing-facility services. Beneficiaries who have Medigap insurance to redress these gaps face additional costs from supplemental premium payments.[6]

If HMOs save money through cost-effective medical care, the savings can be used to offer broader benefits than Medicare currently provides by covering services such as routine physicals, outpatient prescription drugs, and even long-term care (Iglehart 1985). Benefit expansions that are financially (and politically) problematic for FFS Medicare may be easier to achieve in HMOs (Schlesinger and Drumheller 1988). It is also believed that HMOs will provide more preventive services for Medicare beneficiaries than FFS insurance plans because it is in their financial interest to keep enrollees healthy in order to avoid the subsequent higher costs of treating illnesses (Luft 1981). Moreover, because HMOs generally use only nominal copayments, beneficiaries will have reduced out-of-pocket costs and, in contrast to traditional Medicare, a fixed annual bill for their medical expenses. This broader coverage can eliminate the need for Medicare HMO enrollees to purchase Medigap policies.

Third, advocates argue that HMOs may improve the quality of care received by Medicare beneficiaries. HMOs avoid the financial incentives inherent in FFS medicine for unnecessary services. Budgetary constraints, it is claimed, lead HMO physicians to provide cost-effective care and avoid inappropriate treatments. HMOs may also reduce unnecessary institutionalization of patients, and freed from the biases of indemnity coverage for inpatient care, they may instead offer alternative treatment options, including home care and outpatient services (Schlesinger 1986). In addition, HMOs may provide case management of complex diseases or chronic conditions by coordinating care from multiple providers and facilitating integration of acute and long-term services in a way that is not common in FFS insurance (Kane 1995; Spitz and Abramson 1987). Finally, Medicare beneficiaries may benefit from the convenience of "one-stop shopping" available at those HMOs where multiple services can be obtained at one location (Iglehart 1985).

The fourth advantage claimed for Medicare HMOs is that they may reduce the regulatory burden on the federal government. Medicare currently regulates physicians and hospitals through complex administered pricing arrangements (diagnosis-related groups for hospitals and the

relative value scale for physicians) that are based on estimates of resource use, difficulty of procedure, practice patterns, and treatment costs
(ProPAC 1995; Physician Payment Review Commission 1995a). These
regulations have in turn produced sophisticated efforts by providers to
"game" the system and preserve their incomes. In contrast, HMOs can be
paid a flat capitation fee by the government or by beneficiaries (in the
form of a voucher) without federal regulation of HMOs' internal prices.
Decentralizing decision making over health care to HMOs may, according to some analysts, end the necessity of Medicare administrators pursuing a potentially "unwinnable" battle to keep up with medical providers (Enthoven 1980).

Concerns: Rationing and Overpayment

Critics of HMOs have voiced two main concerns about their extension to
Medicare. The first is that HMOs' rationing of medical services will erode
the quality of care provided to beneficiaries. The elderly require, on
average, substantially more medical treatment than the younger, employed enrollees who have historically constituted the bulk of HMO
memberships. The fear is consequently that HMO cost-containment
strategies, such as reducing hospitalization and restricting access to specialists, will have especially adverse effects on health care for the elderly
(Gillick 1987). Underprovision may be a greater problem in HMOs than
in indemnity insurance, as prepayment and capitation provide stronger
incentives to constrain utilization of medical services than does FFS
payment. HMOs may also have nonfinancial barriers to access, such as
obtaining the permission of gatekeepers for specialist care, which pose
problems for the elderly. HMOs in which the elderly do not represent a
substantial percentage of enrollees may lack the experience in managing
their health problems and fail to develop special programs to accommo-
date their needs (Newcomer, Harrington, and Preston 1994; Schlesinger
and Mechanic 1993). These concerns were fueled by a study from the
Rand Health Insurance Experiment that found worse health outcomes
for another vulnerable population—sicker, low-income patients—in prepaid than in FFS settings (Ware et al. 1986).

Elderly patients with chronic illness may be at particular risk in
HMOs. The supposed safeguard against underprovision in prepaid plans
is that it is in their financial interest to provide early, appropriate medical
treatment to patients in order to avoid the subsequent higher costs associated with untreated illnesses. HMOs keep patients healthy, in other
words, because they will bear the costs of not doing so (Luft 1981). This

logic, however, does not hold for chronic conditions, because the costs of not providing such care may not fall on the plan, but instead may be shifted to family caregivers, public insurers, and social agencies (Schlesinger 1986). For example, home care that is not provided by a health plan may be provided by a patient's family, whereas seriously ill elderly patients can be placed in nursing homes at cost to Medicaid. As a consequence of not having to bear all these costs, HMOs may underprovide care to chronically ill elders.

The reliance of managed care plans on primary care gatekeepers may also adversely affect care for the chronically ill. There is evidence that primary care physicians lack sufficient expertise to diagnose and treat some chronic conditions (Mechanic 1994; Schlesinger and Mechanic 1993; Gillick 1987). This problem is compounded by HMOs' reluctance to pay for medical care where the norms of treatment are vague, as they often are with chronic illness. The absence of clear standards is used by health plans to justify not paying for "unnecessary" medical services for chronically ill patients. But critics note that it cannot be assumed "services are unnecessary simply because norms of treatment are poorly defined" (Schlesinger and Mechanic 1993: 129). Finally, the variability of costs for the chronically ill puts pressure on capitated providers that have higher-cost patients (Kane 1995; Schlesinger and Mechanic 1993; Gillick 1987). Under such payment arrangements, physicians have incentives to underprovide services, encourage patients to disenroll, or avoid taking on chronically ill elders as patients (Schlesinger and Mechanic 1993).

The second concern regarding HMOs is that capitated payment will lead to federal overpayment of HMOs, negating any potential cost savings to Medicare. HMOs contracting with Medicare receive a capitation payment based on average expenditures for non-HMO Medicare beneficiaries. Medicare expenditures, however, are highly skewed; 10 percent of beneficiaries accounted for 70 percent of program expenditures at a per-person average of $28,120 in 1995. The average Medicare expenditure in 1995 for all beneficiaries was $4,020, and 18 percent of beneficiaries accounted for no program expenditures (Kaiser Family Foundation 1995). If HMOs disproportionately enroll healthier beneficiaries and avoid the most expensive 10 percent, this favorable selection will allow them to make large margins on capitation payments based on average Medicare expenditures. Medicare could lose money on HMOs if the capitation payment exceeds the medical expenditures that relatively healthy beneficiaries would have had under Medicare FFS (Iglehart 1985, 1987; Brown 1983). In theory, risk adjustment that alters payments to reflect enrollees' expected medical expenditures can prevent this outcome, but concerns have persisted over the adequacy of Medicare's AAPCC risk-adjustment system.

HMOs and Medicare: Assessing the Evidence

Do HMOs provide adequate care to elderly enrollees? How much savings can prepaid plans generate for Medicare? Medicare's current HMO program offers significant evidence bearing on the claims of HMO advocates and critics. The following section reviews the existing empirical literature on Medicare and HMOs from 1982, when the TEFRA risk program began. I summarize the evidence on three dimensions of HMO performance: financial savings, benefit coverage, and quality of care. This section focuses on Medicare's experience with HMOs prior to 1997. The 1997 BBA revised program policy toward managed care in several crucial respects; these new policies are discussed later in this chapter.

Financial savings

The evidence suggests that HMOs can provide medical care to Medicare beneficiaries at less cost than FFS insurance. It has been estimated that, after controlling for patient mix, expenditures on medical care services for Medicare HMO enrollees were 11 percent less than they would have been under Medicare FFS (Brown et al. 1993). Reductions in the duration of hospital stays accounted for most of the savings, with additional savings from reductions in home health visits and restrictions on access to specialists (Schlenker, Shaugnessy, and Hittle 1995; Clement et al. 1994; Brown et al. 1993).[7]

The performance of HMOs in restraining expenditures for elderly enrollees indicates the potential for Medicare savings from HMO enrollment. However, HMO expenditure reductions relative to FFS care do not necessarily guarantee these savings. Program savings depend on the government's ability to "capture" HMOs' cost savings through a payment mechanism that adequately adjusts for the health status of enrollees. The Medicare capitation rate is set at 95 percent of the AAPCC, so in theory, HMOs should lower costs to Medicare by 5 percent (Brown et al. 1993). However, most studies conclude that Medicare has lost rather than saved money from the TEFRA HMO program. It is estimated that Medicare paid approximately "5.7% more per [HMO] beneficiary per year than would have been paid in reimbursements for these individuals had they received their Medicare-covered care on a FFS basis" (Brown and Hill 1994: 36).

The main reason for Medicare's overpayment of HMOs is biased selection. A long list of studies has found program beneficiaries enrolled in HMOs to be significantly healthier than those in Medicare FFS (Clement et al. 1994; Brown et al. 1993; Retchin and Clement 1992; Langwell and Hadley 1989; Luft and Miller 1988; Eggars and Prihoda 1982). The finding of favorable selection of healthier beneficiaries to HMOs has proven robust, holding constant throughout a decade of operation for the TEFRA risk program, and across different health plans and geographic regions. Favorable selection has been detected in pre-enrollment comparisons of FFS and HMO enrollees' medical expenditures, beneficiaries' self-reported health status, and in the severity and complexity of illnesses for HMO and FFS patients presenting at hospitals and physician offices with identical conditions. Medicare HMO enrollees are consequently less likely to receive medical care than FFS beneficiaries and when they do require treatment, are likely to need less care than nonenrollees.

There are two major sources of biased selection in Medicare. The first is beneficiary self-selection. Healthier individuals are more willing to change physicians and health plans than sicker individuals (Luft and Miller 1988). Sicker individuals are likely to have established relationships with physicians and may be reluctant to disrupt their continuity of care. A recent review of the literature concludes that all "health plans which restrict an enrollee's choice of provider (i.e., HMOs and exclusive provider organizations) attract relatively healthy individuals" (Hellinger 1995: 135). This dynamic may be especially strong among the elderly population. As medical care utilization is higher for the aged than for the general population, there may be greater fear of changing medical care providers, often a prerequisite for joining an HMO (Sofaer and Hurwicz 1993). Medicare enrollees who do decide to leave FFS care for an HMO can then be expected to be healthier than the average beneficiary, and beneficiary self-selection may be the single largest factor explaining HMO favorable selection of Medicare enrollees (Lichenstein et al. 1991, 1992).

A second source of biased selection is the marketing practices of health insurance plans. In a competitive health system, all types of insurers compete to sign up the best risks. An insurance pool of sicker individuals will lead to higher premiums, placing insurers at a competitive disadvantage and jeopardizing their ability to maintain market share. These pressures may be even stronger in HMOs, where capitation and prepayment create particularly strong incentives for HMOs to enroll healthy individuals whose costs will not exceed fixed payments. In the employer insurance market, HMOs may seek out healthy enrollees by pursuing contracts with firms whose employees are considered low risks for high medical expenditures. Medicare, however, is an individual insurance market, necessitating somewhat different strategies to attract healthy beneficiaries. HMOs have pursued selective marketing of Medicare beneficiaries at get-acquainted meetings and other community events that are likely to reach disproportionately healthier segments of the aged population (Luft and Miller 1988). HMOs may also tailor their insurance products to induce favorable selection, for instance, by avoiding benefits that attract sicker enrollees (e.g., prescription drug coverage), while covering services that appeal to healthier elders (e.g., health education; Lichenstein et al. 1992; Luft and Miller 1988).

The HMO option in Medicare is structured in ways that exacerbate the potential for biased selection. First, HMOs market directly to beneficiaries, in contrast to insurance systems such as the Federal Employees Health Benefit Program (FEHBP), that centralize marketing through an employer or government "sponsor" (Butler and Moffit 1995; Enthoven 1980). Direct marketing, through telephone calls and face-to-face meetings, enhances the opportunity for health plans to learn about an individual's health status and encourage or discourage enrollment, depending on the customer's perceived risk factors (Luft and Miller 1988). Second, in contrast to the convention in the employer market, Medicare enrollees are not "locked in" to health plans for a whole year, but may switch to a different plan, or back to Medicare FFS, on a monthly basis. This allows plans to encourage high-cost enrollees to switch to another plan by creating barriers to medical treatment or administrative hassles that lower enrollees' satisfaction with the plan (Schlesinger and Drumheller 1988; Luft and Miller 1988). Third, both health plans and physicians can receive Medicare reimbursement either through capitation or FFS. Consequently, medical providers and insurers may game the system by selecting the payment option that maximizes their revenues. An HMO with a relatively costly Medicare enrollment can switch to a cost contract. Physicians who both serve Medicare FFS patients and contract with HMOs may recruit patients into the financially appropriate health plan (Langwell, Nelson, and Nelson 1988). For example, a low-cost patient could be directed to an HMO, where expected medical expenditures will be less than capitation so that the physician can keep the surplus, whereas a sicker patient who may exceed capitation limits could be directed to Medicare FFS. The close relationships that many elderly persons have with their physicians and their comparatively greater hesitance to change doctors makes differential physician recruitment a particularly difficult problem for Medicare.

Medicare's AAPCC is supposed to compensate for risk selection by adjusting payment according to health status. By all accounts, though, the AAPCC has performed poorly and had low predictive value for individual health expenditures (Rossiter, Chiu, and Chen 1994; Brown 1983). The variables used by Medicare to adjust capitation payments have proven inadequate to predict differences in individuals' health expenditures; AAPCC risk categories have explained less than 1 percent of the variance in expenditures for Medicare FFS beneficiaries (Dowd et al. 1992). The Medicare capitation fee is based on average expenditures for beneficiaries, but HMOs are enrolling elderly persons with less-than-average medical expenses. Consequently, Medicare has overpaid HMOs for providing medical care to a relatively healthy group of beneficiaries.

In addition to producing direct savings by providing cheaper medical care to enrollees, Medicare HMOs may also save the program money by indirectly influencing providers' treatment practices or creating competitive pressures for FFS providers to lower prices. At least one study has found evidence of such spillover effects on Medicare FFS costs, indicating that the rate of growth in Medicare program outlays will decrease as Medicare HMO market share increases (Welch 1994). However, determining the precise extent of spillover effects in Medicare depends on distinguishing the impact of higher enrollment in Medicare HMOs from higher enrollment of the non-Medicare population of a given market in HMOs (Christianson 1994). Without such a distinction, it is impossible to know if it is Medicare HMOs, or rather HMOs more generally, that are impacting Medicare FFS costs.

Benefits

Virtually all HMOs provide Medicare enrollees with benefits in addition to basic Medicare coverage. As Table 2 reveals, the most common extra benefit is the annual physical, offered by 95 percent of risk plans in 1995. Eye exams and immunizations were provided by 90 percent of plans (Kaiser Family Foundation 1995). Other benefits, including extended mental health coverage and hearing aids, were covered by almost no plans. The percentage of plans covering prescription drugs, one of the additional benefits most often associated with HMOs, fell from 71 percent in 1986 to 31 percent in 1993, "suggesting that plans may have perceived that this benefit contributed to reduced profitability and unfavorable selection" (McMillan 1993: 146). Since 1993, however, the percentage of plans offering a prescription drug benefit has risen substantially (to 47 percent), perhaps an indicator of the competitive behavior of health plans that are now entering the Medicare HMO market.

Table 2. Percentages of HMOs Offering Benefits in Addition
to Basic Medicare

Benefit	1986	1993	1995
Annual physical	NA	97	95
Eye exam	69	85	88
Immunization	NA	90	86
Ear exam	37	66	73
Prescription drugs	71	31	47
Foot care	NA	24	34
Dental care	15	26	34
Extended mental health	35	0	NA

Sources. McMillan 1993, Kaiser Family Foundation 1995.
Note. NA means data were not available.

Medicare allows risk plans to charge program enrollees additional premiums for any extra benefits that are covered on top of basic Medicare. However, plans that make excess profits on Medicare enrollees must invest the profits toward broader benefits or reduced premiums for beneficiaries. In 1993, about one-half of Medicare risk plans did not charge any additional premium for extra benefits. Twenty-four percent of plans charged $40 per month or less in premiums, whereas 27 percent of plans charged over $40 a month (Kaiser Family Foundation 1995).[8]

Quality of care

Most studies have found that the quality of care received by Medicare beneficiaries in HMOs is comparable to or better than that received in FFS settings, although the evidence on chronically ill elders in prepaid plans has been less favorable.[9] No difference was detected between HMO and FFS settings in health outcomes for Medicare beneficiaries with colorectal cancer, strokes, chest pain, diabetes, hypertension, and urinary incontinence (Coffey et al. 1994; Clement et al. 1994; Brown et al. 1993; Preston and Retchin 1991; Retchin and Preston 1991; Retchin and Brown 1990a, 1990b). The similarity in outcomes occurred despite significantly lower HMO utilization rates of laboratory tests, diagnostic procedures, hospital stays, and specialist utilization, suggesting that for many conditions discretionary services can be eliminated without adverse health outcomes (Brown et al. 1993). Medicare enrollees with heart attacks (acute myocardial infarction) and congestive heart failure received better process of care in HMOs than in FFS settings, while HMOs provided higher levels of recommended routine care and preventive services such as screening tests, enabling, for example, earlier detection of cancer in prepaid plans than in FFS settings (Riley et al. 1994; Carlisle et al. 1992; Retchin and Brown 1990a, 1990b, 1991). The higher level of preventive care conforms with expectations that HMOs have financial incentives to encourage more utilization of preventive services than FFS plans.

However, some studies have found worse health outcomes in HMOs for Medicare beneficiaries with particular diagnoses, or raised questions about the appropriateness of treatment in prepaid settings. A recent report from the Medical Outcomes Study concluded that over a four-year period, chronically ill elders in HMOs were twice as likely to experience a decline in their health status than chronically ill elders in Medicare FFS, and that low-income elders fared particularly badly in prepaid settings (Ware et al. 1996). Medicare FFS outcomes for patients in home health care were superior to those in HMOs (Shaughnessy, Schlenker, and Hittle 1994). Medicare enrollees with persistent joint pain in HMOs were less likely to have symptomatic improvement than their FFS counterparts (Clement et al. 1994). For some dimensions of surgical care, HMO colon cancer patients were less likely than Medicare FFS patients to receive treatment in accordance with medical guidelines (Brown et al. 1993). And elderly stroke patients in HMOs were released with more neurologic (e.g., speech or motor) deficits at discharge than FFS patients, without compensating higher rates of posthospital rehabilitation (Retchin, Clement, and Brown 1994). Virtually all of these negative results were in treatment of chronic conditions, raising doubts about whether HMOs consistently provide adequate care to chronically ill elders.

In addition to health outcomes, beneficiary satisfaction may also serve as a measure of quality of care as perceived by health plan enrollees. The record of HMOs on Medicare enrollee satisfaction has been mixed. A 1985 survey found that although similar proportions of HMO enrollees and FFS beneficiaries were "very satisfied" with their health care, HMO enrollees were significantly less satisfied with the professional competence of their physicians and with the willingness of the medical staff to discuss their health problems. However, Medicare enrollees were more satisfied with their waiting times and claims-processing experience than nonenrollees (Rossiter, Langwell et al. 1989). A 1990 survey raised more serious questions regarding satisfaction in Medicare HMOs, concluding that "on virtually every dimension examined except cost . . . [HMO] enrollees were significantly less likely than non-enrollees to rate their care as excellent," including attention received as a patient, physician explanations, ease of obtaining care, waiting times, thoroughness of examinations, and overall results of care (Brown et al. 1993: 17; Clement et al. 1994). Yet HMO enrollees were more satisfied with their out-of-pocket costs, and 93 percent would recommend their HMO to a friend or relative (Brown et al. 1993). More recently, a 1996 survey found that the vast majority of Medicare HMO enrollees were satisfied with their plans and reported no problems with access. At the same time, however, 25 percent of Medicare HMO enrollees would not recommend their health plan to families and friends with serious or chronic conditions (Nelson et al. 1997).

A second measure of enrollee satisfaction is disenrollment rates. Early studies found that approximately one of every five Medicare HMO enrollees disenroll from their health plan in a given year, with 75 percent returning to Medicare FFS (Brown et al. 1993; Langwell and Hadley 1990). Medicare HMO disenrollees are less satisfied with their medical care and less healthy than enrollees who remain in prepaid plans (Sullivan 1990; Rossiter, Wan et al. 1988). However, it is difficult to know to what extent high rates of enrollee exit indicate serious problems in Medicare HMO care or rather, are the consequence of the program's permissive rules for changing plans. And a recent survey concluded that the proportion of HMO enrollees returning to Medicare FFS, as opposed to switching to another managed care plan, was quite low (3 percent) (Nelson et al. 1997). Grievances against health plans also offer a barometer of enrollee satisfaction. Medicare HMOs operate their own complaint processes and enrollees can submit their grievances to federal review after exhausting two levels of internal HMO appeals (Anders 1996). Federal complaints from Medicare beneficiaries declined from 3,271 in 1994 to 3,151 in 1995, with patients winning 32 percent of appeals. However, it is difficult to know if variation in complaint rates over time and between HMOs reflects real differences in the quality of care or differences in the accessibility of internal grievance procedures. If the latter is the case, plans that make it easier for enrollees to file complaints may be penalized by appearing to have lower quality of care than plans with substantial barriers to filing a grievance.

HMOs and Medicare: Summarizing the Evidence

The empirical evidence on HMOs and Medicare from 1982–1995 supports four propositions:

1 Medicare has lost money on its HMO patients.
2 HMOs have enrolled relatively healthy beneficiaries.

3 HMOs have a mixed record on quality of care. Most studies show health outcomes in Medicare HMOs that are comparable or superior to those in FFS, but less-adequate care has been found for chronically ill elders enrolled in HMOs.

4 Virtually all HMOs provide additional benefits to basic Medicare.

On balance, then, HMOs have not yet lived up to their promise in Medicare. They have not produced program cost savings (the primary justification for the adoption of the TEFRA risk program) or consistent improvements in the quality of medical care for the elderly. Nor have they alleviated the regulatory burden on the federal government and associated problems with gaming of federal reimbursement rules by the medical industry. Rather, the difficulties experienced with Medicare's capitation policies and the AAPCC suggest that HMOs simply replaced one set of regulatory dilemmas with another. These shortcomings have been a function both of incentives inherent in prepaid plans and particular features of Medicare policy. Shortcomings that are produced by quirks of program policy may prove amenable to reform; changes in payment practices to risk plans, for instance, could generate savings for Medicare from HMO enrollment. However, problems that are more inherent in prepaid care, such as inadequate treatment of the chronically ill, may prove harder to remedy.[10]

On the more positive side, it is evident that HMOs can provide high-quality medical care to many segments of the elderly population, care that for some conditions and services is superior to that in FFS settings. And HMOs have generally offered enrollees broader benefits than those available in the traditional Medicare package. However, it should be noted that the ability of prepaid plans to provide these additional benefits is partly a function of overpayment from the AAPCC. The federal government has, in effect, subsidized broader benefits for Medicare HMO enrollees who represent a healthier segment of the program population. These funds might be better used to finance benefit expansions in FFS Medicare, which enrolls a greater proportion of sicker beneficiaries who are more in need of improved coverage (Schlesinger and Drumheller 1988).

The Limits of Existing Evidence

If research on the TEFRA risk program can be extrapolated to the future, we have a reasonable picture of what HMO performance will look like under Medicare. Yet there is good reason to believe that past experience is not a reliable guide to the future of Medicare managed care. Existing research studied Medicare HMOs under a particular set of financial, market, organizational, and enrollment conditions. The current transformations of the health care system and Medicare policy are altering these conditions, raising doubts about the limitations of the evidence discussed in the previous section.[11]

Financial changes

Medicare HMOs were studied during a period when they were overpaid by the federal government by an estimated 5.7 percent per beneficiary (Brown et al. 1993). It is likely in the future, however, that in the context of political concerns over the federal budget and Medicare's financial insolvency, as well as technical concerns over the accuracy of the AAPCC, the Medicare capitation rate will not be as generous. Elimination of overpayment in the AAPCC has been widely endorsed by policy analysts, and reduced capitation payments to Medicare HMOs are a major source of program savings in the 1997 BBA (CBO 1997, 1995; Physician Payment Review Commission 1995b; Brown et al. 1993).

The quality of care provided to program beneficiaries under excess capitation may not be the same as that provided at reduced payment levels. Lower payments may lead HMOs to further curtail the utilization of medical services by Medicare enrollees, possibly inducing the rationing of access to medically beneficial services. Incentives also will be stronger to shun sicker enrollees and to encourage disenrollment of high-cost enrollees. Finally, lower capitation rates may diminish the ability of HMOs to provide benefits in addition to the basic Medicare package. To the extent that price affects quality, then, lowering the Medicare capitation payment may adversely impact HMOs' quality of care.

Market changes

Medicare HMOs were studied in a health market characterized by the predominance of indemnity insurance, limited market penetration by managed care plans, and HMO shadow pricing of indemnity insurers. The current health insurance market is alternatively characterized by the decline of indemnity insurance, the spread of for-profit HMOs, and substantially higher levels of competition for HMOs from the increased market penetration of other managed care plans. These new market conditions are generating pressures on health plans to reduce costs and maintain profitability, raising the same concerns about potential effects on quality of care as lower capitation payments. For example, an HMO facing competition from other managed care plans could attempt to hold down its costs by requiring physicians to increase the number of patients they see in a day. This could have particularly harmful consequences for Medicare beneficiaries, because the elderly have more complex health conditions than younger patients and require more time for accurate diagnosis (Kane 1995; Schlesinger and Drumheller 1988).

Alternatively, the new market may induce greater competition among plans for Medicare beneficiaries. Competition could take the form of an escalating contest to offer higher benefits to attract Medicare enrollees. This dynamic, in fact, may already be at work in the Medicare HMO market, accounting for the recent upturn in the percentage of risk plans offering outpatient prescription drug coverage.[12]

Organizational changes

Studies of Medicare HMOs have focused disproportionately on non-profit, staff, and group-model HMOs, such as Kaiser Permanente and Group Health Cooperative of Puget Sound. HMO growth in the private sector, though, is not in this type of HMO, but in looser forms of individual practice association (IPA) and network-model HMOs. Although program beneficiaries have disproportionately joined staff- or group-model HMOs, Medicare enrollment can be anticipated to follow the move toward IPA and network-model HMOs.

Yet it is not clear that evidence drawn from the staff- or group-model experience with Medicare can be generalized to other HMO forms. For instance, whereas staff- and group-model HMOs typically pay their physicians on a salaried basis, IPA and network models often put the physician at direct financial risk through capitation, creating stronger incentives for restraining utilization of services. Moreover, even Kaiser is now departing from its own model of health care delivery, calling into question whether evidence based on past performance is a valid guide to its own future, let alone to that of other plans (Olmos 1995).

The changing organizational composition of Medicare HMOs will differentially affect various dimensions of performance. In some markets, decentralized HMOs are outperforming staff models in reducing utilization of medical services and expenditures, so Medicare might expect greater cost savings. In addition, HMOs with larger physician panels than staff or group models typically employ may prove more attractive to beneficiaries, perhaps making it easier for sicker beneficiaries to join risk plans without losing their doctors. On the other hand, staff- and group-model HMOs have broader coverage of preventive services than other plans. The advantage in preventive services (including early screening for cancer) that has been observed for HMOs relative to FFS may not exist in nonstaff or nongroup models. Finally, centralized plans such as Kaiser may offer greater convenience (one-stop shopping) and potential for coordination of health services than decentralized plans.

Enrollment changes

Medicare HMOs were analyzed with an enrollment of beneficiaries that was healthier than the program average. If enrollment in the Medicare HMO program increases substantially, HMOs may enroll more seriously ill beneficiaries. Due to the favorable selection in Medicare HMO enrollment, however, it remains unclear how large numbers of sicker beneficiaries would fare in prepaid settings. Medicare's experience with HMOs has not eased concerns about inadequate care for chronically ill enrollees in prepaid plans. Even the social health maintenance organizations (SHMOs), which were specifically designed to enhance prepaid care for the chronically ill, have experienced problems in treating this population (Harrington, Lynch, and Newcomer 1993).[13]

In addition, much of the commentary on Medicare policy proceeds as if the elderly are the sole beneficiary group in the program. Yet 10 percent of Medicare beneficiaries qualify for the program through disabled status and produce, on average, more program expenditures per person than the elderly (Moon 1993). Studies of Medicare HMOs, though, typically exclude the disabled from the study population, since the disabled are, as a proportion of Medicare, underrepresented in HMOs and often constitute a minuscule percentage of a given sample (e.g., Clement et al. 1994). Consequently, not much is known about how disabled Medicare beneficiaries fare in HMOs. However, analyses of risk plans that discontinued their Medicare contracts have raised doubts about HMOs' abilities to care for the disabled. One of the primary variables associated with HMO exit from Medicare was the percentage of disabled patients enrolled in a health plan (Porell and Tompkins 1993). The more disabled beneficiaries a plan enrolled, the greater the chance it terminated its Medicare contract, suggesting problems of adverse selection.

The problems associated with HMO care for sicker Medicare enrollees may be exacerbated by putting elderly and disabled beneficiaries with little experience in using HMOs into HMOs with little experience in treating elderly and disabled patients. Medicare HMO enrollment is highly concentrated, so substantial increases in growth assume bringing new beneficiaries and health plans into the risk program. It is uncertain how new plans will perform compared with more established HMOs experienced in treating Medicare beneficiaries. Alternatively, an increase in enrollment could have beneficial effects on health care for the elderly and disabled if it leads HMOs to devote more resources to developing health services that cater to the needs of Medicare beneficiaries. To date, however, HMOs have been slow to incorporate geriatric-trained physicians with expertise in diagnosing and coordinating elderly health problems (Friedman and Kane 1993).

HMOs and Other Managed Care Plans

As much uncertainty as there is regarding the performance of various types of HMOs in different dimensions of medical care for the Medicare population, the uncertainty is even greater for other types of managed care plans. A recent study concluded that there were too few observations to produce any reliable data on the performance of PPO and POS plans (Miller and Luft 1994b). We do not yet understand how different organizational features of managed care affect physician behavior and shape medical care in health plans; existing research does not distinguish the varying effects of particular forms of managed care that range from utilization review to myriad financial incentives. Findings from HMOs cannot, then, be generalized to PPO and POS plans, and because we do not understand the performance of such plans in caring for the general population, there is no basis for assessing their impact on Medicare beneficiaries.

This issue is crucial because under the 1997 BBA, much of the projected growth in Medicare managed care will come in precisely these types of plans, in addition to the newly minted provider-sponsored organizations. There is tremendous uncertainty as to how much, if any, savings other managed care plans can generate for Medicare and how beneficiaries will fare in such plans. In fact, many Medicare beneficiaries will join managed care plans that actually do not manage care at all, but simply contract with a selected network of providers at reduced fees (White 1997).

The Challenges Ahead: The Future of Medicare Managed Care

Regardless of the uncertainty surrounding the future performance of Medicare managed care plans, or the very real concerns over how poor, chronically ill beneficiaries will fare in such plans, public policy is dramatically expanding the role of managed care in the program. As already noted, the 1997 BBA, by broadening the range of managed care options available to beneficiaries, will increase managed care enrollment (though the legislation's reduction of capitation fees may put a brake on some of that growth). However, the strongest impetus to the growth of Medicare managed care comes from two private-sector developments. The first is the retiree health policies of employers. In 1995, virtually all growth in employers' outlays for health insurance was due to increases in the costs of medical care for retirees. In response, employers are curtailing retiree health coverage and increasingly requiring retired workers to receive their health coverage (either as a pre-Medicare benefit or as a Medigap wraparound) in managed care plans. Forty percent of under-sixty-five retirees and 69 percent of Medicare-eligible retirees in firms with at least ten workers currently remain in indemnity plans, but that figure is expected to plummet as employers embrace managed care plans (Findlay and Meyeroff 1996). Consequently, many beneficiaries who face the loss of Medigap coverage if they choose public Medicare can be expected to enroll instead in managed care plans. The second development that will increase Medicare managed care is the changing character of the private insurance market. Managed care plans are experiencing high rates of growth, whereas the market position of traditional indemnity plans is declining. As more employees join managed care plans, the presence of managed care in Medicare will inexorably increase because workers will seek to maintain the same health coverage in retirement that they carried while employed. Moreover, future cohorts of Medicare recipients will be more experienced with managed care than current beneficiaries, and consequently, more amenable to opting out of Medicare FFS.

Regardless, then, of the direction of public policy, the participation of private managed care plans in Medicare will expand substantially in the coming years. This expansion, as well as the new Medicare market established by the 1997 BBA, creates a number of challenges for the program. There are four such challenges that will help to define the future of Medicare.

Regulating marketing
In the past, HMOs marketed directly to Medicare beneficiaries through mail and phone solicitations, as well as community social events. The 1997 reforms both increase the burden on federal policy makers to regulate plan marketing and create new responsibilities for operating a centralized marketing system similar to the one used by the FEHBP. Under the new system, each year program beneficiaries will choose whether they wish to enroll in public Medicare or in one of the private plans contracting with Medicare under the Medicare+Choice option. The legislation requires the Department of Health and Human Services (pre-

sumably through HCFA) to provide beneficiaries with comparative information on all the available plans during the enrollment process. That information will contain data about plan features, including cost, quality of care, and grievance procedures. In addition, HHS is charged with orchestrating a nationwide education campaign to inform beneficiaries about the Medicare+Choice program and the new enrollment process.

The centralization of Medicare marketing has been widely endorsed by policy analysts as the key to reducing abusive marketing practices and efforts at favorable selection, as well as to enhancing beneficiaries' knowledge about health coverage options (Claxton and Levitt 1996; Moon and Davis 1995; Luft and Miller 1988; Schlesinger and Drumheller 1988). However, HCFA lacks experience in operating a centralized marketing plan and the numerous types of plans that will participate in Medicare+Choice will exacerbate the problems in establishing such a scheme by the targeted deadline and maintaining it in the future. In addition, many beneficiaries will not understand the numerous coverage options and a public education campaign is probably not sufficient to remove the confusion and anxiety many beneficiaries will experience in coping with the new program. As a result, beneficiary assistance programs with individual counseling are needed to aid Medicare beneficiaries in navigating through the enrollment process.

Finally, the 1997 reforms require Medicare+Choice plans to submit marketing materials to HHS in order to ensure they meet federal standards for fair marketing. In other words, it appears that the centralized marketing information will coexist along with some forms of direct marketing. The sheer number of plans that HCFA will contract with will make monitoring of these marketing standards difficult. And given the experience of private insurers in evading rules and using marketing for selection purposes, it is not clear that HCFA has the administrative capacity to prevent such behavior.

Managing risk selection

A second challenge will be coping with the consequences of risk selection. As noted, selection effects are largely responsible for Medicare's losing money on its HMO program. These problems, however, will only get worse in the new Medicare+Choice market. With the enrollments in Medicare HMOs expected to increase, the failure to develop adequate risk adjustment methods will be a costly one for the program. Given Medicare's financial problems, it is crucial that the program eliminate overpayment to managed care plans that stems from biased selection. In theory, an effective risk adjuster could redress this problem by accurately modifying payments to reflect an enrollee's health status and expected medical consumption. Yet while the shortcomings of the AAPCC are well-known, the technical barriers to creating an effective risk adjuster are considerable and a working alternative has not been developed anywhere in the world. Risk adjustment remains very much a "holy grail."

The addition of new managed care plans, including PPOs, and other enrollment options such as PSOs and MSAs, will intensify the impact of selection effects on the program. As the number of Medicare beneficiaries who opt out of public Medicare increases, the program's risk pool will fragment in multiple directions and the corresponding requirements of accurate risk adjustment will thereby multiply. Moreover, a number of the new plans available to beneficiaries, including medical savings accounts and provider sponsored organizations, are expected to induce favorable selection (CBO 1997). PSOs pose a particular problem because they give physicians both the incentives and opportunity to direct healthy patients to their capitated practice (PSOs), while keeping sicker, more expensive patients in traditional FFS Medicare. These risk dynamics will continue to undercut the ability of the program to realize financial savings from managed care.

Protecting quality

A third challenge will be to protect the quality of care provided to Medicare beneficiaries by managed care plans. To date, the record of the federal government in this area is not encouraging. Both HCFA and the local peer-review organizations (PROs) that HCFA contracts with have been sharply criticized for lax oversight of the quality of care provided to Medicare HMO enrollees. The U.S. General Accounting Office (1995) has charged that, although health plans contracting with HCFA must submit proposals for internal quality assurance programs, HCFA often does not check to see if these programs have actually been implemented. Federal administrators have been reluctant to use their enforcement authority: HCFA has been slow to impose sanctions (ranging from contract termination to freezing enrollment and financial penalties) on HMOs that violate quality guidelines—giving them repeated chances to improve performance while renewing their contracts—and has not required risk plans to report data that might provide evidence of inappropriate care. Moreover, on-site HCFA evaluation teams frequently lack personnel with the medical expertise to assess quality issues and have instead focused on health plans' compliance with financial and administrative requirements (U.S. GAO 1995). Similar questions have been raised about the capacities of PROs to monitor care effectively in HMOs and the absence of coordination between PROs and HCFA (U.S. GAO 1991b; Schlesinger and Drumheller 1988).

HCFA is currently revamping its quality oversight program with substantial attention to improving quality regulation in Medicare HMOs. The agency's new strategy, known as the Health Care Quality Improvement Program, is focused on adapting private sector performance measures such as the Health Plan Employer Data and Information Set version for Medicare, initiating collaborative efforts between PROs and HMOs to improve quality of care, and monitoring beneficiary satisfaction with health plans (U.S. GAO 1996b; Hanchak et al. 1996). As part of the new approach, HCFA and PROs have moved away from identification of quality problems through medical review of individual cases and providers in favor of cooperative projects to enhance overall quality of care. It is expected that this cooperative strategy will alleviate adversarial tensions between regulators and HMOs, as well as provide a more effective framework than individual case review for ameliorating health plans' delivery of medical care to Medicare beneficiaries (Jencks and Wilensky 1992; U.S. GAO 1996b).

It is unclear, though, how this program will provide enhanced quality protection for chronically ill elders and other beneficiaries who are most at risk in prepaid systems. In fact, without compensating action, it is likely that oversight of the care provided to such patients will decline, as HCFA's quality initiative is explicitly premised on the notion of shifting regulatory attention away from "occasional, unusual deficiencies in care" in favor of more aggregate-level analysis, leaving "providers to conduct the more intrusive and detailed study of who, when, and why" (Jencks and Wilensky 1992: 900).

As a consequence, several reforms are needed to protect quality of care for at-risk enrollees. First, cooperative projects could be focused on improving quality for precisely those conditions where evidence exists that HMOs are providing less-than-adequate care. Second, HMOs might be encouraged through subsidies to hire geriatric-trained providers who could serve as effective gatekeepers by coordinating services for the elderly. Third, HMOs should be required to develop grievance procedures that reduce the barriers for elderly and disabled patients to register complaints. Attention to the effective soliciting and fair resolution of grievances as a mechanism for enrollees to voice dissatisfaction with their care is particularly important, given the reluctance of many elderly patients to leave health plans once they have an established physician (Schlesinger and Drumheller 1988). Mandatory satisfaction surveys of enrollees, with the information provided to all beneficiaries, would also provide indicators of quality problems. At present, proposed regulations mandate such surveys only if plans place physicians at "substantial financial risk"; this requirement should be broadened to include all contracting health plans. Medicare could also require health plans to hire externally based patient advocates who could help elderly and disabled enrollees navigate health plans and provide assistance in pursuing grievances. The 1997 reforms give broad discretion to administrators to pursue some of these policies through requirements that plans meet quality assurance requirements that will track, for example, high-risk services and chronic conditions. These are clearly steps in the right direction. What remains to be seen, however, is if these provisions are implemented with any more effectiveness than past quality regulations.

Preserving medicare fee-for-service

While Medicare is moving toward managed care, managed care plans are not, as the evidence of poor outcomes for chronically ill and lower-income patients reveals, appropriate forms of medical care for all program beneficiaries. Therefore, it is essential that Medicare maintain a stable FFS component. However, perhaps the most vexing problem in Medicare's long-term future is how to incorporate a growing managed care enrollment without destabilizing Medicare FFS. With growing numbers of enrollees opting out of traditional Medicare, and HCFA offering a broader choice of managed care plans to beneficiaries, Medicare will soon resemble a multiple insurance system. The experience of the private sector and other public-sector insurers shows that indemnity plans often face difficulties in such systems. Confronted with financial penalties for choosing more expensive plans, healthier enrollees typically switch to lower-cost managed care plans, leaving indemnity insurers with sicker and more-expensive risk pools. Indemnity premiums then rise in a "death spiral" because of their adverse selection, causing even more enrollees to switch plans. Eventually, indemnity premiums may be so high as to drive the plan out of business. This dynamic has been observed recently in the University of California health system and the FEHBP, as well as previously in Blue Cross/Blue Shield plans (Evans 1995; Buchmueller and Feldstein 1995).

The danger is that Medicare will be left holding sicker beneficiaries while private health plans attract good risks. What can be done to prevent Medicare FFS from collapsing financially as a consequence of biased selection? The most important safeguard is to maintain pooled financing where all Medicare beneficiaries pay the same premium regardless of their health plan selection. Medicare can afford some fragmentation of health plan choice as long as its financing is not similarly fragmented. If financial incentives such as vouchers are implemented, then there is a real danger of a death spiral in Medicare FFS. However, even with pooled financing, there will be political pressures on Medicare FFS if its costs substantially exceed those of private plans contracting with Medicare, regardless of whether the differential is due to efficiency or risk selection. In addition, if healthier and wealthier enrollees join private insurance plans, beneficiary support for the program may fragment, and the political constituency for Medicare FFS may consequently be weakened (Schlesinger and Drumheller 1988).

Conclusion

Medicare was designed to bring the elderly into the mainstream of American medicine. With the ascendance of managed care, that mainstream has changed, and a political consensus now exists that Medicare should follow suit. The enthusiasm for managed care is driven, in part, by its potential to hold down program costs and to provide broader benefits than traditional Medicare. These are surely worthwhile goals. But this chapter suggests that the new consensus also carries with it substantial risks for beneficiaries and tremendous uncertainty for the program. There is a mismatch between the arguments made for expanding managed care in Medicare—based on the experiences of nonprofit, staff-model HMOs—and the enrollment patterns that are likely to define the new Medicare market. We simply do not know how the vast array of new managed care plans will perform with Medicare patients and how successful policy makers will be in managing the new regulatory challenges, particularly risk selection. We do know, however, that Medicare's past experience with HMOs indicates that the financial savings expected from the move to managed care will not be easy to secure. Moreover, there is reason to fear that segments of the elderly and disabled population will not cope well in a competitive insurance environment of managed care plans. In sum, managed care is unlikely to fulfill policy makers' aspirations as the "magic bullet" of Medicare policy.

Notes

This essay was originally prepared as a paper for presentation to Health Care into the Next Century: Markets, States, and Communities, spring 1996 conference, 3–4 May, Durham, NC, and was supported by a grant from the Robert Wood Johnson Foundation, Princeton, NJ. Special thanks to Mark Schlesinger for his exceptional advice throughout this project. I would also like to thank Mark Peterson for his excellent suggestions on revising an earlier draft, and Harold Luft and Caroll Estes for their insightful comments.

1 For an analysis of the politics of Medicare reform in the 104th Congress, see Cathie Jo Martin's chapter in this volume.

2 There is, of course, widespread disagreement over the precise meaning of *managed care*. This essay follows Miller and Luft (1994a) in focusing on managed care plans whose defining characteristic is their reliance on restricted networks of medical providers. This definition of managed care includes HMOs, preferred provider organizations, and point-of-service plans, and excludes indemnity insurers that employ utilization review but not restricted provider networks. This exclusion makes sense for the present purposes, as proposals for moving Medicare beneficiaries to managed care do not generally have in mind indemnity plans.

3 HMOs are, however, legally entitled to make profits on Medicare beneficiaries that do not exceed the profit margins they earn on non-Medicare beneficiaries. This profit margin is figured into the adjusted community rate (ACR) that plans submit to HCFA as a projected premium.

4 Medicare enrollment in managed care is also substantially lower than Medicaid, where 30 percent of recipients were in managed care plans in 1994 (Grimaldi 1995).

5 A recent Lewin-VHI study found that 80 percent of cost savings in network HMOs came from price discounts (Freudenheim 1994).

6 Medigap premiums account for 25 percent of elderly out-of-pocket expenses on health care; about one-third of Medicare beneficiaries have employer-sponsored Medigap plans; an additional 12 percent of Medicare beneficiaries receive Medicaid coverage (Kaiser Family Foundation 1995).

7 HMOs typically "do not limit initial access to services but do control costs by reducing the intensity of the service rendered" (Brown et al. 1993: 17).

8 Supplemental premiums are another way for risk plans to induce favorable selection.

9 Quality of care was evaluated by measuring the health outcomes of patients treated for specific conditions or by assessing the extent to which medical treatments complied with recommended "process-of-care" standards (Brown et al. 1993): For inpatient care, outcomes measured included mortality, hospital readmission, and postadmission complication rates; for ambulatory and chronic care, measures included access to medical services, changes in functional status, and symptomatic improvement. Process-of-care standards to measure appropriate treatment were developed by panels of physicians or gleaned from existing literature on medical treatment norms.

10 The final section of this essay discusses options for reforming Medicare policy toward HMOs.

11 In addition to these changes, present research is limited by a number of methodological problems, including the absence of many randomized studies, the limited time duration of studies, the limited number of conditions analyzed, and difficulties in performing adequate case-mix adjustment to control for biased selection into health plans.

12 However, there is reason to be cautious about long-term trends in benefit coverage. After entry into the Medicare market slows, HMOs may not be as aggressive in offering new benefits. Furthermore, health plans will try to avoid offering any benefits that could produce adverse selection in their enrollment.

13 SHMOs were started as a demonstration project in 1985. The idea was to overcome HMOs' disincentives for caring for the chronically ill by providing for broad coverage integrating acute and long-term care services.

Markets and Medicaid: Insights from

Oregon and Tennessee

Marsha Gold

This essay builds on two parallel state efforts to construct health reform for low-income populations using the Medicaid program, with a view to identifying what we can learn about issues related to their implementation and effects. Specifically, the essay describes the early experiences of Oregon and Tennessee with health reform based on the Medicaid program under federal Section 1115 waivers. The analysis is drawn largely from in-depth case studies based on document review and site visits to each state in late 1994 to assess their first-year experience, with limited follow-up in August 1996 and later.

In sum, the analysis suggests that Medicaid managed care and market strategies in concept are neither "magic bullets" nor "poison pills" for achieving public policy objectives. The way these strategies are formed, the context in which they are conceived, and the way in which they are implemented can markedly influence their accomplishments. As a public program, Medicaid has features that influence the way market strategies develop and their ultimate effects. These include objectives that are broad in scope, multifaceted, and sometimes unacknowledged or conflicting; political processes that influence the speed and form of implementation; and administrative features both external and internal to the program that constrain the flexibility of the design and adoption. These features apply to all states, but they often operate differently in each.

Many of these concerns also exist in Medicaid fee-for-service. Thus our research suggests that in moving to managed care and market-based solutions, states gain some tools but remain faced with the same challenge: How to achieve more for less and for whom, when support falls short of the amount needed to achieve policy goals. Medicaid is the major national program that promotes access to health care for low-income people (Rowland et al. 1992). A product of the federal social welfare system, Medicaid is explicitly designed as a federal-state partnership (CRS 1993). Medicaid programmatic features have always varied widely across states, which differ in eligibility requirements, benefit levels, provider payments, and administrative structures and processes.

Spurred by concerns over rising costs and responding to other changes in the health care market, many states are now introducing more emphasis on managed care and market processes in the design of their Medicaid programs, often through federal Section 1115 waivers of standard federal Medicaid provisions (Rowland and Hanson 1996). The 1997 Balanced Budget Act (BBA) provides states with further flexibility to contract with managed care plans that serve the Medicaid population alone and also to implement managed care initiatives outside of the waiver requirements that historically have applied to these programs (Rosenbaum 1997). The BBA also allows states that currently have Section 1115 waivers (as do Oregon and Tennessee) to seek a three-year continuation following the expiration date. In addition, the BBA creates a new Child Health Insurance Program to be implemented by states. Managed care is likely to factor heavily in this major coverage expansion for low-income children that states have considerable flexibility to design, either within or outside the Medicaid program.

At the end of 1996, one-third of Medicaid beneficiaries (13.3 million individuals) were enrolled in some form of Medicaid managed care, 9 million in at-risk health maintenance organizations (HMOs), prepaid health plans, or health-insuring organizations. Today, all but a few states have some contracts with such organizations. By mid-1996, twenty-nine states and the District of Columbia had one-quarter or more of their population in them (KFF 1997). Most commonly, they involve capitated at-risk arrangements with organizations, like HMOs, which assume responsibility for providing or arranging needed health services.

Pursuing Medicaid managed care strategies fundamentally shifts the role of government in important ways, and thus, is of considerable interest. Traditionally, Medicaid agencies were directly responsible for running a public insurance program. State agencies saw themselves, for the most part, as bill payers, with little role in actively shaping health care delivery even though Medicaid, through its scope, has great influence in this area. As enrollment and costs in the Medicaid program have grown markedly, Medicaid activities have moved toward more activist roles. In most states through the 1980s, the focus was on structuring individual provider and utilization payment policies to achieve spending targets or constraints and other goals, including those external to the Medicaid program, like securing funds to finance care for previously fully state-funded health programs.

By introducing managed care strategies within their programs, the state role is yet further broadened and deepened. A focus on payment policies to providers and such mechanisms as utilization review or coverage policies emphasizes discrete services in individual sectors of the health care system. In contrast, the focus on managed care potentially shifts the interest more broadly both to the way the system functions as a whole, and also to an emphasis on its effects on individuals or populations for whom the state is accountable.

Most managed care strategies also tend to distance state agencies from directly affecting the way the state policies influence both the health system and the population covered by managed care. This is because managed care strategies work through managed care organizations charged by the state with responsibility for systemwide reconfiguration and population-based interventions. In using managed care, by which I refer to risk-based arrangements with organizations like HMOs or their equivalents, states are structuring contract arrangements with organizations that, in turn, mediate the delivery of health services and financial risk for their costs. In doing so, states typically also today are relying more explicitly on the market and competition to help them, with the health plans, achieve their objectives. This was less the case historically. In effect, as Rosenbaum and colleagues (1997) have observed, a managed care strategy means that the legal framework in which states function shifts the paradigm of law that rests in regulation and administrative law to the law of contract, with the latter yielding states much less authority and discretion for interpretations not explicitly laid out in the contract.

Thus, the movement to Medicaid managed care strategies provides a two-edged sword from the perspective of the national or state policy maker. On one hand, Medicaid managed care provides the potential to enhance the performance of the health system because a managed care focus, by its nature, is more broadly based, and at least in theory, is more closely linked with ultimate outcomes because of its focus on accountability for defined care to defined populations. On the other, Medicaid managed care has the potential to allow states more easily to divest themselves of responsibility, in reality or in perception, as they contractually transfer authority to private entities and charge them with carrying out obligations that will greatly influence how well the state meets its public policy objectives under Medicaid.

For these reasons, the way in which states structure their Medicaid managed care strategies and how they operationally carry them out become vitally important from a public policy perspective. Whereas some may view the shift in state responsibilities under Medicaid managed care as a limiting influence on the role of public agencies, there is another perspective—based on the points noted previously—that leads one to conclude that state roles change with Medicaid managed care, but become no less important and potentially more so. This perspective, which I share, views the challenges of Medicaid managed care as considerably more demanding on states because the goalpost has been moved: Medicaid agencies now can be judged not only by their ability to pay bills on time and keep expenditures within the budget, but also by their success in encouraging the employment of well-structured and cost-effective care systems to address the needs of populations for whom they are accountable. This calls for state staff with considerable skills and great appreciation for the complexity of the health care system, as well as for the subtle nuances that can make the difference between effectively motivating private behavior toward public ends or failing in this regard, either because the agency removed the flexibility private organizations need to work or, alternatively, provided so much flexibility that private ends dominated.

These issues are particularly relevant when there is considerable diversity across states, each of which has a somewhat unique infrastructure in its health system, distinct historical features associated with the Medicaid program, particular characteristics of the population and the sociopolitical milieu, and uniquely configured administrative processes and financial structures. States differ in how they see the role of the Medicaid program, and also in how they see the role of the public sector more generally. The variation across states also influences the capacity of states to carry out policy and the consistency with which the implemented programs match the original design. Interstate variability will only grow larger as Congress enhances state flexibility and makes concurrent changes such as the decoupling of welfare and Medicaid.

All this raises questions about what states will achieve through their Medicaid programs in the years ahead, and how this will affect the ability, nationwide, to meet national goals relating to coverage and access for low-income people. There is, of course, disagreement on the form of these goals (President's Commission 1983) and how expansive they should be. Yet despite the disagreement, most would concur that some form of national goals on access and coverage is appropriate. Given Medicaid's historical importance in promoting access for low-income populations, there is thus great interest in understanding the potential effects from a shift to Medicaid managed care and a market-based approach within the state-context influence on these issues.

This article is intended to provide insight into these issues by contrasting the experience of two states seeking to reform their Medicaid programs to enhance access and control costs. Oregon and Tennessee have received federal Section 1115 demonstration and research waivers of provisions of the Social Security Act. Subject to federal constraints, these two states exemplify the flexibility in program development and efforts to engage the market that is a part of Medicaid's future. Both states mounted initiatives to implement capitated managed care to contain costs, and linked the initiatives to a major expansion in coverage for low-income populations. This article builds on case studies on the first-year experiences of each of these states, shedding light on the similarities and differences in state contexts and how they may influence people in the states and the policy issues that come to the forefront. I review the case study data sources and methods, summarize the efforts in each state, and discuss the lessons that their experience teaches us.

Source of Information and Approach

The information in this article comes from a broader study conducted to develop case studies of seven states that are currently restructuring their health care systems for low-income populations: California, Florida, Minnesota, New York, Oregon, Tennessee, and Texas (Gold, Sparer, and Chu 1996). Funded by the Henry J. Kaiser Family Foundation and the Commonwealth Fund, these case studies are designed to provide information and analyses that will yield a better understanding of how the shift to managed care is affecting low-income individuals and their access to health care services. The studies focus on early insight and timely analyses that will be useful to other states and other efforts to shape the rapidly evolving managed care systems and health reforms for low-income populations.

This essay draws on the findings reported in the cases prepared for Oregon and Tennessee (Gold, Chu, and Lyons 1995; Gold, Frazer, and Schoen 1995). We focused on these two states because their objectives are broad and parallel in many ways, with similar timing, yet their approaches are highly distinct, making them very useful as foils for one another. These cases are based largely on interviews conducted in late 1994, supplemented by a review of documents and other written materials. This time frame allowed us to capture the first year's operational experience under the Section 1115 waivers in each state. During a four-day site visit, the project team interviewed individuals at the state and local levels to get both perspectives. We interviewed state policy makers and others who are attempting to influence policy from the standpoint of consumers, providers, and insurers/health plans. The local perspective came from participating health plans, consumers, and providers affected by the initiatives. Various interests are represented in these cases, including physicians in private practice and traditional safety-net providers, such as public hospitals, county health services, and community health centers. For this essay, we have selectively updated the case studies to reflect changes that have occurred since our visit, particularly in major features of the states' programs or their experience in terms of key issues prominent after the first year. This included press-clipping searches and limited telephone follow-up with states in August 1996, as well as a more limited search of national newsletters and state Web sites conducted in October 1997 for purposes of revising this essay for publication here. While we were not able to conduct the detailed study inherent in the initial assessment, the updates confirm the relevance of the insights and issues identified initially, with both state initiatives continuing with core features intact, and many of the state issues still at stake.

The Oregon Initiative: Development, Experience, and Prospects

Oregon is a relatively small state with 2.8 million residents, two-thirds of whom live in the Portland-Salem corridor. More homogeneous than the nation as a whole, the state has a lower proportion of people in poverty (10.3 percent) and a smaller nonwhite population (9 percent). Before Oregon implemented its health care reform initiative, lack of insurance was perceived to be the major barrier to health care. Of the estimated 400,000 to 450,000 Oregonians who had no health insurance, about one-third had an income below the federal poverty level (Oregon Department of Human Resources [DHR] 1991). Oregon also has a long history with managed care in private insurance and in Medicaid.

Goals, general design, and context

The Oregon Health Plan (OHP) is a major state initiative for health care reform. The purpose of the Medicaid component of the OHP is to expand coverage to all Oregonians with an income below the poverty level. Savings would be generated both by the design of the benefit package, which is based on a priority list of conditions and treatments,[1] and by managed care for beneficiaries. The Medicaid component was implemented in two phases, the first of which was operational in 1994.

A key feature of the OHP is that it rations health care and uses the savings to expand coverage and access within budget constraints. A priority list of 696 condition/treatment pairs is the formal mechanism used for resource allocation, that is, deciding which services to cover given budget constraints. These pairs are ranked by a legislatively established Health Services Commission composed of clinicians and consumers.

The pairs are given priority on the basis of three major criteria: the ability of the specified treatment to prevent death, the average cost of the treatment, and twelve other considerations based on community values. Among these considerations are the importance of interceding early before the condition develops, comfort care, and the public health goal of ensuring healthy mothers and infants through prenatal care (Oregon Health Services Commission 1993).

The goals of the OHP are to (1) expand coverage and access; (2) constrain costs and reduce cost shifting across payers; (3) evaluate critically the relative effectiveness of medical services and obtain public participation by setting priorities to guide health care funding decisions; and (4) enable all Oregonians to access a basic level of health services (Oregon DHR 1991, 1993).

As enacted in 1989, the OHP includes:

- expanded Medicaid coverage for all Oregonians with an income below the federal poverty level (Coverage within Medicaid is made affordable through the use of a standard benefit package and enrollment in managed care plans. The standard benefit package is based on the ranked condition/treatment pairs.);
- expanded private sector coverage based on an employer mandate applying first to employers with more than twenty-five employees, and a year later, to smaller businesses (In 1993, the legislature delayed the expansions until 1 March 1997 and 1 January 1998, respectively; however, the entire mandate would expire unless an exemption of the federal Employee Retirement Income Security Act [ERISA] was received by 1 January 1996.);
- an Oregon medical insurance pool for high-risk individuals (Legislation passed in 1991 further addressed issues of insurance availability by creating a Small Employer Carrier Advisory Committee to design a basic benefit package similar to the Medicaid benefit package that all small-business insurance carriers must offer.).

Because the employer mandate was never implemented (and the high-risk pool so far includes only a small number of individuals), the Medicaid component of the OHP has been the major component of the initiative driving changes in care patterns and access for the low-income population.

Phase 1 of the OHP was implemented in February 1994, following approval of the federal Section 1115 waiver in March 1993. This delay was caused by a series of federally initiated reviews and controversial negotiations that spanned the multiyear period that began when the waiver request was submitted in 1991. Phase 1 involves the removal of categorical and asset restrictions on Medicaid eligibility and extends coverage to residents with an income below 100 percent of the poverty level. This level compares with a previous income threshold estimated to have ranged from 50 to 65 percent of the poverty level, depending on the group and family size (Oregon DHR 1991).[2] The aged, blind, and disabled were initially excluded, but are being included under Phase 2 starting in January 1995, as are foster children. From a previous base enrollment of about 283,000 in fiscal year 1991, the OHP is estimated to cover an additional 160,000 persons, 75 percent of whom (120,000) would participate (OTA 1992). The program proved to be popular, with about 100,000 new enrollees added by the end of 1994.

Coverage is provided through managed care plans under full capitation (i.e., through prepaid health plans) in most counties, through a combination of fully capitated and partially capitated plans in a few counties, and through primary care case managers in the rest. More than 70 percent of the OHP enrollees are in fully capitated health plans (FCHPs). Individuals select a plan, and the number of choices varies by county. As mentioned, the benefits are defined on the basis of a ranked list of condition/treatment pairs. Mental health and chemical dependency benefits, carved out in Phase 1, are paid on a fee-for-service basis. Enrollees are not charged a premium, and there was no cost sharing in 1994. The program is administered by the Office of Medical Assistance Programs (OMAP) within the DHR. Other components of state government are also involved.

To a large extent, the OHP managed care system rests on a foundation of experience and preexisting plans in the commercial and Medicaid markets, especially in urban areas. When the waiver proposal was submitted in 1991, Oregon had nine HMOs with more than 770,000 enrollees: 26 percent of the state's population. By 1993, just before the plan became effective, enrollment had grown to 960,000 in seven HMOs: 32 percent of the population (GHAA 1992, 1994).

The Oregon Medicaid program also had an extensive, and generally successful, experience with Medicaid managed care prior to the waiver (GAO 1992). Although there had been earlier demonstrations, the major pre-OHP managed care initiative began in mid-1985 under a Section 1915(b) waiver for a mandatory managed care program in eight counties, all but one in metropolitan areas.[3] By 1991, when the Section 1115 waiver was submitted, about 54 percent of all recipients of Aid to Families with

Dependent Children (AFDC)—31 percent of all Medicaid enrollees—were in managed care plans (OTA 1992). Except for Kaiser Permanente, with 11,600 fully capitated enrollees, all of these plans were partially capitated, generally for physician services. Partially capitated plans are called physician care organizations (PCOs); some fifteen served about 56,400 AFDC eligibles by 1991.

This experience with managed care worked to the OHP's advantage, as did the small size of the state and relative homogeneity of the population and additional time made available for program planning and implementation because of the delay in waiver approval. While Oregon waited for approval of the federal waiver, many Medicaid beneficiaries were enrolled in managed care plans in anticipation of the OHP. By January 1993, mandatory Medicaid managed care programs had expanded to fourteen counties and were voluntary in two others, and a total of four HMOs and twenty-two PCOs were serving almost 83,000 AFDC enrollees, or about 35 percent of all Medicaid enrollees (GAO 1993).

Development of the initiative

Equity and access to care appear to be the main impetus for the development of the OHP. The initiative has its roots in the legislature's July 1987 decision to cut off Medicaid funding for organ transplants with relatively little discussion. In December 1987 the highly publicized death of a young man who had not received a transplant spurred a lengthy debate about whom and what to cover. The incident drew the attention of John Kitzhaber, then president of Oregon's senate, and a physician and supporter of managed care; his leadership played a key role in the OHP's development.

The OHP evolved through an extensive process of formal and informal discussions essentially involving, at some level, everyone in the state who potentially had a stake in the initiative. The public participated as press attention shifted from the transplant story to broader issues of the uninsured. As a state administrator remarked during our visit, "In Oregon you need to get the right answer and you need to get it the right way. . . . Both product and process have to be credible."

Providers were a key force driving the initiative, and from the start, there was greater consensus on the Medicaid component of the OHP than on the employer mandate. A primary argument for the OHP was that the current system entailed a cost shift, resulting in added expenses for many stakeholders. In addition, there was concern about the amount and high cost of care being inappropriately provided in emergency rooms. The perception that rationing of health care services already occurred under the existing system also made the acceptance of a priority list possible.

Provider groups told us that the Oregon legislature, faced with a five-year recession in early 1980, had cut both eligibility and benefits for Medicaid. By the mid- to late 1980s, the providers believed that these cuts had added considerably to their costs. The Oregon Hospital Association—a key player because hospitals in Portland are said to be very powerful—was concerned about costs under the current Medicaid system and a decrease in hospitals ability to shift these costs after the implementation of Medicare's diagnosis-related group system. The cost shift (which the industry thought might be at least tens of millions of dollars) stemmed from low Medicaid eligibility levels—only about half the poverty level—and low Medicaid rates, which hospitals said covered only 60 percent of their costs.

The physician community, represented by the Oregon Medical Association, also supported the initiative: Physicians believed that they were already subsidizing the Medicaid program because of low payment rates. The burden of uncompensated care was another motivating factor. In the mid-1980s, provider groups, along with Blue Cross and Blue Shield (BCBS) of Oregon, supported a survey of the uninsured and an analysis of the cost shift that could be used in discussions with the legislature.

Employers (through the Association of Oregon Industries) were also on board, spurred by a concern that they were already absorbing the cost of uncompensated care and by Senator Kitzhaber's argument that universal coverage was necessary to control costs. Advocacy groups and safety-net providers that traditionally serve low-income groups were apparently less involved in the evolution of the OHP, although they supported it because of the expansion in eligibility. Resistance to the OHP by elderly and disabled individuals was avoided by excluding them altogether, at their request, from Phase 1. Meanwhile, legislative approval was encouraged because both liberals and conservatives could support the initiative. Broadly speaking, Democrats (who controlled both houses) viewed it as a way to expand services, whereas Republicans were attracted to the rationing arguments.

Senator Kitzhaber, said to be a "good process player" by a state administrator, gained the support of the various interests before introducing the first draft of the bill in 1989. Legislation to expand Medicaid and use the priority list "passed handily"; the employer mandate was enacted by a slimmer margin and was viewed as more of an achievement by legislative staff members with whom we spoke. The passing of the bill was followed by meetings of the Health Services Commission to develop a methodology for determining which benefits to cover, which resulted in the condition/treatment pairs list. This process in Oregon has been well documented elsewhere (OTA 1992; Oregon Health Services Commission 1993).

The national controversy over the OHP focuses on the priority list, begun when the waiver proposal was submitted. However, by then, conflict over this issue seemed largely resolved within Oregon, thanks to the process used by the Health Services Commission, which was composed of five physicians, four health care consumers, a social worker, and a public health nurse. In generating the ranked list, the commission enhanced its credibility because the group involved physicians, was relatively open, and was insulated from political pressures. Indeed, the priority list was not an issue in Oregon at the time of our visit, and the major result of the federal-level controversy has arguably been a closing of ranks within the state. Oregonians were reportedly less likely to voice concern over specific features of the OHP because of the process used to develop it and the possible political ramifications of opposition within the state.

The need to revise the priority list as a result of federal negotiations, with changes purportedly made in response to the ADA, was difficult for Oregonians to accept. Although they ultimately agreed to the changes to get the OHP moving, the compromise was perceived as a violation of the state agreement that politics would not be allowed to interfere with the process of establishing the list, especially with Kitzhaber's election as governor in 1994. Nonetheless, despite the constraints on the debate, the OHP (particularly its Medicaid component) seems to have broad support in Oregon.

The slowdown in implementing the OHP caused by the delay in obtaining the federal waiver had several effects. On the one hand, it added valuable time to build support and develop necessary administrative processes and managed care arrangements. On the other hand, it deferred implementation at a time most auspicious for the OHP's success: During the interim, party control of the state legislature shifted, as did public sentiment. In 1991 (when the request for the Section 1115 waiver was submitted), Republicans assumed leadership of the Oregon House. Kitzhaber left the senate before the 1993 legislative session, and that body switched to Republican leadership in 1995.[4] Since 1993, the political climate in Oregon has become increasingly conservative, with greater state budgetary constraints and what one state administrator termed a more cynical voter population, partly attributable to the sour taste left by last year's failed national health reform effort. These changes have influenced Phase 2 efforts and the employer mandate feature of the OHP.

Implementation

The implementation of the first phrase of the OHP in 1994 is widely perceived to have been a success, although certain concerns are outstanding. Some 269,000 people, including about 90,000 new eligibles, were enrolled from February 1994 to November 1994 (Oregon DHR 1994). Both they and the existing Medicaid population eligible because of AFDC or related criteria (mostly children and mothers) were enrolled in managed care plans involving a new benefit package. An extensive educational effort was mounted, with a contractor used to handle most information dissemination and preliminary eligibility screening. Enrollment materials were prepared in eight languages. A simplified eligibility form was developed to encourage enrollment. Although there was some inevitable confusion, about 90 percent of enrollees were said to have selected their plans voluntarily.

The experience with managed care plans was also better than expected. Under the plan, all organizations that meet plan standards on access, quality, and financial solvency (as well as others) are eligible to participate. Payment rates were set using actuarial analysis obtained from an actuarial firm that used fee-for-service Medicaid data to calculate estimated cost-to-charge ratios for providing the care called for in the benefit package. The objective was to be fair to plan actuarially while also capturing savings to the state for managed care (assumed at 20 percent of per capita inpatient and outpatient service costs excluding maternity for an FCHP and 10 percent for a partially capitated plan) and adding an allowance for plan administrative costs (6 percent for FCHPs and $4 per member per month for PCOs). The state was able to rely much more on FCHPs than it had expected. Contracts were established with sixteen FCHPs (including all of the state's federally qualified HMOs) and with four PCOs. In all but eleven counties, FCHPs are the only participants in the OHP. The exceptions are three counties with a mixture of FCHPs and PCOs, and eight generally very small counties with few physicians that rely only on mandatory primary care case management.

The priority list has not tended to be a major issue for health plans or providers in Oregon to date, although differences of opinion exist about its value. To address providers' questions, the state operates a benefit hotline staffed by registered nurses. In addition, medical directors meet monthly with Medicaid staff to discuss issues. Some providers view the list as a valuable tool, whereas others say it is confusing. Provider support appears to have been increased by the willingness of health plans to allow their associated physicians to respond flexibly to concerns over services below the cutoff line.

The OHP deliberately leaves to each plan decisions on any special care efforts for low-income vulnerable populations. Differences in plan philosophy about whether payer status or other characteristics should be considered in an equitable system appear to exist. Translation services and the interpretation of state requirements were issues we heard about in our visit. We also heard that the issue of how to handle special needs will be more prominent in Phase 2, both because of the types of people added, and because state officials from service programs will be involved and may want greater specificity in mandating program features.

To support it in implementing the program, OMAP, charged with its implementation, reorganized its functions and hired staff with needed expertise. A cross-agency implementation committee was established to provide oversight and guidance. The smooth implementation of Phase 1 is attributed to the state's extensive prior experience with managed care, deliberate planning, cooperation between the public and private sectors, and the high caliber of the staff from OMAP, who are clearly respected by those within and outside the state. There was some concern that staff would be recruited away by health plans, particularly when there were legislative efforts to reduce the salaries of state staff.

Although we found little concrete information on the first-year effects of the OHP on access to care, there is broad consensus that access is better because more people are covered. In addition, some perceive that the newly covered are prouder seeking care, and that their providers are more comfortable when coverage exists than when it does not. For those who had been covered already, the perception was that little changed, although some benefits were expanded. The perception is that access was reasonably good to medical care under Medicaid for eligibles before the OHP despite some problems, including provider supply in rural areas and dental services.

It was too early to assess other spillover effects from the OHP on other important policy goals. Oregon's safety net consists of a variety of providers, including private physicians who see low-income patients, hospital emergency rooms, community health centers, and county health departments (some of which provide primary care services). These providers, particularly the center and county providers, participate in the OHP, which has also spurred some creative arrangements including one between Multnomah County (Portland) and the Oregon Health Sciences University. Yet, the perception also is that demand for care from these providers among the uninsured exceeded available supply. Even though the OHP has expanded those with coverage, safety-net providers had not experienced a decline in the number of uninsured seeking their services at the end of 1994. The OHP has reduced revenue for some of these providers and thus there is concern for the impact on the safety net if Oregon's goal of more universal coverage is not successful. As this appears likely, given the failure to enact an employer mandate or to develop alternative sources of support for more broad-based systemwide reform, the spillover effect of the OHP on the safety net is more worrisome than otherwise.

Prospects

In late 1994 we perceived strong political support for the continuation of the Phase 1 component of the OHP, although some changes in the program seemed possible. Most of these changes have now been implemented or are being developed. A three-month rather than one-month test of income eligibility is now in place in response to fiscal constraints and the heightened concern for fraud inherent in more simplified eligibility. Some cost sharing for premiums or services is being introduced. The benefit package has been reduced and the total number of condition/treatment pairs covered in February 1997 is 578 out of 745 (Miller 1997).

In late 1994 the larger issues involved how far the state would be able to move forward, both politically and fiscally, with the rest of the OHP (including Phase 2). Phase 2 of the OHP, developed in 1993, calls for

- including persons who are aged, blind, and disabled, and who receive Supplemental Security Income, as well as children in foster care;
- phasing in the integration of mental health services under managed care instead of the current carve-out, fee-for-service arrangements and an expansion of the mental health benefit;
- adding chemical dependency treatment services to the managed care benefit package.

The expansion for the aged, blind, and disabled was added at the request of advocates and provides a measure of the acceptance of the OHP's Phase 1 experience.[5] We also were told that advocates supported inclusion of mental health services as a means to both improve the quality of these services and expand benefits either directly or through legal action. At the time of our visit, there was concern that turf battles among various public and private mental health providers and fiscal problems could lessen the chances for expansion and integration of the mental health and substance abuse benefits.

Implementing Phase 2 means setting a number of features in motion and resolving controversial issues. Phase 2 began in January 1995. Aged and disabled individuals were phased in over eight months starting in

March 1995; children in substitute care were phased in next. State officials and advocates (who worked with them in implementation) say the expansion went generally smoothly despite some problems. Effective 1 January 1995, chemical dependency benefits were added to the OHP package. Enhanced mental health benefits are being added on an incremental basis. This part of the process focuses first on about 25 percent of the OHP enrollees who live in twenty counties (Multnomah County, where Portland is located, is excluded). The goal was for all OHP enrollees to receive mental health services through managed care arrangements by July 1996. However this has been delayed, with execution of many contracts currently scheduled for early 1998. The state share of Phase 1 expansion was funded by a combination of new state spending and savings from the redesigned benefit package and managed care. The state's financial commitment was greater than expected because of the growth of managed care while the waiver was being debated in Washington. Another problem is that the waiver assumed future savings because of the employer mandate. However, support for this has eroded, and authority for it sunsetted when Congress did not grant the ERISA preemption needed to execute the mandate.

A key question that was prominent at the end of the first year involved how far Oregon will get in reaching its coverage goals. In August 1996, enrollment in the OHP stood at 373,000, up from 269,000 in November 1994. This includes 115,000 newly covered individuals, more than the 90,000 to 100,000 covered in late 1994, but below the 120,000 new eligibles originally projected under the Medicaid component. Although Oregon has started to implement Phase 2, financing continues to be a major concern and a point of debate. Fiscal issues are especially worrisome because of the passage in 1990 of Measure 5, which limits property taxes and has increased the demand on state general fund revenues. Alternatives to the employer mandate were considered in the next legislative session in 1995. In order to continue movement toward universal coverage, Oregon passed Measure 44, whose levy of thirty cents per pack of cigarettes will be used to extend health care coverage to low-income populations (American Health Line 1997a). The Family Health Insurance Assistance program will help low-income working people pay for health care coverage beginning in March 1998. These state actions, together with funding from the BBA will expand the OHP to more low-income groups although universal coverage still presents a challenge. We were told in late 1994 that Governor Kitzhaber would fight hard to maintain a broader OHP. As he is said to have stated, "I didn't sign up for an expanded Medicaid program." However, the coalition supporting the employer mandate has broken down, and much employer support has been lost. Most wondered how far Oregon could progress beyond the Medicaid component of the program in moving toward universal coverage. We heard some concern that if the program involved a Medicaid expansion only, support for it could erode, narrowing the eligibility criteria and reducing coverage over time in response to budget crises.

The Tennessee Initiative: Development and Prospects

Tennessee is small to medium in size, has 5.1 million residents, and is geographically and demographically diverse. Roughly 2 million of Tennessee's residents live in counties associated with four urban centers: Memphis, Nashville, Knoxville, and Chattanooga. Overall, 39 percent of the population resides outside an urban area, which is considerably above the U.S. average of 25 percent. Like the state's demographic profile, the health care system varies substantially throughout the state. A shortage of providers is a major issue in many rural and some inner-city areas of Tennessee. The state Medicaid program had very little experience with managed care before the initiative, and experience in the private sector also was relatively limited. HMO penetration was very small, and most experience was based on the basically discounted fee arrangements inherent in Tennessee's BCBS preferred provider plan for state and some other large-account employees.

Goals, general design, and context

TennCare, a major Medicaid demonstration project, is using Section 1115 waiver authority under the Social Security Act to rapidly reconfigure Tennessee's Medicaid program, and potentially along with it, to make major changes in Tennessee's health care delivery and financing systems.

The goals of TennCare are to increase access within the limits of the state budget, improve quality of care, encourage preventive care, give enrollees incentives for appropriate utilization, incorporate charity funds, encourage coverage for the uninsured, remove disincentives to work for recipients of AFDC, and provide continuity of coverage. TennCare expands coverage up to 400 percent of poverty, requires the rapid development of a managed care infrastructure, and substantially revises the state funding streams for health care.

Implemented on 1 January 1994, TennCare is intended to expand coverage to roughly 500,000 additional people while restraining state spending through managed care and alternative financing strategies. Although it continues to evolve in response to long-standing issues and concerns,

TennCare was conceived and implemented in less than a year. In the first year of operation, total enrollment grew from 770,000 to more than 1.1 million. All 1994 enrollees were in managed care. This shift away from fee-for-service plans generated considerable controversy nationwide, and at least short-term transitional issues. Only one of the participating managed care entities with expanded enrollment had previous Medicaid experience (one small plan with 35,000 enrollees), and few had any managed care experience. Immediately before TennCare began, only 300,000 people (or 5.7 percent of Tennessee's total population) were in HMOs, and another million or so were in preferred provider plans operated by BCBS (GHAA 1994). Within a year, the percentage of the total population statewide in managed care organizations (MCOs) basically doubled to include about half the state's population.

TennCare's scope is considerably broader than virtually any other state's Section 1115 waiver demonstrations. Using a sliding scale to determine premiums and patient cost sharing to pay for services, TennCare removes categorical and asset test restrictions on Medicaid eligibility, expanding eligibility to the uninsurables (such as those denied coverage after applying) and the uninsured. There are premium subsidies with limitations for those with incomes up to 400 percent of the poverty level. Enrollees are required to join any one of twelve managed care plans, two of which are statewide. TennCare covers everyone who is eligible, including the disabled. However, long-term care (covered by both Medicare and Medicaid for dual eligibles) and, at least initially, selected mental health benefits and special children's program services for those in custody, continue as in the past. The program is operated by the TennCare bureau within the Department of Health.

The designers of TennCare assumed that at least a rudimentary managed care infrastructure could be developed rapidly. Before TennCare, managed care experience in the private sector and in Medicaid was quite limited. Tennessee had eleven HMOs, none of which were very large. Most privately insured managed care enrollees were in relatively loosely structured preferred provider organizations (PPOs) offered by BCBS to state employees and other large-employer groups. Medicaid contracted with only one managed care plan, an HMO with a Medicaid enrollment of 35,000. Tennessee has a history of generally unsuccessful legislative battles involving anti–managed care provider-protection legislation.

The impetus for TennCare was largely fiscal (Coughlin and Lipson 1994). Tennessee made extensive use of provider donations and taxes in conjunction with disproportionate share (DSH) payments to finance the expansion of Medicaid and the required state contribution (Holahan and Liska 1995). (The DSH payment adjustment is made under the Medicaid program to hospitals that serve a relatively large volume of low-income patients.) This financing arrangement became increasingly untenable because of growing provider resistance and changes in federal policy. To balance the budget, the state needed to generate substantial savings or extensively cut back the program. Citing an urgent fiscal crisis that would otherwise require tighter eligibility rules and major reductions in provider payments, state officials developed TennCare to retain federal funds. In January 1995, incoming Governor Don Sundquist announced that he would move the administration of the program to the Department of Finance and Administration, constrain state spending, sustain current Medicaid eligibility and benefit levels, and expand coverage. State officials aimed to expand coverage through savings from managed care, hard-nosed contracting, and alternative financing drawn from the Medicaid program, other state programs, and the private sector.

Development of the initiative

TennCare was developed and implemented quickly, with limited involvement by most key stakeholders. The concept was approved in April 1993, and the Section 1115 waiver was submitted in June 1993. The program was implemented six months later in January 1994, less than two months after the Health Care Financing Administration (HCFA) approved the waiver. This schedule was viewed as being critical to generate the necessary savings immediately. There was also a desire to have the program well under way when the legislature was out of session, making it less likely that opponents would lobby against TennCare. TennCare developers were well aware of the operational challenges of the schedule, but thought that they could address short-term problems as they arose. They also believed that these problems would be offset by the long-term gains in coverage and fiscal control expected from the initiative.

Legislation with broadly permissive language authorized Tennessee's executive branch to design and define the program through administrative regulations. These regulations, which are the legal authority for the TennCare waiver, were established using a streamlined rule-making process. The legislation was adopted in April 1993: Debate was limited and there were no public hearings. When the waiver application was submitted in June 1993, the details were not widely known, although state officials say that discussions were held with legislators and major stakeholders. Our impression is that these talks were limited. The most extensive discussions appeared to have taken place with BCBS and key advocates for beneficiaries.

The state's ability to show that TennCare could offer a credible statewide managed care network hinged on participation by BCBS. The state also had considerable leverage with BCBS because its employees' contract represented a large share of BCBS's business. Discussions within the Tennessee bureaucracy were also relatively limited in scope. For example, neither the Department of Commerce and Insurance (DCI), charged with licensing HMOs, nor other parts of the Department of Health and the commissioner's officer appear to have been extensively involved in program planning. TennCare officials did, however, meet weekly with advocacy groups to identify and address issues of concern. Major provider groups, such as the Tennessee Medical Association (TMA) and the Tennessee Hospital Association, were not included, however. Furthermore, although providers (especially physicians) were reportedly consulted, they were not influential in the program-planning process, perhaps because they continued to support a fee-for-service alternative to the program and its managed care features.

Major opposition to TennCare has come from physicians speaking mainly through the TMA, which has been unsuccessfully battling the initiative in court. The TMA argues that it supports the concept of TennCare but not the speed of its implementation. The reason for the opposition appears mainly to be the broad-based imposition of managed care, including both the level of the capitation payments and what physicians have termed the cram-down provision. This provision makes physician participation in the BCBS state employees' PPO network conditional on their participation in the BCBS TennCare plan.

Our interviews suggest that the physician community's views may be more mixed than the TMA has conveyed, with physician attitudes differing on the basis of location and specialty. Some rural primary care physicians, for instance, have benefited financially from TennCare, especially if they had been seeing a substantial number of uninsured persons. Meanwhile, some specialists (like orthopedists) may still be boycotting TennCare, especially in certain areas of the state: Only 13 of the 394 licensed orthopedic surgeons had agreed to contract with Access MedPlus, the second largest managed care organization in TennCare, as of August 1994. Of 291 licensed orthopedists in the state's seven urban counties, only 8 were in Access MedPlus. Although considerably more orthopedists contract with BCBS in these seven urban counties, BCBS also had extremely few in some of the individual counties as of August 1994. In Hamilton, Sullivan, and Washington counties, where there are 73 such surgeons, only 5 participated in BCBS.

Other interests appear to have given TennCare at least lukewarm support in its first year. In government, sister agencies have been reluctant to disagree publicly with this key initiative of the governor. The Tennessee Hospital Association has not opposed TennCare for two reasons: First, hospitals were to benefit from TennCare because it eliminates the provider tax. Second, the financing structure initially included additional funding through pools to facilitate the transition from DSH payments and for expenses such as graduate medical education and adverse selection that vary across providers and their plans.

However, not all hospitals benefited equally from the changes TennCare introduced, faring differently according to location, how they participate in TennCare, and whether they have traditionally relied heavily on DSH payments. Urban hospitals have historically depended most heavily on DSH payments, and these funds have also helped some rural facilities. Still, rural hospitals have generally supported TennCare because they would benefit from the elimination of the DSH-associated provider taxes. Hospitals that do not participate extensively in TennCare have benefited from the elimination of provider taxes and have not incurred additional obligations. The Tennessee Primary Care Association, which represents community health centers and similar providers, including the state Department of Health, did not oppose the initiative. It did, however, express concern about the dependence on too few providers with insufficient attention to the development of delivery systems. The association also attempted, not completely successfully, to address some of its members contractual and payment concerns.

Advocates for beneficiaries expressed support for TennCare because they were able to address particular beneficiary issues related to implementation. Key advocates have supported the program even though their position has been at odds with some national advocacy groups for low-income beneficiaries. The reasons for their support appear to be multifaceted. Expanded coverage and its ability to enhance access are key attractions. Rapid implementation is viewed as an essential part of this access strategy, creating an irrevocable entitlement. TennCare also has components that are seen as being able to remove some of the welfare stigma traditionally associated with Medicaid. In addition, and perhaps most important, advocates perceive the alternative, because of fiscal and DSH issues, to be much tighter eligibility criteria.

Implementation

Assuming that enrollees in TennCare are appropriately classified, the program expanded coverage to 400,000 people in 1994, its first year. This accounts for about one-third of the approximately 1.2 million people enrolled in TennCare in October 1994. Current eligibles were enrolled in managed care plans through the mail, with people asked to indicate their top three choices. New eligibles could enroll in a variety of locations.

The enrollment process generated considerable confusion. Contributing factors included the speed of the change, limited enrollee and provider education, and difficulty in handling the substantial volume of telephone inquiries. Most communication was in writing, which was hard because some were illiterate, even though TennCare officials worked closely with advocates to make the materials clear. Because of the pace of implementation, plans had not fully formed their provider panels, making it impossible for beneficiaries to get lists of providers associated with the plans or consult with their providers, as advised, to determine which plans they were affiliated with. State officials reportedly received 50,000 telephone inquiries in one day early after the initiative started, and ultimately responded with an 800-number staffed, in part, by state employees drawn from throughout the state government, many of whom had no previous involvement in health programs.

Only about 50 to 60 percent of those previously eligible for Medicaid selected a plan, requiring many to be assigned to plans. We heard reports that many got none of their choices or found it difficult to transfer from one plan to another to retain their providers, keep the family in one plan, or attain other objectives, although such movement was authorized in the program. At least one plan enrolled individuals not eligible (e.g., state prison inmates) and employed marketing practices that were regarded as abusive. MCOs were responsible for notifying individuals about the plans in which they were enrolled and for providing membership information. However, shortcomings in both state and plan administrative processes meant that some notifications were delayed or multiple notifications were sent.

As noted previously, the program involved two statewide plans and ten others. Each plan was paid a monthly capitated rate. A single statewide rate was used in the first year, with demographic adjustments based on age, sex (for those of childbearing age), and disability. There were offsets for excluded services and anticipated managed care savings. Capitation payments were reduced by estimated cost sharing from providers, savings in provider bad debt, and savings to local government, with a 10 percent withhold. Thus, the rates appear to include only about two-thirds of the estimated costs, taking the withhold into account.

Starting from a base of limited managed care, TennCare predictably did not shift in the first year to a system with fully functioning and well-developed MCOs. Many of those interviewed perceive that, so far, TennCare is basically much more about managed costs than managed care, with limited change in the delivery system. The BCBS plan, which has half the statewide enrollment, essentially is a discounted fee-for-service payment system with utilization review. It was given three years to adopt a primary care case management program, and was still implementing grievance and quality systems at the end of 1994. However, it could pay claims well. In contrast, Access MedPlus, the other statewide plan, had targeted to grow from 35,000 to 100,000–150,000, but grew to almost twice that when TennCare implemented an assignment process that allocated assignments proportional to those among self-selectors. The plan was ill-prepared for this growth, with only fifty staff members, no claims processing systems, and no specialty contracting. Despite the commitment and hard work by staff to make the transition, we heard many complaints from consumers and providers about limited provider networks, delays in claims payment, and other problems.

Our interviews suggest that care delivery problems existed in the first year, although our methods are ill-suited to assessing their magnitude, and data constraints and timing limit empirical verification. Reported problems include the handling of formulary issues involving medical necessity overrides and communication of policies to both providers and pharmacists, barriers created by deductibles, disruptions in existing referral and traditional care systems, and burdensome prior approval systems. Provider and specialty availability within the TennCare plan networks also appears problematic in some areas of the state, due to general physician shortages and network design; for example, a plan might have a surgeon at one hospital but no anesthesiologist. These issues could be related as much to start-up and provider confusion about managed care as to flaws in design. TennCare officials expect some sorting out among participating plans, perhaps including changes in market share, consolidations, or even failures. They view this as an important part of the evolution of a well-functioning managed care system.

With the rapid speed of development, TennCare officials had little administrative structure in the first year with which to implement the plan. Many key policies and procedures do not appear to have been recorded, or at least widely available and known, and we heard conflicting reports on the policies. The speed of implementation appears to have required a primary focus on urgent administrative needs, with only limited work on more generic systems. For example, TennCare officials were embarrassed by press attention in late 1994 about the failure to bill for required premiums. Yet, TennCare officials appear committed to resolving problems that arise on a case-by-case basis, generally deciding in the beneficiary's favor.

To administer TennCare, state officials reorganized, but according to their waiver application, proposed no change in staff. Oversight for TennCare plans was split in the first year among participating HMOs; oversight by the DCI, which oversees financial status, marketing, and complaints, and requires plans to comply with the health care delivery requirements of the Department of Health; and TennCare itself, which oversaw other plans (PPOs) authorized under the TennCare program. These arrangements proved problematic and have been subsequently revised, as discussed later.

TennCare financed its program through a complex set of arrangements. A key objective was to retain federal Medicaid funds despite policy changes limiting the use of DSH payments and provider taxes to generate federal matching payments. Funds for the state match essentially are drawn from a variety of sources with the objective of maintaining core state funds at no more than historical Medicaid spending levels. Other sources include state funds for indigent care problems (including the state share of various federal block grants), public hospital charity care expenses, and other state, local, and private sources. TennCare established financing pools as a key component to the first-year strategy. These involved a combination of explicit funding and anticipated savings. The pools were designed to smooth the transition to TennCare by providing flexible funds to deal with issues like protecting essential providers, compensating for adverse selection, supporting graduate medical education, and covering uncompensated care. At our visit, the distribution of these funds was still being negotiated, but the key issue was what would happen in future years when they no longer existed.

The available information shows effects on access and the safety net that are similar to Oregon's, but less positive. Satisfaction with insurance coverage decreased from 82 percent to 61 percent, with marked differences associated with respondents' pre-TennCare coverage, according to a state-funded study (Fox and Lyons 1994). Among those previously uninsured, 59 percent were more satisfied with TennCare, 10 percent were less so, and the rest reported no change. The dissatisfaction may be explained by several factors: the negative publicity about TennCare, start-up problems of access, disruption to some preexisting care arrangements with safety-net providers, and provider shortages unaffected by TennCare. Among those covered by Medicaid in 1993, about half were less satisfied with TennCare, 12 percent were more satisfied, and 37 percent reported no change. Whenever assignments are made, research shows initial increases in dissatisfaction, but this may have been lessened if there had been fewer start-up problems, including disruptions in continuity of care, particularly for those vulnerable to adverse outcomes. The impact of these problems was probably mitigated by providers' efforts to respond, especially to problems experienced by patients they had seen before TennCare.

As in Oregon, it is too early to assess the spillover effects. On the positive side, TennCare reportedly has stepped up the level of formal physician participation in the program and has provided an impetus for enacting legislation giving nurse practitioners and physician assistants expanded roles and also adding to their supply. However, some specialists (such as orthopedists) appeared to be opting out, and there was some disruption to informal care arrangements. Revenue streams for public health services have been disrupted by TennCare, so that these revenues could be credited toward the state match. In Memphis, the Regional Medical Center, colloquially referred to as "the Med" (a public hospital almost one-half Medicaid and one-quarter self-pay or nonpaying patients), reported extensive loss of revenue and a deteriorating situation that has since brought further attention and action.

In addition, the scope of TennCare has had spillover effects on virtually all components of the Tennessee health system. Most broadly, TennCare appears to have dramatically transformed Tennessee from a state with little managed care activity to one with features typically found in more developed markets. However, after the first year, there was relatively limited growth in private sector managed care, with employers said to be waiting for TennCare's effects on the health care system to stabilize. Lack of change also could reflect the fact that medical inflation dropped in Tennessee, as it did elsewhere, in 1994.

Prospects

TennCare has begun to stabilize from its rocky first year. The *Washington Post* reported results from a state-funded survey showing greater consumer acceptance of TennCare in the second year than in the first year, particularly among those previously covered by Medicaid where acceptance increased from 49 percent to 68 percent between 1994 and 1995: Waiting times for appointments have declined, formularies remain an issue, and other problems remain.

TennCare also survived a change in political leadership, managed to get physicians into a more cooperative relationship with the state, and took steps to strengthen management. TennCare was a major issue in the November 1994 elections, with physicians contributing substantially to the successful campaign of Governor Sundquist. Despite election year pressure, the new governor supported TennCare. The so-called cram-down provision requiring physicians in the BCBS PPO to participate in TennCare has been retained. A proposed regulation prohibiting providers from limiting TennCare enrollees in their practice (unless the regulation is applied to all new patients) was withdrawn (Snyder and Cromer 1995). TennCare underwent an administrative shake-up early in 1995 and its administration continues to evolve. Governor Sundquist moved the TennCare Bureau from the Department of Health to the Department of Finance and Administration and gave DCI additional oversight responsibility for PPOs. (In January 1997 TennCare was moved back to the Department of Health.) New appointees were put in place. A Governor's Roundtable was convened in early 1995 and its recommendations for the program are being implemented now. All TennCare MCOs will have to be HMOs and have primary care gatekeeping by 1 January 1997. The state's telephone system has been improved as well. It remains to be seen how the latest change in administrative leadership (Governor Sundquist's appointments have moved on of their own accord) will influence these efforts at administrative restructuring. With the aim of smoothing the transition at the top, Corker (1996) and his staff prepared a TennCare Transition Document summarizing the status of the program and current issues.

TennCare efforts to influence the delivery system continue to evolve. Despite assurances from state officials in 1995 that there are no issues of fiscal viability of MCOs or the program at this point in time (Martins 1995), press reports confirmed that fiscal problems represented a growing concern for at least one plan, Access MedPlus. However, steps have been taken to strengthen the plan, and the short-term crisis appears to have been resolved. The structure of managed behavioral health continues to evolve. It was expected that mental health and substance abuse services for the chronically ill would be incorporated into the MCO capitation rate by 1 July 1995. However, this move proved to be controversial, and was not implemented until mid-1996 after some changes in basic features. In TennCare, behavioral health services are provided through one of two Behavioral Health Organizations (BHO) who are capitated under contract with the TennCare Partners Program administered by the Tennessee Department of Mental Health/Mental Retardation. The rates were $22.93, which is beyond the $113 per enrollee per month under TennCare. Each managed care organization is aligned with one of two of the BHOs.

More fundamental challenges face TennCare, especially whether TennCare's financing or political support will remain sufficient to achieve the expanded coverage objectives used to support its development. In

TennCare's case, this is particularly crucial, as some of the funding used to support the program was deliberately taken from existing state-funded efforts, thus potentially undercutting the safety net. New enrollment in TennCare was closed to anyone not otherwise Medicaid eligible or uninsurable in January 1995. At the same time, individuals have been dropped for reasons of eligibility, for nonpayment of premiums, or for other reasons. As a result, enrollment continued to shrink slowly, reaching 1.17 million in June 1997. Beginning in April 1997 enrollment was reopened for uninsured children under eighteen and enrollment was opened for eligible dislocated workers in May 1997. In October 1997, enrollment stands at 1.21 million, including a reported 838,728 Medicaid eligibles and 369,456 in uninsured or uninsurable categories.

There also are outstanding issues about the safety net. TennCare included various special financing pools in the first year to address expected problems, such as adverse selection. The elimination of these pools in 1995 reportedly threatened the fiscal viability of a few key hospitals, such as the Med (Snyder 1995; National Association of Public Hospitals 1995). Funding has been provided to fill the gap, but the Med is still working to develop a viable strategy for long-run survival.

Discussion

Oregon and Tennessee illustrate what can be conceptualized as two very different processes for implementing reform initiatives. Yet their experience also shares many similarities, suggesting that states pursuing Medicaid managed care strategies based on private-sector competition would do well to consider both their unique features and their commonality with other state experiences.

Oregon's approach to health care reform for its low-income population can be viewed as a "classical planning model" applied within a political context. Oregon reflects, in many ways, what Mohr (1976) termed the "rational model," characterized by considerable analysis and persuasion, with high goal compatibility across participants. The initiative was developed over time with the substantial involvement and consensus of key stakeholders. The decision to establish a priority list explicitly supports rationing as the most equitable means for dealing with limited resources and disparities in coverage across the population. The concept of equity carries through the initiative. There is wide agreement that the implementation experience in Phase 1 was relatively smooth and reasonably scheduled. However, the future of Oregon's efforts are uncertain, given the technical challenges involved in Phase 2, state funding constraints, a more conservative political climate, and a lingering number of individuals who remain, and may continue to remain, uninsured. Despite the focus on equity, Oregon's health reform effort remains largely grounded in a Medicaid initiative, with considerable uncertainty about how far funding will allow it to progress. (Recent enactment of new financing, however, provides some encouragement. Oregon, as other states, also should benefit from the introduction of children's health insurance.)

In contrast to Oregon's approach, Tennessee's approach, at least in the first year, can be viewed in terms of a political model, characterized by contention, struggle, and force to dominate decision making. This is particularly apparent in the initial domination of physician interests through speed and brute force, in an environment in which rapid achievement of short-term goals is key. In the political arena, domination was also possible, at least in its initial stages, because there was a strategic agglomeration of interests (as is typified by the garbage-can model of decision making) through which TennCare leadership obtained the support of advocates, and the acquiescence of other major providers and insurers, including BCBS and the hospitals. TennCare was very deliberately developed with limited involvement of most key stakeholders. The decision process was relatively undocumented, focusing on rapid development and implementation, and on the policy flexibility created by the absence of disclosure or formal promulgation of most rules. The implementation experience can only be characterized as chaotic: widespread confusion among beneficiaries, providers, and health plans; reported problems of access; undeveloped administrative systems; physician opposition; and deal making through funding pools to fix problems on an ad hoc basis. The approach was a gamble: a decision made by a few individuals with the tacit consent of other stakeholders to accept short-term problems as the price for immediate savings and potential long-term gains through change in the health system. The outcome of this bet is uncertain. A key question is whether there ever was, or will be, sufficient funding to support the goals established through the initiative, and if not, what will happen, particularly given the complex financing arrangements that underlie the initiative.

What can we learn from these states about the effects of Medicaid managed care and competition on public policy objectives, and also about the balance between common and state-specific features in determining these effects? We conclude that, despite their differences, several common lessons can be drawn from both states.

No Free Lunch. One fundamental lesson from the experience of Oregon and Tennessee is that there is no "free lunch." Both these states and the others we have studied show strongly that all states implementing these kinds of initiatives need to address the same kinds of operational issues relating to eligibility and enrollment, plan and provider participation policies, and state oversight (Gold, Sparer, and Chu 1996). Education of those new to managed care, whether consumers, providers, or health plans, is a strong imperative, and even with it, confusion is unlikely to be totally avoided. Oregon had more than Tennessee to build upon because of its greater experience with managed care, but it still faced the same technical tasks. In both cases, success in these tasks was influenced by planning, attention to details, and available administrative resources.

Yet, success requires more than attention to details. It requires resources (i.e., money). In neither state was managed care or competition sufficient on its own to generate the magnitude of resources necessary to cover fully all the uninsured. Not only are the numbers too large, but the populations of initial focus in almost all states were women and children—those least expensive to cover. Tellingly, Tennessee had the most expansive initial focus in terms of the current Medicaid population and also in terms of new eligibles. Yet in Tennessee, as in Oregon, there are outstanding issues about how adequate the financing will prove over time, even with some infusion of new state funds (which occurred in Oregon).

Markets and Public Process. Medicaid is a public program whose size gives it considerable market clout, as witnessed in Tennessee. Yet, the Medicaid program is also one that involves substantial roles for both federal and state governments. This lessens Medicaid officials' flexibility to draw on market forces, particularly when both federal and state processes are involved. Because this more limited flexibility also has the potential to delay, it makes market strategies for public programs particularly dependent on timing and influenced by shifts in the political environment and public mood. In both Oregon and Tennessee, support for eligibility expansion and the funding for it were lower at the end of 1994 than previously. The effects of this were particularly obvious in Oregon because its initiative had developed over time. The delays in federal approval of Oregon's plan—due more to national than state politics—created more time to plan, but probably jeopardized the ultimate success of the initiative because certain concrete steps were postponed until support for them eventually eroded. Conversely, Tennessee policy makers were probably right in perceiving that only prompt implementation would elicit and sustain support. It is worthy of note that TennCare, through its speedy implementation, managed to neutralize physicians and to buy time to address problems, and ultimately, to gain at least their acquiescence. In terms of concrete outcomes, speedy implementation created to some extent an "irrevocable entitlement," making it hard to dismantle the program. At the same time, the speedy and dominating way in which TennCare was developed also meant there was less underlying support developed for it outside the advocacy constituency. Thus, the irrevocable entitlement potentially may erode, particularly by restricting new eligibles and whittling down the number of current eligibles through less politically obvious administrative mechanisms.

Markets and Distributional Equity. Each state's initiative created winners and losers, although the data were typically not there to confirm which was which. Among the low-income populations, there are trade-offs among those previously covered by Medicaid both inside and outside the initiative, and also among those in the low-income population who may be newly enfranchised, remain uninsured, or lose coverage indirectly through incentives created for those from whom they receive coverage. There are also trade-offs involving providers: between hospitals and physicians, and between hospitals of different types (safety-net providers versus others).

Medicaid serves, explicitly or implicitly, an increasingly broad and sometimes conflicting set of goals. Cross-subsidies play a large role in financing care for low-income populations, and have become increasingly important in the absence of more direct sources of support for universal coverage. This is particularly so in state legislatures when Medicaid provides at least a one-to-one match for each state dollar and state expenses, for a substantial period, have been increasing, in part because of nationally mandated expansions of coverage.

The issue of distributional equity is a particularly germane one when the decision-making model means that some stakeholders or parties bring more political capital to the bargaining table than others. Given the way in which the initiatives were developed, these issues were less central at the start in Oregon and Tennessee, but recent evidence suggests that they will grow over time. Despite Oregon's consensus style used to develop the initiative, its initial base was in low-income women and children, not the more politically mobilized disabled and chronically ill populations. And as resources shrink, there is growing pressure to ratchet down capitation rates and benefits, which may limit the willingness by some plans and providers, who are stronger in the market and have alternatives, to participate. Oregon's inclusion now of the disabled and others with more active constituent groups may serve to exert pressure against this trend, but it also raises the potential that, with scarce resources, the result will be competition between groups, rather than cooperative efforts to gain support for additional resources.

In Tennessee, the amount of short-term disruption and potentially serious health care access issues initially might arguably never have been acceptable if the beneficiary constituency were politically stronger. As it was, advocates in TennCare probably had disproportionately more power initially than they might have had, because the state probably wanted to avoid protests that might have jeopardized federal approval of the waiver, upon which their fiscal health was perceived to depend. It is striking that Tennessee advocates have not succeeded since then in encouraging the state to move forward with actions that would expand the rolls in the program. TennCare also illustrates, relatively dramatically, the potential trade-offs among those already on Medicaid (who may have something to lose, especially if access is already good or care patterns established), those newly enfranchised (who stand to gain most), and the remaining uninsured (who stand to lose most because they remain uncovered in a state where expanded entitlement has been financed by removing some of the cross-subsidies and direct grant funding from the system).

Preexisting Managed Care and Provider Infrastructure. State infrastructures and experience with managed care vary, and this influences the feasibility of Medicaid managed care initiatives. Oregon's relatively smooth transition to a managed care system was considerably expedited by its preexisting managed care infrastructure within the Medicaid program and the health care system in general. The fact that managed care is common in Oregon created a comfort level among both providers and beneficiaries. In addition, experience with Medicaid managed care meant that the state had an infrastructure upon which to build its managed care elements and strategy. Tennessee had no such infrastructure. Indeed, TennCare spurred the development of a managed care market in Tennessee. This generated controversy among providers and confusion among providers and beneficiaries.

Furthermore, both Oregon and Tennessee found that the form and feasibility of managed care varied across their states, reflecting differences in the in-state care systems. Area-specific provider shortages constrained access and the development of managed care in both states, most typically in rural areas but also in some inner cities. The form of managed care plans also varied across urban areas, less by design than by the type of infrastructure in place and the way physicians practice.

Similarly, the way the initiatives affect safety-net providers differs across communities in each state, reflecting differences in state programs and the way in which safety-net providers were positioned to participate in them. From the perspective of beneficiaries, effects on the safety net were most damaging in communities like Memphis, where safety-net providers (i.e., the Med) are heavily utilized. In other communities, beneficiaries may be less affected even if safety-net providers are adversely selected, because alternative sources of care exist or are created. In most communities, the most critical negative effects on safety-net providers stemmed from the inherent cross-subsidies that support care for the uninsured.

State Administrative Capacities. Both a state's prior experience with managed care and also the general form of support for its state administrative bureaucracy vary. Without an established managed care base, state officials had less local expertise to draw upon in Tennessee and, most important, few plans upon which to build. The differences in context, together with a short implementation schedule, led to many more first-year problems in Tennessee than in Oregon.

In sum, we conclude from this analysis that the factors that contribute to success or failure with Medicaid managed care and market strategies are the same in each state, but that the way in which these factors are brought to bear will differ across states depending on state characteristics. For example, the political and cultural styles in Oregon and Tennessee differ greatly from one another. Thus, it is hard to imagine Oregon stakeholders accepting an OHP without benefit of debate and consensus building, particularly with respect to the priority list. Conversely, it is not clear that TennCare officials could have gained support from the medical community for a TennCare-like initiative within a policy-relevant time frame, given the strong opposition to precedent-setting managed care. Administrative structures in the states also differ, varying with the degree of prior experience, salary levels, and the stability of the staff.

Yet, in fundamental ways, Oregon's and Tennessee's outcomes will be influenced by how the same factors play out in today's environment. That is, each state initiative's ultimate success, at least in terms of the access objectives, will depend on the ability to secure adequate resources and gain support for access-enhancing interventions sponsored by public bodies, and the distribution of political capital as this bears on issues of distributional equity. And in both cases, trade-offs already are evident between those newly enfranchised and those remaining outside the system to be served by a safety net weakened to varying extents by the strategies each state found politically necessary to employ in order to secure the capital needed to finance the initiatives. All these issues also apply, of course, in the traditional Medicaid program. Thus, in moving to managed care and market-based solutions, states gain some tools but remain faced with the same challenge: How to achieve more with less and for whom, when support falls short of the amount needed to achieve policy goals.

Notes

This chapter is a revision of a paper presented at the Health Care into the Next Century: Markets, States and Communities conference, convened by the *Journal of Health Politics, Policy and Law*, Durham, NC, 3–4 May 1996, and is based on a study funded by the Henry J. Kaiser Family Foundation and the Commonwealth Fund. Internal funding from Mathematica Policy Research partially underwrote the costs of preparing this chapter, which builds on case studies of Oregon and Tennessee released in July 1995. The individual cases are available. We include here selected factual updates in August 1996 and October 1997 with help from Jessica Mittler. The Oregon case is authored by Marsha Gold, Karyen Chu, and Barbara Lyons and is entitled *Managed Care and Low Income Populations: A Case Study of Managed Care in Oregon*. The Tennessee case is authored by Marsha Gold, Hilary Frazer, and Cathy Schoen and is entitled *Managed Care and Low Income Populations: A Case Study of Managed Care in Tennessee*. The cases were prepared as part of a project involving case studies of seven states that is being directed by Marsha Gold. Michael Sparer of Columbia University is a coinvestigator on the project and leader of several of the other cases. The perspectives presented here are solely mine, and not necessarily those of Mathematica Policy Research, the Kaiser Family Foundation, or the Commonwealth Fund.

1   An example of a condition/treatment pair is appendicitis (condition)/appendectomy (treatment). The priority list was modified to meet federal concerns related to compliance with the Americans with Disabilities Act (ADA).

2   Pregnant women and children younger than age six whose family income is below 133 percent of the poverty level were previously eligible for Medicaid and continue to be eligible for the OHP if their family income is below 133 percent of the poverty level.

3   By 1991, this initiative had been expanded to nine counties, with a voluntary managed care program in one additional county.

4   Oregon has biennial legislative sessions.

5   The exclusion of the aged, blind, and disabled in Phase 1 was based on a concern about how the priority process would affect the ability of these populations to receive services and keep medical benefits.

Part 3 *Reflections on the Road Ahead*

The Limits of Social Learning:

Translating Analysis into Action

Mark A. Peterson

Unusual political dynamics, extraordinary fiscal pressures, and concerted private-sector change in the U.S. health care system have placed enormous decision-making demands in the 1990s on public policy makers at all levels of government. In a period of just a few years, they have been called upon to attempt intelligent and informed decisions on a range of health policy issues of considerable import. First there was the momentum toward proactive comprehensive health care reform. In the wake of the political failure of reform initiatives at the national level and the stalling or reversing of them within the states, the charge to policy makers now is to react sensibly to the unprecedented shifts in the private health care market. To policy makers in Washington, DC, or their counterparts from Albany, New York, to Salem, Oregon, the health care domain has thrust upon their agendas decisions of extraordinary import, unyielding complexity, and swirling politics.

Whether in a proactive or reactive policy environment, we naturally expect (or certainly hope) that policy makers will identify potential policy options and decide among them guided by good evaluative information—choosing the best policy alternatives, including taking no action at all, on the basis of what Rose (1993) would call tested ideas borrowed across time (from previous experiences) and space (from the experiences of governments in other settings). That involves seizing the opportunity for *social learning,* meaning "a deliberate attempt to adjust the goals or techniques of policy in response to past experience and new information" (Hall 1993: 278). The evidence that such learning can and does take place in the United States, or that it has the impact dispassionate observers would desire, is not reassuring. In the midst of the debate over comprehensive health care reform, after nearly a half century of being able to observe functioning systems in practice across the globe, much of what was actually proposed and deliberated as potential reform had more to do with theory and the chalkboard than with actual experience and the lab coat (Marmor and Mashaw 1993; White 1995a). Recent policy making in response to market change does not immediately strike one as being necessarily more enlightened. Using state and federal laws to ensure that women and their new babies have two-day hospital stays following birth, for example, *may* produce desirable health care results, but we know that such legislation is more a response to unsettling anecdotes and powerful symbols than good clinical information. As some of the hundreds of bills proposed in state legislatures to regulate managed care make their way into the statute books, it is worth worrying about what lies behind lawmakers' decision making.

How much and in what ways is social learning affecting these policy choices? Stepping back, can we ascertain what kinds of lessons generally affect decisions of policy makers and under what conditions? What might our recent experiences suggest about the nature of social learning in the United States and its potential role in government responses to the market transformation of the health care system? Indeed, can any of the analyses presented in this book or in other health policy publications be expected to have any meaningful impact as we slide into a new century in health care? What can we conclude conceptually about the operational limits of social learning?

Here I address those questions by first examining the role of policy legacies—the results of past policy decisions—and how their effects work through the policy-making system. I then present a more fully specified process model of social learning embedded within the larger policy-making process, which includes the effects of its constitutional context, technological change, and political factors exogenous to social learning. I begin by drawing an important distinction between two different types of policy legacies—structural effects and social learning effects. At the next stage I identify a second core distinction, separating substantive learning (the usual meaning given to social learning) from situational learning. The effect that each of these has on policy making then depends on the relative position of three categories of participants in the policy-making process (experts, organized interests, and politicians), as well as on the scope of the policy issue being considered (ranging from routine change to major reform). This analysis reveals the full extent to which social learning is often a decidedly political struggle over ideas and information in which policy advocates and opponents strategically pursue their best advantage within a given institutional context and political setting. Finally, I use this schematic to consider the implications of social learning for three market-related policy issues currently of some moment: the government's role in overseeing managed care in the private insurance market; the rapid transformation by states of their Medicaid programs from fee-for-service public insurance to publicly financed contracts with competing private managed care organizations; and the federal effort to promote incentives for individuals to establish medical savings accounts.

The Recognition of Policy Legacies

Not all that long ago, one might have derived from the social science and public policy literatures the impression that specific policy-making events could be well understood without reference to anything beyond the immediate political, institutional, and interpersonal contexts in which they transpired. Identify the players in the game, their vantage points and institutional resources, as well as the vectors of interest-group influence and general electoral incentives, and one had a sufficient explanation of the process of policy deliberation and choice.

Because of more historically based institutional analyses, mixed with cross-national studies comparing divergent policy outcomes in nations that otherwise confront similar immediate circumstances, we recognize that such approaches are too simplistic. We need to add enhanced appreciation for the consequences of what has come before—the motivating and constraining legacies created by previous policy debate, action, and implementation (Hall 1986; Morone 1990; Pierson 1992; Skocpol 1992; Walker 1991; Weir and Skocpol 1985; Weir 1992). As stated by Theda Skocpol,

> Too often social scientists who study national systems of social provision forget that policies, once enacted, restructure subsequent political processes. Analysts typically look only for synchronic determinants of policies—for example, in current social interests or in existing political alliances. In addition, however, we must examine patterns unfolding over time (and not only long-term macroscopic processes of social change and polity reorganization). We must make social policies the starting points as well as the end points of analysis: As politics creates policies, policies also remake politics. . . . Policies not only flow from prior institutions and politics; they also reshape institutions and politics, making some future developments more likely, and hindering the possibilities for others. (1992: 58, 531)

Paul Pierson (1992) adds to this process the direct impact of legacies on agenda setting. Previously implemented (or defeated) policies "lock in" future policy choices by solidifying social and economic networks that threaten the political viability of particular options that might have been sustainable in an earlier policy environment. Consider how the noisy demise of President Clinton's Health Security Act shifted attention from policy options involving the public sector to those predicated on nurturing the market. The public-choice literature, too, which has been accused in the past of static modeling based on the assumption of independent and stable preferences, now incorporates a dynamism reflecting ongoing interactions among changing institutions, shifting incentives, and evolving preferences (see Shepsle 1986, 1989). Policy legacies thus continuously transform the decision matrix of each participant in the policy-making process, as well as the capacity of governments to implement and administer particular kinds of public-sector interventions.

Imagine trying to explain the passage of Medicare and Medicaid in 1965, and particularly why they are so different from successfully implemented universal health care systems in other nations, without fully embracing the legacy of previous health care reform debates. One could suggest, quite legitimately, that Medicare as enacted was the product of presidential influence over the legislative agenda, the unusual liberal congressional majorities created by the 1964 election, a vibrant economy feeding the federal treasury, and the countering political influence then enjoyed by organized medicine. However accurate in its own terms, however, this characterization begs the question, why Medicare? Why a program of health insurance coverage for the elderly alone? And why did President Johnson, heir to the martyred Kennedy's legacy, victor in a historic landslide, and leader of a party possessing the largest majorities on Capitol Hill since the Roosevelt-era 75th Congress (1937–1938), initially proceed so tepidly with his predecessor's cautious plan, which offered no more than extremely limited hospital coverage?

The answers, of course, are obvious. The partisan struggles over President Truman's failed effort to enact compulsory national health insurance in the 1940s, inflamed with the antagonists' rhetoric of protecting American freedoms against socialized tyranny, and in which the opposing American Medical Association (AMA) could credibly claim victory, colored what everyone thought they knew about health care financing and what they considered to be viable in the American system (Marmor 1973; Peterson 1993a, 1994, 1995b; Poen 1979; Skidmore 1970). To borrow from Pierson's construction, for too many policy makers in the 1960s, the merits of a fully publicly financed or publicly organized system remained in doubt. The AMA and its allies had convincingly demonstrated their political muscle. The federal government lacked a sufficiently tangible record of directly administering such large-scale programs (at least in official perceptions of what the public believed; see Jacobs 1993). The cumulative message of past experience, reified in the established networks of policy makers and advocates, suggested that ours was not a society in which a comprehensive, inclusive, and government-constructed system of financing health care for the entire population was politically feasible, or even worth seriously discussing. In its place, a program directed at a deserving population that was beyond its years of productive employment and income generation and that required relatively few public dollars and much reliance on existing private-sector administration seemed compatible with the policy legacy as it was widely understood.

Policy Legacies as Social Acts

Our analytical task, however, is far more demanding than these general reminders about policy legacies suggest. For better or for worse, cogent and colorful brochures reporting on the ramifications of policy legacies relevant to the present are not widely distributed to all the officials and advocates who will determine the next round of policy decisions. Learning, interpreting, defining, and projecting policy legacies and the lessons embedded within them is a collective social act, with all of its implications, both intellectual and political. It has to be done by someone or some many typically engaged in vibrant political contention. Inevitably, who that someone is, or the many are, will have some impact on how the legacy is perceived and how it affects current policy choices.

Quite often, it seems, social learning and its product are the province of public officials, especially the career bureaucrats who manage the central activities of the state (Heclo 1974). That this kind of social learning is to be found in the bowels of government itself makes a good deal of sense (see Hall 1993). After all, of all the myriad players in the political system, bureaucrats are likely to have the longest, least disrupted, and most systematically cumulative exposure to the information, analysis, decisions, and implementation effects that constitute an evolving policy legacy (Aberbach, Putnam, and Rockman 1981: chap. 4). Theirs may well also be the kind of policy-making experience most imbued with what Hugh Heclo identifies as the "power" and "puzzle" of government, requiring "both deciding and knowing" (1974: 305), inseparable activities joined in "political reason" (Stone 1988). Further, while political scientists of an earlier era may have seen the state (a term they did not use) as merely doing the bidding of whatever social and political forces were at work, there is now considerable evidence that the permanent government retains a substantial degree of latitude, if not autonomy, in its actions (Heclo 1974; Nordlinger 1981; Skocpol 1985). It should therefore not be surprising that an individual like Wilbur Cohen, a permanent fixture in the Social Security and health care reform scenes and often in the ranks of government itself, played an instrumental role in formulating the initial national health insurance proposals, learning the lessons of their political failure, and defining the course of subsequent Medicare initiatives (see Marmor 1973, 1990).

If social learning and its incorporation in new policy making were accomplished solely by career officials, one might anticipate a couple of implications for policy innovation. Internally codified policy analysis should take precedence over explicit judgments about electoral politics. Institutional memories would be long and easily sustained. At the same time, public accountability could be limited, with diminished responsiveness to changing public demands. A natural stodginess or small-*c* conservatism is also likely to pervade policy making and constrain creativity, commonly producing, at best, incremental adjustments to the status quo. These attributes of social learning and policy making certainly have been witnessed in the actual practice of governance in the United States (and other democratic systems), but they hardly characterize the entire domain of public-sector deliberation and action (Baumgartner and Jones 1993). How do we explain the effects of social learning on the initial passage of Medicare and Medicaid and the repeated and frequently heated public debates about comprehensive reform strategies? How would something as grand as national health insurance ever have been placed on the national agenda and its merits assessed?

Peter Hall offers an invaluable clarification in identifying the more elaborate circumstances that need to be considered in evaluating social learning and the process by which it is introduced in policy decisions:

> Recent theories of the state can be divided into two types. On one side is a set of analyses that might be described as state-centric in that they emphasize the autonomy of the state from societal pressure. These works suggest that policy is generally made by public officials operating with considerable independence from organizations like interest groups and political parties that transmit societal demands. On the other side is a range of theories that might be called state-structural. They, too, emphasize the impact on policy of the state's structure and its action, but they are less inclined to insist on the autonomy of the state vis-à-vis societal pressure. Instead, they accord interest groups, political parties, and other actors out-

side the state an important role in the policy process. Their main point is that the structure and past activities of the state often affect the nature or force of the demands that these actors articulate. (1993: 276)

Recognizing that variations in state autonomy are not only possible but likely, Hall goes on to show that the level of state autonomy in social learning, and the range of involvement and degree of influence exhibited by other actors in the political system, vary in accordance with the nature of the policy change at issue. Adjustments of existing policy "instruments" that do not challenge the established order of priorities, for example, are likely to be dominated by agency officials responding to new information and programmatic experience.

However, when policy change involves what Hall refers to as a shift in the policy paradigm—the "interpretative framework" in which policy issues are judged—then social learning and its effects are an entirely more public and inclusive affair, typically played out in the mass media and assessed according to a mixture of merit and power:

> The process whereby one policy paradigm comes to replace another is likely to be more sociological than scientific. That is to say, although the changing views of experts may play a role, their views are likely to be controversial, and the choice between paradigms can rarely be made on scientific grounds alone. The movement from one paradigm to another will ultimately entail a set of judgments that is more political in tone, and the outcome will depend, not only on the arguments of competing factions, but on their positional advantages within a broader institutional framework. (ibid.: 280)

Thus far I have tried to advance this synthetic analysis from a recognition of the general impact of policy legacies to an emerging understanding of the process of social learning. The past matters because previous policy shapes institutions and the rules governing their procedures, and because it alters the meaning of interests and the contours of power in the political system. The past further matters because it presents current policy makers in those institutions, and those influencing them, with information—indeed, ideas in all of their meanings—about what may or may not happen when policies are designed in certain ways. Both the structural and informational effects of the past constitute a form of feedback; the latter introduces the process of policy-relevant social learning. It raises the question of who is generating and acquiring information, receiving ideas, learning, as well as interpreting and communicating (and manipulating) their message, and how that varies across settings and types of policy change.

A Model of Social Learning

We are now ready to develop a more precise conceptualization of the generic social learning process and its component parts, operating at the intersection of three external dynamics. The first is the overall constitutional context in which policy making takes place. The second involves changes in technology, be they new ways of performing services (e.g., the latest in diagnostic imaging), new policy instruments (e.g., provider reimbursement methodologies), or new techniques for mobilizing political resources (e.g., computer-generated phone calling).[1] The third encapsulates the variations in political factors that may influence policy making but that do not derive from a policy legacy of specific relevance to the issue at hand. Figure 1 presents graphically a model of social learning that begins with the legacy of past policies and depicts the path of learning to a later stage of policy outcomes. They, in turn, create new policy legacies and allow for a feedback loop returning to the start of the model. This characterization of the social learning process can be adapted to the policy-making process in any democratic system.

Structural effects

The figure depicts the two kinds of effects policy legacies can have, both of which influence the learning process but in distinctly different ways. The first involves the *structural* changes that a previous policy event has introduced. New institutions are created or existing ones are altered; administrative capacity is expanded, improved, or disrupted; procedural rules are recrafted; new groups are mobilized, the influence of extant organizations changes, or power arrangements are reordered. These structural effects indirectly influence the social learning process by interacting with the overall constitutional context of a society—the formal arrangements of government—and the existing governing and political institutions that have evolved within it, including executive agencies, legislative committees, interest groups, and political parties. Because, as I will explain shortly, different types of participants in the policy-making process have distinct roles in social learning, and their numbers, activities, and importance in policy making vary according to the institutional settings in which they work (broadly conceived), structural

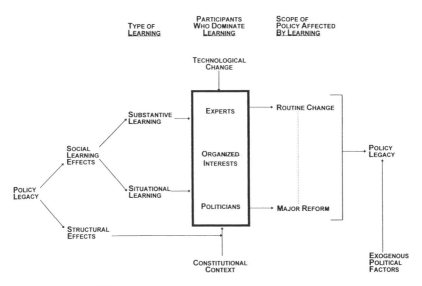

Figure 1. Model of the Social Learning Process

changes reshape the social learning process by altering the position and power of significant players in the system.

The passage of Medicare in 1965, for example, required the development of new executive offices and staffs with responsibilities that were not previously associated with the federal government and that ultimately prompted the authorization of additional congressional support agencies. Prior to Medicare, the government had essentially no indigenous expertise on health care financing (nor did much exist outside of government). In designing Medicare, White House aide Wilbur Cohen, as recounted to me by one of his associates, made crude calculations on a legal pad. By the 1980s, however, program management and evaluation became the province of a sophisticated army of government specialists, many trained in health services and policy research, and their innumerable counterparts throughout the health policy community (Brown, 1991; Peterson 1995a). The institutional epiphenomena of the Medicare program's enactment served to expand the administrative experience and analytic capacity of the federal government. It also became the basis for what James Morone calls "the bureaucracy empowered." Much of health-policy making now "operates with the language, methodology, and mind-set of bureaucratic actors. Even highly politicized judgments are coded in dense, complex, technical constructions" (Morone 1994: 149). That could be used to describe President Clinton's Health Security

Act, formulated with the assistance of myriad health care reform task force working groups populated by dozens of health financing specialists from the Health Care Financing Administration (HCFA), the Office of Planning and Evaluation in the Department of Health and Human Services, the Office of Management and Budget, and other agencies.

The new Congress of the 1980s and 1990s had its own health specialists, many of whom were invited to participate in the Clinton administration's working groups. New and old, but much changed, congressional agencies—such as the General Accounting Office (GAO), Congressional Budget Office (CBO), Office of Technology Assessment (OTA), as well as the Medicare-specific Prospective Payment Assessment Commission (ProPAC) and Physician Payment Review Commission (PPRC)—furnished legislators with an unprecedented amount of analytical material on issues related to health care financing. Between January 1990 and September 1994, for instance, the specialists within GAO alone issued thirty-two analytical reports on the performance of the Medicare program (Peterson 1995a: 100). In addition, under the prevailing congressional budget rules, to survive politically, any health initiative has to ensure neutral impact on the federal deficit. The CBO, established in 1974, and its dozen or so health experts, carry out the function of "scoring" legislative proposals in these and other terms, with tremendous consequences for what approaches remain viable (White 1995b).[2]

Social learning effects: two types

Policy legacies also affect social learning directly. We learn lessons from our past and the experiences of others. But it is essential to differentiate between two conceptually distinct streams of social learning, which together set the stage for advancing or deferring policy innovation. As shown in Figure 1, the first involves *substantive learning*. It incorporates the results of practice, experimentation, observation, analysis, education, planning, and adjustment in policy, argued on the basis of facts. Scholars in the health care field publish unending streams of such substantive work. Government agencies, university research centers, think tanks, and other institutions issue an even greater number of comparable reports. They enter the mass of material available to policy makers (Peterson 1995a).

Policy change can and does occur because over time, in some sense, we know more about what has worked and not worked, where, why, and under what conditions. Because experience has yielded a better understanding of disability and needs, for example, any national long-term care financing program introduced in the future, like many current private long-term care insurance plans, is going to have a different kind of trigger for allocating benefits than would have been true fifteen years ago. The inability to perform activities of daily living, or perhaps even a more precise score on a cognitive ability scale, will replace a prior hospitalization threshold, which had been the norm.

Even substantive learning, however, is not a matter of pure science. Although participants may make claims to thoroughgoing objectivity, Hall harks back to Heclo in stating that "the important point . . . is that 'powering' and 'puzzling' often go together" (1993: 289). That proposition is, in fact, the core theme of Deborah Stone's volume, *Policy Paradox and Political Reason* (1988):

> This book has challenged the dichotomy of analysis and politics. . . . My central argument is that the categories of thought behind reasoned analysis are themselves constructed in political struggle, and nonviolent political conflict is conducted primarily through reasoned analysis. It is not simply, therefore, a matter that sometimes analysis is used in partisan fashion or for political purposes. Reasoned analysis is necessarily political. It always involves choices to include some things and exclude others and to view the world in a particular way when other visions are possible. Policy analysis *is* political argument, and vice versa. (307, emphasis in original)

Because of sometimes sharp differences in the worldviews held by participants in the policy-making process, disputes over ideology and values, the potentially obtuse metaphysics of particular policy issues, and divergent interests, there is an inescapable ambiguity that surrounds the meaning of empirical, analytic policy experience, or the applicability of abstract policy theory. That ambiguity provides the invitation and the means for analysis and politics (or values) to merge. Witness the intense analytical sparring evident among the health economists in the earlier chapters and commentaries of this book. Knowledge is power, goes the old adage, but power also emerges as knowledge of the desired sort.

How else can one account for the astounding diversity of conclusions about the observable workings of particular health care systems, such as Canada's? One would think that the Canadian provincially run system either has life-threatening queues, or it does not. Either the quality of care is high, or it is not. Either the public is satisfied with the system, or it is not. These should be issues open to careful empirical assessment and determination. Instead they are fodder for a cottage industry of myth-making and rebuttal (Marmor and Mashaw 1990). A significant feature of social learning is the opportunity and incentive for "information," "knowledge," and "analysis" to reflect the interests and biases of whoever is communicating the conclusions.

But I wish to portray the subjective side of social learning more starkly than the necessary recognition that puzzling and power, analysis and politics, and framing and facts are commonly joined in the actual practice of substantive learning and deliberation. There is, in fact, a distinct second type of learning. It also requires information and judgment, a capacity to calibrate and recalibrate, and it is also open to interpretation. But it is explicitly political. It pertains to what we know, learn, and communicate about what can be accomplished politically. Let us call it *situational learning*. No matter what works as policy, the question becomes, What is enactable and sustainable as a political and social exercise? Historical experience, perceptions of norms, purported cultural differences across nations, vote counts in legislatures, and measures of public attitudes through focus groups and surveys are among the ways situational lessons are derived.

Let me illustrate the practical implications of these two types of social learning. During the health care reform debate, opponents of reform plans like the president's that relied on employer mandates to expand coverage had two distinct quasi-analytical strategies of opposition, *in addition to exerting direct political influence.* One was to use their institutional capacity and resources to generate and promote analytic information that credibly and compellingly demonstrated that the mandates would have serious negative repercussions on employment and lead to a large number of lost jobs (see O'Neill and O'Neill 1993, as one example). Rather than getting much desired health care coverage, people would in fact be losing their livelihoods.

The other strategy, which could be carried out simultaneously, did not challenge the performance of an employer-mandated system, but rather argued its lack of fit with our society's values and institutions. The objective here was to "teach" policy makers and the people to whom they listen that such a program is not socially or politically palatable because of its dependence on "big government" and interference with the market and individual responsibility (Johnson and Broder 1996). Just as with substantive learning, situational learning was advertised as being built upon empirical evidence derived from past experience. The battles over national health insurance in the 1930s, 1940s, and 1970s (and implicitly the 1960s) reveal, according to the opponents (and even some advocates), that our society, whatever Canadians and Germans may choose to do, is not prepared to accept either a government-financed system of health insurance or even one that requires employers to provide private insurance coverage to their employees (see Brecher 1992, especially the essay by Brown; Peterson 1993a, 1993b).

Because of their conceptually distinctive qualities, substantive and situational lessons could be promoted by different sets of actors. Frequently they are. But in practice the process by which substantive learning and the overtly political situational learning get defined and communicated often force a convergence of the two. First, especially to the extent that learning and action must be either accomplished or ratified by elected officials, lessons drawn in the situational stream can foreclose certain options in the substantive stream, including options thought by many specialists to have analytical merit, even superiority (Pierson 1992). If you can't sell it, it's useless to the politician. Move on to the next best alternative that you can sell. Given the inclination to believe that the institutions of government and distribution of power in a political system are relatively stable, these determinations, once "learned," can be extremely difficult to reassess, even when it is warranted (Peterson 1993a, 1993b).

Second, all successful policy making requires that specific leadership tasks be performed. Elsewhere I have labeled these policy entrepreneurship, politics entrepreneurship, and mobilization (Peterson 1992b; see also Oliver and Paul-Shaheen 1997). Policy entrepreneurship involves the generation, promotion, and brokerage of ideas. Politics entrepreneurship either recognizes and promotes an understanding of the political landscape or actually transforms the landscape, creating entirely new opportunities for particular kinds of policy options (see Baumgartner and Jones 1993). Mobilization supplies the leadership that is instrumental for building and motivating the broad-based coalitions needed to pass legislative initiatives.

If the chores of policy entrepreneurship and politics entrepreneurship were accomplished by independent sets of leaders, then the separation of the substantive and situational streams could be maintained and one set of interests or perspectives would have a more difficult time dominating the process of social learning. Often, however, these leadership tasks end up resting in the same hands. Senator Edward Kennedy, long an experienced policy entrepreneur who promoted national health insurance, is also a politics entrepreneur who became convinced that the single-payer approach, regardless of its substantive merits, did not conform with the situational parameters of U.S. politics (Peterson 1992b). Nothing could be more debilitating to the prospects of a policy approach than to have its leading protagonists conclude that it lacks political viability.

It is worth emphasizing that nothing about the process of social learning—whether substantive or situational—requires that the lessons be accurate, only that they count (Hall 1993: 278, 293). For example, I would suggest—indeed have suggested (1993b)—that the political lessons so many took away from the failed attempt at national health insurance in the 1970s were decidedly miscast but became self-fulfilling. What I wish to emphasize here is that opponents of particular policy approaches have two opportunities to promote lessons that reduce the attractiveness of those approaches—on substance and on viability—that elevate the hurdles for beneficial policy change. This vastly complicates, in particular, the kind of lesson drawing to be derived from "searching across space" because arguments can always be mounted that the attributes of one setting make policies conceived within it appropriate for another (Rose 1993: chap. 5; Klein 1997; Marmor 1995a).

The participants who dominate social learning

Because we are able to separate substantive and situational learning, we can also elaborate upon which types of participants in the policy-making process are likely to emphasize one or the other (or both) sorts of social learning. That will give us some clues about what happens when state autonomy breaks down or other kinds of less severe institutional changes occur, as well as furnish a basis for assessing U.S. health-policy making in a comparative context.

Any democratic system has three broad categories of direct participants in policy making (excluding, for now, the public): experts, organized interests, and politicians. *Experts* are knowledgeable policy specialists inside government (the core of the state policy apparatus) and outside government (in think tanks, on university campuses, in consulting firms, etc.). Their currency is policy information and analysis, producing special knowledge about specific features of existing policy and alternatives to it.

As Deborah Stone argues, politics and analysis can never be fully separated, so no expert is entirely divorced from the bias of interest or politics. They can also range from the nonpartisan professional—such as the civil servants who gather health expenditure data in the Office of National Cost Estimates located deep within the bowels of HCFA, itself an agency within the Department of Health and Human Services—to congressional staff closely associated with the political interests of their bosses. One senior Republican congressional staffer, for example, who works in a policy position, commented to me that the political advisers viewed him as a policy person unversed in politics, the media people considered him a neophyte when it came to developing the message to sell a policy, but that other policy people thought him more political because of the position of his prominent employer. Despite this range of individuals, however, there is a center of gravity among experts that values professional standards about knowledge acquisition and use.

For this set of participants, persuasion is to be accomplished as a result of the power of argument, analysis, and information, which in turn are derived with some fidelity to objective, disinterested research, or at least the framing of questions in ways that allows the testing of competing hypotheses. If an expert becomes too closely associated with a particular ideological bent—say, a priori devotion to either public-sector salvations or market theology—he or she risks losing credibility as an expert. Experts pride themselves on faithfulness to ideas and the data, if you will. They cannot garner influence on the basis of votes controlled, money contributed, or responsiveness to constituencies. As suggested by their location in Figure 1, in a world that they controlled, substantive policy learning would dominate (though not preclude) situational learning or even conscious concerns about situational dynamics.

Organized interests have discernible stakes in or positions on the policy status quo or policy alternatives to it. They each naturally wish to manipulate policy making to the advantage of their group or clients. Given the power of ideas in policy discourse (Stone 1988), their positions, to be credible, require full participation in substantive social learning. As legislatures like Congress have developed more analytical tools and become more adept at using policy-analytic knowledge, organized interests, in order to lobby effectively, have had to nurture the capacity to support or produce professional quality research (Brown 1991; Peterson 1995a). But projecting their political advantage also means being able to exploit situational social learning to beneficial effect. As representatives of legitimate interests embedded in the larger public, they make a special claim to reflect the political and social contours of the society or represent activities vital to economic advances and improving the quality of life. Its link to employment and economic growth, for example, gives business a "privileged position" with policy makers (Lindblom 1977).

Just as with experts, organized interests can range widely on the substantive dimension. Some groups have the resources and capabilities to play a major role in the development of substantive knowledge. Few in Congress, for example, would attempt to write long-term care legislation without making use of the expertise acquired by specialists at the American Association of Retired Persons. The research division of the American Association of Health Plans (AAHP), the trade association for managed care organizations, has long employed experienced health policy researchers, and furnishes outside scholars and policy makers with valuable information about enrollments and practices within the managed care industry.

At the other end of the spectrum, the impact of ideology can be greater than that of analysis. When Senate Majority Leader George Mitchell sought in the summer of 1992 to forge a Democratic consensus bill on health care reform, one of the challenges he and his colleagues faced was trying to reduce the opposition of small business to employer mandates. The National Federation of Independent Business (NFIB) met with the Senate Democrats' small business task force. The NFIB demanded that the government be able to demonstrate that the public sector could contain health care costs before imposing any mandates. Its representatives agreed that global budgets and negotiated reimbursement rates could achieve that end (substantive learning from the international experience). They objected to them, however, on the grounds that such mechanisms violated their philosophical commitment to free markets and opposition to government intervention. They pursued those objections right through the defeat of the Clinton health care plan, in which they played a major role (Johnson and Broder 1996: chap. 10).

Most organized interests gain leverage by being credible on both counts—the information they provide about what works and does not work as a matter of policy and perspectives they offer about what is and is not politically viable. They also confront inherent limits about how far substantive analysis can possibly take them. Even if there were a profound consensus among health policy specialists that public financing was the optimal way to organize the financing of health insurance, the Health Insurance Association of America (HIAA), representing hundreds of commercial private insurance carriers, could never ratify putting private insurance out of business.

Politicians, in the best sense of the word, are the elected officials who possess the formal public authority to decide the course of government policy and who regularly suffer the consequences of their decisions by standing for reelection in their constituencies. Certainly they have substantive interests and thus a desire to benefit from that kind of social learning, but the direct link between their fate and their constituents' evaluations causes them to emphasize situational social learning (noted in Figure 1) and to look for what is doable, can pass, can attract a majority (see Arnold 1990). Politicians like what is possible. Their common refrain is to not let the perfect become the enemy of the good. Books entitled *Profiles in Courage* are written for a reason.

Not all politicians are the same, however, or consistently give the same emphasis to substantive and situational issues. Although they place a premium on being generalists, since they are called upon to make decisions about the full scope of public policy, many also develop niches of expertise. Anyone who watched former Senator Dave Durenberger (R-MN) actively and substantively participate in Senate Finance Committee hearings on issues as dense as the fusion of capital reimbursements to hospitals in the Medicare Prospective Payment System, or worked with former Senate Majority Leader George Mitchell on long-term care issues, or witnessed Speaker Newt Gingrich negotiate the final intricate details of the Republican Medicare reform package, knows that politicians are sometimes capable of performing with the knowledge base of quasi experts. Many politicians are comfortable with substantive issues and the analysis on which such decisions are based, although they are also far more likely than "pure" experts to use analytical information to buttress conclusions that have already been drawn than to learn from it in an unadulterated sense (Sabatier 1987). Theirs is a world primarily of "struggles, not seminars," and of all the players involved in policy making, politicians and organized interests share the ultimate need for "victory, not illumination" (Marmor 1995a: 4).

At the other end of the spectrum are the unalloyed politicians in the worst sense of the word. In Mayhew's famous phrase, they are "single-minded seekers of reelection" (1974: 5). Nothing else matters but staying in office. But even these politicians, for whom situational concerns would seem to be everything, have a demand for substantive learning. If reelection depends on receiving the most votes, and if voters at least partially come to judgment about incumbents in reaction to the effects of governmental policies on their lives and welfare that the incumbents helped to enact (or tried to defeat), then even the pure reelection seekers need a way to reduce uncertainty about what programs can and will do once in place (Krehbiel 1991: 62).

For politicians of any stripe to operate effectively in a world of both information and values, merits and politics, each policy decision must represent a balance of ordinary knowledge (commonsense judgments that "feel" right even if they are empirically wrong), distributional knowledge (the impact of policy options on different groups and constituencies of political importance to the politician), and policy-analytic knowledge (research-based conclusions about what works and why) (Peterson 1995a; see also Lindblom 1979 and Schick 1991). Politicians thus aggregate the perspectives of the expert and the organized interest, as well as their own perceptions and those of the electorate about what makes sense.

When there is conflict among these three kinds of knowledge, or when an issue is so salient that the public's sensibilities are particularly well known, ordinary knowledge, and then distributional knowledge, are likely to prevail at the expense of analysis.

None of these policy makers and influentials operates in a vacuum. The public, naturally, constitutes an essential feature of the policy-making context—as the source of societal demands when the issues are salient, as the boundary setters when alternatives are being deliberated, and as the constituencies to which politicians respond or anticipate (Arnold 1990; Kingdon 1992: chap. 2). An issue of no concern to the public is not likely to motivate politicians, and the core of the policy game, as well as the social-learning enterprise, may be left to either experts alone, or experts together with organized interests.

There are also the media, which function as "both a mirror of public opinion and a magnifying glass for the issues that it takes up" (Hall 1993: 288). What the press covers and how the subject is presented can influence the position and role of experts, organized interests, and politicians in the aggregate and individually, as well as affect the character and consequences of social learning (Page and Shapiro 1992). Particular experts who attract the camera and the reporter more than others (say, Stanford economist Alain Enthoven), and representatives of organized interests who can sell a persuasive combination of substantively and situationally "learned" policy perspectives (perhaps insurance companies represented by the HIAA) can torque the policy debate in certain directions. The status of public attitudes and behavior, along with media activities, thus establish variations in the relevance of experts, organized interests, and politicians—and the social learning they bring with them—to policy change.

Compared to parliamentary systems with strong parties, highly decentralized, open policy-making systems, such as in the United States, are more likely on average to highlight the role of organized interests and individual entrepreneurial politicians in social learning, giving greater weight to situational lessons drawn from more parochial perspectives. Such systems also enhance sensitivity to the locus and intensity of public attention to an issue, as well as to the character of media coverage. For technical issues of little salience to the public and with little press exposure, social learning in the parliamentary and separation-of-powers systems may be quite similar—led by experts and oriented to substantive issues (albeit within the confines of whatever biases dominate the expert community). When the policy concerns are of intense interest to the public, the atmospherics are different in *both* systems, to be sure, but the

American-style arrangements are likely to give more attention to situational social learning as a result of specific organized interests and individual politicians possessing greater analytical resources and political leverage (see Wilensky 1997).

The scope of policy

We can now turn to the final dimension of variation in the social learning process. As noted earlier, the scope of the policy one is evaluating affects what aspect of social learning gets emphasized because of the difference in involvement and relative influence of distinct populations of participants. Fine-tuning policy instruments in response to new data occurs within the realm of the autonomous state—among civil servants and other experts who emphasize substantive over situational learning. Politicians may set the overall theme in enabling legislation. Organizations that have a stake in the outcome obviously try to protect their interests. But in the actual design and implementation of policy, experts are prominent.

A classic example in the health domain is the revision of the provider reimbursement mechanisms in Medicare during the 1980s (see Smith 1992). President Reagan, his political appointees, and Congress came to agreement on legislative provisions that authorized the creation of new approaches for paying providers and defined the general conceptual frameworks within which they were to be developed. No longer would hospitals be granted cost-based retrospective reimbursements, nor would physicians be paid according to established customary, prevailing, and reasonable rates. The specifications of the new payment methodologies—the prospective payment system (PPS) for hospitals based on paying fixed rates for treatments that fell into predesignated diagnosis-related groupings (DRGs) and a Medicare fee schedule (MFS) for physicians using an empirically established resource-based relative-value scale (RBRVS)—were determined by policy specialists inside and outside of HCFA. Further enhancing the substantive nature of these changes, Congress established the ProPAC and PPRC, each staffed with professional analysts, to monitor the progress of these new systems of payment (Oliver 1993; Peterson 1995a).

Organized interests, to be sure, were involved at two levels. First, they furnished a considerable amount of information to the program designers about provider practices. Medical associations cooperated with Dr. William Hsiao at the Harvard Public Health School who led the development of the RBRVS. Second, they approached Congress—the politicians—for protection when at the implementation stage, in the case of physician payment reform, they concluded that the Bush administration was exploiting the new system to advance its own budget-cutting agenda (see Peterson 1995a). Nonetheless, these new features of Medicare were crafted largely by experts, guided mostly by substantive assessments of what works and does not work (within the decision opportunity framed by the enabling legislation). Few people outside of HCFA, some members of the congressional committees of jurisdiction, hospital trade associations, physician societies, and a circumscribed set of health policy specialists knew enough about DRGs or the RBRVS to even recognize that a change had occurred.

Major policy changes—"paradigm shifts" or "punctuated equilibria"—introduce a social learning process that may comprise all kinds of participants, reflecting broad social and economic demands and interests (Baumgartner and Jones 1993; Hall 1993). A few years ago, whether and how the government could ensure universal access to medical care and effectively contain health care costs were undoubtedly subject to much intense discussion in the back corridors of HCFA and other locales of expertise within the Department of Health and Human Services. The discussions were just as intense, however, in union halls and trade association conference rooms, at community forums and town meetings, and across kitchen tables in homes throughout America. Health care reform broadcasts on television drifted from a few specialized productions on PBS to being part of regular programming on the commercial networks, a sure sign that this was not a debate confined to the state.

Experts were certainly plentiful and important in the process of formulating proposed reform bills. They used information gathered about current experiences with federal programs like Medicare and Medicaid, the ill-fated Medicare Catastrophic Coverage Act, and state programs, as well as the practices of countries around the world, especially Canada (the quintessential public-financing single-payer model), Germany (used to illustrate the all-payer model of regulated private insurers), and the Netherlands (which poked around with formulations comparable to managed competition among private plans) (White 1995a). The Clinton administration employed hundreds of experts, but even legislation drafted by one or a few members of Congress reached out to a considerable number of qualified specialists (Peterson 1995a: 108–112).

Organized interests naturally played a central role. These groups did just what one would expect for an issue of this magnitude. They used all means necessary to protect their valuable stakes, including seeking to affect the interpretations of both substantive and situational lessons to their benefit. Groups across the political spectrum released studies of everything from the effects of employer mandates on jobs to the administrative costs of the current health care system, from the implications on choice of plans in mandatory versus voluntary health alliances to the likely impact of specific reform plans on the numbers of uninsured Americans. Quite frequently groups—many with little else in common—contracted with Lewin-VHI, the most prominent consulting firm, to run the numbers based on its models. All of this work was intended to show the analytical validity of each organization's policy agenda. The same organizations used both surveys of public opinion and methods for influencing popular attitudes to bolster their claims that one or another policy option did or did not comply with the wishes of the American public.

They also drew lessons from the previous periods of reform debate to argue what has already been proven impossible to enact in this country given its values and institutions. The No Name Coalition, an alliance dominated by insurance and small business interests, drove home through repetition and a major media campaign that Clinton was set to burden Americans with "government-run health care" (Johnson and Broder 1996; Skocpol 1996). The most important lesson they wanted politicians to learn, of course, was that they had the resources—campaign contributions and, more important, influence over large numbers of voters—to make the lawmakers' lives miserable, should they proceed with legislation that ran counter to the groups' interests.

Given its scope (the redesigning of one-seventh of the economy, with consequences for every man, woman, and child, most likely today and not just in the future), health care reform was ultimately, of necessity, going to be dominated by politicians making very careful political judgments. Because of the paramount role of politicians in the process, situational learning dominated substantive learning. The public discourse emphasized representations of values, public philosophy, and common sense far more than the analytical works of the General Accounting Office, the Brookings Institution, or the myriad studies financed by the Robert Wood Johnson Foundation. Analysis became a weak reed against the tide of political forces.

Proponents of reform tried to convince elected officials that it was in their political interest to join the reform bandwagon. Voters were going to decide the fate of members of Congress, they argued, based more than trivially on what the senator or representative did to affect the passage of a reform initiative. Opponents worked just as hard, and in the end far more effectively, to persuade politicians that the data—past experience and current opinion—offered learning of the situational sort that favored stalling proposals for reform. Concern about flagging popular support and the implied electoral calculus probably ultimately doomed health care reform in the 1990s. To the extent that social learning mattered in the health care reform debate, it was the intersection of organized interest activities with the sensibility of politicians, emphasizing situational as opposed to substantive learning, that stood in the way of major policy change (see Wilensky 1997). It was not the machination of experts (although divisions among policy specialists, who communicated the substantive lessons, and the capacity of some advocates to capture the mantle of "expert," helped confuse the debate and the public [Marmor 1995b]).

The associations among the scope of the policy change being considered, the types of participants involved, and the form of social learning likely to be highlighted are not always so easily determined as I have suggested thus far. Politicians may view some issues as so contentious or politically problematic that however salient they are, it would be most advantageous to deal with them by means other than the politicians' having to make explicit decisions. Issues that require difficult political choices over competing values can be made safer—avoiding blame—by transforming them into technical decisions either left to the specialists in the bureaucracy or resolved with automatic formulas (see Weaver 1988: chap. 2).

For example, situational lessons about the risks associated with tampering with Medicare may have helped motivate elected officials to transform the tricky problem of rapidly rising Medicare expenditures from a major reform issue into a "technical" problem to be left to experts. As Morone argues (1994: 155), the provider reimbursement approaches imposed in the 1980s "appear[ed] (and in politics, appearance is crucial) to operate automatically, scientifically—without visible decisions by politicians or bureaucrats. The illusion of self-enforcing, automatic, scientific process is important in a nation that is suspicious of its own public officials."

The new policy legacy

At the end of the model presented in Figure 1, a new policy legacy is formed by the intersection of the contributions of social learning with the influence of political factors exogenous to the previous policy legacy. This is where raw politics again enters the scene. It serves as a reminder that the social learning process is a necessary addendum to the understanding of policy making, but is neither a sufficient nor necessarily even dominant explanation for policy outcomes.

I have suggested that the mechanics of social learning in the U.S. context probably did little to advance deliberation over proposals to comprehensively reform the health care system. Although various reform proposals reflected aspects of substantive learning, little entered the public debate, and situational lessons complicating the politics of reform tended to dominate. The main determinants of what transpired in the 103rd Congress, however, producing the defeat of Clinton's Health Security Act and all other alternatives, probably had more to do with a number of other political and strategic factors. We can be certain that whatever combination of factors produced the defeat of health care reform, and a defeat of its particular character, created a new policy legacy with structural and social learning effects that are likely to influence future federal (as well as state) health care politics and policy making (note Skocpol 1996).

Policy toward Markets: Anticipating the Role of Social Learning

The market has now taken over as the principle engine of health care system change. How are policy makers likely to respond to the transformations of the medical care market, and what is the likely impact of social learning?

One answer is that policy makers, burned by the recent health care reform experience, may try to avoid political confrontations altogether by ceding decision making again to what could be perceived as an automatic, apolitical, and technocratic process. This time protection is not to be found in diverting issues to the civil servants in the public bureaucracy but rather to private actors operating in the presumed realm of technical proficiency. As Gary Belkin argues in his chapter, this "technocratic wish" recognizes the political merits of allowing the health care system to transform itself and reallocate medical resources under market guises, with the rise of managed care and greater reliance on outcomes research and other methods justified as scientific. The claimed "objectivity of standardized measures" can be used "to broker disagreement" (1997; see also Morone 1993). Substantive learning in this context will be a private act, not a social one.

That impulse cannot be completely sustained, however. First, as Judy Feder commented at a 1996 forum, in a world of competing managed care networks, the government has an important role to play in ensuring consumer protection and requiring the accountability of private plans (1996). There are enough anecdotes about problems with managed care to have already prompted elected officials to respond to perceived constituent worries. The operation of the market in practice also does little to mitigate the electorate's fears about losing health insurance coverage. So from federal policy makers we get modest measures like the Health Insurance Portability and Accountability Act of 1996 (the Kassebaum-Kennedy bill), essentially ratifying similar state-level statutes (Hacker and Skocpol 1997; Oliver and Fiedle 1997; Peterson 1998). Second, with nearly half of health care spending involving public dollars, and under the gun of mounting pressure on state and federal budgets, fulfillment of the technocratic wish—bringing managed care and market competition into public programs like Medicaid and Medicare—actually requires proactive policy making.

So government policy makers have acted and will act. But how are they approaching their decision-making responsibilities? How much is this next round of public policy making to be informed by social learning, and in what ways? Will substantive learning leave its mark? A significant component of the work published in this book and health policy journals has been designed to lend analytical perspective to issues of importance in the health care market. Will these studies, or any others, influence the course of public policy?

I have contended in this essay that the social learning process is complex, nuanced, and variable, suggesting serious limitations on the effects substantive lessons can have on policy making. Those limitations, however, also vary in reasonably predictable ways. To illustrate how one might anticipate the role of policy analysis in the course of policy making on market-related topics, I will briefly discuss three issues almost certain to be continuously on the public agenda: expanded federal and state regulation of private managed care plans; promotion of managed care in Medicaid by state governments; and federal encouragement of medical savings accounts.

Managed care in private insurance

There is a general consensus that with a movement toward competing managed care networks, entirely new requirements are being made of consumers (or of their employers' benefit managers, who in many cases make the fundamental decisions about which health plans will be available) and providers. As a general proposition, along the lines explored by Thomas Rice in his chapter, there are a number of reasons why health care decision making in a market environment is potentially problematic. More specifically, managed care organizations, most of which are now commercial enterprises having to pay close attention to the bottom line, can easily and understandably be led down the path of denying the public the kind of insurance coverage it might expect (Buchanan 1998). There are two ways for insurers to make money in a competitive environment. The first is to lead in innovation, attracting more enrollees by developing an insurance product that provides better, higher-quality coverage at a lower cost. The second is to engage in practices that enroll the healthy while discouraging the sick, the minority of the population in any particular year that accounts for the vast majority of health care costs. Given the enormous financial stakes involved and the difficulty of ensuring sustained innovation, the temptation is to choose the second strategy.

Theoretically, policy makers could concentrate on a number of approaches to facilitate workable competition among private managed care plans while minimizing the effects of these deleterious incentives. For example, they could promote the use of performance measures of managed care organizations to help consumers choose wisely among plans on the basis of availability of services, quality of care, and effectiveness of outcomes. They could reduce incentives for plans to cherry-pick the healthy by facilitating the incorporation of risk adjustment in payment to insurers to ensure that plans receive appropriate funding for the risk population they cover. They could require that consumers as patients be permitted to obtain full information about plausible treatments and the incentive structures built into physician compensation agreements. Overall, they could impose a regulatory regime that strikes a balance between protecting legitimate consumer interests and preserving the capacity of managed care organizations to offer cost-effective care (see Zelman 1997).

All of these remedies are under serious consideration, but none, however, is easy to accomplish. By all accounts, quality measures are still in their infancy, including one of the most widely recognized instruments, HEDIS, the Health Plan Employer Data and Information Set, sponsored by the National Committee for Quality Assurance (Anders 1996; Measuring 1995; Rules Changes 1997). Managed care plans have thus far been unable to ensure consistent performance across the whole range of services and activities. The variance in quality within plans may generally be greater than across plans (Report Card 1995). Progress has been made on risk adjusters, but there, too, we are only beginning to develop basic practical techniques that could be widely implemented (see Physician Payment Review Commission 1994; Shewry et al. 1996; and the excellent summary provided in Lee and Rogal 1997). Even though three-quarters of people are covered through their employers, more than a third (and rising rapidly) of Medicaid recipients, and 13 percent of Medicare beneficiaries are in managed care, public officials have little basis for intelligent intervention in the managed care market, however appropriate and needed it may be. In this instance the limits of social learning rests at the hands of experts. Even if public officials wished to legislate on the basis of policy-analytic knowledge, they are having to act in response to the rapid changes in the market before suitable expertise is available. As a senior state official commented at a meeting I attended, they are having to make it up as they go along.

Elected officials have a clear interest in these issues, especially since just about every constituent of every legislator will ultimately experience the effects of managed care, both positive and negative. But the intensity of policy maker involvement is also certain to vary. The process of learning about quality measures or risk adjusters, for example, is going to be the province of specialists in the field. As with the reforms in Medicare reimbursement systems, politicians are likely to establish the foundation for public-sector intervention (e.g., mandating that federally qualified health maintenance organizations perform at adequate levels on federally recognized quality measures), but the precise measures and their application will have much more to do with the evolving work of experts inside and outside of government. Analysis in the conventional sense—and the substantive social learning that goes with it—will probably ultimately have a significant effect.

On other issues relating to the regulation of private managed care plans, organized interests and politicians (and with them situational learning) can be expected to be more influential. States have already enacted a large number of restrictions on selective contracting with providers, including "any willing provider" laws that limit the degree to which managed care outfits can restrict providers from their panels and thus from access to their beneficiaries (Marsteller et al. 1997). Politically influential state medical associations have naturally been active in keeping managed care plans as open as possible, no doubt supported by consumers who are far more concerned about choice over providers than overall health care cost reductions. In the same vein, although no one knows how pervasive a problem it ever was, a number of states have passed legislation to inhibit the use by managed care organizations of financial incentives and "gag" rules to keep primary care physicians from recommending that patients receive more advanced (and more expensive) levels of care (similar federal rules have been issued for Medicare and Medicaid). Managed care plans, on the other side of the equation, have an enormous financial stake in retaining as much control over contracting with providers as possible. That is why the AAHP prefers voluntary industry efforts to promote consumer protection, despite the willingness of some nonprofit plans to call for limited federal requirements (Pear 1997b). As the emerging six-hundred-pound gorillas of the health care industry, the managed care industry has the resources and clout to push its own political agenda.

Very little is actually known about the empirical substantive impact of the restrictions on managed care contracting, in terms of quality of care, market efficiencies, or cost control. At best, one can propose policy strategies that *arguably* protect the viability of managed care while stemming the worst abuses of consumers (see Marsteller et al. 1997). Even if we had more extensive and better empirical evidence, the needs of organized interests and ultimately of politicians are likely to rise above and subvert the message of experts. Hence the state and federal initiatives focusing on specific health insurance benefits, such as limiting "drive-through deliveries" by requiring coverage for a forty-eight-hour hospital stay for women who have given birth, if the woman and her obstetrician desire it. Whatever their individual substantive merits, laws like these represent an extraordinary micromanagement of the core administration of managed care plans. In the words of one industry representative, "There seems to be a shoot-from-the hip tendency to create laws based on anecdotes that are not representative of a trend" (Pear 1997a: A12). Politicians are naturally going to be most concerned about the situational lessons—what happens when elected officials ignore what are perceived to be popular outcries. They are apt to react to horror stories, especially very specific ones, and the media coverage they engender. Regulatory interventions were thus initially episodic, fragmented, and incoherent. If there is a real shift taking place in state legislation, moving away from regulation of managed care coverage by body part and treatment toward more comprehensive consumer protection frameworks, we may in fact be witnessing the beginning of an unusual improvement in the social learning process.

Medicaid managed care

The rapidly accelerating trend among states to move Medicaid beneficiaries into managed care plans also demonstrates the limits of the social learning process and the relatively feeble impact of analysis on policy making (almost all states have such initiatives; Gold, Sparer, and Chu 1996: 153). The diffusion of Medicaid managed care spread so quickly across the states that it outran any assessment of how well it worked or its impact on the affected population groups. Expectations were high among state officials, or at least were announced, that shifting to managed care coverage for beneficiaries would produce substantial and reasonably rapid savings. Some states initially assumed the economies would be sufficient to cut budgets *and* expand substantially insurance coverage through the Medicaid program, an approach announced in many early waiver requests to HCFA.

This collective line of reasoning, however, did not have a foundation in substantive learning. Indeed, it overlooked a number of crucial issues. For example, although a substantial majority of current Medicaid beneficiaries are women and children receiving acute care coverage, most Medicaid expenditures go to finance acute and long-term care for the elderly and disabled. Few states were attempting to introduce managed care into long-term care, where there is very limited experience to guide policy (see Weissert et al. 1998, however, for an evaluation of the Arizona experience). As a result, actual savings have now proved far less plentiful than originally anticipated, early coverage expansions had to be curtailed, and more recent waiver submissions to HCFA excluded such bold ambitions (Vladeck 1996). In addition, success with Medicaid managed care (at least early on) depended on the state and providers having previous experience with managed care in the private insurance market. The analysis presented by Marsha Gold in her essay shows that Tennessee, without any such prior experience, tried to make these changes overnight and confusion ensued.

Why the incongruence between the accelerated restructuring of the Medicaid program in so many states and what was actually known about how to effect such a change? Elected officials felt the political pressure to wrest control of Medicaid expenditures. Politically, they had to act. They acted in a political environment that increasingly favored private institutions and market instruments, even in government programs. And the character of the program's recipients, most of whom were linked to Medicaid through welfare, permitted a social (not analytical) consensus to develop about how that population ought to be treated, along with recognition that they would not offer effective political opposition (Grogan 1997; Kronebusch 1997). Analysis and experience were not entirely absent from this major recasting of a core social program. Nonetheless, the transformation of Medicaid in the 1990s is more the product of situational factors than of substantive learning. What we cannot determine yet is whether future adjustments in Medicaid managed care will be more analytically grounded. On the one hand, such policy adjustments are more likely to be the province of career officials, suggesting a greater role of expertise. On the other hand, a system built around huge public contracts with large, private, often commercial health plans introduces both problems of oversight and promotes vast financial stakes that are certain to be forcefully protected by powerful interests.

Medical savings accounts

Medical savings accounts (MSAs) offer a third interesting example. Proposals to write federal tax provisions to stimulate the establishment of MSAs have been around for a number of years (Jensen and Morlock 1994). Although they have few meaningful tax incentives to offer, by 1996 twenty states had laws on the books to encourage MSAs, and many employers already offered them even without federal support (Medical Savings Accounts 1996; Pauly and Goodman 1995). But MSAs suddenly arrived foursquare on the agenda—as an experimental part of the Health Insurance Portability and Accountability Act (HIPAA) enacted in 1996 and as an additional experiment for the Medicare population authorized by the 1997 budget act—not because of an obvious substantive lesson based on widely recognized analysis or experience, but rather as a result of situational politics.

Republicans swept the congressional elections in 1994, took control of the legislature for the first time in forty years, and advanced MSAs as a feature of conservative market orthodoxy (Peterson 1998). This approach to financing health care had been promoted by a number of organizations with close ties to the Republican Party. They include the libertarian and market-oriented Cato Institute, which has provided much of the intellectual groundwork for MSAs; the American Medical Association, which views them as an opportunity to avoid both managed care and Medicare regulations that cap reimbursement rates; and parts of the commercial insurance industry that offer the high-deductible insurance that is partnered with MSAs.

So far there has been little new, solid analytical work to justify the prominence of medical savings accounts on the policy agenda. At best, the substantive learning process for MSAs has been played out on the field of conceptualization. MSA advocates turn to the traditional principles of market choice and consumer sovereignty to argue the merits of their flexibility and efficiency. Individuals using MSAs could maximize their preferences within their budget constraints. Because they would be using their own dollars for all but catastrophic medical services, they would become more cost conscious and careful to search for the best value for their money (Jensen and Morlock 1994; Goodman and Musgrave 1992; Pauly and Goodman 1995). Overall health care costs would thus come down.

The opponents return to the issue of incentives and how they affect individual behavior to judge what types of people would be drawn to MSAs and what their impact would be on existing insurance arrangements. They typically conclude that the healthy and wealthy would gravitate toward MSAs, sucking resources out of standard insurance in which the chronically ill (and others who remained) would face escalating insurance premiums (Shear 1996). Within the private insurance market, for example, if half of the healthy population participated in MSAs, premiums for conventional health insurance would double (Nichols, Moon, and Wall 1996). Critics argue that the MSA provision for Medicare would have a similar, even more troubling, effect. Appealing to the more than half of the beneficiary population that generates $500 or less in medical expenditures per year (accounting for less than 2 percent of overall program expenditures), an MSA option risks withdrawing money from the Medicare system that currently pays for the medical services received by the sicker beneficiaries who would remain in the traditional program. The per capita costs of traditional Medicare would be driven up (Statistical Supplement 1996: 31; Moon and Davis 1995: 36).

A prime motive for promoting MSAs—cost containment through cost consciousness—is also not so easy to sustain. A simulation analysis by reasonably sympathetic analysts concluded that "medical savings account legislation . . . would have little impact on health care costs of Americans with employer-provided insurance" (Keeler et al. 1996: 1667). Hsiao notes that a decade ago, to hold down health care costs, Singapore instituted a system comparable to MSAs and catastrophic insurance. Its experience shows that "the theory has not been supported by the evidence" (1995: 266). Others offer contrary assessments of the Singapore results (Massaro and Wong 1995). A major source of contention is disagreement about what is the primary source of health care cost increases. Is it individuals' excess demand for unnecessary medical services, especially routine services, which in an MSA scheme would fall within the deductible and be entirely financed out of account? Or is the problem on the supply side, the product of induced demand by providers, and the costs of expensive procedures linked to advanced technologies, for which high-deductible health insurance under the MSA scheme would provide first-dollar coverage and thus no individual cost-consciousness?

At the moment, it does not matter which side is analytically correct. A year of experience with the HIPAA experiment produced few and ambiguous results. In one sense the deepest worries of the MSA opponents (and the hopes of the advocates) were not fulfilled. One of the issues that tied up the debate over the HIPAA was the size of the MSA experiment.

Democrats struggled to keep the number of potential participants limited. The compromise agreement settled on a figure of about 750,000, 375,000 of whom could be signed up by 30 April 1997. The IRS reported that only 10,000 had done so, far too few people to affect any characteristic of the insurance market (Unintended Consequences 1997). Yet in specific places the potentially negative effects of MSAs apparently were realized. In 1996 Ada County, Idaho, became one of the first public employers to offer MSAs as an option for its employees. In less than a year the option was dropped. Among other things, because the MSA option attracted healthier individuals, the other insurance plans ended up with a higher concentration of people with greater medical needs producing increased costs. If the MSA option were retained, premiums for these plans were going to rise 15 percent the next year, well above typical premium trends (Idaho's Most Populous County 1997).

The initial enactment of the MSA experiments was decided in terms of situational dynamics and which set of politicians had the most votes. Will future congressional decisions about whether to extend and expand the MSA initiatives be influenced by the substantive lessons to be derived from these pilot programs? There is reason to be concerned. Because the experiments are not of long enough duration (four years) and any enrollees are not concentrated enough in any given region, it will be difficult to assess the potential impact of unrestricted MSA availability on the insurance market, insurance premiums, Medicare, and overall health care costs (Finally, a Health Bill 1996).

A final note. Social learning as a foundation for policy making in response to market changes is further circumscribed by the very nature of the issues. No one else in the world has organized their health care systems in ways at all comparable to the United States. Although many countries have introduced various forms of "competition" into the provision of medical care, as discussed by Lawrence Brown in the next chapter (see also Jacobs 1998), none has relied on markets as the central organizing device. None has developed, as yet, vast integrated managed care networks of providers. For judging MSAs, all we have is Singapore.

When the policy debate was about global budgeting, rate regulation, negotiated reimbursement systems, and the like, the international scene offered a fount of analytically useful information about how such arrangements can and do work, and under what conditions. An international standard emerged that gained currency because of its robustness within many different types of institutional settings (White 1995a; Marmor 1995a: 5). That is simply not the case with market-based and managed-care oriented changes in health care financing and delivery. Learning across space, therefore, becomes far more difficult. Substantive learning is necessarily narrowed and more dependent upon competing conceptual arguments rather than empirical experience. And the presumed uniqueness of the United States, a well-worn situational lesson, takes on greater import than ever before (Klein 1997), at least in the foreseeable future. That is a most important brake on translating analysis into action.

Conclusion

The way societies are able to "do better" is to learn from their own past experiences or from the relevant experiences of others. Because of the range of participants that has to be involved in a democratic policy-making process, however, and the ways in which issues of substance intersect with the dynamics of politics, there is nothing straightforward about the social-learning process.

In the U.S. system, as with all others, experts do not and cannot reign. Indeed, since popular legitimacy in a democracy is at least as important as policy intelligence, that is often a very good thing. Despite the increasing availability of sophisticated policy analysis, and the enhanced capacity of legislators and executives to use it, in the end, the core practical challenge for any policy supporter—proponents of single-payer financing, patrons of managed competition, or enthusiasts for the market—is to win the situational social-learning battle, not the substantive debate. While organized interests and politicians certainly try to score points in substantive discourse, which all too often becomes dueling sound bites or a "dialogue of the deaf" in a "universe with multiple versions of the truth" (Sabatier 1987: 676–678; Klein 1997; Marmor 1995a), they can often simply dominate the enterprise of establishing situational verities. They are able to articulate quite persuasive lessons derived from the policy legacy both of health care policies in particular and of social policy considerations in general.

In this context, current antitax, antigovernment, and promarket perspectives enjoy considerable influence and advantage. For many health policy specialists (but not all), the substantive empirical record of market mechanisms is thus far mixed at best and disquieting at worst, but the political viability of the market in the United States at the close of this century is decidedly robust. With organized interests that hold huge stakes in the existing system and individual politicians being such easy participants in the situational social-learning process, it is extremely difficult for the president or other policy advocates to identify and work with safe lessons, other than to gravitate toward strategies that shun taxes and more than marginal government involvement. On health care reform, President Clinton's commitment to universal access, portability of coverage, and budget caps arguably derived more from what has been learned on the substantive front than from what he felt compelled to accept within the situational constraints, as he and others understood them. On the other hand, the core design features of his Health Security Act—including employer-based benefits and competition among private health plans—represented his effort to achieve his policy objectives by combining the fruits of health services research within politically defensible institutions. It did not work. Political lessons guided the parameters, the parameters constrained substantively informed policy choices, and the restricted policy choices yielded a complex policy initiative that ended up easy prey to situational politics (Peterson 1998). The proponents of market-oriented changes, such as managed care and medical savings accounts, do not encounter the same tensions between substantive lessons (often nonexistent or confused in the health domain) and situational dynamics.

Without understanding the force of policy legacies, one cannot possibly explain either the debate over health care reform or the current machinations over the health care market. Simple policy-making models incorporating public opinion, partisan debates, electoral outcomes, and interest-group influence fail to set the context in which these factors operate. We have to know why taxation, government involvement, markets, and organized interests of particular types become such significant issues at various points in time. We have to recognize why substantive analysis of various kinds either lacks currency or gains a foothold, as well as where and when analysis can have a meaningful role. Absent a careful elaboration of the two types of social learning, one cannot fully appreciate the opportunities that exist in the United States to frustrate certain kinds of policy innovation and promote others, and the likelihood of finding discontinuities between analytical and political judgments.

Notes

This chapter is based on a paper presented at the *Journal of Health Politics, Policy and Law* Conference: Health Care into the Next Century: Markets, States, and Communities, Duke University, 3–4 May 1996, and published in the *Journal of Health Politics, Policy and Law*, Vol. 22, No. 4, August 1997. The analysis reported here derived from an overall project given generous support by a number of institutions, including funding from the Robert Wood Johnson Foundation, the Russell Sage Foundation, the Dirksen Congressional Leadership Center and Caterpillar Foundation, the William F. Milton Fund and Faculty Aide Program at Harvard University, and the Graduate School of Public and International Affairs at the University of Pittsburgh; an American Political Science Association Congressional Fellowship; and time as a guest scholar at the Brookings Institution. Thanks are owed Senator Tom Daschle, as well as Rima Cohen and Peter Rouse of his staff; Thomas Mann; Ranjan Chaudhuri for research assistance; and William Brandon, James Morone, and Paul Pierson for insightful comments on earlier incarnations of this essay.

1   I appreciate William Brandon's suggestion to incorporate technological change into this analysis.
2   Since the health care reform debate, Congress terminated the Office of Technology Assessment and consolidated ProPAC and the PPRC into a single body, the Medicare Payment Assessment Commission (MedPAC).

Exceptionalism as the Rule? U.S. Health Policy

Innovation and Cross-National Learning

Lawrence D. Brown

For the American left, the phrase "the U.S. health system in cross-national perspective" tends to stimulate a (by now) nearly instinctive response: Every other comparable country has implemented affordable universal coverage and the United States has not. The United States should (obviously) learn from others how to do it, but for any number of reasons—among them culture, politics, and market ideology—remains contentedly mired in exceptionalism.

This familiar litany faces a discordant fact, however: Many other comparable nations want to learn from the United States the ins and outs of managed care, managed competition, diagnosis-related groups (DRGs), medical practice guidelines, and kindred strategic innovations. The contradiction could be more apparent than real. The United States is highly inventive in all respects except the truly important ones—affordability and universal coverage—and other nations look here for innovations to install at the edges of sound and solid systems.

Arguably, however, cross-national convergence around U.S.-inspired innovations reflects deeper forces facing both the political economies of nations that enjoy coverage for all at affordable cost and the political economy of the nation that does not. Strategic fancies and fashions that are sometimes dismissed as indigenous American schemes to paper over the unhappy consequences of exceptionalism are becoming policy "rules" in nations that are often held up for American emulation. This article explores the roots of this paradox.

Sources of Innovation: Cost as Motive

It is indeed strange, prima facie, that nations spending "only" 9 to 10 percent or so of their gross domestic products on health care while covering nearly all their citizens should seek policy wisdom from a nation that devotes 14 percent of its GDP to health care while leaving more than 40 million citizens with no health insurance at all. Compared to the United States, other Western nations have an admirable record. The problem is that compared to themselves (so to speak), the record is less reassuring. In nation after nation, ministers of finance, social affairs, and health struggle to counter the "insupportable" rates of growth in spending on health care and other social benefits. Everywhere one hears the weary refrain: "We can no longer afford the system that we have."

This image of health care costs soaring beyond the control of hapless policy makers is certainly open to question. In Germany, health care spending as a percentage of GDP has been fairly stable (around 8 percent) since 1975 (Greiner, Graf, and Schulenburg 1997: 79). Sweden devoted about 7.9 percent of GDP to health services in 1975, and 7.6 percent in 1992 (Hakansson and Nordling 1997: 207). The French share in 1980—7.6 percent—rose to nearly 10 percent in 1995, but the system was hardly running amok: An average annual increase of 10.4 percent between 1980 and 1990 slowed to a 5.6 percent between 1990 and 1994 (Pascal-Pomey and Poullier 1997: 65).

That these seemingly unspectacular numbers trigger talk of a health cost "crisis" cannot be imputed to hysteria or rhetorical cunning, however. The macroeconomic context in which policy makers work is much more complex than summary GDP statistics suggest. France, for example, faced a deficit of 35.5 billion francs (about $400 per capita) in health insurance funding within the social security system in 1995, and an accumulated debt since 1992 of 230 billion francs. That the response—a special flat income tax to help cover the gap—conforms to pressures from the European Union to cut the public deficit presumably does not ease the political pain (Pascal-Pomey and Poullier 1997: 51). Between 1991 and 1993, Sweden faced its worst economic recession since the 1930s. Under a national budget deficit amounting to nearly 15 percent of GDP in 1993, the national government told county councils to cut their budgets, which are the main funding source for the country's public health system (Hakansson and Nordling 1997: 206–207). Israel struggles with chronic public budget deficits, generated mainly by defense spending but aggravated by annual payments to bail out the nation's largest sickness fund.

These enfolding circumstances leave budget makers little chance to savor their successes in health cost containment. Making social policy in general has grown harder. Slow economic growth depletes revenues for taxes and social insurance contributions and increases claimants for benefits. High unemployment (now around 12 percent in France, Germany, and Sweden) aggravates the tension between revenues and expenditures in social budgets. The high tax rates that sustain these programs are said to discourage entrepreneurship, burden smaller firms, and slow the creation of jobs, and the critics who say so are no longer dismissed as ideological curmudgeons. These stresses by no means spell the end of welfare states, nor even a crisis within them, but they powerfully complicate their political and economic management.

In this context health care costs are especially enervating not only because they rise steadily but also because leverage on the sources of these increases seems so elusive. Everyone knows the usual suspects: demographic trends that make the elderly a growing proportion of populations and (supposedly) raise the demand for health services; immigration (and in Germany, unification), which obliges national health insurance plans to assimilate sizable new groups with significant health needs; the political influence of special populations such as the disabled and those with specific diseases such as AIDS; consumer expectations of bigger and better drugs, devices, and procedures; and—perhaps most important—the advances of medical technology, whose wonders never cease (Gelijns and Rosenberg 1996).

Health care costs in Europe and Canada, although indeed reasonable on such familiar measures as percent of GDP and spending per capita, throw fuel on fiscal fires forever threatening to escape control. There are of course several ways of coping. Policy makers can raise existing taxes, adopt new ones, reduce benefits, raise cost sharing, and cut payments to providers, for example, but these steps are as distasteful politically as the incessant shoveling of money into the status quo.

Cost-containment policy in Europe is an arduous and unending political exercise in bargaining, legislating, implementing, and fine-tuning—processes whose intensity and complexity naturally have inspired inquiries into alternatives. In the 1970s, costs were controlled mainly by means of structured negotiations between payers (sickness funds) and providers (associations of sickness fund physicians and hospitals) while governments set the rules of the game, watched from the sidelines, and sometimes intervened to shape the settlement (Glaser 1978). As costs rose unacceptably, nations began to constrain bargaining by linking increases in health spending to targets and ceilings—for example, rates of growth of GDP, the Consumer Price Index (CPI), or worker wages (Kirkman-Liff 1994, Glaser 1993, U.S. GAO 1991). These innovations slowed spending growth, but the ceaseless elaboration and enforcement required to hold health costs within the allowable bounds of political economies stressed by macroeconomic circumstances, competition among spending priorities, and pressures of European integration seem to have triggered regulatory exhaustion, and with it, demands for strategic relief. As van de Ven and Schut note in the Dutch case, "Only government was responsible for cost containment," which allowed all other stakeholders to "oppose regulation without committing themselves in any way" (van de Ven and Schut: 98). By realigning economic incentives, Dutch reforms of 1990 aimed to engage providers, insurers, and consumers—along with government—in the struggle to contain costs. Economics, then, supplies a constant and continuing motive for policy innovation. Makers of public policies and budgets are, in effect, constant authors of requests for proposals that will somehow relieve regulatory exhaustion and deliver bright new ideas that will contain costs without extensive political damage.

Sources of Innovation: Knowledge as Opportunity

Nations bedeviled by health costs can increasingly satisfy their economic urges by embracing strategic opportunities that accompany rapidly accumulating knowledge about the workings of health care systems, and about where they are broken and in need of repair. Over the past twenty-five years the findings of scholarly investigations of health systems have been welcomed and made comfortable within the policy mainstream. Practice variations across small areas, technology assessment, cost-effectiveness analysis, medical practice guidelines, outcomes research, randomly controlled clinical trials, and patient satisfaction surveys have all triggered a barrage of corrosive questions—and purported answers—about quality of care and value for money in conventional practice patterns. To policy makers this weighty information has delivered the message that large stretches of the system make no clinical or economic sense and invite correction by means of strategic innovation.

Studies of variations in rates of medical procedures across small areas in the United States and Canada (Wennberg 1984; Roos and Roos 1994) suggest that many such practices are "much more loosely connected with science . . . than the official rhetoric would suggest" (Evans, Barer, and Marmor 1994: 30). Cross-national comparisons find variations indicating clinical uncertainties that seem to derive from "the procedure or diagnosis itself, rather than the health system through which it has been provided," which naturally invites attention to the determinants of utilization (McPherson 1990). Persistent discrepancies in health status among socioeconomic groups and regions despite the equalizing efforts of national health insurance plans (Stronks and Gunning-Schepers 1993) add ethical insult to economic injury, fortify the sense that "so much of total health expenditure is impossible to justify" (Jerome-Forget and Forget 1995: 194), and argue for more evidence and better evaluation of the system's workings.

In the United States the symbiosis between corrosive findings and constructive strategies finagling has become a little industry of its own. For example, small area analyses unearth rates of medical procedures that are far too divergent to explain by invoking such "objective" factors as demography and case mix. Government budget makers infer (rightly or wrongly) that the system indulges vastly excessive use. The policy maker's imagination naturally starts to wander to whether changes in payment rates might encourage parsimony, whether practice guidelines authored by experts might lay a professional foundation for quality, and whether close studies of the outcomes of clinical procedures might help providers sort out what works from what falls short. Corporate financial officers and benefit managers conclude that a hefty portion of their health premium payments underwrites pointless procedures; they resolve to tighten management controls on providers and squeeze waste. Meanwhile foundations launch demonstrations and (then) evaluations that fund academic analysis to fill the literature with findings that animate further debate and offer helpful hints for saving money by curbing clinical excesses.

In the last ten years or so, public and private policy makers and budget setters in most Western nations have grown increasingly intrigued by and fluent in the theories, methods, findings, and implications of these research endeavors. It is this intellectual development, not cost pressure, that is the big "new" news in contemporary health policy. Much of the evidence and argument originates in the United States, but this intellectual capital, like investment capital, has gone global. It is a fairly safe bet that even as the reader turns the learned pages of this book, some health official or analyst in another country (quite possibly bearing a master's degree in public health from a U.S. university) is pondering whether sickness funds should encourage providers to form "integrated service networks" or how diagnosis-related groups (DRGs) might enhance the performance of the nation's hospitals. Other countries contemplate American research, add to it, adapt it, and apply it at home. Thus arises the European and Canadian attraction to such analytic enterprises as technology assessment (Gelijns and Rosenberg 1996), DRGs (Kimberly, Pouvourville, and Associates 1993; Casas and Wiley 1993), quality-of-life indicators as a basis for setting health policy priorities, evidence-based medicine, practice protocols (Rodwin forthcoming: 15–16), and of course market incentives (Jerome-Forget, White, and Weiner

1995), and managed competition (Ham and Brommels 1994). Spurred by costs, modern polities increasingly launch health policy innovations with a confidence born of the legitimacy that accompanies the sense that one finally knows what one is doing.

Sources of Innovation: Generational Change Generates Change

Evidence and information gain force in the search for cost-containment policies not because they self-evidently reveal correct answers, but because new ways of looking at public policy encourage them. Images of what constitutes good policy change over time, in health as in other arenas. For example, in the French system that evolved after 1945, the dominant sickness fund, governed by a board composed of labor and business representatives, negotiated with providers about payments and recommended payroll tax increases to the government. Government, meanwhile, supervised these negotiations, promulgated global budgets for public hospitals, set payroll taxes, and covered deficits. In the postwar political context, arrangements that delegated duties to "social partners" (labor and business) and left the government's role ambiguous helped ease social conflict by parceling out pieces of power. In the late 1990s, however, policy analysts who know the 1940s and 1950s only from books confront rising costs, mounting evidence of excess and inefficiency, and chronic governmental anxiety over a "crisis of legitimacy" (Rodwin forthcoming: 12–13). Unsurprisingly, they wonder why sickness funds that have "neither the authority nor the financial incentive to manage their funds judiciously" (ibid.) should be the "administrative focal point" of a system in which government is the "decisional focal point" (Wilsford 1996: 235); why labor, which represents a declining portion of the French working population, should dominate the board of the largest sick fund; why business should be so slow to exert its purchaser leverage; why "budgeting, financing, quality assurance, and educational functions" should be dispersed among six different ministries (Fielding and Lancry 1993: 752), leaving policy to emerge from endless back-and-forth exchange among health, budget, and other officials; and why, in general, French health policy should be so pervasively *mal gérè* (badly managed).

The growth of health spending steadily encourages government intervention, but for critics the tentative character of the interventions highlights the lack of accountability in the system as a whole. The political virtues of an earlier day—pluralism, participation, and accommodation—conjure up the economic vices of the present and seem to demand infusions of efficiency, rationality, and systems thinking that transcend such traditional tools of budget regulation as negotiations and caps. The interplay of cost and knowledge, as contemplated by policy and budget makers who view the system's institutional inheritance as an artifact of ancient history, trigger a potent managerial imperative. The costs of fragmentation are high, the refinement of regulations is wearying, and the knowledge to rationalize the system lies at hand, so new structures and incentives must be devised to make stakeholders collaborate in "managing care."

In Europe, as in the United States, "managed care" covers a broad menu of interventions, from which nations choose according to their policy tastes. At the simplest end of the continuum, every society clamors for innovations that promise to improve the management of care by means of more and better information (Wiley 1992). Beyond "mere" information lies the limited manipulation of financial incentives within the status quo. France, for instance, has debated higher payments for physicians and consumers who enter into "gatekeeping" arrangements (Rodwin forthcoming: 16; Wilsford 1996: 254). A more stringent strategy empowers public purchasing agents (for example, British District Health Authorities and budget-holding general practitioners) to contract selectively with providers, favoring those who measure up on such criteria as price, quality, and responsiveness to consumer preferences (Klein 1995; Light 1997; Glennerster 1995).

At the farther frontier of managed care one finds managed competition, which beams its incentives at payers as well as providers. Consumers are induced to join health plans that contract selectively with providers who (like the plans themselves) must improve their performance on pain of losing market share. By its nature this approach applies most readily to systems with multiple sickness funds (unlike the system in the United Kingdom, whose area-based public purchasing agencies compete mainly in the quest for larger budget allocations from higher authorities in the National Health Service) and not all such systems find it appealing (France, for example). Other nations—the Netherlands, Germany, and Israel are leading cases in point—have studied managed competition carefully and their parliaments have passed ambitious legislation to try it out (Kirkman-Liff 1994; Schut 1995; U.S. GAO 1993; Chinitz 1995).

Although American boosters may interpret these cross-national doings as a dazzling display of diffusion of U.S. innovation, the most striking feature of the distribution of selections along the strategic continuum is the absence of the modal American approach to managed care, namely, unmanaged competition among managed care organizations of diverse age, origin, ownership, and organizational character. Although Europeans cheerfully embrace fuller information, sharper incentives, and even competition that drives providers and plans, they seem never to have imagined that such "reforms" could work in the absence of universal coverage, or for that matter, without aggregate budget limits on health spending (White 1995). Other nations expect efficiencies realized by means of competition to improve the allocation of resources within such limits, not substitute for them. In the European context, simply "encouraging HMOs" for the sake of their internal and competitive efficiencies, without detailed policy fine-tuning of their market setting, is too absurd to contemplate. Unlike the United States, European nations have in place the policy rules and institutional basics that give theories of managed care and competition a fair chance to develop into plausible practice. For them, the trick is less policy than politics.

New Policies, New Politics

In several very important particulars, managed care challenges norms and expectations long settled into European systems. Unlike the United States, comparable nations have for decades followed explicit policies aimed at containing health care costs, and these generally rely on budgetary regulation—structured negotiations between payers and providers, within state-set constraints, over the content, levels, and growth rates of fee schedules for physicians and prospective or per-unit payments to hospitals. Though this approach addresses part of the health cost equation—price—it leaves the other key ingredient—volume— largely off-limits to policy. This selective focus is far from accidental: By acceding to limits on (and negotiations over) their incomes, providers won from governments assurance that freedom of clinical practice would be respected and clinical micromanagement averted. Cost pressures and proliferating literature that documents (or alleges) substantial waste of care now trigger a near-universal temptation to break the old social compact with providers by pushing for policies that manage patterns of use, which is why, of course, U.S. flailings evoke such strong cross-national fascination. Economic encouragement, intellectual inspiration, and policy predispositions, do not, however, automatically ensure political success.

If managed care were solely an impulse driven by costs and an analytical hubris grounded in research, societies with well-working systems might well define it down to the least-challenging end of the continuum or trot out more audacious variants and then reject them as politically unworkable. To be sure, the mixed record of competitive reforms in the United Kingdom's National Health Service and the slow progress of managed competition in the Netherlands suggest that the reform glass may be less than half full, but the bigger picture indicates that the managerial imperative and its strategic expressions draw strength from a deep and powerful institutional development, namely, the atrophy of traditional political coalitions in the health sphere and the gradual consolidation of new ones. Innovative reconciliations of solidarity and efficiency that draw on fresh images of the requisites of equity and the promise of markets now challenge policy traditions in systems that American reformers are wont to cite as bedrocks of consensus and stability. These policy departures gain ground (unevenly yet persistently) because they not only express but also lubricate political agreements between the left and the right.

The new policy paradigm that purports to honor the managerial imperative rests on three central, interdependent strategic pillars (see also Chernichovsky 1995). The first is a redefinition of national health insurance to require uniform coverage of the entire population for a defined benefit package. For the Left, this modification in the terms of coverage corrects an egalitarian anomaly, that health insurance systems can be national yet less than universal in the terms that define membership in sickness funds. In Germany and the Netherlands, for example, compulsory health insurance applied to workers who earned less than a specified amount annually, while the wealthier had a broader range of coverage options. This disparity made plain enough sense in the days of old-style working class politics: Workers' parties and labor movements fought for new policy protections for society's most vulnerable members. In the 1990s, however, unions are no longer the heart and soul of labor parties, and the adjective "working class" means less and less when applied to consciousness, movements, politics, and policies.

In this different social setting, institutional customs long accepted as fair and proper have begun to evoke incredulity and contempt. In France, as noted above, apportioning governance of the health system among business and labor "social partners," which had allowed conflicting groups, classes, and parties to cooperate in expanding national health coverage, came to look like the essence of bad planning and management to a new generation of stakeholders, including young analysts in government ministries, struggling to shrink the public deficit, and the business leader who observed in an interview that "in 1945, France had to choose between Beveridge and Bismarck," and wondered whether the latter had been the better choice after all (interview with the author, July 1994). Such musings bore modest political fruit in 1996 when the government's plan to introduce a modicum of managed care survived a general strike that scuttled most of the broader economic package of which it was part (Wilsford 1996: 254).

In some nations, coalition shifts carry straight through to managed competition. In Israel, for instance, several government commissions met in the 1980s to ponder a means of weaning the Kupat Cholim Chalit (KHC), the major sickness fund, from its dominance by the Labor Federation and its dependence on government bailouts. Proposals for leveling the proverbial insurance playing field floated around, but none passed. In the early 1990s, support for reform ran high, but opposition by the Labor Federation and consequent vacillating within the Labor Party stalled action. In 1994 the logjam broke in flamboyant Israeli fashion: Haim Ramon, minister of health in the Labor government, publicly endorsed separation of the KHC from the Labor Federation, met opposition from predictable quarters, and responded by resigning his state post in order to run as a reform candidate for the secretary generalship of the Labor Federation itself. His victory signaled that the old networks linking the Labor Party, the KHC, the Federation, and parliament had largely unraveled and that reform could finally proceed (Chinitz 1995: 919–921).

Coalition dynamics produced different policy outcomes in different national settings, but in general, as their historical and cultural supports weakened, variations in national health coverage found less favor on the left. A fixed and explicit benefit package to which all citizens are entitled enhances equity and lets consumers see more clearly the content of the coverage to which they can lay claim. Uniformity of benefits also attracts the European right (which does not share the conviction of some American conservatives that citizens' health benefits should be defined solely by employers' willingness to pay). For one thing, at least in principle, a standard package permits more accurate estimation of health costs and budgets. For another, it is crucial for the creation of the "level playing field" on which fairly managed competition depends.

The second fundamental element of the new approach calls for free choice (by newly "standardized" citizens) among competing sickness funds. To the left, choice among plans helps replace class-based distinctions (such as occupation-based assignments to funds in Germany) with irreproachable universality. To the right, competition will oblige insurers to manage resources more efficiently, respond more readily to customer demands, and—a precondition of these objectives—control more closely the providers with whom they deal.

The third piece of the paradigm is capitation payment to the competing sickness funds, adjusted to reflect the risks of enrollees. Like the other elements, this stratagem appeals both to the left, which approves of payments that take explicit account of need (and thus reinforce solidarity) and deter that competitive Achilles' heel—preferred risk selection—and to the right, which believes that fixed global sums for sickness funds will compel them to compete "properly," that is, by delivering high quality care efficiently.

Although adherents of the left and right obviously differ, managed competition is a theme with many variations, and no simple paradigm of politics or policy fits all cases. Nonetheless, Schut's analysis of the "ingenious political compromise" contrived by health reformers in the Netherlands captures pretty well—mutatis mutandis, of course—tendencies that have grown "central":

> [T]he proposed reform had appealing aspects for all interest groups and political parties. The Christian Democrats were happy with the reconciliation of cost containment within the principles of social solidarity and subsidiarity. The Conservative Liberals were pleased with the idea of market competition and the dismissal of the planning model. The Social Democrats and the unions were content with national health insurance and the consequent removal of the class distinction between sickness funds and private health insurance. Health care providers enjoyed the prospect of eliminating detailed government planning. Sickness funds applauded the increased freedom and responsibilities. And private insurers were pleased with the opportunity to expand their market. (1995: 638)

Implementation and Implications

This image of managed and competitive medical services implies new roles for stakeholders. Insofar as the paradigm takes hold, consumers may find their traditional freedom to choose individual providers giving way to choice among competing health insurance plans. Providers, long accustomed to treating any willing patient as they deemed medically appropriate, may face closed panels, selective contracting, and closer clinical scrutiny. Sickness funds will no longer merely negotiate with providers, pay bills, and ask governments for subsidies but will also struggle to plan and manage care rendered by "their" providers. Governments will go on setting the rules of the game—defining the structure of negotiations, establishing frameworks for planning of facilities, and experimenting with diverse payment methods—but their tasks will expand dramatically.

Needless to say, these players are not obliged to honor the theoretical requisites of managed competition. Little is known in the United States or Europe about how consumers weigh prices, how far they can (or even try to) judge the quality of services, how much information of what types they seek and use, and how far loyalty to familiar funds and providers—or ignorance or inertia—shape shopping and switching in a competitive context. Under competitive scrutiny providers may work earnestly to perfect their practices, or they may send up blizzards of rhetoric, documents, and protocols that reveal less than they conceal from befogged monitors. Sickness funds and public-purchasing authorities may throw around their weighty new powers to contract selectively, or they may hesitate to disturb consumer expectations or to sever or strain long-standing ties to providers whose livelihoods are on the line (James 1995). Even assertive purchasers may lack the data, or the tools to make sense of them, needed to steer confidently along the new market byways. Nor is it clear that competitive reforms will save money. Donald Light observes that since turning to managed competition, the British have had to find "more and more funds to pay for more managers, more consultants, more data, more marketing, more consumer pressures, more consumer complaints, more underbudgeted areas, and more demands for high quality" (Light 1997: 334).

Governments will face especially bracing challenges because managed competition assigns to the state a wide range of roles that enter terra incognita—a point often overlooked by Americans who steadfastly refuse to manage the competition they celebrate. Defining a package of benefits is not simple if "basic" means that some salient services will be left out. Putting an accurate price on the basic package and updating price and package over time are taxing tasks. Services omitted from the basic list but available to those who can buy them privately raise equity issues and complaints that "reform" retracts with one hand the universalism it expands with the other. Cutting across all these conundrums is the progress of medical technology, the fruits of which must be assessed, priced, and regulated. Government ministries have little experience in ensuring that funds play fair—avoiding preferred risk selection, collusive pricing, and other anticompetitive practices—and have little clue about how to give consumers the information they (presumably) need. Setting risk-adjusted capitation payments that cover the costs of bad risks without rewarding bad management by plans is no small feat; current methods of risk adjustment are notoriously limited and frustrating (Van de Ven et al. 1994).

Administrative realities compound and confound these technical perplexities. Few officials in ministries of health have trained or practiced in these arcane spheres, and budget makers in ministries of finance may be slow to get with the new program. Health ministries can be magnets for aggressive leaders when the agency basks in the glow of imminent "reform," but once legislation passes and the fabled "hard choices" top the agenda, prime ministers may have trouble giving the top jobs away. These institutional lags and vacuums are the more ominous because in most nations the "progressive" course entails writing ambitious but ambiguous legislation, appointing various expert bodies to figure out what it means (or conceivably might have meant), and hoping that the details come out right. And, ironically, Europeans tantalized by theories of managed care and competition have usually given short shrift to U.S. literature on implementation as a rich and problematic set of processes worthy of sustained examination. Moving managed competition from legislation to implementation—not to mention understanding how the move works out—will entail hasty translations from economics into the exotic tongues of psychology, sociology, organizational analysis, and politics.

Managed care and competition may not deliver fully on their promises, but they are also unlikely to wreak harm and havoc on national health systems that (critics say) could have left well enough alone but instead have unwittingly put financial considerations above professionalism, solidarity, and equity. The erosion of legitimacy in systems that suffer high costs, contentious relations with providers, and growing doubts about the wisdom of patterns of use of services is not a small cost; reforms that may address these problems while dodging the excesses of unmanaged competition in the United States could yield major benefits. Careful observers of internal markets in the United Kingdom suggest that medical professionals have been not so much "disempowered" as obliged to revise and recapitalize their power around plausible answers to pointed (and overdue) questions about the merits of their practices (Light 1997; Klein 1995). Innovative accommodations between government and market, and between state and society, have come widely into vogue (Ruggie 1996), and for good reason: The distribution of power between "sectors" is not always best viewed as a zero-sum game. In health policy, the more one expects of the market, the more one must ask of government and (as the turn to internal markets and managed competition in Europe itself argues) vice versa. Finally, as Klein (1995: 313) remarks, risk-adjusted capitation payments may enhance equity, not impair it. Budget makers could cut payments to insurers who discourage poorer risks; conversely, properly designed payments can offer incentives to accept the least healthy patients. In short, it all depends on interplay among actors, fields, and forces still feeling their way. Abstract social philosophy no more foreordains the failure of these innovations than standard economic logic ensures their success.

American Exceptionalism?

Dissecting the cross-national diffusion of ideas that increasingly make the exceptional United States a source of reform "rules" is a subtle business. Contrary to familiar interpretations, American theories of managed care and competition are neither revelations that replace statist confusion with market enlightenment nor blinders that credulous foreigners have bought because they fell among evil companions. The key cross-national reform dynamic is the emergence of new political coalitions, dominated by new generations with fresh images of what solidarity, equity, efficiency, and markets mean, how they are interdependent, how government should address them, and how innovative syntheses of these elements can ease agreement between left and right. These reformist developments have rather little to do with American inspiration or instruction. Indeed reformers elsewhere recoil from the American prospect of sharper-edged market forces injected into a system lacking universal coverage and budget controls. This said, however, U.S. theories of managerial and market reform offer stimulus and encouragement, and an off-the-shelf vocabulary, for fertilizing strategies whose roots are firmly planted in native soil. To shift metaphors, American teachings are, in effect, the icing on a homemade cake.

In health affairs the United States would seem to be at once less eccentric and less inspirational than is sometimes supposed. Indeed, if new coalitions generate successful reforms abroad, cross-national health policy might in time come full circle as the exceptionalist United States learns from other nations how to design and implement health policy innovations made (but so far muddled) in America.

Notes

Conversations with David Chinitz, Philippe DuPrat, and Annetine Gelijns much improved this essay, as did comments by James Morone and Mark Peterson on an earlier draft.

Forecasting American Health Care: How We Got Here and Where We Might Be Going

Theodore R. Marmor

Introduction

Americans once lived in the glow of a Golden Age of Medicine. The two decades following World War II were ones of expansion and prosperity. American medicine was an emblem of the seemingly limitless capabilities for progress of the modern era. Federal programs generously aided medical research and hospital construction and helped build up the infrastructure of a highly technological system of medical services centered in schools of medicine and their affiliated institutions. With the assistance of federal aid and the growth of private health insurance, American hospitals and medical care became progressively more elaborate, sophisticated and, in the absence of countervailing pressures, inevitably more expensive.

How long ago that now seems. By the time of the oil crisis of 1973–74, complaints about the relentlessly increasing costs of medical care had become commonplace. Whether it was the effect on government finances of rising Medicare and Medicaid expenditures or the annual reports that (yet again) medical care inflation would outstrip the general inflation rate in the economy, the threat to American competitiveness caused by increased health insurance premiums or the risk of financial catastrophe faced by the uninsured—all became standard concerns from the 1970s to the early 1990s. Medical care in America came to be regarded as so costly and troubled that assertions of system crisis became increasingly routine in this period. With the profound changes of the 1990s, the topics of discussion have changed once again. Though we are living in the twilight of the earlier Golden Age, the changes during the 1990s in organizational form, the sources of power and regulation, and the very shifts in locus of medical authority have been nothing short of staggering (Kassirer 1997).[1] We have come from the blithe extravagance of the postwar era, with its fee-for-service arrangements that at worst overprovided and overcharged for medical care, to the more tightly regulated insurance plans of the 1990s—labeled "managed care"—that at worst profit by excessively constraining patient choices and physician judgments and incomes. The memory of the period of crisis talk and reform stalemate—from roughly 1970 to 1990—has for a time been suppressed by the magnitude of changes in the regulation of American medical practices by the recently invigorated private payers (Ginzberg and Ostow 1977). Given such a disjuncture, the impulse to try to chart the future is practically irresistible. Hence, the request of this book's editor to discuss how we got here and where we might be going.

A short digression on futurology

Efforts to anticipate the future are ubiquitous—across time, space, and culture. The purposes that motivate predictive efforts are highly varied. For some, the point of forecasting the future is to change it. To imagine what the world might be like is to imagine ways to alter it. Sometimes, this takes the form of jeremiads, honest laments about what, in the absence of determined reform effort, the years to come will be like. For others, futurology is more a weapon in policy warfare. Used that way, predictions easily transform the desirable into the inevitable, as, for example, when proponents claim that the recent expansion of managed care indicates both its inevitable predominance and its unquestioned desirability. Likewise, the undesirable can just as easily be converted into the infeasible, as was the case, for example, for opponents of Canadian national health insurance during the American health reform debates of 1992–93 (Marmor 1994: chap. 12). This sort of manipulative futurology is rhetoric dressed up as social science.

There is, however, a more restrained form of futurology. It is simply a form of conditional causal analysis, an exploration of alternative scenarios. Such work can suggest paths of change and stability that a given configuration of forces are likely to produce. In that sense it is applied social science, done prospectively rather than retrospectively.

This essay is an effort of this latter type. Its topic is how to think about the likely shape of American medical care in the first decades of the twenty-first century. I begin, however, by setting the stage, reminding readers of the enormous changes in American medicine in the half century since the end of World War II. I go on to revisit an exercise in conditional forecasting that Paul Starr and I presented in 1980. We were asked then to try to anticipate what American medical care would be like a decade and a half later, in 1995. We devoted an entire essay to what we called the "trends in progress" and linked them to four possible combinations of political and economic settings. After reviewing (and seeing the weaknesses of) that earlier forecasting effort, the present essay takes up the challenge of anticipating some plausible medical futures in the America of the early twenty-first century.

The most common vice in futurology is simple extrapolation. All of us know all too many failures of even the most sophisticated economic and demographic forecasts to think we can accurately anticipate the structure of institutions and practices even a few years hence. As one economist put it bluntly once, his disciplinary colleagues were able to predict nine of the last three recessions. Why go on with such a difficult task, one might well ask. To do so plausibly means, to my mind, sharply distinguishing between point predictions and conditional forecasts. Point predictions are estimates of what precisely will be the case at some time in the future. Statements like "The United States will/will not have universal health insurance in 2005" illustrate the type. By *conditional* forecasting, I mean statements of the form, "There is high probability that the United States will have universal health insurance if, in the first decade of the twenty-first century, it has a Congress with substantial majorities of liberal Democrats and a combination of low unemployment and a reasonable growth rate of the economy." If the conditions obtain, the forecast seems very similar to a point prediction. But what the conditional mode emphasizes is the substantial uncertainty we necessarily have about the future. We can neither be sure whether a particular configuration will emerge nor can we anticipate how factors outside our present field will come into play. Put this way, conditional futurology (which can be helpful) seems far more sensible than confident extrapolation and point predictions (which are almost sure to be wrong), even though there are plenty of the latter attempts in the seminar and board rooms of modern life.

American Medicine in the Period after World War II: An Overview

American medicine after World War II was, as noted above, a golden age for most medical professionals and many of their patients. For two decades, health expansionism proceeded without a major change in the government's role in financing care. But in the mid-1960s that transformation took place not only in the enactment of Medicare and Medicaid in 1965, but also in the adoption of programs to increase the number of physicians, to set up community mental health centers and other neighborhood clinics, and in a variety of programs to redress class and racial inequities. In the late 1960s, extending into the 1970s, there were massive legal efforts to change both the conditions of work and environmental conditions.

Looking back on the 1970s from the perspective of the 1990s, the striking feature is discontinuity. The economic environment of the early 1970s was a stunningly disappointing reversal of sustained postwar growth. "Stagflation" ushered in an era of fiscal strain, dampened expectations for social amelioration, and, in many instances, generated efforts to cut back if not do away with the reform programs and aspirations of the earlier period. In the 1980s there were virtually no major efforts in national politics to extend the coverage of health insurance to all Americans or to transform the fundamental rules of American medicine. But, in the early 1990s, such an effort was made with dramatic flourish in the Clinton Administration's proposed Health Security Bill.

This is not the place to offer an extensive description or appraisal of this unusual episode in medical politics, already certain to become one of the most cited controversies in postwar American politics (Hacker 1997). For present purposes, one might simply say that during the 1992–94 period Americans witnessed a process of "choice without change": a massive amount of public discussion of what might be changed that ended in congressional stalemate by September 1994. On the other hand, what ensued through the rest of the decade could rightly be termed "change without choice." That context—the aftermath of the Clinton reform stalemate—will be the starting point of this essay's futurology. But we will first review the core elements of the forecasts for 1995 made in the 1980s.

Trends and Forecasts: 1995 As Seen from the Vantage Point of 1980

The forecasting question Paul Starr and I first asked in 1980 was deceptively simple: "What types of changes may we expect to see in the next fifteen years?" But we approached that question with a number of qualifications in mind. We knew that the trends in progress were but the starting point, and stressed that forecasting trends "falls short of predicting the future." We emphasized that besides the trends, which could well change, there were "major unpredictable contingencies." And that meant we had to examine "several possible alternative scenarios under varying political and economic conditions" (Starr and Marmor 1984).[2]

And that is precisely what we did. As background to our scenarios, we cited three trends in progress in the early 1980s: the demographic, professional, and organizational developments that would affect the conflicts over cost control and access to care. We noted then that the anticipated aging of the population would increase the inflationary pressures already at work in American medicine; we emphasized that the increased number of women physicians had the potential to change the professional culture of medicine in the direction of more primary care and more caring; and we highlighted the variable impact of increasing numbers of physicians, suggesting that the result depended on whether the greater supply of doctors took place in traditional fee-for-service settings or in the newly emerging forms of so-called organized care. In fact, we emphasized the institutional consolidation of American medicine and predicted then that it would continue over the two decades. Beyond that, we called attention to what was obvious to most observers of American medical care in the early 1980s: namely, that the inflationary pressures everywhere in the system also left a large proportion of the population either uninsured or underinsured.

In our thinking about scenarios we concentrated on two sources of major influence on medical care—the political and economic context. Growth or stagnation provided two economic options; liberal or conservative political auspices provided the two political possibilities. Combined, of course, that produced a fourfold set of possible determinants of the future states of American medical care.

First we asked what medical austerity would look like overseen by a regime that believed in government efficiency. The tendency under such circumstances, we thought, would be to move toward a more centrally budgeted system along the lines of the British model, although it would surely stop short of a national health service. The great advantage of this system would have been the controlling of costs by introducing a single national budget for medical care and eliminating the inflationary incentives of fee-for-service by paying practitioners on a capitation basis. This model offered the greatest possibility of controlling costs while pursuing the traditional liberal objectives of social equality and public health. Forecasted in 1980, this combination of factors obviously did not come to pass. But that did not make asking the question useless. Indeed, it highlighted what was a low probability future.

Our second question was this: What would happen should a conservative political coalition preside in a time of economic and medical austerity? We claimed to know then that American liberals seek to control costs while bolstering equality, and that American conservatives seek to control costs while limiting state control and preserving the prerogative of private enterprise. For many conservatives, the most attractive reforms involve the suppression of demand through greater patient cost sharing and greater business supervision of (and participation in) management and decision making in the medical care industry.

This scenario of austerity and conservative prominence comes close to characterizing what happened in the early 1980s. The Reagan administration came into office in a time of great economic unrest. It ushered in an era of celebrating "competition" in medicine, getting government off the industry's back, and letting the fresh air of deregulation solve the problems of access, cost, and quality. This picture captured the ideological direction that debates over American medicine took in most of the 1980s—dropping the political agenda of universal health insurance, dismantling some of the regulatory programs assembled in the 1970s. But it is worth remembering the gap between the pro-competition public rhetoric and the reality of efforts to control the government's Medicare and Medicaid costs by administering prices for hospitals through DRGs and the steady development of tougher fee schedules for physicians.

Medical austerity, however, was but one economic future. We also considered the possibility that a return to relative affluence and rapid economic growth could reduce the clamor for cost controls. In that situation, medical care's future might, we anticipated, shift focus from how to control costs to how to respond to demands for broader and more secure health insurance coverage.

From the perspective of the early 1980s, we presumed that such an economy would produce very different results under liberal or conservative auspices. Had Democratic liberals presided over an expanding economy, we anticipated that its inclination in health policy would most likely have been a move in the direction of the Canadian system of government health insurance. In a sense, that would have meant resuming the course of development that began in the 1960s with Medicare, a national health insurance system for America's retired designed by liberal reformers. Cost controls under the Canadian option are less centralized than under the British model. And had the United States followed the Canadian model, American medical professionals would have retained greater autonomy, and fee-for-service would have continued for those physicians who preferred it. There was also the possibility of universal coverage accompanied by increased social investment for prevention. These policies, we suggested, might have drawn support from the reform elements within the medical professions, and expanded that class at the same time.

What transpired in the mid-eighties was a brief return to prosperity, presided over by conservative presidential leadership—a version of our fourth possible scenario. Our prediction was this: Were conservatives to lead a period of renewed economic growth, their inclination would be either to celebrate the status quo, or possibly to introduce reforms along the lines of the German model. The German system provides for near-universal health insurance, but under nongovernmental management and public regulation. Many conservative health insurance proposals in America during the late 1980s and early 1990s actually assumed this orientation, though in varying forms. Such an approach, in one sense, would have rounded out America's private health insurance system, just as the Canadian option would have rounded out our public system.

Such was the world as it appeared to two analysts of health policy and politics in the early 1980s. Our temptation then was to predict that a conservative ideological orientation would dominate policy debates for some years. But just the opposite prediction would have been made in 1946 or 1966—and in both cases would have turned out to be quite wrong. So we ended our forecasting exercise by emphasizing the uncertainty about what configuration of forces would prevail by 1995.

How successful was our forecasting in light of what actually transpired? Did the structure of our analysis hold up even if the precise forecasts differed from the historical record in detail. Or did we miss both what happened and why? If so, the outcome has obvious implications for looking forward.

A retrospective analysis of the earlier forecasts

The description of trends in progress during the early 1980s was the least demanding task, one should admit candidly. But the earlier essay was especially accurate in anticipating a continuation of the trend toward consolidation in American medical institutions. On questions of magnitude, the forecasts were sensible about the ambiguity of the effects of increased physician supply on costs. The increased use of market power to constrain physician practices and incomes—while anticipated as a possible outgrowth of HMO expansion—has proven in the 1990s to be far more dramatic than we anticipated. Finally, on trends, we identified the changing position of women in medicine as a potentially profound development, but had no clear idea then about how much the occupational socialization and professional practices would shape female professionals rather than the other way around. Still, the setting out of trends in progress seems on balance, to this self-interested reviewer at least, as a helpful starting point for someone in the early 1980s thinking about the future of American medicine fifteen years hence.

It might be useful to remember what the less restrained extrapolators had been predicting throughout the mid to late 1970s. The growth of national and regional hospital chains prompted some to anticipate a simple takeover in due course of the community nonprofit hospital by such chains—whether for profit or not. In that period, Hospital Corporation of America and Humana were the rage in the investment community. For others, especially the advocates of reform who stressed vertical and horizontal integration as the panacea for inefficiency in American medicine, the future was going to one of far-reaching consolidation. As Paul Ellwood repeatedly predicted in the 1970s, American medicine would be dominated by six or seven national firms, vertically integrated from insurance to tertiary care. It was a vision of competing giants, massive firms on the scale of MCI, Sprint, or NYNEX, serving national customers a menu of health services. Needless to say, vertical integration of this sort is not the kind of consolidation that became dominant in the 1990s. Humana, for example, unsuccessfully tried this course of action and pulled back into the delivery of hospital and related services. Hospital Corporation of America (HCA) went through its own turbulent growth, merged with the expansionary Columbia system, and in 1997, found itself in enormous economic and legal difficulties. In short, the futuristic vision of huge vertically integrated firms is an object lesson in the limits of extrapolation.

The next issue, quite obviously, is whether our fourfold presentation of possible futures proved helpful. Here, the picture is considerably more mixed. The combination of economic austerity and liberal Democratic political control did not come to pass. Likewise, there was in the Reagan and Bush years no obvious combination of conservative political domination and either recession or a spurt of growth. To be sure, there was Republican control of the White House but, at least over any sustained period, there was not a corresponding unified party control of Congress. There was enormous economic dislocation in the early 1980s, to be sure, and there was improvement of this in the latter part of the decade, but never a transformative political coalition of the right or the left. So, we were more simple-minded about political auspices than we should have been. Unified national government has turned out to be the rare American circumstance in the postwar period. By that I mean periods of ideological and partisan compatibility between the president and the majority of both houses of Congress, circumstances like 1964, when President Johnson won in a landslide and had an overwhelming majority of like-minded Democrats in the Congress to enact much of his agenda. President Reagan, by contrast, had a Democratic Congress for most of his tenure and, though he was able to push through important tax and spending changes in the early 1980s, there were, as we only partly anticipated under the predictive scenario, no major transformations of either private medicine or the public programs like Medicare and Medicaid.

The remaining option was liberal political control amidst a buoyant economy: That never happened. A fusion of the economic circumstances of 1994–97 with the agenda of the campaign Clinton ran in 1992 might have justified this description. But the Clinton presidency, unlike the campaign for it, cannot plausibly be described as liberal. Moreover, the overall political circumstances of the 1990s, like those of the 1980s, were ones of mixed government. American politics were not stalemated on all issues by any means, but hedged in by fundamental differences enough to make major reform in health care highly unlikely. What remains, then, are the limits of our fourfold conception of possible contexts in American politics. While illuminating as a set of possibilities, it missed what turned out to be the political reality for most of the period. That context was one of oscillation from mixed government without an ideological domination of liberals or conservatives or, as in 1994–96, a sharp shift in the ideological composition of the Congress that did not bring with it either the capitulation of the Democratic president or the election of a Republican president in 1996. So far, then, there is much to be said for the importance of unanticipated events (and contexts), a reminder we acknowledged in the original article but which was not emphasized enough in our conditional predictions.

Looking Forward: A Possible Forecast of the First Decades of the Twenty-first Century

The preceding discussion should be enough to make even the most confident prognosticator hesitant. And, indeed, that is precisely what has happened in the course of revising this essay for publication. My conclusions about futurology in 1997 turned out to be even more skeptical than what we expressed in 1984. Conditional forecasting still is surely better than simple extrapolation. But neither is able to deal with the enormous uncertainty that remains about the configuration of economic circumstance, political setting, and unexpected events and actions. What then is to be said?

The case against simple extrapolation remains valid and is all the more worth reviewing because it is both rampant and seductive. One continues to observe the widespread tendency to take the present as the basis for anticipating what will be. Moreover, in the face of uncertainty, there is an understandable human tendency to follow the lead of those who claim they have expertise that justifies their speaking assertively about the future. Sensible futurology continues to require a critique of unjustified extrapolation and its accompanying rhetoric.

Looking toward the twenty-first century:
misleading images, possible futures

Three developments in the 1990s have had a profound (and misleading) effect on the discussion of American medicine and its future. One is the spread of what is conventionally called managed care. A second is the growth in appeals to global economic developments as guides to medicine's future. And the third one to which I want to draw attention is the appeal to managerial theory and jargon—from "integrated delivery systems" to information systems to organizational consolidation—as sources of resolution for the tensions in modern medical care. Each development has its extrapolators and many of the extrapolators regard their projected future with the enthusiasm purveyors of panaceas regularly effuse.

Managed care enjoyed a marketing boom in the first half of the 1990s. Although the Clinton health reform collapsed in 1994, audiences have been repeatedly (and rightly) told that change in American medicine has taken place at a breathtaking pace ever since. Managed care—the world of medical networks, competing plans, and complex choices—has shaken up the medical lives of Americans to a degree and in ways that no one predicted even a few years ago. According to promoters, these changes promise major benefits in getting more value per dollar in the American medical care industry.

But what is one to make of these claims about managed care? One 1997 article, entitled "The New Dominance of Managed Care: Insurance Trends in the 1990s," illustrates the ambiguity about what is actually going on (Jensen, Morrisey, Gaffney, and Liston 1997). "Managed care isn't coming," the authors rhetorically emphasize, "it has arrived" (ibid.: 125). One might reasonably ask, however, what precisely does "it" refer to? And beyond that, does it make any meaningful sense to describe the referents as managed care? The survey ignores any conceptual discussion of what is meant by "managed care." Instead, it simply announces that nearly three-quarters of U.S. workers with health insurance now receive their coverage through a health maintenance organization (HMO), a preferred provider organization (PPO), or a point-of-service plan (126)—and all of these are labeled managed care plans. In fact, what has arrived without a doubt are these new corporate forms of health finance organizations. But adding the expression *managed care* tells us nothing additional about who manages what or how. Moreover, the understanding of these developments is blocked, not enhanced, by the connotations of this term. For the trends actually described by the article show not managerial innovations so much as convergence in benefit structure and patient cost sharing among these "insurance products."

This survey also illustrates the dramatic changes in the very language used to describe American medical care. Increasingly, that language reflects the conventions of American corporate life, not those of either traditional physicians or biomedical scientists. Sometimes Madison Avenue exaggeration accompanies the antigovernment rhetoric of free markets and beneficent competition. This style of discourse is nicely illustrated by the chief executive of the Cigna Insurance Company at a 1995 conference on health care. Reform at the national level failed, Mr. Larry English claimed, but there was nevertheless an extraordinary "revolution" under way in American medicine. Market-based change would transform the medical cottage industry of the past into a competitive, cost-effective marvel of the future. Indeed, the free market would be the "toughest" regulator and would produce "better care and lower costs," Mr. English concluded, if only allowed to do so with minimal government interference (Marmor and Mashaw 1995). Cigna, like Aetna, he said, would be in the forefront of change as managed care firms, not health insurance companies.

Managed care is an expression that implies both competence and concern. It epitomizes the use of persuasive definitions in the new language of corporate medical care. Managed care in practice mostly has meant cutting back on payment levels, medical choices, and covered services, sometimes wisely, sometimes not. It has been largely the "managing" of costs, not the micromanaging of care. None of the developments in PPOs, HMOs, or POSs noted in the 1997 survey emphasize the management of care, the finding of new modes of organizing services, or different ways of motivating providers or patients to improve their health. Heralded in 1995, questioned increasingly in 1996 and after, the short-term future of these organizations involves regulatory battles in the states about what can and can not be rationed by the policies of private firms.

The shift in language fashions has truly been extraordinary. Marketing firms generate cute but misleading labels for health firms to catch the eye of potential enrollees. So, for example, we find a health maintenance organization called Maxicare, when the obvious incentives of such organizations are to restrain rather than "maximize" the use of medical services. The labels now come from a remarkably different set of sources than we appreciated in the early 1980s. This is obvious in the case of medical care quality. Executives of insurance firms advertise the wonders of "medical report cards" that claim to sort out the good from the bad among hospitals and doctors.

Orwellian doublespeak and the exaggerations of American management commentators are hardly new to American audiences. Numerous management theories have been developed, marketed, applied, and then abandoned as ways to deal with familiar problems in the organization of medical care provision. Two decades ago, HMOs were celebrated as the antidote to fee-for-service's inflationary pressures. Decentralization was in vogue for a time, as were health-planning agencies, to decide what was needed medically in local areas. More recently, management fashions have shifted to "total quality management," "integrated delivery systems," and the promise of the "information age." Some years big is better and the emphasis is on synergy, economies of scale, coordinated or unified central management. A few years later, small is beautiful: downsizing, decentralization, and divestiture become the buzzwords of management strategy. At the time of this writing (1997), there is again considerable emphasis on "consolidation," shifts from nonprofit to for-profit forms, and management by performance measures.

These slogans are less for the broad public than for other managers, the ones who decide which health plans their employees can join. What we have is the language of Madison Avenue linked to the managerial jargon of American business schools. And just as the rhetoric of fee-for-service medicine obscured the dangers of overproviding and overcharging for medical care in earlier periods, so does managerial medicine mask the dangers of its key features: bureaucratic and financial constraints on patient choice and physician judgment, and consequent loss of professional morale and patient trust.

The difficulty with sloganeering lies not only in increasing the likelihood of future disappointments but also in the confusion that the language of marketing can sow if not seen for what is. (The same sloganeering can arise from public sources, too.)[3] There could be, of course, a very substantial but unintended consequence. Over time, the gap between what Americans expect and what they experience could become a catalyst of change. More Americans may come to reject medical care being marketed to them in attractive terms if and when they experience troublesome realities behind the advertising hype. The complexities of choosing health plans amid the jumble of competing claims has already provoked demands for simpler and more protected choices. Indeed, the fears generated by the changes of the 1990s may well be impetus for pushing health care back toward the top of the nation's political agenda within a very short period. But it will take political sponsorship to do so. The underlying pressures are already present in the widespread critiques of the recent changes in the rules of American medicine. Yet, the frustrations that the initial Clinton campaign on health reform brought out had been present for years before any presidential candidate was able to give it vigorous expression. As John Kingdon emphasized years ago, large changes in public policy occur when there is a convergence of special opportunities, accepted problems, and available policy responses (Kingdon 1984).

Alledged worldwide developments as the future's predictors

A second source of confusion and futuristic overconfidence is the increased appeal to international experience as a guide to the future. It is impossible, as Rudolf Klein noted, to escape the "bombardment of information about what is happening in other countries" (Klein 1997). But there is an extraordinary gap between the magnitude of the information flows and the capacity to interpret or learn useful lessons from it. Indeed, I suspect that the speed of communication about developments abroad has actually reduced the likelihood of credible cross-national learning. There is little doubt about the salience of health policy on the public agenda of each of our nations—and indeed, of most industrial democracies. The puzzle is not whether there is such widespread interest in health policy, but why now. And why has international evidence (arguments, claims, caricatures) seemed more prominent in this period of "reform" than, say, during the fiscal strains of the early 1970s?

There is a simple answer to this question: Medical care policy has come to the forefront of public agendas for quite obvious reasons. First, the financing of personal medical care has everywhere become a major financial component of the budgets of mature welfare states, and when fiscal strain arises—especially from prolonged recession—policy scrutiny is the predictable result. Second, mature welfare states come under almost all circumstances to have less capacity for bold fiscal expansion in new areas. This means managing existing programs has necessarily assumed a larger share of the public agenda. Thirdly, there has been what might be termed the wearing out (perhaps wearing down) of the postwar consensus about the welfare state. By that I mean the effects of more than two decades of fretting about the affordability, desirability, and governability of the welfare state.

Begun in earnest during the 1973–74 oil shock, sustained by stagflation, and bolstered by electoral victories of parties opposed to welfare state expansion, critics assumed bolder postures and the public came increasingly to hear challenges to programs that had for decades seemed sancrosanct. From Mulroney to Thatcher, from New Zealand to the Netherlands, the message of necessary change was heard. Accordingly, when economic strain reappears, the inner rim of programmatic protection—not interest group commitment, but social faith—is weaker and the incentive to explore transformative but not fiscally burdensome options becomes relatively stronger, of the international pattern of welfare state review—including health policy—over the past decade. And further, times of policy change sharply increase the demand for new ideas, or at least new means to old ends.

Yet as Klein reminds us, policy learning in practice is not so much about transferring ideas as adapting them to local circumstances. It is that central fact that makes so unrealistic the efforts of institutions like the World Bank (World Bank 1993) to promote all-purpose models of health policy supposedly applicable to all countries. Worldwide "forces" may well be at work, but the shape of American medical care (or that of any other nation) cannot be deduced from them. The very "process of naturalizing foreign experience," Klein (1977) notes, tends also to transform it into forms that are suitable for the national environment. The vocabulary may be international, but the "way in which [ideas are] translated into policy remains national."[4]

Management technique is not a panacea

The proliferation of management techniques is the third trend in progress that prompts misleading extrapolation and misplaced confidence. As we operate in a world often characterized by management rhetoric and enthusiasm for market competition, we would be wise to remember the remarkably cyclical history of such enthusiasms. The heralded initiatives of one era regularly have given way to the enthusiasms of the next. It is worth recalling that almost every management innovation of the last half century launched itself with high hopes and inflated rhetoric only to be abandoned later without much admitted regret. Better understanding of why the world of management commentary produces such cycles of enthusiasm followed by declarations of failure will probably never prevent the distribution of the managerial equivalent of snake oil. But some realism about what management can and cannot accomplish might guard against the more unrealistic predictions of innovation and also help moderate disappointment that good management can not and will not rid societies of their medical care problems.[5]

There is great danger in believing that managerial techniques are the equivalent of solutions. The point here is quite simple. The issue of good management is not what slogan medical administrators decide to proselytize but how well managers balance the demands prompted by the multiple purposes of health institutions. The demands of institutions like hospitals and clinics are contradictory and shifting. They have multiple tasks that require different organizational structures and techniques—in short, different managerial approaches. Furthermore, managerial technique is intimately related to the existence of multiple objectives: Every upside has a downside. As we confront the private regulations managed care organizations employ, we should reflect not only on what may be lost as well as gained, but also on the countervailing reactions that will be increasingly provoked. Whether the technique is preapproval for specialist care or hospitalization, or movement to a staff-model HMO for providing services, medical organizations in the 1990s have increasingly concentrated on eliminating unnecessary physician-patient encounter, diagnostic procedures, surgical interventions, and pharmaceutical prescriptions. The bureaucratic routines necessary for these activities may well control costs to some firms, but the losses of patient and physician autonomy, control over quality, and profit-driven innovation are significant and already provoking countervailing pressures.

Deeply embedded in managerial theory is the ambivalence concerning the efficacy of technological versus cultural solutions to organizational problems. Ever since "Taylorism" provoked a reaction based on that particular model's desire to treat people and machines as interchangeable, theorists have oscillated between recommendations based on structures, processes, and technologies and those based on learning, motivation, and culture. One cannot sensibly decide which managerial strategy to believe in because both work some of the time, but not all of the time.

The same is true in the reorganization of America's medical care system. It is hard to believe that a cultural approach will be attractive from the standpoint of cost containment. Cost control in practice is about information systems, statistical testing, and economic rewards for scientifically determining what works or what is cost effective. On the other hand, in a medical world increasingly dominated by large organizations, Americans are likely to want to retain the cultural vision of Marcus Welby—doctor, counselor, friend. Demands will continue for some internal structures that emphasize professional autonomy, team effort, group responsibility for care, and patient involvement in an overall culture of "wellness." Our managerial arrangements may work at cross-purposes—

the technocracy of cost containment confronting the professional culture of patient care. The trick of good management, in the future as in the past, will be to balance these perspectives in ways that cope with our conflicting purposes and inconsistent desires. And as Deborah Stone and Gary Belkin emphasize in their chapters, there is a terrific tension for physicians between their role as professionals giving care without regard to financial considerations, and demands that they be businesslike in considering both economic and medical issues in their decisions.

Preparing for the multiple futures

How then should the sensible prognosticator proceed? Can we assess how broader currents of change in American society impinge on the trends in progress *within* medicine. Can we predict what types of change, external to medicine, one could expect to see over the next decade or so?

Our temptation in 1980 was to predict that conservative ideology would dominate policy debates for the foreseeable future. The same was true for many soothsayers in 1994. But, as already mentioned, just the opposite ideological prediction would have been made in 1946 or 1966, and in both cases would have turned out to be quite wrong. Moreover, the scenarios we projected earlier also failed to anticipate the major reform actions of the period: both the ambitious, but stalemated Clinton proposal and the dramatic increase in nongovernmental reform. It follows then that very hesitant anticipation is all one can reasonably assume. The medical world of the next decade is strikingly uncertain, one for which a remarkable number of futures could plausibly be forecasted and defended. Simple extrapolation into the future based on recent history has already been shown to be misguided (Ginzberg and Ostow 1997). Instead, we have to be prepared for a multiplicity of different futures.

Conclusion: The Medical World of the Next Decade Is Uncertain

The first requirement, then, is to imagine what those multiple futures might be. The second is to sort out what these possible futures mean both for analysts of American medical care and those responsible for health institutions.

Will governmental health reform disappear from the national agenda? That seems unlikely under almost any combination of political and economic circumstances. But while the changes of the 1990s have made certain that regulatory issues will continue to arise in both the Congress and the states, the direction of their political resolution is by no means clear. National stalemate could easily coexist with radical state reforms.

Would a continuation of economic growth into the next century dramatically alter my predictive hesitancy? Here, the answer for the end of the century is very different from what seemed plausible amid the economic strains of the early 1980s. The context of national politics appears transformed by the commitment to balanced budgets over the foreseeable future. Just as the fiscal requirements of the European Monetary Union constrain national governments from Britain to Belgium and from Spain to Sweden, so do the terms of the 1997 budget agreement restrict the ambitions of any new American administration. It is of course possible that growth will prove so dynamic that the budget deal will not be the straitjacket it now appears. But that in turn is highly improbable.

The picture of the future in 1997 is one of turbulence, hard-to-chart adjustments, and little prospect of dramatic policy reform. Even if the economy grows at a healthy rate, the fiscal constraints will most likely remain. There is little reason to expect a major departure from the pattern of divided government we have seen for most of the period after World War II. That does not mean stasis in policy. Rather, it means that dramatic, transformative shifts constitute a lower probability than marginal adjustments. By "marginal adjustments" I mean changes in the rules of Medicare that began in the summer of 1997, or continued restrictions on the autonomy of health care plans, and incremental increases in who is covered by Medicare or Medicaid. Modest changes over time can, of course, add up to transformations. And there is no denying the possibility of situational factors—of leadership, context, and happenstance— that could end up in large programmatic changes. There is a good case for claiming that American political processes exhibit both "incrementalism and rapid policy change" (Hacker 1997). For a very wide range of policies, there "are long periods of stability in public policy understandings punctuated by short periods of when dramatic changes take place" (Baumgartner and Jones 1993). Scholars should be able to anticipate ideological inclinations, but the conditions that prompt dramatic change do not appear predictable.

The implications of such futuristic caution are very different, however, for those practicing in the institutions of American medical care. With such great uncertainty about what the future might bring, the sensible posture seems quite clear: Whatever the immediate pressures, act to the extent possible on the basis of core medical values that could be defended in quite varied contexts.

By core values in medicine, I mean the following: (a) the use of least cost means to arrive at any given medical effect; (b) the use of ability to benefit as a rationing device, where necessary, rather than ability or willingness to pay or some other nonmedical criterion; (c) determined effort to avoid doing harm in the interests of institutional fame, research experimentation, and organizational marketing; and more generally, (d) applying not only the cost effectiveness test of (a), but using in a commonsensical way the benefit-cost test for selecting what to do and to whom. In practice, that means not only avoiding sheer waste (activities with no known benefit) and fraud (seeking payment for tasks not done), both of which may be lucrative but wrong. It also means encouraging the doing of more important things first and of less important things second or not at all.

The prudent and resourceful reformer faces other imperatives under the conditions of uncertainty we have highlighted. Every method of payment, oversight, and sanctioning has the vice of its virtues. The virtuous and successful agent of change, accordingly, would attend to the inherent vices of any system of financing or provision. Consider, for illustrative purposes, the medical executive facing both fee-for-service and capitation methods of reimbursement for different client groups. Prudence requires anticipating that fee-for-service payment prompts overprovision and capitation the opposite. Institutional review, then, should anticipate the risks of both dangers. Institutional prudence suggests having salaried physicians overseeing patterns of care provided under fee-for-service terms and fee-for-service physicians monitoring the patterns or care given capitated patients. These suggestions, quite obviously just examples, are nonetheless the opposite of trying to maximize financial gain under differing systems of finance and provision.[6]

From this perspective, managed care initiatives already underway should be evaluated, and where possible restructured, to pursue these core medical values. The emphasis on assuring cost effective care should surely continue. But the administrative hassles, attempts at cost shifting, and other impediments to quality care that many in the medical care community associate with the managed care movement will continue to be challenged. In short, the institutions that call themselves managed care plans will be charged with living up to their promises of sensible and effective care—care that upgrades the average quality now available for most patients. The managers who achieve these goals will flourish under any set of assumptions.

The reform struggles of the 1990s have been and will continue to be substantively complex, politically conflictual, and conceptually befuddling (Ginzberg and Ostow 1997). Health care is in an ever-changing state, driven in the mid-1990s by the frenzy of large scale mergers and acquisitions, like that of US Healthcare and Aetna. But the very market forces that produced such turbulence will unsettle the deals struck. And the task of anticipating the future of American medical care will become even harder than it was in past decades.

Notes

1 For a short but helpful summary of those changes in the 1990s, see J. P. Kassirer 1997.

2 See Starr and Marmor 1984. This chapter in *The End of Illusion* was first written in 1980 and edited and revised in 1983.

3 The expression *managed competition* was so much in vogue after Clinton's use of the tag late in the presidential campaign that one speaker at the January 1993 retreat for congressional staff members said, "I don't know what we are going to do, but whatever it is, we'll call it managed competition." See Marmor 1994, chap. 1.

4 The case of competition in health care—what Klein calls the "new master idea sweeping the globe"—illustrates his point well. "The meaning given to [competition] . . . has been very different in the various countries that have seemingly embraced it" (Klein 1997).

5 One reader wondered why management fads rise and fall so dynamically. With powerful interests backing particular notions, why do these interests not settle on a formulation that serves their purposes and stick with it? The short answer to this question is simple: The changing fortunes of firms in turbulent times, whatever the cause, require continually changing explanations. Moreover, to the extent that new ideas play a motivating role in organizations, the incentives to acquire ever new ones does not decline.

6 The institutional forms this sort of anticipatory management might take are quite varied. One would be to encourage state regulators to make use of contrasting expertise in their oversight. Another would be for organizations to plan explicitly in their advisory boards for different sources of expertise. The backlash against the practices of health plans in the mid-1990s has already sparked public relations responses, exemplified by the initiative of the American Association of Health Plans' "Putting Patients First" (Kassirer 1997). What prompts such reactions could prompt as well more far-reaching policy adjustments.

Bibliography

Aaron, H. J. 1994. Distinguished Lecture on Economics in Government: Public Policy, Values, and Consciousness. *Journal of Economic Perspectives* 8(2):3–21.

Aaron, H. J., and R. D. Reischauer. 1995. The Medicare Reform Debate: What Is the Next Step? *Health Affairs* 14(4):8–30.

Abel-Smith, B. 1985. Who Is the Odd Man Out: The Experience of Western Europe in Containing the Costs of Health Care. *Milbank Quarterly* 63:1–17.

———. 1992. Cost Containment and New Priorities in the European Community. *Milbank Quarterly* 70:393–416.

Abel-Smith, B., and E. Mossialos. 1994. Cost Containment and Health Care Reform: A Study of the European Union. *Health Policy* 28:89–132.

Aberbach, J. D., R. D. Putnam, and B. A. Rockman. 1981. *Bureaucrats and Politicians in Western Democracies.* Cambridge: Harvard University Press.

Akerlof, G. A. 1995. *Social Distance and Social Decisions.* Fischer-Schultz Lecture, Econometric Society World Congress, September.

Akerlof, G. A., and W. T. Dickens. 1992. The Economic Consequences of Cognitive Dissonance. *American Economic Review* 72:307–319.

Albury, R. 1983. *The Politics of Objectivity.* Victoria, New South Wales, Australia: Deakin University Press.

American Academy of Actuaries. 1996. *Medicaid Managed Care: Savings, Access, and Quality.* Washington, DC: American Academy of Actuaries.

American Health Line. 1997a. *The Daily Briefing of the National Journal.* Washington, DC: National Journal. 29 July.

———. 1997b. *50-State Report.* Washington, DC: National Journal, p. 181.

American Hospital Association. 1981. *Hospital Statistics.* Chicago: American Hospital Association.

———. 1993. *Annual Survey of Hospitals* (unpublished tabulations). Chicago: American Hospital Association.

———. 1994. *1993 Annual Survey of Hospitals.* Chicago: American Hospital Association.

———. 1995a. *Annual Survey of Hospitals.* Chicago: American Hospital Association.

———. 1995b. *Hospital Statistics.* Chicago: American Hospital Association.

American Medical Association. 1934. Proceedings of the Cleveland Session. *Journal of the American Medical Association* 102(26):2199–2201.

American Medical Association: Power, Purpose and Politics in Organized Medicine. 1954. *Yale Law Journal* 63 (May):938–1029.

Anders, G. 1996a. Medicare HMOs Get Fewer Complaints. *Wall Street Journal,* 14 March, p. B5.

——. 1996b. Polling Quirks Give HMOs Healthy Ratings. *Wall Street Journal,* 27 August, p. B1.

Apple, R. 1980. To Be Used Only under the Direction of a Physician: Commercial Infant Feeding and Medical Practice, 1870–1940. *Bulletin of the History of Medicine* 54(1):401–417.

Arneson, R. J. 1990. Liberalism, Distributive Subjectivism, and Equal Opportunity for Welfare. *Philosophy and Public Affairs* 19:158–197.

Arnold, R. D. 1990. *The Logic of Congressional Action.* New Haven, CT: Yale University Press.

Aronson, E. 1972. *The Social Animal.* San Francisco: W. H. Freeman.

Arrow, K. J. 1951. *Social Choice and Individual Values,* rev. ed. 1963. New York: Wiley.

——. 1963. Uncertainty and the Welfare Economics of Health Care. *American Economic Review* 53:941–973.

——. 1976. Welfare Analysis of Changes in Health Coinsurance Rates. In *The Role of Health Insurance in the Health Services Sector,* ed. R. Rosett. New York: National Bureau of Economic Research.

Ashmore, M., M. Mulkay, and T. Pinch. 1989. *Health and Efficiency: A Sociology of Health Economics.* Milton Keynes, U.K.: Open University Press.

Barer, M. L., T. R. Marmor, and E. Morrison. 1995. Editorial: Health Care Reform in the United States: On the Road to Nowhere (Again). *Social Science and Medicine* 41:453–460.

Barer, M. L., V. Bhatia, G. L. Stoddart, and R. G. Evans. 1994. *The Remarkable Tenacity of User Charges.* Toronto: Premier's Council on Health, Well-Being, and Social Justice.

Baumgartner, F. R., and B. D. Jones. 1993. *Agendas and Instability in American Politics.* Chicago: University of Chicago Press.

Becker, G. S., and K. M. Murphy. 1988. A Theory of Rational Addiction. *Journal of Political Economy* 96:675–700.

Belkin, G. 1994. The New Science of Medicine. *Journal of Health Politics, Policy and Law* 19:801–808.

——. In press. Shifting the Focus: The Historical Meaning of Managed Care and the Search for Ethics in Mental Health. In *Rationing Sanity: Ethics, Resource Allocation, and Managed Health Care,* ed. P. Boyle. Washington, DC: Georgetown University Press.

Bell, N. 1991. From the Trenches: Strategies That Work. *Business and Health* 9(5):19–25.

——. 1992. Pros and Cons of Point-of-Service Plans. *Business and Health* 10(1):34.

Berenson, R. 1987. In a Doctor's Wallet: Financial Confessions of a Sawbones. *New Republic,* 18 May, pp. 11–13.

Berger, J. 1996. In One New York County, Welfare Meets Managed Care, and Wins Praise. *New York Times,* 9 September, p. A13.

Bergthold, L. A. 1990. *Purchasing Power in Health: Business, the State, and Health Care Politics.* New Brunswick, NJ: Rutgers University Press.

———. 1994. American Business and Health Care Reform. In *Health Care Reform in the Nineties,* ed. P. V. Rosenau. Thousand Oaks, CA: Sage.

Berk, M. L., and A. C. Monheit. 1992. The Concentration of Health Expenditures: An Update. *Health Affairs* 11(4):145–149.

Bernheim, B. D. 1994. A Theory of Conformity. *Journal of Political Economy* 102:841–877.

Big Business vs. the GOP? 1995. *Wall Street Journal,* 13 March, p. A14.

Bipartisan Commission on Entitlement Reform. 1994. *Staff Report on Entitlement Reform Options.* Washington, DC.

Bjornstad, D. J., and J. R. Kahn, eds. 1996. *The Contingent Valuation of Environmental Resources: Methodological Issues and Research Needs.* Brookfield, VT: Edward Elgar.

Blackorby, C., and D. Donaldson. 1990. A Review Article: The Case against the Use of the Sum of Compensating Variations in Cost-Benefit Analysis. *Canadian Journal of Economics* 23:471–494.

Blendon, R. J., J. Benson, K. Donelan, R. Leitman, H. Taylor, C. Koeck, and D. Gitterman. 1995. Who Has the Best Health Care System? A Second Look. *Health Affairs* 14(4):220–230.

Blendon, R. J., R. Leitman, I. Morrison, and K. Donelan. 1990. Satisfaction with Health Systems in Ten Nations. *Health Affairs* 9(2):185–192.

Bloom, B. 1986. Controlled Studies in Measuring the Efficacy of Medical Care: A Historical Perspective. *International Journal of Technology Assessment in Health Care* 2(2):299–310.

Bloor, D. [1976] 1991. *Knowledge and Social Imagery.* 2d ed. Chicago: University of Chicago Press.

Blues Growth Tied to Managed Care: Plans Reorganize to Compete. 1996. *Medical Benefits* 13, 30 June, p. 7 (summary of Robert Kazel, Business Insurance, 3 June 1996).

Blumenthal, D. 1996. Effects of Market Reforms on Doctors and Their Patients. *Health Affairs* 15(2):170–184.

Bodenheimer, T. S., and K. Grumbach. 1995. *Understanding Health Policy.* Norwalk, CT: Appleton and Lange.

Boston Dispensary Quarterly. 1913. Vol. 1, no. 2 (January). Codman Papers, box 1, folder 5. Countway Library of Medicine, Boston.

Boulding, K. E. 1969. Economics as a Moral Science. *American Economic Review* 59(1):1–12.

Bowman, J. G. *Standardization of Hospitals.* (ACS pamphlet) 15 January 1918. Codman Papers, box 1, folder 1. Countway Library of Medicine, Boston.

Brecher, C., ed. 1992. *Implementation Issues and National Health Care Reform.* Washington, DC: Josiah Macy Jr. Foundation.

Bresnahan, T. F. 1989. Empirical Studies of Industries with Market Power. In *Hand-*

book of *Industrial Organization,* ed. R. Schmalensee and R. Willig. Amsterdam: North-Holland.

Brown, L. D. 1983. *Politics and Health Care Organization: HMOs as Federal Policy.* Washington, DC: Brookings Institution.

———. 1991. Knowledge and Power: Health Services Research as a Political Resource. In *Health Services Research: Key to Health Policy,* ed. E. Ginzberg. Cambridge: Harvard University Press.

Brown, R. S., D. G. Clement, J. W. Hill, S. M. Retchin, and J. W. Bergeron. 1993. Do Health Maintenance Organizations Work for Medicare? *Health Care Financing Review* 15(1):7–23.

Brown, R. S., J. Bergeron, D. G. Clement, J. W. Hill, and S. M. Retchin. 1993. *Does Managed Care Work for Medicare? An Evaluation of the Medicare Risk Program for HMOs* (December). Princeton, NJ: Mathematica Policy Research.

Brown, R. S., and J. W. Hill. 1994. The Effects of Medicare Risk HMOs on Medicare Costs and Service Utilization. In *HMOs and the Elderly,* ed. H. S. Luft. Ann Arbor, MI: Health Administration Press.

Buchanan, A. 1998. Managed Care: Rationing Without Justice, But Not Unjustly. *Journal of Health Politics, Policy and Law* 23:617–634.

Buchanan, J. M. 1997. Political Equality and Private Property: The Distributional Paradox. In *Markets and Morals,* ed. G. Dworkin, G. Bermant, and P. G. Brow. Washington, DC: Hemisphere.

Buchanan, J. M., and G. Tullock. 1962. *The Calculus of Consent.* Ann Arbor: University of Michigan Press.

Buchmueller, T. C., and P. J. Feldstein. 1995. *The Effect of Price on Switching among Health Plans.* Working paper, Graduate School of Management, University of California, Irvine.

———. 1996. Consumers' Sensitivity to Health Plan Premiums: Evidence from a Natural Experiment. *Health Affairs* 15(1):143–151.

Burner, S. T., and D. R. Waldo. 1995. National Health Expenditure Projections 1994–2005. *Health Care Financing Review* 16(4):221–242.

Butler, S. M., and R. E. Moffit. 1995. The FEHBP as a Mode for a New Medicare Program. *Health Affairs* 14(4):47–61.

Cantor, J., N. Barrand, R. Desonia, A. Cohen, and J. Merrill. 1991. Business Leaders' Views on American Health Care. *Health Affairs* 10:99–101.

Carlisle, D. M., A. L. Siu, E. B. Keeler, E. A. McGlynn, K. L. Kahn, L. V. Rubenstein, and R. H. Brook. 1992. HMO vs. Fee-for-Service Care of Older Persons with Acute Myocardial Infarction. *American Journal of Public Health* 82:1626–1630.

Casas, M., and M. M. Wiley, eds. 1993. *Diagnosis-Related Groups in Europe: Uses and Perspectives.* Berlin: Springer-Verlag.

Center for Studying Health System Change. 1996a. *The Community Tracking Study.* Issue Brief No. 1 (July). Washington, DC: Center for Studying Health System Change.

———. 1996b. *Policy Implications of Risk Selection in Medicare HMOs: Is the Federal*

Payment Rate Too High? Issue Brief No. 4 (November). Washington, DC: Center for Studying Health System Change.

Chernichovsky, D. 1995. Health System Reforms in Industrialized Democracies: An Emerging Paradigm. *Milbank Quarterly* 73(3):339–372.

Chinitz, D. 1995. Israel's Health Policy Breakthrough: The Politics of Reform and the Reform of Politics. *Journal of Health Politics, Policy and Law* 20:909–932.

Chinitz, D., and J. Cohen, eds. 1998. *Governments and Health Systems: Implications of Differing Involvements.* Chichester: John Wiley.

Christensen, L. 1991. Change of Hearts. *Business and Health* 9(6):18–26.

Christianson, J. B. 1994. Responses and Discussions: Premium Levels. In *HMOs and the Elderly,* ed. H. S. Luft. Ann Arbor, MI: Health Administration Press.

Christianson, J., B. Dowd, J. Kralewski, S. Hayes, and C. Wisner. 1995. Managed Care in the Twin Cities: What Can We Learn? *Health Affairs* 14(2):114–130.

Claxton, G., and L. Levitt. 1996. *Risk Selection Issues under Medicare Reform Proposals.* Menlo Park, CA: Kaiser Family Foundation.

Clement, D. G., S. M. Retchin, and R. S. Brown. 1994. Satisfaction with Access and Quality of Care in Medicare Risk Contract HMOs. In *HMOs and the Elderly,* ed. H. S. Luft. Ann Arbor, MI: Health Administration Press.

Clement, D. G., S. M. Retchin, R. S. Brown, and M. H. Stegall. 1994. Access and Outcomes of Elderly Patients Enrolled in Managed Care. *New England Journal of Medicine* 271:1487–1492.

Clinton, President B. 1996a. Remarks by the President to the Community of the Pittsburgh Area, Robert Morris College, Coraopolis, PA, 25 September 1996; available from the Internet (Publications–Admin@WhiteHouse.gov).

———. 1996b. Statement by the President, upon signing of H.R. 3666, *Departments of Veterans Affairs and Housing and Urban Development, and Independent Agencies Appropriations Act, FY 1997,* the White House, Washington, DC, 26 September; available from the Internet (Publications–Admin@WhiteHouse.gov).

Clymer, A. 1995a. Health Lobby Starts Taking Aim at G.O.P. Plan. *New York Times,* 10 October, pp. A1, A18.

———. 1995b. Republicans Choose Vote on Medicare Cut. *New York Times,* 18 October, p. B8.

———. 1995c. House Votes to Curb Costs on Medicare by $270 Billion; President Promises a Veto. *New York Times,* 20 October, pp. A1, A27.

———. 1995d. Americans Reject Big Medicare Cuts, a New Poll Finds. *New York Times,* 26 October, pp. A1, D23.

Cochrane, A. 1971. *Effectiveness and Efficiency.* Abingdon, Berks.: Burgess and Son.

Codman, E. A. 1914. *A Study in Hospital Efficiency as Demonstrated by the Case Report of the First Two Years of a Private Hospital.* Codman Papers, box 3, folder 123, Countway Library of Medicine, Boston.

———. c. 1915. *Fundamental Differences in the Problem of the Management of a Manufacturing Business and That of a Charitable Hospital.* Codman Papers, box 6, folder 114. Countway Library of Medicine, Boston.

Coffey, E., I. Moscovice, M. Finch, J. B. Christianson, and N. Lurie. 1994. Capitated

Medicaid and the Process of Care of Elderly Hypertensives and Diabetics: Results from a Randomized Trial. *American Journal of Medicine* 98:531–536.

Collins, H. M. 1974. The TEA Set: Tacit Knowledge and Scientific Network. *Science Studies* 4:165–186.

Competitive Edge HMO Industry Report. 1997. *Medical Benefits* 14, 30 May, p. 6 (summary of InterStudy Publications, April 1997).

The *Competitive Edge* Regional Market Analysis. 1996. *Medical Benefits* 13, 30 August, p. 5 (summary of InterStudy Publications, June 1996).

Cone, T., Jr. 1979. *History of American Pediatrics*. Boston: Little, Brown.

Congressional Budget Office (CBO). 1995. *Cost Estimate for HR 2485 (Medicare Preservation Act of 1995)*. Washington, DC.

——. 1997a. *Budgetary Implications of the Balanced Budget Act of 1997*. Washington, DC.

——. 1997b. Budget baseline estimate, unpublished memo.

Congressional Research Service (CRS). 1993. *Medicaid Source Book: Background Data and Analysis (A 1993 Update)*. Washington, DC: U.S. Government Printing Office.

——. 1997. *Medicine Provisions in the Balanced Budget Act of 1997*. Washington, DC.

Corker, B. 1996. TennCare Transition Document, 21 January 1995 to 30 June 1996. Nashville: Tennessee Department of Finance and Administration.

Coughlin, T., and D. Lipson. 1994. Tennessee: TennCare. In *Increasing Coverage through Medicaid Waiver Programs: Case Studies*. Washington, DC: Urban Institute.

Craig, J., Jr. 1985. Private Foundations' Role in Coalitions. In *Private Sector Coalitions: A Fourth Party in Health Care,* ed. Jon Jaeger. Durham, NC: Duke University Press.

Cronin, C. 1988. Business Wields Its Purchase Power. *Business and Health* 6(1): 14–17.

Culyer, A. J. 1982. The NHS and the Market: Images and Realities. In *The Public-Private Mix for Health: The Relevance and Effects of Change,* ed. G. McLachlan and A. Maynard. London: Nuffield Provincial Hospitals Trust. 23–55.

——. 1989. The Normative Economics of Health Care Finance and Provision. *Oxford Review of Economic Policy* 5:34–58.

Culyer, A. J., and R. G. Evans. 1996. Mark Pauly on Welfare Economics: Normative Rabbis from Positive Hats. *Journal of Health Economics* 15(2):243–251.

Danziger, K. 1990. *Constructing the Subject: Historical Origins of Psychological Research*. Cambridge: Cambridge University Press.

Davis, K., K. S. Collins, and C. Morris. 1994. Managed Care: Promise and Concerns. *Health Affairs* 13(4):178–185.

Davis, K., K. S. Collins, C. Schoen, and C. Morris. 1995. Choice Matters: Enrollees' Views of Their Health Plans. *Health Affairs* 14(2):99–112.

Debreu, G. 1979. *Theory of Value: An Axiomatic Analysis of Economic Equilibrium*. New York: Wiley.

Derbyshire, R. 1965. What Should the Profession Do about the Incompetent Physician? *Journal of the American Medical Association* 194:1287–1290.

———. 1969. *Medical Licensure and Discipline in the United States.* Baltimore: Johns Hopkins University Press.

———. 1974. Medical Ethics and Discipline. *Journal of the American Medical Association* 288:59–62.

Donabedian, A. 1969. An Evaluation of Prepaid Group Practice. *Inquiry* 6:3–27.

Donlon, J. P., and B. Benson. 1996. The New Anatomy of Health Care. *Chief Executive* 110 (January):52.

Dowd, B., J. Christianson, R. Feldman, C. Wisner, and J. Klein. 1992. Issues Regarding Health Plan Performance under Medicare and Recommendations for Reform. *Milbank Quarterly* 70:423–453.

Dranove, D. 1995. A Problem with Consumer Surplus Measures of the Cost of Practice Variations. *Journal of Health Economics* 14:243–251.

Dreifus, C., ed. 1977. *Seizing Our Bodies: The Politics of Women's Health.* New York: Vintage.

Duesenberry, J. S. 1952. *Income, Saving, and the Theory of Consumer Behavior.* Cambridge: Harvard University Press.

Easterlin, R. A. 1974. Does Economic Growth Improve the Human Lot? Some Empirical Evidence. In *Nations and Households in Economic Growth: Essays in Honor of Moses Abramovitz,* ed. P. David and M. W. Reder. New York: Academic Press.

Eckholm, E. 1996. HMOs Are Changing the Face of Medicare. *New York Times,* 10 January, p. A1.

Eggars, P. W., and R. Prihoda. 1981. Pre-enrollment Reimbursement Patterns of Medicare Beneficiaries Enrolled in "At-Risk" HMOs. *Health Care Financing Review* 4:55–73.

Ellis, R. P., and T. G. McGuire. 1993. Supply-Side and Demand-Side Cost Sharing in Health Care. *Journal of Economic Perspectives* 7:135–151.

Ellwood, P. 1970. *The Health Maintenance Strategy.* Minneapolis, MN: Institute for Interdisciplinary Studies.

———. 1973. *Assuring the Quality of Care.* Minneapolis, MN: InterStudy.

———. 1988. Shattuck Lecture—Outcomes Management—A Technology of Patient Experience. *New England Journal of Medicine* 318(23):1549–1556.

Ellwood, P. M., and A. C. Enthoven. 1995. Responsible Choices: The Jackson Hole Group Plan for Health Reform. *Health Affairs* 14(2):24–39.

Emanuel, E. J., and L. L. Emanuel. 1997. Preserving Community in Health Care. *Journal of Health Politics, Policy and Law* 22(1):147–184.

Enthoven, A. C. 1978a. Consumer-Choice Health Plan (2 parts). *New England Journal of Medicine* 298:650–658, 709–720.

———. 1978b. Shattuck Lecture: Cutting Cost without Cutting the Quality of Care. *New England Journal of Medicine* 298:1229–1237.

———. 1980. *Health Plan: The Only Practical Solution to the Soaring Costs of Medical Care.* Reading, MA: Addison-Wesley.

———. 1989. What Can Europeans Learn from Americans about Financing and Organization of Medical Care? *Health Care Financing Review* (Annual Suppl.): 49–63.

———. 1993. The History and Principles of Managed Competition. *Health Affairs* 12 (Suppl.):24–48.

Etheredge, L. 1998. The Medicare Reforms of 1997: The Headlines You Didn't Read. *Journal of Health Politics, Policy and Law* 23(3):153–159.

Evans, A. 1995. *The Federal Health Benefits Program, Managed Competition, and Considerations for Medicare.* Washington, DC: National Academy on Aging.

Evans, R. G. 1984. *Strained Mercy.* Toronto: Butterworth.

Evans, R. G., M. L. Barer, and G. L. Stoddart. 1993. *It's Not the Money, It's the Principle: Why User Charges for Some Services and Not Others?* University of British Columbia, Vancouver: Centre for Health Services and Policy Research.

———. 1994. *Charging Peter to Pay Paul: Accounting for the Financial Effects of User Charges.* Toronto: Premier's Council on Health, Well-Being, and Social Justice.

Evans, R. G., M. L. Barer, and T. R. Marmor, eds. 1994. *Why Are Some People Healthy, and Others Not? The Determinants of Health of Populations.* New York: Aldine de Gruyter.

Executive Order 13017. 1996. Advisory Commission on Consumer Protection and Quality in the Health Care Industry. The White House, Washington, DC, 5 September.

Ezrahi, Y. 1990. *The Descent of Icarus.* Cambridge: Harvard University Press.

Families USA. 1996. *HMO Consumers at Risk: States to the Rescue.* Washington, DC: Families USA.

Feder, J. M. 1995. Double Whammy for the Elderly. *Washington Post,* 20 December, p. A25.

———. 1996. Keynote address at the forum on "Health Care: Does the Government Matter Anymore? A Special Roundtable Discussion." The H. John Heinz III School of Public Policy and Management, Carnegie Mellon University, Pittsburgh, PA, 26 April.

———. 1977. *Medicare: The Politics of Federal Hospital Insurance.* Lexington, MA: Heath.

Fein, E. 1995. Public Hospitals Facing Deep Cuts by Medicare Bill. *New York Times,* 21 October, pp. P1, P8.

Feinstein, A. 1967. *Clinical Judgment.* Baltimore: Williams and Wilkins.

Feldman, R., and B. Dowd. 1991. A New Estimate of the Welfare Loss of Excess Health Insurance. *American Economic Review* 81:297–301.

———. 1993. What Does the Demand Curve for Medical Care Measure? *Journal of Health Economics* 12:193–200.

Feldman, R., and F. A. Sloan. 1988. Competition among Physicians, Revisited. *Journal of Health Politics, Policy and Law* 13:239–261.

Feldman, R., and M. A. Morrisey. 1990. Health Economics: A Report on the Field. *Journal of Health Politics, Policy and Law* 15:627–646.

Feldstein, P. J. 1988a. *Health Care Economics.* New York: Wiley.

———. 1988b. *The Politics of Health Legislation: An Economic Perspective.* Ann Arbor, MI: Health Administration Press.

Field, M., and H. Shapiro. 1993. *Summary.* In *Employment and Health Benefits,* ed. M. Field and H. Shapiro. Washington: National Academy.

Fielding, J. E., and P.-J. Lancry. 1993. Lessons from France—Vive la Difference. *Journal of the American Medical Association* 270(6):748–756.

Finally, a Health Bill. 1996. *New York Times,* 27 July, p. 18.

Findlay, S. 1995a. Block Grants for Sale. *Business and Health* 13(8):55.

———. 1995b. Will Big HMOs Stamp Out Competition? *Business and Health* 13(10):52.

Findlay, S., and W. J. Meyeroff. 1996. Health Costs: Why Employers Won Another Round. *Business and Health* 14(3) (March):49–51.

Fisher, M. J. 1995a. Both Parties Turning Medicare into Huge Political Football. *National Underwriter,* 14 August, p. 8.

———. 1995b. Kennedy Charges Industry with Medicare "Conspiracy." *National Underwriter,* 14 August, p. 1.

———. 1995c. Coalition Holding "Medicare University" Briefings. *National Underwriter,* 4 September, p. 36.

———. 1995d. Medicare Reform Is Turning Congress into a Circus. *National Underwriter,* 9 October, p. 10.

Fleck, L. [1935] 1981. *Genesis and Development of a Scientific Fact.* Trans. Fred Bradley. Chicago: University of Chicago Press.

Folland, S., A. C. Goodman, and M. Stano. 1993. *The Economics of Health and Health Care.* Upper Saddle River, NJ: Prentice-Hall.

Foster Higgins. 1992. *Health Care Benefits Survey; Managed Care Plans.* New York: Foster Higgins.

———. 1994. *National Survey of Employer-Sponsored Health Plans.* New York: Foster Higgins.

———. 1995. *National Survey of Employer-Sponsored Health Plans.* New York: Foster Higgins.

Fox, D. M., and H. M. Leichter. 1993. The Ups and Downs of Oregon's Rationing Plan. *Health Affairs* 120(2):66–70.

Fox, W. F., and W. Lyons. 1994. *A Survey to Determine Insurance Status for Tennessee Residents.* Report prepared for the Tennessee Department of Finance and Administration, 25 August, Nashville.

Frank, R. H. 1985. *Choosing the Right Pond: Human Behavior and the Quest for Status.* New York: Oxford University Press.

Frankford, D. M. 1992. Privatizing Health Care: Economic Magic to Cure Legal Medicine. *Southern California Law Review* 66(1):1–98.

Frankford, D. 1994. Scientism and Economism in the Regulation of Health Care. *Journal of Health Politics, Policy and Law* 19:773–799.

Freeman, R. B., and J. L. Medoff. 1984. *What Do Unions Do?* New York: Basic Books.

Freidson, E. 1975. *Doctoring Together.* New York: Elsevier.

———. 1986. *Professional Powers.* Chicago: University of Chicago Press.

Freudenheim, M. 1994. To Economists, Managed Care Is No Cure-All. *New York Times,* 6 September, p. A1.

———. 1995a. Business May Pay More for Health as Congress Cuts. *New York Times,* 4 November, p. 49.

———. 1995b. Survey Finds Health Costs Rose in '95. *New York Times,* 30 January, p. D1.

———. 1996. Managed Care Empires in the Making. *New York Times,* 2 April, p. D1.

Frieden, J. 1991. Hershey's Newest Nonfat Product: Wellness. *Business and Health* 9(12):56–60.

Friedland, R. 1987. Introduction and Background. In *The Changing Health Care Market,* ed. Frank McArdle. Washington, DC: Employee Benefit Research Institute, 15.

Friedman, B., and R. L. Kane. 1993. HMO Directors' Perceptions of Geriatric Practice in Medicare HMOs. *Journal of the American Geriatric Society* 41:1144–1149.

Friedman, M. 1962a. *Capitalism and Freedom.* Chicago: University of Chicago Press.

———. 1962b. *Price Theory.* Chicago: Aldine Press.

Friedman, M., and S. Kuznets. 1954. *Income from Independent Professional Practice.* New York: National Bureau of Economic Research.

Fuchs, V. R. 1996. Economics, Values, and Health Care Reform. *American Economic Review* 86:1–24.

Fuchs, V. R., and J. S. Hahn. 1990. How Does Canada Do It? A Comparison of Expenditures for Physicians' Services in the United States and Canada. *New England Journal of Medicine* 323:884–890.

Garret, M. 1997. How to Behave Like a Majority Party. *Weekly Standard,* 5 May, p. 20.

Gelijns, A. C., and N. Rosenberg. 1996. Making Choices about Medical Technology. In *Fundamental Questions about the Future of Health Care,* ed. L. J. Gunning-Schepers, G. J. Kronjell, and R. A. Ipasoff. The Hague: Netherlands Scientific Council for Government Policy.

Gerdtham, U.-G., and B. Jönsson. 1991. Price and Quantity in International Comparisons of Health Care Expenditure. *Applied Economics* 23:1519–1528.

Gifford, F. 1996. Outcomes Research and Practice Guideline——Upstream Issues for Downstream Users. *Hastings Center Report* 26(2):38–44.

Gillick, M. R. 1987. The Impact of Health Maintenance Organizations on Geriatric Care. *Annals of Internal Medicine* 106(1):139–143.

Ginsburg, P. B. 1996. The RWJF Community Snapshots Study: Introduction and Overview. *Health Affairs* 15(2):7–20.

Ginsburg, P. B., and J. D. Pickreign. 1996. Tracking Health Care Costs. *Health Affairs* 15(3):140–149.

Ginsburg, P. B., and J. M. Grossman. 1995. Health System Change: The View from Wall Street. *Health Affairs* 14(4):159–163.

Ginsburg, P. B., and N. J. Fasciano, eds. 1996. *The Community Snapshots Project: Capturing Health System Change.* Princeton, NJ: Robert Wood Johnson Foundation.

Ginzberg, E., and M. Ostow. 1997. Managed Care—A Look Back and a Look Ahead. *New England Journal of Medicine* 336(14):1018–1020.

Glaser, W. A. 1978. *Health Insurance Bargaining: Foreign Lessons for Americans*. New York: Gardner.

———. 1993. How Expenditure Caps and Expenditure Targets Really Work. *Milbank Quarterly* 71(1):97–127.

Glennerster, H. 1995. Internal Markets: Context and Structure. In *Health Care Reform through Internal Markets*, ed. M. Jerome-Forget, J. White, and J. W. Wiener. Washington, DC: Brookings Institution.

Gold, M. 1997. Markets and Public Programs: Insights from Oregon and Tennessee. *Journal of Health Politics, Policy and Law* 22:663–666.

Gold, M., H. Frazer, and C. Schoen. 1995. *Managed Care and Low Income Populations: A Case Study of Managed Care in Tennessee*. Washington, DC: Kaiser Family Foundation.

Gold, M., K. Chu, and B. Lyons. 1995. *Managed Care and Low Income Populations: A Case Study of Managed Care in Oregon*. Washington, DC: Kaiser Family Foundation.

Gold, M., M. Sparer, and K. Chu. 1996. Medicaid Managed Care: Lessons from Five States. *Health Affairs* 15(3):153–166.

Gold, M., R. Hurley, T. Lake, T. Ensor, and R. Berenson. 1995. A National Survey of the Arrangements Managed-Care Plans Make with Physicians. *New England Journal of Medicine* 333:1678–1683.

Goldsmith, J. 1994. Perspective: Impact of Technology on Health Costs. *Health Affairs* 13(3):80–81.

Goldstein, A. 1997. Medicare Recipients to Face a Dizzying Array of Choices. *Washington Post*, 8 August, p. A1.

Goldwater, S. S. 1916. *Modern Hospital* 7 (October–November):4–5. Codman Papers, box 3, folder 42. Countway Library of Medicine, Boston.

Goodman, J. C., and G. Musgrave. 1992. *Patient Power: Solving America's Health Care Crisis*. Washington, DC: Cato Institute.

Gorovitz, S., and A. MacIntyre. 1976. Toward a Theory of Medical Fallibility. *Journal of Medicine and Philosophy* 1:51–71.

Gottlieb, M. 1995. Health Lobbyists Win Adjustments to Medicare Plan. *New York Times*, 10 December, pp. A1, A26.

Gottlieb, M., and R. Pear. 1995. Beneath Surface, New Health Bills Offer some Boons. *New York Times*, 15 October, pp. A1, 20.

Gqabel, J., S. DiCarlo, C. Sullivan, and T. Rice. 1990. Employer-Sponsored Health Insurance, 1989. *Health Affairs* 9:161–175.

Graaff, J. de V. 1971. *Theoretical Welfare Economics*. London: Cambridge University Press.

Gray, B. 1992. The Legislative Battle over Health Services Research. *Health Affairs* 11(4):38–66.

Gray, J. 1995a. Gingrich, Long Seen as a Purist, Proves His Worth as Pragmatist. *New York Times*, 27 October, pp. A1, D21.

———. 1995b. Senate Moderates Gain Concessions in Big Budget Bill. *New York Times*, 28 October, pp. A1, A8.

Green, M., J. Kohn, and C. G. Lee. 1995. *Managed Confusion: How HMO Marketing*

Materials Are Tricking the Elderly and the Poor. New York: Office of the Public Advocate.

Greiner, W., and J.-M. Graf von der Schulenburg. 1997. The Health System of Germany. In *Health Care and Reform in Industrialized Countries,* ed. Marshall W. Raffel. University Park: Pennsylvania State University Press.

Griffin, J. 1986. *Well-Being: Its Meaning, Measurement, and Moral Importance.* Oxford: Clarendon.

Grimaldi, P. L. 1995. Medicaid Switching to Managed Care. *Nursing Management* 26(7):12–17.

Grobman, M. 1993. UR Only as Good as What You Save. *Business and Health* 9(7):21–30.

Grogan, C. 1997. The Medicaid Managed Care Policy Consensus for Welfare Recipients: A Reflection of Traditional Welfare Concerns. *Journal of Health Politics, Policy and Law* 22:815–838.

Group Health Association of America (GHAA). 1992. *1992 National Directory of HMOs.* Washington, DC: GHAA.

———. 1994. *1994 National Directory of HMOs.* Washington, DC: GHAA.

Haas-Wilson, D., and M. Gaynor. 1996. Antitrust Policy and the Transformation of Health Care Markets. Presentation at the Policy Roundtable, "Managed Care: Prospects for Success and Failure," at the Annual Meeting of the Robert Wood Johnson Investigator Awards in Health Policy Research Program, Ft. Lauderdale, FL, 15–17 October.

Hacker, J. S. 1997. *The Road to Nowhere: The Genesis of President Clinton's Plan for Health Security.* Princeton, NJ: Princeton University Press.

Hacker, J., and T. Skocpol. 1997. The New Politics of U.S. Health Policy. *Journal of Health Politics, Policy and Law* 22:315–338.

Hacking, I. 1990. *The Taming of Chance.* Cambridge: Cambridge University Press.

Hahnel, R., and M. Albert. 1990. *Quiet Revolution in Welfare Economics.* Princeton, NJ: Princeton University Press.

Hakansson, S., and S. Nordling. 1997. The Health System of Sweden. In *Health Care and Reform in Industrialized Countries,* ed. M. W. Raffel. University Park: Pennsylvania State University Press.

Hall, P. 1986. *Governing the Economy: The Politics of State Intervention in Britain and France.* Oxford: Oxford University Press.

———. 1993. Policy Paradigms, Social Learning, and the State: The Case of Economic Policymaking in Britain. *Comparative Politics* 25 (April):275–296.

Ham, C. 1994. *Management and Competition in the New NHS.* Oxford, U.K.: Radcliffe Medical Press for the National Association of Health Authorities and Trusts.

Ham, C., and M. Brommels. 1994. Health Care Reform in the Netherlands, Sweden, and the United Kingdom. *Health Affairs* 13(4):106–119.

Hanchak, N. A., S. R. Harmon-Weiss, P. D. McDermott, A. Hirsch, and N. Schlackman. 1996. Medicare Managed Care and the Need for Quality Measurement. *Managed Care Quarterly* 4(1):1–12.

Harrington, C., M. Lynch, and R. J. Newcomer. 1993. Medical Services in Social Health Maintenance Organizations. *Gerontologist* 33:790–800.

Harris, J. 1997. Bipartisanship Reigns at Budget Signing. *Washington Post*, 6 August, p. A1.

Hausman, D. M., and M. S. McPherson. 1996. *Economic Analysis and Moral Philosophy*. New York: Cambridge University Press.

Hausman, J. A., ed. 1993. *Contingent Valuation: A Critical Assessment*. Amsterdam: Elsevier.

Havighurst, C. 1974. Hearings on Competition in the Health Services Market—Testimony before the U.S. Senate, Subcommittee on Antitrust and Monopoly. Washington, DC, 17 May.

———. 1977. Controlling Health Care Costs: Strengthening the Private Sector's Hand. *Journal of Health Politics, Policy and Law* 1:471–498.

———. 1986. The Changing Locus of Decision Making in the Health Care Sector. *Journal of Health Politics, Policy and Law* 11:697–735.

Health. 1997. *Forbes*, 13 January, p. 167.

Health Action Council of Northeast Ohio. n.d. *Rethinking the Health-Care Marketplace*, p. 3.

Health Care Is Poised for an Increase in Rates. 1997. *Medical Benefits* 13, 15 August, p. 5 (summary of Rodd Zolkos et al., *Business Insurance*, 7 July 1997).

Health Care Study Group. 1994. Understanding the Choices in Health Care Reform. *Journal of Health Politics, Policy and Law* 19:499–541.

Heclo, H. 1974. *Modern Social Politics in Britain and Sweden*. New Haven, CT: Yale University Press.

Hellinger, F. J. 1995. Selection Bias in HMOs and PPOs: A Review of the Evidence. *Inquiry* 32:135–142.

Henderson, J. M., and R. E. Quandt. 1980. *Microeconomic Theory*, 3d ed. New York: McGraw-Hill.

Henke, K.-D., M. A. Murray, and C. Ade. 1994. Global Budgeting in Germany: Lessons for the United States. *Health Affairs* 13(4):7–21.

Herder-Dorneich, P. 1965. *Analyse der Gesetzlichen Krankenversicherung* [Analysis of statutory health insurance]. Berlin: Erich Schmidt.

Herzlinger, R. 1985. How Companies Tackle Health Care Costs. *Harvard Business Review* 85(5):108–120.

———. 1997. *Market-Driven Health Care: Who Wins, Who Loses in the Transformation of America's Largest Service Industry*. Reading, MA: Addison-Wesley.

Hibbard, J. H., and E. C. Weeks. 1989a. The Dissemination of Physician Fee Information: Impact on Consumer Knowledge, Attitudes, and Behaviors. *Journal of Health and Social Policy* 1:75–87.

———. 1989b. Does the Dissemination of Comparative Data on Physician Fees Affect Consumer Use of Services? *Medical Care* 27:1167–1174.

Hibbard, J. H., and J. J. Jewett. 1996. What Type of Quality Information Do Consumers Want in a Health Care Report Card? *Medical Care Research and Review* 53:28–47.

Hill, A. 1962. *Statistical Methods in Clinical Research*. New York: Oxford University Press.

Hillman, A. 1987. Financial Incentives for Physicians in HMOs: Is There a Conflict of Interest? *New England Journal of Medicine* 317:1743–1748.

Hillman, A., M. V. Pauly, and J. J. Kerstein. 1989. How Do Financial Incentives Affect Physicians' Clinical Decisions and the Financial Performance of Health Maintenance Organizations? *New England Journal of Medicine* 321: 86–92.

Hillman, A., P. Welch, and M. V. Pauly. 1992. Contractual Arrangements between HMOs and Primary Care Physicians: Three-Tiered HMOs and Risk Pools. *Medical Care* 30:136–148.

Himmelstein, D., and S. Woolhandler. 1995. Extreme Risk——The New Corporate Proposition for Physicians. *New England Journal of Medicine* 333:1706–1708.

Hirschman, A. O. 1970. *Exit, Voice, and Loyalty: Responses to Decline in Firms, Organizations, and States*. Cambridge: Harvard University Press.

HMO Industry Report. 1996. *Medical Benefits* 13, 30 April, pp. 1–2 (summary of InterStudy Competitive Edge 6.1, April 1996).

HMO-PPO Digest, 1995. 1996. *Medical Benefits* 13, 15 March, p. 2 (summary of Hoechst Marion Roussel, Inc., and SMG Marketing Group, Inc., report, January 1996).

——. 1996. 1997. *Medical Benefits* 14, 30 January, p. 6 (summary of Hoechst Marion Roussel, Inc., report, December 1996).

Hodgson, G. 1996. *The World Turned Right Side Up*. Boston: Houghton Mifflin.

Hoerger, T. J., and L. Z. Howard. 1995. Search Behavior and Choice of Physician in the Market for Prenatal Care. *Medical Care* 33:332–349.

Hogle, L. F. 1995. Standardization across Non-standard Domains: The Case of Organ Procurement. *Science, Technology and Human Values* 20:482–500.

Holahan, J., and D. Liska. 1995. *State Variations in Medicaid: Implications for Block Grants and Expenditure Growth Tapes*. Kaiser Commission for the Future of Medicaid Policy brief. Washington, DC: Kaiser Family Foundation.

Howell, J. 1995. *Technology in the Hospital*. Baltimore: Johns Hopkins University Press.

How Good Is Your Health Plan? 1996. *Consumer Reports* 61(8):28–42.

Hsiao, W. 1995. Medical Savings Accounts: Lessons from Singapore. *Health Affairs* 14(2):260–266.

Hunter, K. M. 1991. *Doctor's Stories——Narrative Structure of Medical Knowledge*. Princeton, NJ: Princeton University Press.

Huskamp, H., and J. Newhouse. 1994. Is Health Spending Slowing Down? *Health Affairs* 13:32–38.

Idaho's Most Populous County Dropping Medical Savings Accounts. 1997. Summary of *BNA Pension and Benefits Reporter*, 4 August 1997. *Medical Benefits* 14(18):6–7.

Iglehart, J. K. 1985. Medicare Turns to HMOs. *New England Journal of Medicine* 312(2):132–136.

——. 1987. Second Thoughts about HMOs for Medicare Patients. *New England Journal of Medicine* 316:1487–1492.

Industry Report. 1994. *Training,* October, p. 30.

Inman, R. P. 1987. Markets, Governments, and the "New" Political Economy. In *Handbook of Public Economics,* ed. A. J. Auerbach and M. Feldstein. Amsterdam: North-Holland.

Institute of Medicine. 1996. *The Nation's Physician Workforce: Options for Balancing Supply and Requirements.* Washington, DC: National Academy Press.

InterStudy. 1996. HMO Directory 6.1. Excelsior, MN: InterStudy.

Ivins, M. 1995. Washington's Looking Glass. *Sacramento Bee,* 26 August, p. 136.

Jacobs, A. 1998. Seeing Difference: Market Health Reform in Europe. *Journal of Health Politics, Policy and Law* 23:1–33.

Jacobs, L. R. 1993. *The Health of Nations: Public Opinion and the Making of American and British Health Policy.* Ithaca, NY: Cornell University Press.

——. 1995. Politics of America's Supply State: Health Reform and Technology. *Health Affairs* 14(2):143–157.

Jaeger, J., ed. 1985. *Private Sector Coalitions: A Fourth Party in Health Care.* Durham, NC: Duke University Press.

James, J. H. 1995. Reforming the British National Health Service: Implementation Problems in London. *Journal of Health Politics, Policy and Law* 20:191–210.

Jasperse, P. 1995. Medicare Forces Mobilize to Do Battle over Reforms. *Milwaukee Journal Sentinel,* 21 September, p. 4.

Jayaram, G., A. Y. Tien, P. Sullivan, and H. Gwon. 1996. Elements of a Successful Short-Stay Inpatient Psychiatric Service. *Psychiatric Services* 47:407–412.

Jencks, S. F., and G. R. Wilensky. 1992. The Health Care Quality Improvement Initiative. *Journal of the American Medical Association* 268:900–903.

Jensen, G. A., M. A. Morrisey, S. Gaffney, and D. K. Liston. 1997. The New Dominance of Managed Care: Insurance Trends in the 1990s. *Health Affairs* 16(1):125–136.

Jensen, G. A., and R. J. Morlock. 1994. Why Medical Savings Accounts Deserve a Closer Look. *Journal of American Health Policy* 4(3):14–23.

Jerome-Forget, M., and C. E. Forget. 1995. Internal Markets in the Canadian Context. In *Health Care Reform through Internal Markets: Experience and Proposals,* ed. M. Jerome-Forget, J. White, and J. M. Weiner. Washington, DC: Brookings Institution.

Johnson, H., and D. S. Broder. 1996. *The System: The American Way of Politics at the Breaking Point.* Boston: Little, Brown.

Jones, D. 1995. Firms Surprised at Managed Care Study Results. *National Underwriter Property and Casualty-Risk and Benefits Management,* no. 30 (24 July):33.

Joskow, P. L. 1981. *Controlling Hospital Costs: The Role of Government Regulation.* Cambridge: MIT Press.

Jost, T. S., D. Hughes, J. McHale, and L. Griffiths. 1995. The British Health Care Reforms, the American Health Care Revolution, and Purchaser/Provider Contracts. *Journal of Health Politics, Policy and Law* 20:885–908.

Kaiser Family Foundation. 1995. *Medicare Chart Book*. Menlo Park, CA: Kaiser Family Foundation.

———. *Kaiser Commission for the Future of Medicaid 1997: Medicaid and Managed Care Fact Sheet*. Washington, DC: Henry J. Kaiser Family Foundation, June.

Kane, R. L. 1995. Health Care Reform and the Care of Older Adults. *Journal of the American Geriatric Society* 43:702–706.

Kassirer, J. P. 1997. Managing Managed Care's Tarnished Image. *New England Journal of Medicine* 337(5):338–339.

Keeler, E. B. 1995. A Model of Demand for Effective Care. *Journal of Health Economics* 14:231–238.

Keeler, E. B., J. D. Malkin, D. P. Goldman, and J. L. Buchanan. 1996. Can Medical Savings Accounts for the Nonelderly Reduce Health Care Costs? *Journal of the American Medical Association* 275(21):1666–1671.

Kemper, P., D. Blumenthal, J. M. Corrigan, P. J. Cunningham, S. M. Felt, J. M. Grossman, L. T. Kohn, C. E. Metcalf, R. F. St. Peter, R. C. Strouse, and P. B. Ginsburg. 1996. The Design of the Community Tracking Study: A Longitudinal Study of Health System Change and Its Effects on People. *Inquiry* 33 (summer):195–206.

Kessel, R. A. 1958. Price Discrimination in Medicine. *Journal of Law and Economics* 1(2):20–53.

———. 1970. The AMA and the Supply of Physicians. *Law and Contemporary Problems* 35:267–283.

Kimberly, J. R., G. de Pouvourville, and Associates, eds. 1993. *The Migration of Managerial Innovation: Diagnosis-Related Groups and Health Care Administration in Western Europe*. San Francisco: Jossey-Bass.

King, G. 1994. Health Care Reform and the Medicare Program. *Health Affairs* 13(5):39–43.

Kingdon, J. W. 1984. *Agendas, Alternatives, and Public Policies*. New York: Harper Collins.

———. 1992. *Congressmen's Voting Decisions*, 3d ed. Ann Arbor: University of Michigan Press.

Kirkman-Liff, B. L. 1994. Management without Frontiers: Health System Convergence Leads to Health Care Management Convergence. *Frontiers of Health Services Management* 11(4):3–48.

Kisner, K. 1992. A Partnership Takes a Gamble to Measure Quality. *Business and Health* 10(4):20–27.

Klarman, H. E. 1963. Effect of Prepaid Group Practice on Hospital Use. *Public Health Reports* 78:955–965.

Klein, R. 1995. Big Bang Health Care Reform—Does It Work? The Case of Britain's 1991 National Health Service Reforms. *Milbank Quarterly* 73(3):299–337.

———. 1997. Learning from Others: Shall the Last Be the First? *Journal of Health Politics, Policy and Law* 22:1267–1278.

Knickman, J. R., R. G. Hughes, H. Taylor, K. Binns, and M. P. Lyons. 1996. Tracking Consumers' Reactions to the Changing Health System: Early Indicators. *Health Affairs* 15(2):21–32.

Knorr-Cetina, K. 1981. *The Manufacture of Knowledge*. Elmsford, NY: Pergamon.

Kosterlitz, J. 1987. Transplanted Industry. *National Journal* 19(16):936.

———. 1997. Betting on Good Times. *National Journal* 29(25):1266.

KPMG Peat Marwick. 1996. *Health Benefits in 1996*. Tysons Corner, VA: KPMG Peat Marwick.

———. 1997. *Health Benefits in 1997*. New York: KPMG Peat Marwick.

Krehbiel, K. 1991. *Information and Legislative Organization*. Ann Arbor: University of Michigan Press.

Kronebusch, K. 1997. Medicaid and the Politics of Groups: Recipients, Providers, and State Policymaker Choices. *Journal of Health Politics, Policy and Law* 22:839–878.

Krueger, A. O. 1974. The Political Economy of the Rent-Seeking Society. *American Economic Review* 64:291–303.

Kuhn, T. [1962] 1970. *The Structure of Scientific Revolutions*. 2d ed. Chicago: University of Chicago Press.

Kuran, T. 1995. *Private Truths, Public Lies: The Social Consequences of Preference Falsification*. Cambridge: Harvard University Press.

Kuttner, R. 1984. *The Economic Illusion: False Choices between Prosperity and Social Justice*. Boston: Houghton Mifflin.

———. 1996. *Everything for Sale: The Virtues and Limits of Markets*. New York: Knopf.

Labelle, R. J., G. L. Stoddart, and T. H. Rice. 1994. A Re-examination of the Meaning and Importance of Supplier-Induced Demand. *Journal of Health Economics* 13(3):347–368.

Lamm, R. D. 1994. Healthcare Heresies. *Healthcare Forum Journal* (September–October):45–46, 59–61.

Lange, O. 1938. On the Economic Theory of Socialism. In *The Economic Theory of Socialism*, ed. Lange and Taylor. Minneapolis, MN: B. E. Lippincott.

Langwell, K., and J. Hadley. 1989. Evaluation of the Medicare Competition Demonstrations. *Health Care Financing Review* 11(2):65–80.

———. 1990. Insights from the Medicare HMO Demonstrations. *Health Affairs* 9(1):74–84.

Langwell, K., L. Nelson, and S. Nelson. 1988. Direct Physician Capitation under the Medicare Program: Evidence and Feasibility. In *Lessons from the First Twenty Years of Medicare*, ed. M. V. Pauly and W. L. Kissick. Philadelphia: University of Pennsylvania Press.

Latour, B. 1983. Give Me a Laboratory and I Will Raise the World. In *Science Observed*, ed. K. D. Knorr-Cetina and M. Mulkayo. Thousand Oaks, CA: Sage.

———. 1988. *The Pasteurization of France*. Cambridge: Harvard University Press.

Latour, B., and S. Woolgar. 1979. *Laboratory Life: The Social Construction of Scientific Facts*. Beverly Hills, CA: Sage.

Leape, L. 1989. Unnecessary Surgery. *Health Services Research* 24:351–407.

Leape, L. L., L. H. Hilborne, J. P. Kahan, W. B. Stason, R. E. Park, C. J. Kamberg, and R. H. Brook. 1991. *Coronary Artery Bypass Graft: A Literature Review and Ratings of Appropriateness and Necessity*. Santa Monica, CA: Rand.

Lee, C., and D. Rogal. 1997. Risk Adjustment: A Key to Changing Incentives in the

Health Insurance Market. Special Report, Changes in Health Care Financing and Organization Program. Washington, DC: Alpha Center.

Leffler, K. B. 1978. Physician Licensure: Competition and Monopoly in American Medicine. *Journal of Law and Economics* 21:165–186.

Lerner, A. P. 1946. *The Economics of Control*. New York: Macmillan.

Levinson, M. 1996. Profit Motive. *Newsweek,* 22 April, pp. 56–57.

Levit, K. R., and C. A. Cowan. 1990. The Burden of Health Care Costs: Business, Households, and Governments. *Health Care Financing Review* 12 (winter): 127–138.

Levit, K., C. Cowan, H. Lazenby, P. McDonnell, A. Sensenig, J. Stiller, and D. Won. 1994. National Health Spending Trends, 1960–1993. *Health Affairs* 13(1):14–31.

Levit, K., H. Lazenby, S. Letsch, and C. Cowan. 1991. National Health Care Spending, 1989. 1991. *Health Affairs* 10(2):117, 127–129.

Levit, K. R., H. C. Lazenby, and L. Sivarajan. 1996. Health Care Spending in 1994: Slowest in Decades. *Health Affairs* 15(2):130–144.

Lichenstein, R. L., J. W. Thomas, B. Watkins, C. Puto, J. Lepkowski, J. Adams-Watson, B. Simone, and D. Vest. 1992. HMO Marketing and Selection Bias. *Medical Care* 30:329–345.

Lichenstein, R. L., J. W. Thomas, J. Adams-Watson, J. Lepkowski, and B. Simone. 1991. Selection Bias in TEFRA At-Risk HMOs. *Medical Care* 29:318–331.

Liebenstein, H. 1976. *Beyond Economic Man*. Cambridge: Harvard University Press.

Light, D. W. 1995. *Homo Economicus*: Escaping the Traps of Managed Competition. *European Journal of Public Health* 5:145–154.

——. 1997. Lessons for the United States: Britain's Experience with Managed Competition. In *Competitive Managed Care: The Emerging Health Care System,* ed. J. D. Wilkerson, K. J. Devers, and R. S. Given. San Francisco: Jossey-Bass.

Lindblom, C. E. 1977. *Politics and Markets: The World's Political Economic Systems*. New York: Basic Books.

Lindblom, C. E., and D. K. Cohen. 1979. *Usable Knowledge: Social Science and Social Problem Solving*. New Haven: Yale University Press.

Lipson, D. J., and J. M. De Sa. 1996. Impact of Purchasing Strategies on Local Health Systems. *Health Affairs* 15(2):62–76.

Lohr, K. N., R. H. Brook, C. J. Kamberg, G. A. Goldberg, A. Leibowitz, J. Keesey, D. Reboussin, and J. P. Newhouse. 1986. Effect of Cost-Sharing on Use of Medically Effective and Less Effective Care. *Medical Care* 24 (Suppl.S32–38).

A Look at Employers' Costs of Providing Health Benefits. 1996. *Medical Benefits* 13, 30 August, p. 1 (summary of U.S. Department of Labor report issued 31 July 1996).

Lowy, I. 1986. Tissue Groups and Cadaver Kidney Sharing: Sociocultural Aspects of a Medical Controversy. *International Journal of Technology Assessment in Health Care* 2:195–218.

Luft, H. S. 1981. *Health Maintenance Organizations: Dimensions of Performance*. New York: Wiley.

——. 1982. Health Organizations and the Rationing of Medical Care. *Milbank Quarterly* 60:268–306.

——, ed. 1994. *HMOs and the Elderly.* Ann Arbor, MI: Health Administration Press.

Luft, H. S., and R. H. Miller. 1988. Patient Selection in a Competitive Medical System. *Health Affairs* 7(3):97–119.

Managed Care in Medicare and Medicaid. 1997. Fact Sheet. Washington, DC: Health Care Financing Administration.

Mann, J., G. Melnick, A. Bamezai, and J. Zwanziger. 1995. Uncompensated Care: Hospitals' Responses to Fiscal Pressures. *Health Affairs* 14(6):263–270.

Manning, W. G., A. Leibowitz, G. Goldberg, W. Rogers, and J. P. Newhouse. 1984. A Controlled Trial of the Effect of Prepaid Group Practice on Use of Service. *New England Journal of Medicine* 310:1505–1510.

March, J. G. 1978. Bounded Rationality, Ambiguity, and the Engineering of Choice. *Bell Journal of Economics* 9:577–608.

Marcus, R. 1995. Health Care PACs Give Freely. *Washington Post,* 1 December, p. A25.

Marmor, T. R. 1973. *The Politics of Medicare.* Chicago: Aldine.

——. 1990. Entrepreneurship in Public Management: Wilbur Cohen and Robert Ball. In *Leadership and Innovation: Entrepreneurs in Government,* abr. ed., ed. J. W. Doig and E. C. Hargrove. Baltimore: Johns Hopkins University Press.

——. 1994. *Understanding Health Care Reform.* New Haven, CT: Yale University Press.

——. 1995a. Medical Care Reform in Mature Welfare States: Fact, Fiction, and Foolishness in the Transmission of Ideas. Paper presented at the Bremen Conference on Health Care Policies and Reform, 27 April.

——. 1995b. A Summer of Discontent: Press Coverage of Murder and Medical Care Reform. *Journal of Health Politics, Policy and Law* 20:495–501.

Marmor, T. R., and A. Dunham. 1983. Political Science and Health Services Administration. In *Political Analysis and American Medical Care: Essays,* ed. T. R. Marmor. Cambridge: Cambridge University Press.

Marmor, T. R., and J. L. Mashaw. 1990. Canada's Health Insurance and Ours: The Real Lessons, the Big Choices. *The American Prospect* 3 (fall):18–29.

——. 1993. A Little Gridlock Might Help. *Los Angeles Times,* 15 August, p. M5.

——. 1995. Madison Avenue Meets Marcus Welby. *Los Angeles Times,* 19 February, p. M5.

Marquis, S., and S. Long. 1994–95. The Uninsured Access Gap: Narrowing the Estimates. *Inquiry* 31:405–414.

Marshall, A. 1920. *Principles of Economics.* London: Macmillan.

Marsteller, J. A., R. R. Bovbjerg, D. K. Verrilli, and L. Nichols. 1997. The Resurgence of Selective Contracting Restrictions. *Journal of Health Politics, Policy and Law* 22(5):1133–1189.

Martin, C. J. 1994. Together Again: Business, Government, and the Quest for Cost Control. In *The Politics of Health Care Reform: Lessons from the Past, Prospects for the Future,* ed. James A. Morone and Gary S. Belkin. Durham, NC: Duke University Press.

——. 1995. Nature or Nurture? Sources of Firm Preference for National Health Reform. *American Political Science Review* 89:898–913.

——. 1997. Markets, Medicare, and Making Do: Business Strategies after National Health Care Reform. *Journal of Health Politics, Policy and Law* 22(2):557–593.

Martins, M. 1995. Letter to Mathematica Policy Research, Inc., Washington, DC, April.

Massaro, T. A., and Y.-N. Wong. 1995. Positive Experience with Medical Savings Accounts in Singapore. *Health Affairs* 14(2):267–272.

Mayhew, D. R. 1974. *Congress: The Electoral Connection*. New Haven, CT: Yale University Press.

McClellan, M. 1995. The Uncertain Demand for Medical Care: A Comment on Emmett Keeler. *Journal of Health Economics* 14:239–242.

McCombs, J. S., J. D. Kasper, and G. F. Riley. 1990. Do HMOs Reduce Health Care Costs: A Multivariate Analysis of Medicare HMO Demonstration Projects. *Health Services Research* 24:593–613.

McGuire, M. C., and M. Olson. 1996. The Economics of Autocracy and Majority Rule: The Invisible Hand and the Use of Force. *Journal of Economic Literature* 34:72.

McIlrath, S. 1995a. Can MSAs Work for Medicare? *American Medical News* 38(31):1.

——. 1995b. GOP Health Plan Blitz. *American Medical News* 38(38):1.

McLoughlin, C., W. Zellers, and K. Frick. 1994. Small Business Winners and Losers under Health Care Reform. *Health Affairs* (spring):221–233.

McMillan, A. 1993. Trends in Medicare Health Maintenance Organization Enrollment. *Health Care Financing Review* 15:135–146.

McPherson, K. 1990. International Differences in Medical Care Practices. In *Health Care Systems in Transition*. Paris: OECD.

Measuring the Quality of Health Care. 1995. Summary of *Issue Brief* no. 159, Employee Benefit Research Institute, March. *Medical Benefits* 12(7):11.

Mechanic, D. 1979. *Future Issues in Health Care*. New York: Free Press.

——. 1994. Managed Care: Rhetoric and Realities. *Inquiry* 31(2):124–128.

Medical Savings Accounts: The State of State Legislation. 1996. *Medical Benefits* 13(15):6.

Medicare Plan by G.O.P. Has No H.M.O. Mandate. 1995. *New York Times*, 15 September, p. A32.

Meehl, P. E. 1954. *Clinical versus Statistical Prediction*. Minneapolis: University of Minnesota Press.

Mega Managed Care Deal Redefines Market. 1996. *Medical Benefits* 13, 30 April, p. 5 (summary of Joe Niedzielski, National Underwriter, Life and Health/Financial Services Edition, 9 April 1996).

Meldrum, M. 1994. Managed Care Plan Performance since 1980. *Journal of the American Medical Association* 271:1512–1518.

——. 1996. Simple Methods and "Determined Contraceptors": The Statistical Evaluation of Fertility Control, 1957–1968. *Bulletin of the History of Medicine* 70:266–295.

Merton, R., ed. 1973. *The Sociology of Science*. Chicago: University of Chicago Press.

Miller, P., ed. 1997. *American Healthline 50-State Report*, 13th ed. Washington, DC: National Journal.

Miller, R. H. 1996. Competition in the Health System: Good News and Bad News. *Health Affairs* 15(2):107–120.

Miller, R. H., and H. S. Luft. 1994a. Managed Care Plan Performance since 1980. *Journal of the American Medical Association* 271:1512–1518.

———. 1994b. Managed Care Plans: Characteristics, Growth, and Premium Performance. *Annual Review of Public Health* 15:437–459.

Miller, W. 1995. Battle Looms. *Industry Week*, 4 September, 82.

Mishan, E. J. 1969a. *Welfare Economics: An Assessment*. Amsterdam: North-Holland.

———. 1969b. *Welfare Economics: Ten Introductory Essays*. New York: Random House.

———. 1982. *What Is Political Economy All About?* Cambridge: Cambridge University Press.

Mohr, L. B. 1976. Organizations, Decisions, and Courts. *Law and Society* (summer):621–642.

Moon, M. 1993. *Medicare: Now and in the Future*. Washington, DC: Urban Institute.

Moon, M., and K. Davis. 1995. Preserving and Strengthening Medicare. *Health Affairs* 14(4):31–46.

Moon, M., and S. Zuckerman. 1995. *Are Private Insurers Really Controlling Spending Better than Medicare?* Henry J. Kaiser Family Foundation Discussion Paper.

Moore, S. 1979. Cost Containment through Risk-Sharing by Primary Care Physicians. *New England Journal of Medicine* 300:1359–1362.

Moore, W. J. 1994. Scouting for GOP Talent. *National Journal*, 10 December, p. 2912.

Moore, W. J., R. Cohen, and P. Stone. 1995. A Loyalty Test for Lobbyists? *National Journal*, 3 June, pp. 1341–1343.

Morone, J. A. 1986. Seven Laws of Policy Analysis. *Journal of Policy Analysis and Management* 5:817–819.

———. 1990. *The Democratic Wish: Popular Participation and the Limits of American Government*. New York: Basic Books.

———. 1993. The Ironic Flaw in Health Care Competition: The Politics of Markets. In *Competitive Approaches to Health Care Reform*, ed. R. J. Arnould, F. F. Rich, and W. D. White. Washington, DC: Urban Institute Press.

———. 1994. The Bureaucracy Empowered. In *The Politics of Health Care Reform: Lessons from the Past, Prospects for the Future*, ed. J. A. Morone and G. S. Belkin. Durham, NC: Duke University Press.

Morone, J. A., and G. Belkin. 1995. *The Science Illusion and the Triumph of Medical Capitalism*. Paper presented at the American Political Science Association Annual Meeting, Chicago, 2 September.

Morone, J. A., and J. M. Goggin, eds. 1995a. European Health Policies: Welfare States in a Market Era (special issue). *Journal of Health Politics, Policy and Law* 20.

———. 1995b. Introduction—Health Policies in Europe: Welfare States in a Market Era. *Journal of Health Politics, Policy and Law* 20:557–569.

Morrisey, M., G. Jensen, and R. Morlock. 1994. Small Employers and the Health Insurance Market. *Health Affairs* 13:149–152.

Morrison, J. I., E. M. Morrison, and J. N. Edwards. 1991. Large Employers and Employee Benefits: Priorities for the 1990s. In *The Future of American Health Care,* ed. R. J. Blendon and J. Edwards. Vol. 1. New York: Faulkner and Gray.

Mueller, D. C. 1989. *Public Choice 2.* Cambridge: Cambridge University Press.

1991 National Executive Poll on Health Care Costs and Benefits. 1991. *Business and Health* 9(9):61–71.

1995 AAHP HMO and PPO Trends Report. 1996. *Medical Benefits* 13, 30 July, p. 1 (summary of report from American Association of Health Plans, 17 June 1996).

1995 National Hospital Merger and Acquisition Survey. 1996. *Medical Benefits* 13, 15 May, p. 11 (summary of Tribrook report, 12 April 1996).

Nair, C., R. Karim, and C. Nyers. 1992. Health Care and Health Status: A Canada–United States Statistical Comparison. *Health Reports* 4(2):175–183. (Ottawa, ON: Statistics Canada; Cat. No. 82–003).

Nath, S. K. 1969. *A Reappraisal of Welfare Economics.* London: Routledge and Kegan Paul.

National Association of Public Hospitals. 1995. *Tennessee's Failing Health Reform Experiment Is Forcing NAPH Member, the Med, to Cut Employees and Services.* Press release, Washington, DC.

Nelson, L., R. Brown, M. Gold, A. Ciemnecki, and E. Docteur. 1997. Access to Care in Medicare HMOs. *Health Affairs* 16(2):148–156.

Newcomer, R., C. Harrington, and S. Preston. 1994. Satisfaction in the Social/Health Maintenance Organization. In *HMOs and the Elderly,* ed. H. S. Luft. Ann Arbor, MI: Health Administration Press.

Newhouse, J. P. 1993. An Iconoclastic View of Health Cost Containment. *Health Affairs* 10 (Suppl.):152–171.

Newhouse, J. P., and the Insurance Experiment Group. 1993. *Free for All? Lessons from the RAND Health Insurance Experiment.* Cambridge: Harvard University Press.

Ng., Y.-K. 1979. *Welfare Economics.* London: Macmillan.

Nichols, L. M., M. Moon, and S. Wall. 1996. Tax-Preferred Medical Savings Accounts and Catastrophic Health Insurance Plans: A Numerical Analysis of Winners and Losers. April. Washington, DC: Urban Institute.

Niskanen, W. A., Jr. 1971. *Bureaucracy and Representative Government.* Chicago: Aldine-Atherton.

Nordlinger, E. A. 1981. *On the Autonomy of the Democratic State.* Cambridge: Harvard University Press.

North, D. C. 1990. *Institutions, Institutional Change, and Economic Performance.* New York: Cambridge University Press.

Nozick, R. 1974. *Anarchy, State, and Utopia.* New York: Basic Books.

Oberlander, J. B. 1997. Managed Care and Medicare Reform. *Journal of Health Politics, Policy and Law* 22(2):595–631.

Odynocki, B. 1988. Corporate Cost-Containment Strategy and Employee Health Care. *Social Policy* 18 (winter):21–25.

OECD/CREDES. 1996. OECD Health Data 96. Software for the Comparative Analysis of 27 Health Systems. Paris: OECD Health Policy Unit.

OECD/CREDES. 1997. OECD Health Data 97. Software for the Comparative Analysis of 29 Health Systems. Paris: OECD Health Policy Unit.

Office of Technology Assessment (OTA). 1992. *Evaluation of the Oregon Medicaid Proposal.* Washington, DC: U.S. Government Printing Office.

O'Grady, K. F., W. G. Manning, J. P. Newhouse, and R. H. Brook. 1985. The Impact of Cost Sharing on Emergency Department Use. *New England Journal of Medicine* 313:484.

Okun, A. M. 1975. *Equality and Efficiency: The Big Tradeoff.* Washington, DC: Brookings Institution.

Oliver, T. R. 1993. Analysis, Advice, and Congressional Leadership: The Physician Payment Review Commission and the Politics of Medicare. *Journal of Health Politics, Policy and Law* 18:113–173.

Oliver, T. R., and R. M. Fiedle. 1997. How Government Modifies the Medical Market Place: Choices and Influences in the Design of State Insurance Reforms. In *Health Policy in America: Innovations from the States*, 2d ed., ed. H. M. Leichter. Armonk, NY: M. E. Sharpe.

Oliver, T. R., and P. Paul-Shaheen. 1997. Translating Ideas into Actions: Entrepreneurial Leadership in State Health Care Reforms. *Journal of Health Politics, Policy and Law* 22:721–728.

Olmos, D. R. 1995. Kaiser Plans Cost Cutting $800 Million. *Los Angeles Times,* 23 September, p. D1.

O'Neill, J. E., and D. M. O'Neill. 1993. The Impact of a Health Insurance Mandate on Labor Costs and Employment: Empirical Evidence. September. Report issued by the Employment Policies Institute, Washington, DC.

Oregon Department of Human Resources (DHR), Office of Medical Assistance Programs. 1991. *Waiver Application. Oregon Medicaid Demonstration Project.* Salem: Oregon DHR.

——. 1993. *Oregon Health Plan.* Salem: Oregon DHR.

——. 1994. *November 1994 Enrollment and Disenrollment Reports.* Salem: Oregon DHR.

——. 1997. *Oregon Health Plan Policy and Research.* [Online website: http://www.das.state.or.us/ohpa.] Salem: Oregon DHR.

Oregon Health Services Commission. 1993. *Prioritization of Health Services: A Report to the Governor and Legislature.* Salem: Oregon Health Services Commission.

Overheard in the House GOP Cloakroom. 1995. *Washington Post,* 13 December, p. A1.

Page, B. I., and R. Y. Shapiro. 1992. *The Rational Public: Fifty Years of Trends in Americans' Policy Preferences.* Chicago: University of Chicago Press.

Paris, S., and R. Vernick. 1995. Good Managed Care Means Good Health Care. *Boston Globe*, 21 November, p. 21.

Parrish, D., and E. Sloane. 1995. UCI Doctors Told Not to Lure Seriously Ill HMO Patients. *Orange County Register*, 3 August, p. A1.

Parsons, T. 1951. *The Social System*. New York: Free Press.

——. 1975. The Sick Role and the Role of the Physician. *Milbank Quarterly* 53:257–278.

Pascal-Pomey, M., and J.-P. Poullier. 1997. France's Health Policy Conundrum. In *Health Care and Reform in Industrialized Countries,* ed. Marshall W. Raffel. University Park: Pennsylvania State University Press.

Pauly, M. V. 1968. The Economics of Moral Hazard. *American Economic Review* 58:231–237.

——. 1993. U.S. Health Care Costs: The Untold True Story. *Health Affairs* 12(3):152–159.

——. 1994a. Editorial: A Re-examination of the Meaning and Importance of Supplier-Induced Demand. *Journal of Health Economics* 13:369–372.

——. 1994b. Reply to Roberta Labelle, Greg Stoddart, and Thomas Rice. *Journal of Health Economics* 13(4):495–496.

——. 1996a. Reply to Anthony J. Culyer and Robert G. Evans. *Journal of Health Economics* 13(4):495–496.

——. 1996b. Trading Cost, Quality, and Coverage of the Uninsured: What Will We Demand and What Will We Supply? Paper presented at the Eleventh Annual William Campbell Felch Lecture for the American Society of Internal Medicine, Chicago, 10 October.

Pauly, M., and J. C. Goodman. 1995. Tax Credits for Health Insurance and Medical Savings Accounts. *Health Affairs* 14(1):126–139.

Pauly, M., P. Danzon, P. Feldstein, and J. Hoff. 1991. A Plan for "Responsible National Health Insurance." *Health Affairs* 10(2):5–25.

Pear, R. 1995a. Senate G.O.P. Plan for Medicare Uses Benefit Cutbacks. *New York Times,* 28 September, pp. A1, B10.

——. 1995b. Retirees' Group Attacks G.O.P. Health Plan. *New York Times,* 6 October, p. A22.

——. 1995c. Doctors' Group Says G.O.P. Agreed to Deal on Medicare. *New York Times,* 12 October, p. A1.

——. 1995d. For Elderly, Bill Promises Entry into a Market of Shifting Forces. *New York Times,* 20 October, pp. A1, 17.

——. 1995e. Leaders of A.M.A. Critical of Plan to Alter Medicaid. *New York Times,* 5 December, pp. A1, B9.

——. 1996a. U.S. Shelves Plan to Limit Rewards to HMO Doctors. *New York Times,* 8 July, p. A1.

——. 1996b. His Eyes on 2d Term, Clinton to Name Panel. *New York Times,* 5 September, p. A11.

——. 1996c. In Congress, Leaders Agree on Insurance Plans. *New York Times,* 20 September, p. A11.

——. 1996d. Health Costs Pose Problems for Millions, Study Finds. *New York Times*, 23 October, p. A14.

——. 1997a. Clinton Bans HMO Rule for Patients in Medicaid. *New York Times*, 21 February, p. A12.

——. 1997b. 3 Big Health Plans Urge National Standards. *New York Times*, 25 September, p. A1, A14.

——. 1997c. Panel of Experts Urges Broadening of Patient Rights. *New York Times*, 23 October, pp. A1, A12.

Pearlstein, S. 1996. There's Irony and Tragedy in Health System 'Savings.' *Washington Post*, 19 December, p. E1.

Peele, P. B. 1993. Evaluating Welfare Losses in the Health Care Market. *Journal of Health Economics* 12:205–208.

Pemberton, C., and D. Holmes, eds. 1995. Benefits Received by Individuals. In *EBRI Databook on Employee Benefits*. Washington, DC: Employee Benefit Research Institution.

Perkoff, G., L. Kahn, and P. J. Haas. 1976. The Effects of an Experimental Prepaid Group Practice on Medical Care Utilization and Cost. *Medical Care* 19:432–449.

Pernick, M. 1985. *A Calculus of Suffering: Pain, Professionalism, and Anesthesia in Nineteenth-Century America*. New York: Columbia University Press.

Peterkin, G. S. 1914. *Medical Ethics versus Ethical Economics or Efficiency in Medical Practice*. Codman Papers, box 2, folder 37. Countway Library of Medicine, Boston.

Peterson, M. A. 1992a. Report from Congress: Momentum toward Health Care Reform in the U.S. Senate. *Journal of Health Politics, Policy and Law* 17:553–573.

——. 1992b. Leading Our Way to Health: Entrepreneurship and Leadership in the Health Care Reform Debate. Paper presented at the annual meeting of the American Political Science Association, Chicago, IL, 3–6 September.

——. 1993a. Political Influence in the 1990s: From Iron Triangles to Policy Networks. *Journal of Health Politics, Policy and Law* 18:395–438.

——. 1993b. Institutional Change and the Health Politics of the 1990s. *American Behavioral Scientist* 36(6):782–801.

——. 1994a. Congress in the 1990s: From Iron Triangles to Policy Networks. In *The Politics of Health Care Reform: Lessons from the Past, Prospects for the Future*, eds. J. A. Morone and G. S. Belkin. Durham, NC: Duke University Press.

——. 1994b. Institutional Change and the New Politics of Health Care in the 1990s. In *Health Care Reform in the Nineties*, ed. Pauline Vaillancourt Rosenau. Thousand Oaks, CA: Sage.

——. 1994c. From Vested Oligarchy to Informed Entrepreneurship: New Opportunities for Health Care Reform in Congress. Paper presented at the annual meeting of the Midwest Political Science Association, Chicago, IL, 14–16 April.

——. 1995a. How Health Policy Information Is Used in Congress. In *Intensive Care:*

How Congress Shapes Health Policy, ed. T. E. Mann and N. J. Ornstein. Washington, DC: American Enterprise Institute and Brookings Institution.

——. 1995b. *Interest Groups as Allies and Antagonists: Their Role in the Politics of Health Care Reform.* Paper presented at the annual meeting of the Association for Health Services Research and Foundation for Health Services Research, Chicago, IL, 4–6 June.

——. 1995c. Welfare Loss from Variations: Further Considerations. *Journal of Health Economics* 14:253–260.

——. 1998. The Politics of Health Care Policy: Overreaching in an Age of Polarization. In *The Social Divide: Political Parties and the Future of Activist Government,* ed. Margaret Weir. Washington, DC: Brookings Institution/Russell Sage Foundation.

Phelps, C. E. 1992. *Health Economics.* New York: HarperCollins.

Phelps, C. E., and C. Mooney. 1992. Correction and Update on Priority Setting in Medical Technology Assessment in Medical Care. *Medicare Care* 31:744–751.

Phelps, C. E., and S. T. Parente. 1990. Priority Setting in Medical Technology and Medical Practice Assessment. *Medicare Care* 29:703–723.

Physician Payment Review Commission (PPRC). 1994. Risk Adjustment. In *Annual Report to Congress, 1994.* Washington, DC: PPRC.

——. 1995a. *Annual Report to Congress 1995.* Washington, DC: Government Printing Office.

——. 1995b. *Estimated Payment Rates for MedicarePlus Plans.* Washington, DC: U.S. Government Printing Office.

Pianin, E. 1997. Clinton Offers, Seeks Concessions on Tax Cuts. *Washington Post,* 1 July, p. A1.

Pickering, A., ed. 1992. *Science as Practice and Culture.* Chicago: University of Chicago Press.

Pierson, P. 1992. "Policy Feedbacks" and Political Change: Contrasting Reagan and Thatcher's Pension-Reform Initiatives. *Studies in American Political Development* 6 (fall):359–390.

Pigou, A. C. 1932. *The Economics of Welfare,* 4th ed. New York: Macmillan.

Poen, M. M. 1979. *Harry S. Truman versus the Medical Lobby.* Columbia: University of Missouri Press.

Pollak, R. A. 1970. Habit Formation and Dynamic Demand Functions. *Journal of Political Economy* 78:745–763.

——. 1976. Habit Formation and Long-Run Utility Functions. *Journal of Economic Theory* 13:272–297.

——. 1978. Endogenous Tastes in Demand and Welfare Analysis. *American Economic Review* 68:374–379.

Popper, K. 1972. *Objective Knowledge: An Evolutionary Approach.* Oxford: Clarendon.

Popularity of HMOs Grows for Seventh Consecutive Year. 1996. *Medical Benefits* 13, 15 June, pp. 4–5 (summary of Minnesota Council of HMOs report, April 1996).

Porell, F. W., and C. P. Tompkins. 1993. Medicare Risk Contracting: Identifying Factors Associated with Market Exit. *Inquiry* 30:157–169.

Porter, T. 1995. *Trust in Numbers: The Pursuit of Objectivity in Science and Public Life*. Princeton, NJ: Princeton University Press.

Posner, R. 1974. Certificate-of-Need for Health Care Facilities: A Dissenting View. In *Regulating Health Facilities Construction*, ed. C. Havighurst. Washington, DC: American Enterprise Institute.

Power in Numbers: How Businesses Are Ganging Up to Control Health Care Costs. 1992. *Corporate Report Minnesota* 23(11):73.

President's Commission for the Study of Ethical Problems in Medicine and Biomedical and Behavioral Research. 1983. *Securing Access to Health Care: The Ethical Implications of Differences in the Availability of Health Services*. Vol. 1. Washington, DC.

Preston, J. A., and S. M. Retchin. 1991. The Management of Geriatric Hypertension in Health Maintenance Organizations. *Journal of the American Geriatric Society* 39:683–690.

Priest, D. 1995. Cross-Dressing for Success: The Parties Trade Medicare Gowns. *Washington Post*, 1 October, p. C3.

Prospective Payment Assessment Commission (ProPAC). 1995. *Medicare and the American Health Care System*. Washington, DC: ProPAC.

——. 1996. *Medicare and the American Health Care System: Report to Congress* (June). Washington, DC: Prospective Payment Assessment Commission.

Putnam, R. D. 1993. *Making Democracy Work: Civic Traditions in Modern Italy*. Princeton, NJ: Princeton University Press.

Rasell, E., J. Bernstein, and K. Tang. 1993. *The Impact of Health Care Financing on Family Budgets*. Briefing Paper (April). Washington, DC: Economic Policy Institute.

Rasell, E., and K. Tang. 1994. *Paying for Health Care: Affordability and Equity in Proposals for Health Care Reform*. Working Paper No. 111 (December). Washington, DC: Economic Policy Institute.

Rauskolb, C. 1976. *Lobby in Weiß*. Frankfurt: Europaische Verlagsanstalt.

Rayack, E. 1967. *Professional Power and American Medicine: The Economics of the American Medical Association*. Cleveland, OH: World Publishing Co.

Redelmeier, D. A., and V. R. Fuchs. 1993. Hospital Expenditures in the United States and Canada. *New England Journal of Medicine* 328:772–778.

Reinhardt, U. E. 1985. The Theory of Physician-Induced Demand: Reflections after a Decade. *Journal of Health Economics* 4(2):187–193.

——. 1992. Reflections on the Meaning of Efficiency: Can Efficiency Be Separated from Equity? *Yale Law and Policy Review* 10(2):302–315.

Reiss, P. C. 1996. Empirical Models of Discrete Strategic Choice. *American Economic Review* 86:421.

Report Card Pilot Project. 1995. Summary of report from National Committee for Quality Assurance, 23 February. *Medical Benefits* 12(5):7.

Retchin, S. M., and B. Brown. 1990a. Management of Colorectal Cancer in Medicare Health Maintenance Organizations. *Journal of General Internal Medicine* 5:110–114.

———. 1990b. The Quality of Ambulatory Care in Health Maintenance Organizations. *American Journal of Public Health* 80:411–415.

———. 1991. Elderly Patients with Congestive Heart Failure under Prepaid Care. *American Journal of Medicine* 90:236–242.

Retchin, S. M., and D. G. Clement. 1992. How the Elderly Fare in HMOs: Outcomes from the Medicare Competition Demonstrations. *Health Services Research* 27:651–669.

Retchin, S. M., D. G. Clement, and R. S. Brown. 1994. Care of Patients Hospitalized with Strokes under the Medicare Risk Program. In *HMOs and the Elderly*, ed. H. S. Luft. Ann Arbor, MI: Health Administration Press.

Retchin, S. M., and J. A. Preston. 1991. Effects of Cost Containment on the Care of Elderly Diabetics. *Archives of Internal Medicine* 151:2244–2248.

Reverby, S. 1981. Stealing the Golden Eggs: Ernest Amory Codman and the Science and Management of Medicine. *Bulletin of the History of Medicine* 55:156–171.

Rice, T. 1992. An Alternative Framework for Evaluating Welfare Losses in the Health Care Market. *Journal of Health Economics* 11:85–92.

———. 1993a. Demand Curves, Economists, and Desert Islands: A Response to Feldman and Dowd. *Journal of Health Economics* 12:201–204.

———. 1993b. A Model Is Only as Good as Its Assumptions: A Reply to Peele. *Journal of Health Economics* 12:209–211.

———. 1997. Can Markets Give Us the Health System We Want? *Journal of Health Politics, Policy and Law* 22(2):383–426.

———. 1998. *The Economics of Health Reconsidered*. Chicago: Health Administration.

Rice, T., E. R. Brown, and R. Wyn. 1993. Holes in the Jackson Hole Approach to Health Care Reform. *Journal of the American Medical Association* 270:1357–1362.

Rice, T., and K. R. Morrison. 1994. Patient Cost Sharing for Medical Services: A Review of the Literature and Implications for Health Care Reform. *Medical Care Review* 51:235–287.

Rich, S. 1996. Even Tougher Debate on Medicare Expected As Baby Boomers Age. *Washington Post*, 6 February, p. A13.

Riley, G. F., A. L. Potosky, J. D. Lubitz, and M. L. Brown. 1994. Stage of Cancer at Diagnosis for Medicare HMO and Fee-for-Service Enrollees. *American Journal of Public Health* 84:1598–1604.

Robert Wood Johnson Foundation. 1994. *Annual Report: Cost Containment*. Princeton, NJ: Robert Wood Johnson Foundation.

Robinson, J. C. 1991. HMO Market Penetration and Hospital Cost Inflation in California. *Journal of the American Medical Association* 266:2719–2723.

Robinson, J. 1995. Health Care Purchasing and Market Changes in California. *Health Affairs* 14:117–130.

Robinson, J. C., H. S. Luft, L. B. Gardner, and E. M. Morrison. 1991. A Method for Risk-Adjusting Employer Contributions to Competing Health Insurance Plans. *Inquiry* 28:107–116.

Rodwin, M. A. 1993. *Medicine, Money, and Morals: Physicians' Conflicts of Interests.* New York: Oxford University Press.

Rodwin, V. G. Forthcoming. The Rise of Managed Care in the United States: Lessons for French Health Policy. In *Health Policy Reform, National Schemes and Globalization,* ed. C. Altenstetter and J. Bjorkman. New York: St. Martin's.

Roemer, J. E. 1994. *Egalitarian Perspectives.* Cambridge: Cambridge University Press.

Roos, N. P., and L. L. Roos. 1994. Small Area Variations, Practice Style, and Quality of Care. In *Why Are Some People Healthy, and Others Not? The Determinants of Health of Populations,* ed. R. G. Evans, M. L. Barer, and R. R. Marmor. New York: Aldine de Gruyter.

Rose, R. 1993. *Lesson-Drawing in Public Policy.* Chatham, NJ: Chatham House.

Rosenbaum, D. 1995a. The Medicare Brawl. *New York Times,* 1 October, p. 18.

———. 1995b. Past All the Talk, Some True Goals. *New York Times,* 20 October, p. A26.

Rosenbaum, S. 1997. A Comparison of Medicaid Provisions in the Balanced Budget Act of 1997 with Current Law. Paper presented for the National Association of Community Health Centers, Washington, DC, August.

Rosenbaum, S., P. Shin, B. M. Smith, E. Wehr, P. C. Borzi, M. H. Zakheim, K. Shaw, and K. Silver. 1997. *Negotiating the New Health System: A Nationwide Study of Medicaid Managed Care Contracts.* Washington, DC: Center for Health Policy Research, George Washington University.

Rosenberg, C. 1987. *The Care of Strangers: The Rise of America's Hospital System.* New York: Basic Books.

Rosenberg, C., and J. Golden, eds. 1992. *Framing Disease: Studies in Cultural History.* New Brunswick, NJ: Rutgers University Press.

Rosenthal, E. 1996. New York State's Plan to Move Medicaid Recipients into Managed Care Advances. *New York Times,* 15 August, p. A20.

Rossiter, L. F., H. C. Chiu, and J. H. Chen. 1994. Strengths and Weaknesses of the AAPCC. In *HMOs and the Elderly,* ed. H. S. Luft. Ann Arbor, MI: Health Administration Press.

Rossiter, L. F., K. Langwell, T. Wan, and M. Rivnyak. 1989. Patient Satisfaction among Elderly Enrollees and Disenrollees in Medicare Health Maintenance Organizations. *Journal of the American Medical Association* 262:57–63.

Rossiter, L. F., T. Wan, K. Langwell, J. Hadley, A. Tucker, M. Rivnyak, K. Sullivan, and J. Norcross. 1988. *An Analysis of Patient Satisfaction for Enrollees and Disenrollees in Medicare Risk-Based Plans.* Richmond, VA: Report for the Health Care Financing Administration.

Rothman, D. J. 1991. The Public Presentation of Blue Cross, 1935–1965. *Journal of Health Politics, Policy and Law* 16:671–693.

———. 1994. A Century of Struggle: Class Barriers to Reform. In *The Politics of Health Care Reform,* ed. J. Morone and G. Belkin. Durham, NC: Duke University Press.

Rowland, D., J. Feder, B. Lyons, and A. Salganicoff. 1992. *Medicaid at the Crossroads.* Baltimore: Kaiser Commission for the Future of Medicaid.

Rowland, D., and K. Hanson. 1996. Medicaid: Moving to Managed Care. *Health Affairs* 15(3):150–152.

Rowley, C. K., and A. T. Peacock. 1975. *Welfare Economics: A Liberal Restatement*. New York: Wiley.

Rublee, D. A. 1994. Medical Technology in Canada, Germany, and the United States: An Update. *Health Affairs* 13(4):113–117.

Ruggie, M. 1996. *Realignments in the Welfare State: Health Policy in the United States, Britain, and Canada*. New York: Columbia University Press.

Rules Changes Affects HMO Quality Ratings. 1997. Summary of A. Bell, *National Underwriter*, Life and Health/Financial Services Edition, 27 October. *Medical Benefits* 14(22):2.

Rusnock, A. 1995. Revolution to Measure: The Political Economy of the Metric System in France. In *The Values of Precision*, ed. M. N. Wise. Princeton, NJ: Princeton University Press.

Ruzek, S. 1978. *The Women's Health Movement: Feminist Alternatives to Medical Control*. New York: Praeger.

Sabatier, P. A. 1987. Knowledge, Policy-Oriented Learning, and Policy Change: An Advocacy Coalition Framework. *Knowledge: Creation, Diffusion, Utilization* 8 (June):649–692.

Salkever, D. S., and T. W. Bice. 1976. The Impact of Certificate-of-Need Controls on Hospital Investment. *Milbank Quarterly* 54:185–214.

Samuelson, P. A. 1938. A Note on the Pure Theory of Consumers' Behavior. *Economica* 5:61–71.

—— [1947] 1976. *Foundations of Economic Analysis*. New York: Atheneum.

Sanford C. Bernstein and Co. 1996. Unpublished data. New York.

Schelling, T. C. 1984. *Choice and Consequence*. Cambridge: Harvard University Press.

Schick, A. 1991. Informed Legislation: Policy Research versus Ordinary Knowledge. In *Knowledge, Power, and the Congress*, ed. W. H. Robinson and C. H. Wellborn, D. Rueschemeyer, and T. Skocpol. Washington, DC: CQ Press.

Schieber, G. J., J.-P. Poullier, and L. M. Greenwald. 1992. U.S. Health Expenditure Performance: An International Comparison. *Health Care Financing Review* 13:1–87.

——. 1994. Health System Performance in OECD Countries, 1980–1992. *Health Affairs* 13(3):100–112.

Schlenker, R. E., P. W. Shaughnessy, and D. F. Hittle. 1995. Patient-Level Cost of Home Health Care under Capitated and Fee-for-Service Payment. *Inquiry* 32:252–270.

Schlesinger, M. 1986. On the Limits of Expanding Health Care Reform: Chronic Care in Prepaid Settings. *Milbank Quarterly* 64(2):189–215.

——. 1995. Ethical Issues in Policy Advocacy. *Health Affairs* 14(3):23–29.

——. 1997. Countervailing Agency: A Strategy of Principaled Regulation under Managed Competition. *Milbank Quarterly* 75(1):35–87.

Schlesinger, M., B. Gray, and E. Bradley. 1996. Charity and Community: The Role of Nonprofit Ownership in a Managed Health Care System. *Journal of Health Politics, Policy and Law* 21:647–696.

Schlesinger, M., and D. Mechanic. 1993. Challenges for Managed Competition from Chronic Illness. *Health Affairs* 12(Suppl.):123–137.

Schlesinger, M., and P. B. Drumheller. 1988. Medicare and Innovative Insurance Plans. In *Renewing the Promise: Medicare and Its Reform,* ed. D. Blumenthal, M. Schlesinger, and P. B. Drumheller. New York: Oxford University Press.

Schlesinger, M., and T. Wetle. 1988. Medicare's Coverage of Health Services. In *Renewing the Promise,* ed. D. Blumenthal, M. Schlesinger, P. Brown, and P. B. Drumheller. New York: Oxford University Press.

Schumpeter, J. A. 1954. *History of Economic Analysis.* New York: Cambridge University Press.

Schut, F. T. 1995. Health Reform in the Netherlands: Balancing Corporatism, Etatism, and Market Mechanisms. *Journal of Health Politics, Policy and Law* 20:615–652.

Schwartz, W. B. 1994. In the Pipeline: A Wave of Valuable Medical Technology. *Health Affairs* 13(3):70–79.

Scitovsky, T. 1976. *The Joyless Economy.* New York: Oxford University Press.

Sen, A. K. 1970. *Collective Choice and Social Welfare.* San Francisco: Holden-Day.

——. 1982. *Choice, Welfare and Measurement.* Cambridge: MIT Press.

——. 1987. *On Ethics and Economics.* Oxford, England: Basil Blackwell.

——. 1992. *Inequality Revisited.* Cambridge: Harvard University Press.

Seppa, N. 1996. Do Americans Take Their Voting Rights for Granted? *APA Monitor* 27:15–19.

Serafini, M. W. 1995. Turning Up the Heat. *National Journal* 27(32).

Shaked, A., and J. Sutton. 1981. The Self-Regulating Profession. *Review of Economic Studies* 48:217–234.

Shapin, S. 1994. *A Social History of Truth: Gentility, Credibility, and Scientific Knowledge in Seventeenth-Century England.* Chicago: University of Chicago Press.

Shapin, S., and S. Schaffer. 1985. *Leviathan and the Air Pump: Hobbes, Boyle, and the Experimental Life.* Princeton, NJ: Princeton University Press.

Shaughnessy, P. W., R. E. Schlenker, and D. F. Hittle. 1994. Home Health Outcomes under Capitated and Fee-for-Service Payment. *Health Care Financing Review* 16(1):187–221.

Shear, G. 1996. *Medical Savings Accounts: A Growing Threat to Consumers' Health Care Security.* Report. Washington, DC: Consumers Union.

Shepsle, K. A. 1986. Institutional Equilibrium and Equilibrium Institutions. In *Political Science: The Science of Politics,* ed. Herbert F. Weisberg. New York: Agathon Press.

——. 1989. Studying Institutions: Some Lessons from the Rational Choice Approach. *Journal of Theoretical Politics* 1 (April):131–147.

Shewry, S., S. Hunt, J. Ramey, and J. Bertko. 1996. Risk Adjustment: The Missing Piece of Market Competition. *Health Affairs* 15(1):171–181.

Shortell, S. M., and K. E. Hull. 1995. *The New Organization of Health Care: The*

Evolution of Managed Care and Organized Delivery Systems. Baxter II Health Policy Review:1–49.

Simon, C. J., and P. H. Born. 1996. Physician Earnings in a Managed Care Environment. *Health Affairs* 15(3):124–133.

Siu, A. L., F. A. Sonnenberg, W. G. Manning, G. A. Goldberg, E. S. Bloomfield, J. P. Newhouse, and R. H. Brook. 1986. Inappropriate Use of Hospitals in a Randomized Trial of Health Insurance Plans. *New England Journal of Medicine* 315:1259–1266.

Skidmore, M. J. 1970. *Medicare and the American Rhetoric of Reconciliation.* Tuscaloosa: University of Alabama Press.

Skocpol, T. 1985. Bringing the State Back In: Strategies of Analysis in Current Research. In *Bringing the State Back In,* ed. P. B. Evans, D. Rueschemeyer, and T. Skocpol. Cambridge: Cambridge University Press.

——. 1992. *Protecting Soldiers and Mothers: The Political Origins of Social Policy in the United States.* Cambridge: Harvard University Press.

——. 1996. *Boomerang: Clinton's Health Security Effort and the Turn Against Government in U.S. Politics.* New York: W. W. Norton.

Sloan, F. A., and B. Steinwald. 1980. Effects of Regulation on Hospital Costs and Input Use. *Journal of Law and Economics* 23:81–110.

Smith, D. G. 1992. *Paying for Medicare: The Politics of Reform.* New York: Aldine de Gruyter.

Snyder, B. 1995. Hospitals Lose Charity Safety Net. *Nashville Banner,* 11 January, pp. A1, A2.

Snyder, B., and E. Cromer. 1995. TennCare Faces Rehab. *Nashville Banner,* 27 January, pp. A1, A16.

Sofaer, S., and M. L. Hurwicz. 1993. When Medical Group and HMO Part Company: Disenrollment Decisions in Medicare HMOs. *Medical Care* 31:808–821.

Spitz, B., and J. Abramson. 1987. Competition, Capitation, and Case Management: Barriers to Strategic Reform. *Milbank Quarterly* 65:348–370.

Spragins, E. 1996. Does Your HMO Stack Up? *Newsweek,* 21 July, pp. 56–63.

Starr, P. 1982. *The Social Transformation of American Medicine.* New York: Basic Books.

——. 1994. *The Logic of Health Care Reform: Why and How the President's Plan Will Work.* Rev. and exp. ed. New York: Penguin.

Starr, P., and T. R. Marmor. 1984. The United States: A Social Forecast. In *The End of Illusion,* ed. J. de Kervasdoue, J. R. Kimberly, and V. G. Rodwin. Berkeley: University of California Press.

Statistical Supplement. 1996. Health Care Financing Review. Baltimore, MD: Department of Health and Human Services, p. 31.

Steinmo, S., and J. Watts. 1995. It's the Institutions, Stupid! Why Comprehensive National Health Insurance Always Fails in America. *Journal of Health Politics, Policy and Law* 20:329–372.

Stern, L. 1991. What's New in Flex Benefits. *Business and Health* 9(3):14–21.

Stevens, B. 1986. *Complementing the Welfare State*. Geneva: International Labor Organization.

Stevens, R. 1989. *In Sickness and in Wealth*. New York: Basic Books.

Stokey, N. L., and R. E. Lucas. 1989. *Recursive Methods in Economic Dynamics*. Cambridge: Harvard University Press.

Stone, D. 1988. *Policy Paradox and Political Reason*. Glenview, IL: Scott, Foresman.

———. 1993. The Struggle for the Soul of Health Insurance. *Journal of Health Politics, Policy and Law* 18:287–317.

Stone, P. 1995a. From the K Street Corridor. *National Journal* 27(32).

———. 1995b. Rallying the Troops. *National Journal* 27(35):2152.

Stronks, K., and L. J. Gunning-Schepers. 1993. Should Equity in Health Be Target Number 1? *European Journal of Public Health* 3(2):104–111.

Sugden, R. 1993. Welfare, Resources, and Capabilities: A Review of Inequality Reexamined by Amartya Sen. *Journal of Economic Literature* 31:1947–1962.

Sullivan, L. W. 1990. *Disenrollment Experience in the Medicare HMO and CMP Risk Program: 1985–1988*. Report to Congress. Washington, DC: Department of Health and Human Services.

Tanenbaum, S. 1993. What Physicians Know. *New England Journal of Medicine* 329:1268–1271.

TennCare Home Page. 1997. [Online website http://www.state.tn.us.health/tenncare.] Nashville, TN: TennCare.

Thomas, B. 1995. Medicare at a Crossroads. *Journal of the American Medical Association* 274:276–278.

Thorpe, K. E. 1992. Inside the Black Box of Administrative Costs. *Health Affairs* 11(2):41–55.

———. 1997. The Health System in Transition: Care, Cost, and Coverage. *Journal of Health Politics, Policy and Law* 22:339–361.

Thorpe, K. E., A. Shields, H. Gold, S. Altman, and D. Shactman. 1995. *Anticipating the Number of Uninsured Americans and the Demand for Uncompensated Care*. Waltham, MA: Council on the Economic Impact of Health Care Reform.

Thurow, L. C. 1980. *The Zero-Sum Society*. New York: Penguin Books.

———. 1983. *Dangerous Currents: The State of Economics*. New York: Random House.

Toner, R. 1995. Angry Opposition Attacks the Process. *New York Times,* 22 October, p. A26.

Toner, R., and R. Pear. 1995. Medicare, Turning 30, Won't Be What It Was. *New York Times,* 23 July, p. A1.

Towers Perrin. 1992. Managed Care: Employer Perspective, 1992. *Profile* 1(2):2.

———. 1996. *1996 Health Care Cost Survey*. Towers Perrin Employee Benefit Information Center, March 1996.

Traska, M. 1990. The King of Controversy: Joe Duva. *Business and Health* 8(4):12.

Trebilcock, M. J., C. J. Tuohy, and A. D. Wolfson. 1979. *Professional Regulation: A Staff Study of Accountancy, Architecture, Engineering, and Law in Ontario* (prepared for the Professional Organizations Committee). Toronto, Ministry of the Attorney-General of Ontario.

Tullock, G. 1967. The Welfare Costs of Tariffs, Monopolies, and Theft. *Western Economic Journal* 5 (June):224–232.

Unintended Consequences. 1997. Summary of Ron Panko, *Best's Review,* July 1997. *Medical Benefits* 14(18):6.

U.S. Bureau of the Census. 1996. *Current Population Survey, March 1996 Supplement.* Washington, DC: U.S. Bureau of the Census.

U.S. Department of Justice and the Federal Trade Commission. 1996. *Statements of Antitrust Enforcement Policy in Health Care* (August). Washington, DC: U.S. DOJ and FTC.

U.S. Department of Labor. 1994. *Consumer Expenditure Survey.* Washington, DC: U.S. Government Printing Office.

——. Bureau of Labor Statistics. 1995. *Employment Cost Indexes and Levels, 1975–1992.* Bulletin 2466, October. Washington, DC: U.S. Government Printing Office.

U.S. General Accounting Office (GAO). 1991a. *Health Care Spending Control: The Experience of France, Germany, and Japan.* Washington, DC: GAO/HRD-92-9.

——. 1991b. *Medicare: PRO Review Does Not Ensure Quality of Care Provided by Risk HMOs.* Washington, DC: U.S. Government Printing Office.

——. 1992. *Medicaid—Oregon's Managed Care Program and Implications for Expansion.* Washington, DC: GAO.

——. 1993a. *Medicaid: States Turn to Managed Care to Improve Access.* Washington, DC: GAO, March.

——. 1993b. *1993 German Health Reforms: New Cost Control Initiatives.* Washington, DC: GAO/HRD-93-103.

——. 1995. *Medicare: Increased HMO Oversight Could Improve Quality and Access to Care.* Washington, DC: U.S. Government Printing Office.

——. 1996a. *Medicare: Federal Efforts to Enhance Patient Quality of Care.* Washington, DC: U.S. Government Printing Office.

——. 1996b. *Medicare HMOs: Rapid Enrollment Growth Concentrated in Selected States.* Washington, DC: U.S. Government Printing Office.

U.S. Hospitals and the Future of Health Care. 1996. *Medical Benefits* 13, 30 July, p. 2 (summary of Deloitte and Touche LLP report, 24 June 1996).

van de Ven, W. P. M. M., and F. T. Schut. 1995. The Dutch Experience with Internal Markets. In *Health Care Reform through Internal Markets: Experience and Proposals,* ed. M. Jerome-Forget, J. White, and J. M. Wiener. Washington, DC: Brookings Institution.

van de Ven, W. P. M. M., R. C. J. A. van Vliet, E. M. Barnsveld, and L. M. Lamers. 1994. Risk-Adjusted Capitation: Recent Experiences in the Netherlands. *Health Affairs* 13(4):120–136.

van Doorslaer, E., A. Wagstaff, and F. Rutten, eds. 1993. *Equity in the Finance and Delivery of Health Care: An International Perspective.* New York: Oxford University Press.

Varian, H. R. 1974. Equity, Envy, and Efficiency. *Journal of Economic Theory* 9:63–91.

Vibbert, S. 1990. Utilization Review: A Report Card. *Business and Health* 8(2):37–46.

Vladeck, B. C. 1990. *Simple, Elegant, and Wrong.* New York: United Hospital Fund.

——. 1996. Seminar on the Future of Medicaid in the Commonwealth of Pennsylvania. Institute of Politics and the Health Policy Institute, University of Pittsburgh, PA, 26 July.

Voltaire, F. [1759] 1981. *Candide.* Trans. L. Bair. New York: Bantam Books.

Wagstaff, A., and E. van Doorslaer. 1992. Equity in the Finance of Health Care: Some International Comparisons. *Journal of Health Economics* 11:361–387.

Walker, J. L., Jr. 1991. *Mobilizing Interest Groups in America: Patrons, Professions, and Social Movements.* Ann Arbor: University of Michigan Press.

Ware, J. E., M. S. Bayliss, W. H. Rogers, M. Kosinski, and A. R. Tarlov. 1996. Differences in Four-Year Health Outcomes for Elderly and Poor, Chronically Ill Patients Treated in HMO and Fee-for-Service Systems. *Journal of the American Medical Association* 276:1039–1047.

Ware, J. E., R. H. Brook, W. H. Rogers, E. B. Keeler, A. R. Davies, C. D. Sherbourne, G. A. Goldberg, P. Camp, and J. P. Newhouse. 1986. Comparison of Health Outcomes at a Health Maintenance Organization with Those of Fee-for-Service Care. *Lancet,* 3 May, pp. 1017–1022.

Warner, D. 1995. A Medicare Tax Hike's Impact on Business. *Nation's Business,* October, p. 8.

Warner, J. H. 1986. *The Therapeutic Perspective: Medical Practice, Knowledge, and Identity in America, 1820–1885.* Cambridge: Cambridge University Press.

Washburn, F. A., and J. F. Bresnahan. 1915. Medical and Surgical Efficiency in Large General Hospitals. *Modern Hospital* 5(6). Codman Papers, box 2, folder 37. Countway Library of Medicine, Boston.

Washington Business Group on Health. 1994. Paper provided by the administration.

Weaver, R. K. 1988. *Automatic Government: The Politics of Indexation.* Washington, DC: Brookings Institution.

Weir, M. 1992. *Politics and Jobs: The Boundaries of Employment Policy in the United States.* Princeton, NJ: Princeton University Press.

Weir, M., and T. Skocpol. 1985. State Structures and the Possibilities for "Keynesian" Responses to the Great Depression in Sweden, Britain, and the United States. In *Bringing the State Back In,* ed. P. B. Evans, D. Rueschemeyer, and T. Skocpol. Cambridge: Cambridge University Press.

Weisbrod, B. A. 1978. *Competition in the Health Care Sector: Past, Present, and Future,* ed. W. Greenberg. Washington, DC: Bureau of Economics, Federal Trade Commission.

Weissenstein, E. 1995. Provider Networks Gaining in Senate. *Modern Health Care,* 2 October, p. 2.

Weissert, W. G., T. Lesnick, M. Musliner, and K. Foley. 1998. Cost-Savings from Home and Community-Based Services: Arizona's Capitated Medicaid Long-Term Care Program. *Journal of Health Politics, Policy and Law* 22(6):1329–1357.

Welch, W. P. 1994. HMO Market Share and Its Effect on Local Medicare Costs. In *HMOs and the Elderly,* ed. H. S. Luft. Ann Arbor, MI: Health Administration Press.

Wennberg, J. E. 1984. Dealing with Medical Practice Variations: A Proposal for Action. *Health Affairs* 3(4):6–31.

——. AHCPR and the Strategy of Health Care Reform. *Health Affairs* 11(4):66–71.

Wennberg, J. E., et al. 1998. *The Dartmouth Atlas of Health Care 1998*. Hanover, NH: Dartmouth Medical School.

West, D. 1995. Price, Quality Wars Seen Paring Down HMO Market. *National Underwriter* 42(16 October):7.

White, J. 1995a. Budgeting and Health Policymaking. In *Intensive Care: How Congress Shapes Health Policy*, ed. T. E. Mann and N. J. Ornstein. Washington, DC: American Enterprise Institute and Brookings Institution.

——. 1995b. *Competing Solutions: American Health Care Proposals and International Experience*. Washington, DC: Brookings Institution.

——. 1997. Which Managed Care for Medicare? *Health Affairs* 16(5):73–82.

Wiener, J. M., L. H. Illston, and R. J. Hanley. 1994. *Sharing the Burden*. Washington, DC: Brookings Institution.

Wildavsky, A. 1977. Doing Better and Feeling Worse: The Political Pathology of Health Policy. *Daedalus* 106(1):105–124.

Wilensky, G. 1995a. Incremental Health System Reform: Where Medicare Fits In. *Health Affairs* 14(1):173–181.

——. 1995b. The Score on Medicare Reform—Minus the Hype and Hyperbole. *New England Journal of Medicine* 333:1774–1777.

Wilensky, H. L. 1997. Social Science and the Public Agenda: Reflections on the Relation of Knowledge to Power and Policy in the United States. *Journal of Health Politics, Policy and Law* 22(5):1241–1265.

Wiley, M. M. 1992. Hospital Financing Reform and Case-Mix Measurement: An International Review. *Health Care Financing Review* 13(4):119–133.

Wilsford, D. 1995. Path Dependency, or Why History Makes It Difficult but Not Impossible to Reform Health Care Systems in a Big Way. *Journal of Public Policy* 14(3):251–283.

——. 1996. Caught between History and Economics: Reforming French Health Care Policy in the 1990s. In *Policy Making in France in the 1990s*, ed. M. Schain and J. Keeler. New York: St. Martin's.

Winston, G. C. 1980. Addiction and Backsliding: A Theory of Compulsive Consumption. *Journal of Economic Behavior and Organization* 1:295–324.

Wise, M. N. 1995. Morals of Energy Metering: Constructing and Deconstructing the Precision of the Victorian Electrical Engineer's Ammeter and Voltmeter. In *The Values of Precision*, ed. M. N. Wise. Princeton, NJ: Princeton University Press.

Wittgenstein, L. 1956. *Remarks on the Foundations of Mathematics*. Oxford: Blackwell.

Woolhandler, S., and D. U. Himmelstein. 1991. The Deteriorating Administrative Efficiency of the U.S. Health Care System. *New England Journal of Medicine* 324:1253–1258.

World Bank. 1993. *World Development Report 1993.* Oxford: Oxford University Press.

Yang, J. 1997. Surprising Democratic Poll Results. *Washington Post,* 10 August, p. A8.

Zarbozo, C., and J. D. LeMasurier. 1995. Medicare and Managed Care. In *Essentials of Managed Health Care,* ed. P. Kongstvedt. Gaithersburg, MD: Aspen.

Zelman, W. A. 1997. Consumer Protection in Managed Care: Finding the Balance. *Health Affairs* 16(1):158–166.

Zoloth-Dorfman, L., and S. Rubin. 1995. The Patient as Commodity: Managed Care and the Question of Ethics. *Journal of Clinical Ethics* 6(4):339–357.

Zwanziger, J., and G. Melnick. 1993. Effects of Competition on the Hospital Industry: Evidence from California. In *Competitive Approaches to Health Care Reform,* ed. R. J. Arnould, R. F. Rich, and W. D. White. Washington, DC: Urban Institute.

——. 1996. Can Managed Care Plans Control Health Care Costs? *Health Affairs* 15(2):185–199.

Zwanziger, J., G. Melnick, and A. Bamezai. 1994. Cost and Price Competition in California Hospitals, 1980–1990. *Health Affairs* 13(3):118–126.

Contributors

Gary S. Belkin is Instructor, Department of Psychiatry, Harvard Medical School and Clinical Assistant Professor, Department of Psychiatry, Brown University School of Medicine.

Lawrence D. Brown is Professor, School of Public Health, Columbia University.

Robert G. Evans is Professor, Department of Economics, University of British Columbia.

Martin Gaynor holds the E. J. Barone Chair in Health Systems Management and is Professor of Economics and Public Policy at the H. John Heinz III School of Public Policy and Management and the Graduate School of Industrial Administration, Carnegie Mellon University.

Paul B. Ginsburg is President, Center for Studying Health System Change.

Marsha Gold is Senior Fellow, Mathematica Policy Research.

Theodore R. Marmor is Professor of Public Policy & Management, School Management, Yale University.

Cathie Jo Martin is Associate Professor, Department of Political Science, Boston University.

Jonathan B. Oberlander is a visiting scholar and Robert Wood Johnson Foundation Postdoctoral Fellow in Health Policy, School of Public Health, University of California, Berkeley.

Mark V. Pauly is Professor of Health Care Systems, Insurance and Risk Management, and Public Policy and Management, Wharton School, and Professor, Department of Economics, University of Pennsylvania.

Mark A. Peterson is Professor of Policy Studies at the University of California, Los Angeles.

Thomas Rice is Professor and Chair of the Department of Health Services, School of Public Health, University of California, Los Angeles.

Deborah A. Stone holds the David R. Pokross Chair in Law and Social Policy at Brandeis University.

Kenneth E. Thorpe is Professor, Department of Health Systems Management, and Director, Institute for Health Services Research, Tulane University.

William B. Vogt is Assistant Professor at the H. John Heinz III School of Public Policy and Management and the Graduate School of Industrial Administration at Carnegie Mellon University.

Index

Blendon, Robert, 43
Bloom, Bernard, 152
Blue Cross and Blue Shield of Ohio, 206
Blue Cross/Blue Shield plans: advertising,
166; expansion of, 165; as insurers of last
resort, 199; managed care organizations
care enrollment, 7; in Oregon, 293; in
Tennessee, 301–2; transition from non-
profit status, 8, 9; transition to provider-
managed networks, 8
Blumenthal, David, 176
Boehner, John, 245
Boulding, Kenneth, 36
Brown, Lawrence, 20
Business Health Care Action Group, 233
Business Roundtable, 243, 244

California: competitive premiums in
Orange County, 185; health care for low-
income populations, 288; Medi-Cal program, 220
Canada: controlling health care costs, 372;
health care costs, 355; health care services, 329–30; provider reimbursement
mechanisms, 338; satisfaction with
health care services, 72; spending on
health care systems, 94; transition from
inpatient to same-day surgery, 95–96
Capitation fees: and economic incentives,
274; and medical judgment, 173, 174; as a
percentage of adjusted average per capita cost, 258; risk-adjusted, 365–66; in
Tennessee, 304
Capron Commission, 106
Carnegie-Mellon University: healthcare
forum, 2
Casey, Pat, 232
Cato Institute, 347
Child Health Insurance Program, 285
Civic Progress group, St. Louis, 234
Cleveland Health Quality Choice Coalition, 232, 233–34
Cleveland Tomorrow, 233
Clinical judgment: and American political
culture, 167; and economic incentives,
168, 170, 174–75; influence of money on,
168, 170; replaced by health services re-
search, 151

Clinics: owned by insurance companies,
187; as provider-managed networks, 8
Clinton health reform initiative, 197, 198,
199, 235–36, 244, 255
Clinton Health Security Act, 4, 6, 103, 322,
341
Coalition for Change, 244
Coalition movements, 230–32
Coalition to Save Medicare, 247, 248, 249
Codman, Ernest Amory, 142, 152, 153–56
Cognitive dissonance, 50–51, 62, 129
Cohen, Wilbur, 324, 327
Columbia HCA, 8, 206
Commitment: role in preferences, 52
Commonwealth Fund, 288
Community health centers, 193
Community Snapshots Study. See RWJF
Community Snapshots Study
Competitive contracting, 204–7
Competitive equilibrium, 30
Competitive markets. See Market competi-
tion
Competitive theory, 29. See also Market
competition
Comprehensive national health insurance,
54
Comte, Auguste, 158
Condillac, Etienne, 158
Congressional Budget Office (CBO), 203,
240–41, 256, 328
Congressional Research Service, 256
Conspiracy theories, 123–24, 138
Consumer choice: in competitive health
care markets, 196; and managed compe-
tition, 362–63; pitfalls, 46–47, 129; and
preferences, 51–53, 113–14, 116–17, 132;
sanctity of, 36; selecting health care pro-
viders, 48–51
Consumer expectations: and medical tech-
nology, 355
Consumer Expenditure Survey, U.S. De-
partment of Labor, 210
Consumer movement, 170, 171
Consumer tastes: assumptions, 35–38; role
in public policy, 42
Consumer theory, 45–46
Consumption externality, 33–34, 108
Contract medicine, 166

Employers (*cont.*)
cans' coercion of, 244–46; shifting re-
sponsibilities for premiums to em-
ployees, 196–97
End Results System, 154, 155. *See also* Cod-
man, Ernest Amory
Enthoven, Alain, 10, 106, 168–69, 169–70, 231
Entitlements, 239. *See also* Medicare pro-
gram
Epistomological standardization, 142, 149,
150
Equity: and positive externality, 34
ERISA (Employee Retirement Income Se-
curity Act), 243
Ethical medicine, 165
Europe: government intervention in
health care spending, 359; health care
costs, 355
Evaluative science, 151
Evans, Robert, 13, 14, 15, 58
Evidence-based health care, 84, 85
Excise profits tax, 226
Externalities of consumption, 33–34, 108
Extraterritoriality, 69

Family Health Insurance Assistance Program, 298
Favorable selection, 63
FCHP. *See* Fully capitated health plans
Feder, Judith, 239, 341
Federal Employees Health Benefit Pro-
gram (FEHBP), 267, 277–78
Federal Trade Commission: antitrust con-
cerns, 8, 198; resistance to coalitions, 235
Fee-for-service (FFS) payments: biased se-
lection, 281–82; compared to HMOs,
260–63, 265, 269–71; competitiveness,
205; for Medicaid program, 284–85; and
medical judgment, 165, 173; and Medi-
care, 257
Fee-splitting, 167–68
Firm-level market interventions, 226–30.
See also Employers
Fixed-price contracts, 205
Flagg, Don, 232
Flex benefits, 227
Florida: health care for low-income popu-
lations, 288

Food and Drug Administration:
randomized-control trials, 145
Food stamp program, 115–16
Foster Higgins survey, 210, 211, 229, 237
France: gatekeeping arrangements, 359;
health care spending, 354; role of politics
in health care, 361–62
Frank, Robert, 32, 47, 53
Free market: allocating resources, 34
Free-rider effect: and preventive services,
41; public-good aspect of, 62
Friedman, Milton, 36
Fuchs, Victor, 14, 30
Fully capitated health plans, 291, 295. *See
also* Managed care systems; Oregon
Fundamentalist approach of economic
analysts, 90–91, 105

Gag rules, 343
Gatekeeping. *See* Medical gatekeeping
Gaynor, Martin, 14
General accounting Office (GAO), 328
General practitioner (GP) fund-holding
and hospital trusts, 96
Germany: compulsory health insurance,
361; controlling health care costs, 373;
health care spending, 354; health financ-
ing systems, 168; health insurance sys-
tem, 164; health policies, 163; managed
competition, 359; provider reimbursement mechanisms, 338; reimbursement
of prescription drugs, 95; spending on
health care systems, 94
Germ theory, 157
Gingrich, Newt, 244, 256, 335
Ginsburg, Paul, 17
Glaxo: acquisition of Wellcome PLC, 206
Gold, Marsha, 19, 346
Golden Age of Medicine, 367, 369–70
Goldwater, S. S., 155
Government: budget makers, 357–58; cost
control mechanisms, 84, 85; endorsement of managed care systems, 141;
failure of political processes, 123–24, 136;
intervention in health care spending,
358–59; and managed competition, 364;
Medicaid reforms, 208; and Medicare
program, 255–57; and Pareto principle,

114–15; role in health care services, 68, 137; role as purchaser, 198; role in market-based health reform, 106–7, 110; social learning process benefit programs, 226. *See also* Health care policies
Graduate medical education: financing, 214–15; and teaching hospitals, 215–16, 218
Gross domestic products (GDP) statistics. *See* Health care spending: statistics
GroupCare Consortium, 234
Guild free choice system, 106
Guiliani, Rudolph, 209

Hacker, Jacob, 235–36
Hahnel, Robin, 53
Hall, Peter, 324–25
Harvard Public Health School, 337–38
Havighurst, Clark, 168
HCFA. *See* Health Care Financing Administration (HCFA)
Health Action Council of Northeast Ohio (HAC), 232
Health Care Connection (HCC), 230
Health Care Financing Administration (HCFA), 4, 7; actuaries, 210, 214; demonstration projects, 258–59; early waiver requests to, 346; examination of health care expenditures, 213; managed care plans for end-stage renal disease, 208; and Medicare+Choice plans, 278; Office of National Cost Estimates, 332–33; Office of Planning and Evaluation, 328; quality program, 280; and TennCare, 301
Health care industry: economic power of managed care systems, 1; management innovations, 188–89; political influence, 345; social influences, 2; and standardization, 142. *See also* Health care systems
Health care insurance coverage: changes in the marketplace, 207–9; competitive premiums in Orange County, California, 185; controlling costs, 4, 57, 109, 171; co-payment rates, 61; cost burden of, 82–84; cross-national comparisons, 361; disenrollment rates, 271; excess coverage, 54; impact on growth in competitive contracting, 204; indemnity-style coverage,

203, 229, 257, 273; marketing, 177; organizational structure of, 163–64; payment methods, 173; political controversy, 1–3; privatization of, 168; relationship to income level, 81–82; supplementary, 92; switching, 42; third-party, 165–66, 223; trends, 376–77
Healthcare Leadership Council, 247
Health care plans, 204–207. *See also* Blue Cross/Blue Shield plans; Health care insurance coverage
Health care policies: code of ethics, 165; and consumer demands, 189; controlling costs, 360; enacting, 35; and entrepreneurship, 331; in Germany, 163; global developments, 379–80; and individual physician behavior, 149; initiatives, 197–200; legacies, 328–32; and legislation, 319–20; and managed care systems, 141; market-oriented thinking, 172; movement to Medicaid managed care strategies, 286–88; and optional health reform, 224–25; in Oregon and Tennessee, 311–15; and private decision making, 2; role in legacies, 320, 321–26. *See also* Social learning process: advocated by economic theory
Health care providers: competitive market, 97; economic incentives, 63, 96, 172, 179, 343; ethical conduct, 85; financial risks, 205–6; impact on growth in competitive contracting, 204; income linked to decisions, 95, 126; Medicare reimbursement mechanisms, 337, 338; objectivity of, 152; pressure from purchasing cooperatives, 185; public relations strategy, 94; regulated as insurers, 199–200; relationship between money and medicine, 161–68; role of consumer choice in selecting, 48–51, 132; types of, 77
Health care reform: and big-business involvement in managed care systems, 243–46; Clinton initiative, 197, 198, 199, 235–36, 244, 255; cost containment, 225–26; of financing systems, 82–83; instrumentalist case for, 94–95, 135; for low-income populations, 284, 287; market-based, 62, 105, 106–7, 110, 255;

Hill-Burton Act, 39
Hillman, Alan, 173
HMOs. *See* Health maintenance organizations
Hoerger, Thomas, 48
Horizontal mergers, 207
Hospital Corporation of America, 206, 374
Hospital management, 154–55
Hospitals: conversion from nonprofit to for-profit status, 200; evaluating, 232, 233; external forces, 186–89; and graduate medical education, 215–16; and HMOs, 228; length-of-stay rules, 178; managing care, 201; and market competition, 193–95; in Oregon, 293; payment methodologies, 11; provider-managed networks, 8; rate-setting system, 203; safety-net, 209; and trends in health care delivery systems, 205; and uncompensated care costs, 217, 218
Hospital trusts: and general practitioner (GP) fund-holding, 96
Howard, Leslie, 48
Howell, Joel, 152
Hsiao, William, 337–38
Humana, 374

Immaculate Conception of the Indifference Curve, 36
Impossibility theorem analyses, 107
Income-expenditure identity, 134–35
Income tax: economic efficiency, 34
Indemnity-style coverage, 203, 229, 257, 273
Independent hospitals, 8
Independent practice associations (IPAs), 8, 195; capitation fees, 274
Individual utilities. *See* Utility functions
Individual welfare, 53
Industrial Outlook reports, U.S. Department of Commerce, 210
Information technology, 188
In-kind services, 131
Instrumental standardization, 142, 149, 150
Insurance. *See* Health care insurance coverage
Insurance companies: ownership of clinics, 187
Insurers of last resort, 199

Intellectual capital, 357
Intellectual property rights, 69
IQ testing, 147
Israel: managed competition, 359, 362
Ivins, Molly, 247

Jackson Hole group, 236
Jewett, Jacqueline, 62
Joint Commission on the Accreditation of Healthcare Organizations, 154

Kaiser Family Foundation, 288
Kennedy, Edward, 242, 331
Kingdon, John, 379
Klein, Rudolf, 379
Knowledge: and managed care systems, 150–53; as opportunity, 356–58; scientific, 140, 143–44, 146–49, 150–53, 156–59, 168; and social learning process, 335–37, 344
Kuppat Cholim Chalit (KHC), Israel, 362

Laboratory techniques, 147
Labor Federation, Israel, 362
Labor market, 37
Levit, Katharine, 236
Lewin-VHI, 339
Libertarians: and individual sovereignty, 47
Liebenstein, Harvey, 50
Life expectancy statistics, 43
Light, Donald, 41–42
Lump-sum taxes, 34
Luxembourg: spending on health care systems, 94

Managed care systems: changes in, 228–29; and competition, 73–74, 75, 204–7; economic incentives, 96, 172, 179, 343, 344; and eroded power of physicians, 140; expansion of, 229; future of, 377, 382; government endorsement, 141; health policies, 141; hospital standardization, 156–59; influence on Medicare policy, 257; managed competition, 359; market competition, 342–45; marketing materials, 179–80; market reforms, 223; and Medicaid program, 4, 7, 345–47; and Medicaid program based on capitating

Smoking: legislation, 33, welfare losses from, 60

Social choice: and Pareto criterion, 114

Social insurance, 51

Social learning process: advocated by economic theory, 27–28; and health care policies and legislation, 319–20; and market competition, 341–42; and medical savings accounts, 347–50; new policy legacy, 340–41; participants in, 332–37; structural effects, 326–28; types of, 328–32; variation in, 337–40

Social sciences: common element, 35–38; and scientific change, 146

Social Security, 226

Social Security: 1972 amendments, 257–58

Social welfare: improving, 60; maximizing, 46, 53–54; reducing, 33

Southwestern Bell: move to managed care systems, 230

Standardization: for hospitals, 156–59; types of, 142–43

Stark, Pete, 243

Starr, Paul, 21, 140, 165, 368, 370

States: health care policies, 343; Section 115 waivers, 285–87, 301

Statistical inference, 144–45, 148, 158

Statistics: health care spending, 71, 74–75, 353–55; life expectancy, 43

Status, 32. *See also* Wealth

Sticky preferences, 113–14

St. Louis: activist coalition, 234–35

St. Louis Quality Alliance, 235

Stone, Deborah, 16, 329, 332

Stutts, Jim, 235

Subsidies: and mandatory cross-subsidies, 108; with public funds, 199; redistributing income, 34

Substantive learning: conceptual arguments, 350; described, 328; and MSAs, 347; as a private act, 341; process, 331

Sugden, Robert, 44–45

Sundquist, Don, 301, 307, 308

Supplementary insurance coverage, 82, 92

Surveys: and questionable accuracy, 118

Switzerland: spending on health care systems, 94

Tax Equity and Fiscal Responsibility Act (TEFRA): HMO program, 265; risk program, 258

Teaching hospitals, 215–16, 218

Technocratic wish: history of, 153; and managed care systems, 141–43; and problem solving, 159; role in scientific credibility, 146, 147, 148, 149

Tenet Health Care, 206

Tennessee: health care for low-income populations, 288; health care policies, 311–15; health care reform initiative, 299–309; Medicaid waivers, 207–8; political model, 310; Section 115 waivers, 288

Tennessee Primary Care Association, 303

Texas: health care for low-income populations, 288

Third-party insurers, 165–66, 223

Thorpe, Kenneth, 17

Thurow, Lester, 50

Thursday Group, 244

Undesirable events, 62, 63

United Kingdom: controlling health care costs, 372; general practitioner (GP) fund-holding and hospital trusts, 96; health care reform, 361; health care spending statistics, 71; internal markets, 365; satisfaction with health care services, 72

United States: controlling costs, 74–75, 109, 203; culture of medicine, 161; exceptionalism, 366; Golden Age of Medicine, 367, 369–70; government intervention in health care spending, 359; health care spending statistics, 71; health financing systems, 168; health insurance system, 164–65; managed care systems, 359–60; management theories, 378, 380–82; percapita health spending, 125–26; percapita insurance costs, 86, 87; policy-making systems, 336–37; political culture, 167, 374–75; public sector spending on health care systems, 93–94; reliance on private action, 76; satisfaction with health care services, 72, 136; uninsured citizens, 214–15, 216–20

Library of Congress Cataloging-in-Publication Data
Healthy markets? the new competition in medical care /
edited by Mark A. Peterson.
    Includes bibliographical references and index.
ISBN 0-8223-2236-6 (cloth : alk. paper).
ISBN 0-8223-2138-6 (pbk. : alk. paper).
    1. Medical care—United States—Finance.   2. Insurance, Health—
United States.   3. Managed care plans (Medical care)—United
States.   I. Peterson, Mark A.
RA395.A3H4335   1998   362.1′04258′0973—dc21   98-29193 CIP